D0210778

The Last of the Celts

The Last of the Celts

Marcus Tanner

Yale University Press

New Haven and London

For information about this and other Yale University Press publications, please contact:
U.S. Office: sales.press@yale.edu   yalebooks.com
Europe Office: sales@yaleup.co.uk   www.yalebooks.co.uk

Set in Bembo by Northern Phototypesetting Co. Ltd, Bolton, Lancs.
Printed in the United States of America

Library of Congress Cataloging-in-Publication Data

Tanner, Marcus.
The Last of the Celts/Marcus Tanner.
p. cm.
Includes bibliographical references and index.
ISBN 0–300–10464–2 (cl.: alk. paper)
1. Civilization, Celtic. I. Title.
CB206.T36 2004   909'.04916—dc22   2004005520

A catalogue record for this book is available from the British Library.

2 4 6 8 10 9 7 5 3 1

The paper in this book meets the guidelines for permanence and durability of the Committee on Production Guidlines for Book Longevity of the Council on Library Resources

For permission to reprint verse extracts from copyright material the author gratefully acknowledges the following: Nuala Ní Dhomhnaill and the Gallery Press, Loughcrew, County Meath for *Pharaoh's Daughter* (1990) translated by Paul Muldoon; A. P. Watt Ltd on behalf of Michael B. Yeats and Anne B. Yeats for 'Easter 1916' by W. B. Yeats.

Contents

PART THREE

Illustrations

Introduction

This is a book about the disappearance of the non-English-speaking peoples of Britain and Ireland and the non-French-speaking people of northern France – those whom for the past couple of centuries we have called the Celts.

I have confined my attention to people who speak, or within relatively recent history spoke, one of the two branches of the Celtic language known as Goidelic or Brythonic. The former comprises the Irish, Scottish Gaelic and Manx languages and the latter comprises the Welsh, Cornish and Breton tongues. I have not discussed where the Celts came from, or what their culture in central Europe was like many centuries ago, nor have I included all those in the world who might define themselves as Celts in terms of their blood ancestry or their sentimental allegiance. The book is about what happened quite recently to a certain group of communities who can be defined by language, what their position is now and what the future holds for them.

As much of my working life has been spent in the Balkans, I have been asked what made me so interested in the Celts. The answer is that it all began with a search for my family's ancestral graves in mid-Wales. I found them a few summers back, hidden in the long grass in the Nonconformist graveyard in the village of Ceris, near Llanidloes. The cemetery had been closed for years, and foliage had grown up and around the gravestones, concealing many of them from view. I was searching for signs of the presence of my father's family who left Wales for London just before the First World War to work, like many Welsh immigrants, as policemen or milkmen in the British capital. It was a difficult assignment, as I had little information except the knowledge that the trail reached back to a village near the town of Llanidloes. In our family's possession was a collection of now-sepia newspaper cuttings from the 1920s recording family events but they were all in Welsh. It was a language my father had spoken fluently to his siblings and occasionally to us, but we had not learned it. Another clue was a late-Victorian photograph of a formidable-looking man sitting in an armchair beside his prune-faced wife, a vast bible balancing on his knee. This supposedly depicted a great-grandfather who was a Nonconformist minister.

After a futile afternoon spent combing churchyards in and around Llanidloes yielded nothing, I was about to give up when I met an elderly couple who lived next door to a cemetery and who had been observing me hopping around the graves. They said they recollected the name Tanner and they remembered the family as having lived in the nearby village of Ceris. They urged me to search the disused cemetery that lay at the far end of this village, where the houses gave way to open country. Their distant memories were correct (how many city people would remember a family who had left the area so many decades before? I thought). Overgrown and forgotten beside a stone wall, obscured by grass as tall as the stones themselves, was a row of slate-grey tombstones bearing the family name.

But the mystery was not lifted, for the words on the tombstones were, of course, written in the Welsh which, judging by the inscriptions of the other graves, had clearly been the language of the area at least until the Second World War. I could not understand them. I felt that an invisible wall separated me from these long-dead Tanners, a wall not merely of death but of culture. Staring at the letters in the late afternoon sunshine I felt like an Egyptologist who had stumbled across some important but indecipherable hieroglyphics. I photographed the inscriptions with a view to getting them translated later at home.

Back in Llanidloes, I found a phone book and tracked down the address of a family bearing my name. I decided to introduce myself and ask what, if anything, they knew of their namesakes who had left Wales decades ago. But the feeling of a glass wall separating me from this whole world was overpowering and kept me from acting on my resolve. I even found the house and peered through a downstairs window, catching sight of an elderly man seated in a front room with his back towards me, watching a television. But I did not knock or go in. I felt too much part and parcel of the world that had been forged by those victorious Anglo-Saxons, and apart from that of the vanquished Celts to which those Welsh Tanners assuredly belonged. It was somehow embarrassing.

I returned to London determined to learn enough Welsh at least to understand the inscriptions on those gravestones. I followed through on that pledge and spent a week on an intensive language course in the wilds of North Wales, on the Lleyn peninsula. It was a wonderful experience, for the days of intensive learning were followed by evenings in which we all gathered together and listened to storytellers recounting history and legends. A further two weeks of language tuition followed in Bangor. By then, the simple phrases on my ancestors' gravestones were easily decipherable.

My language courses and subsequent travels through Wales awoke in me a powerful sense of longing and nostalgia, which the Welsh call *hiraeth*. Almost everything about me – my personality, my face, my height, my shape – made more sense. I had always felt vaguely dissatisfied with my features and personality in the suburban English milieu in which I grew up, feeling somehow that they did not belong to the setting. Small, dark-haired and powerfully built, even as a child I felt rather distinct from the mostly tall, rangy, blond or sandy-haired boys who sat in class beside me. Even my character did not quite fit in. I was so much more easily moved to tears of joy, or rage, than they were. In England I had developed a sense of watchfulness about my own personality, aware that it needed keeping in check, and that at any moment I might sound unsuitably loud, excitable and over the top. In Wales that feeling of difference from my surroundings fell away. I found myself among a nation of gesticulating, excitable people and the physical similarity between me and the people I saw around me was as striking. Over the years I had got used to people constantly asking if I was Irish, which irritated me, as I knew I had no Irish blood in me at all. In Wales I saw my own features everywhere – a million or so stocky little replicas.

But the sense of recognition could only go so far. For all my new-found enthusiasm for Wales and the Welsh, I knew I would never gain access to the language, culture and the way of seeing and hearing the world that my ancestors buried in Ceris had known. A gate closed behind me. I would never be more than an outsider, looking in, for what has been forgotten cannot be relearned. In that sense, I had found what I sought in the cemetery and had no need to go again.

But the journey was not quite over. The visit to the graveyard in Ceris marked the start of a longer voyage, for the discovery of those graves had made me curious about what happened, not only to that one family but to their world. Why was it that a culture that had survived in our family for so long had come to a full stop after my father's death? There had to be more to it than the fact that the family had moved to England and, in my father's case, had married 'out'. Confident and assertive cultures spread through migration and intermarriage and that had been the experience of Welsh and Irish for centuries.

The story of Wales and Welsh did not make much sense in isolation. Just as my own family history added up only in the context of the wider story of Welsh culture, that story also fitted into a broader narrative about all the Celtic peoples of Britain and Ireland, and the Bretons of France. The fates of the several branches of the Celtic family, the Irish, Scottish and the Manx Gaels of the north and the Brythonic Celts – the Bretons, the Welsh and the Cornish – were similar though not identical.

Books, maps, graphs and theses offered only partial answers to my questions. I needed to see what had happened on the ground. And so, for more than a year, I travelled through the Celtic lands, hugging the west coast of Britain, Ireland and north-west France and the islands that had held out longest against English (or French) penetration, looking, listening and scribbling notes. Starting in the island of Lewis, in the north-west of Scotland, I travelled south, passing through Wales, the Isle of Man, Ireland, Cornwall and Brittany, taking the temperature of a culture to see what history had done to the Celts and hazard some guesses about what lay in store.

I attended language courses in Scottish Gaelic as well as Welsh, went to church services and music festivals, walked around cemeteries, museums and shopping centres, and spoke to priests and ministers, university professors, musicians and storytellers, to people who cared passionately about their traditional culture and to people who didn't care a bit. I was careful not to confine myself to the true believers.

After completing this journey, I still felt the picture was incomplete. English (and in Brittany, French) influence was so pervasive wherever I went that I was unable to discern what the Celts were truly like outside this English, or French, context. I wanted to journey to lands where Celtic emigrants had consciously attempted to plant non-English-speaking colonies outside Europe. And so I included two other Celtic lands in my journey. These were the Scottish Gaelic settlement of Nova Scotia in Canada, and the Welsh colony in Patagonia, in southern Argentina. The number of settlers in each of these places paled in comparison with the number of Irish immigrants to America or Australia, for example. But the Irish in America had moved mostly into English-speaking urban environments and had soon lost their old language. I was more interested in Cape Breton in Nova Scotia and the Chubut valley of Patagonia because they were isolated rural colonies where the incomers had been left alone for generations and to which they had transplanted everything from the old country, from their religion to their language. I wanted to see if these transplanted Celtic cultures had fared better than those at home.

I began with thoughts of Celtic revivals ringing in my ears, for there is nothing that the British or the French love more than a good old Celtic revival. The British, French and North American public who know any-thing of the subject have been lulled into believing a Celtic renaissance is going on. They believe this partly because boosterism and a marked tendency to 'puff' has been a feature of Celtic revivalism since the nine-teenth century, and partly because, quite simply, the word Celt or Celtic has become ubiquitous. This new-baked Celticism owes almost nothing to the traditional culture of Ireland, the Scottish Highlands, Wales or Brittany. It is a marketing device that has attached itself like glue to the worlds of design, spirituality, music, politics and even sport. This informs the vogue for 'Celtic' brooches, jewellery and cutlery (all of which is as much Norse or Anglo-Saxon as Celtic in design), and the Celtic CDs sold in music stores, containing plaintive ballads, often of English origin, but fronted by pictures of interlacing, curling shapes and Christian crosses, sometimes with potted descriptions of what it means to be a Celt. Typical is the blurb that accom-panies *Celtic Journeys*, a CD I picked up on the Isle of Man: 'It means real music with real values, real ideas and real emotions. Celts are spiritual, proud, courageous and believe in meaning what they say. They are born artists, visionaries, warriors.' Vacuous Celticism of this type explains the continued appetite in a fairly non-religious environment for books of Celtic prayers and Celtic saints. It underpins the ideology of nationalist parties of various strengths throughout Britain, Ireland and France, which base polit-ical claims to independent statehood partly on loose theories about the Celtic origins of their societies.

The first leg of my Celtic journey coincided with the golden jubilee of Queen Elizabeth II and naturally prompted reflection on the increasingly fragmented nature of her British and Northern Irish realm. The growing popularity of a loosely defined Celtic identity in Scotland, Wales and Northern Ireland seemed to reflect a marked decline in confidence in British institutions. The sincere applause of the dutiful crowds that attended the Queen on her jubilee travels could not disguise Britain's identity crisis, unsur-prising perhaps, as the patchwork of lands united around Protestantism and empire were no longer Protestant or in charge of an empire. Far more than is the case with the citizens of the United States or France, I found many people were now uncertain what Britain was *for*. The atmosphere of the Queen's disunited kingdom as it moved into the early twenty-first century to me recalled Austria-Hungary in the early twentieth century. Both were fractious collections of peoples united only by a worn-out dynastic principle. Britain rolls on for much the same reason that Austria-Hungary rolled on in its final decades: because it is reasonably comfortable, prosperous, fairly humanely governed and has been around for so long that it is hard to imagine life without it. But as an idea, Britishness is dying on its feet. One only has to witness the ill-concealed hostility shown towards the national flag and national anthem in Scotland, parts of Northern Ireland, to a lesser extent in Wales, and even in Cornwall. Real, old-fashioned, full-blooded Britishness leaves even the English squirming with embarrassment these days. Where the identity has been retained in the old, grand style, as it is in unionist parts of Northern Ireland, complete with flags, drums, high-octane Protestantism and toasts to the Queen, it evokes more shame than admiration among the English. There is little understanding or sympathy among modern English people for values that were virtually automatically held by most of their own grandparents.

The enfeebled self-image of the English has an up-side. It has given ethnic and sexual minorities room to pursue their own identities, which is one reason why England remains so attractive to outsiders – whether they are seeking asylum, or just space to breathe. At the same time, a feeling of cultural weightlessness propels the majority white population to reach out for more nourishing badges of identity. Even in America which has a stronger sense of 'self' than Britain, a less dominant and self-confident white community is full of people seeking an exit from the 'white' label and finding it in other identities. Being Celtic is just one.

Celticism is a way out of membership of undesirable-sounding, oppressive and discredited hierarchies. This also commends it to the churches. Leaving aside fundamentalist Protestant evangelicals, a growing force who feel no need for apology or self-examination, the main British and Irish denominations have rushed to embrace a Celtic identity in a type of manic spiritual flight. One sign of this, which I encountered from Iona in Scotland to St Ives in Cornwall, is the merchandising in church-run souvenir shops of copious quantities of supposedly Celtic gear – from prayers, charms, jewellery and cures to recipes – alongside rows of books on Celtic saints fronted by interlace patterns. The churches hug the Celts to their bosom these days because what they call Celtic spirituality implies a set of favourable cultural references, including a less hierarchical and less sexually censorious form of religion. These they hope will resolve many of the dilemmas that they face in modern Western society.

The enthusiasm for Celtic Christianity is particularly strong in Ireland, where it dovetails with the Irish image of themselves as *the* most Celtic society, the land *par excellence* of saints, scholars, interlace designs, Celtic crosses, fiddles, little people, wild and poetic temperament – in short everything the Western world means by the word 'Celtic'. In Ireland I found the word Celtic applied indiscriminately to most aspects of life, from religion to sticky liqueurs invented in the 1980s; even to the economy – the boom of the 1990s having been popularly baptised the 'Celtic Tiger'.

Celtic spirituality is popular because it is spiritual. Books have spread the idea that the Celts, usually taken as a homogeneous lump, formerly professed a model of Christianity that anticipated modern Western society's relaxed attitudes to sex, as well as its interest in alternative medicine, wildlife, conservation and gender equality. It goes like this. Traditional denominations have said almost nothing about ecology or wildlife. By contrast, the Celtic saints were in touch with nature. Traditional churches are male-dominated and place women in a subordinate, supporting role. The Celtic Church gave women a high profile and was proto-feminist. Traditional churches are stiffly hierarchical, while the Celtic Church was anti-hierarchical. The traditional Church was negatively obsessed with sex, while the Celts were accommodating. The traditional churches sided with the big empires. The Celtic saints were Irish, Welsh and Cornish nationalists.

The interpretation is of course a fantasy. The Irish and British missionary saints of the fifth and sixth centuries, Patrick in Ireland, Columba in Iona, Samson in Wales and Brittany and Petroc in Cornwall, lived long before the rise of nation states and knew nothing of modern nationalism. It is ironic that Irish nationalism has taken for its icon Patrick, a Briton, or as we would now say, a Welshman. That these early evangelists preached a forgiving and permissive Christianity is equally wide of the mark. 'Celtic' Christianity emphasised asceticism and it is no accident that John Calvin's harsh doctrines conquered much of what we now call the Celtic lands during the Reformation. The real inheritors of the Celtic spiritual tradition, I discovered, were the Methodists in Cornwall, the Calvinist Methodists in Wales and the Free Church in Scotland, none of them known for mysticism, an interest in herbal remedies, tolerance of pagan traditions or liberal attitudes to sex. The puritanical strain is equally evident in Ireland, in both the Catholic tradition and in Presbyterian north-east Ulster.

But modern Celtic enthusiasts rarely acknowledge this ascetic tradition. Instead, the 1970s and 1980s saw Celticism emerge as a kind of shorthand expression for almost any unorthodox or non-traditional spirituality. Shirley Toulson, in *The Celtic Alternative* of 1987, was typical of this school, proposing that Celtic Christianity had more in common with Buddhism than modern institutional Catholicism or Protestantism. A 'church without martyrs', at peace with nature and decidedly feminist, it was 'more concerned with celebrating life than with recording death'.[1] Tom Davies, in *The Celtic Heart* in 1997, defined Celticness in terms of restored emphasis on the nuclear family. 'We should duly revive the values of the old Celtic heart, become passionate and proud again, relearn the delights of music, poetry and story-telling', he wrote. 'A revived Celtic heart would . . . put women in their rightful place next to men . . . [for] the old Celt understood the sanctity of life and the sacred interconnectedness of everything.'[2] Peter Cherici in *Celtic Sexuality* advanced the claim that the ancient Celts, again assumed as a homogeneous group, had been a sexually liberated society, featuring women 'dispensing favours as they saw fit'. As he put it: 'Men and women were not ashamed of the urges of their bodies and recognised them as natural, pleasurable and even religious.'[3]

The Celtic revivals that have taken place over many centuries have had little direct connection to the lands or the people they claim as their inspiration. From early hagiographers and historians such as Bede, through the Norman bishops and the sixteenth-century Protestant controversialists, to Matthew Arnold in the 1860s or the recent Celtic Christian writers and sex gurus, outsiders have constructed their own image of Celts. They fashioned Celts to act as a counterweight to what they perceived as deficiencies in their own societies; as symbols and representations of otherness, their factual existence has become increasingly unnecessary.

Celtic revivals more often than not dovetailed with a downturn in the fortunes of the real, live Celts. James Usher, seventeenth-century Archbishop of Armagh, was an important revivalist. He was an important promoter of Ireland as 'the iland of Saints', as he put it, because of 'that innumerable company of Saints whose memory was reverenced here'.[4] He did much to revive interest in St Patrick. At the same time he supported the plantation of Ireland with English Protestants and the suppression of the Irish language, and blocked the promotion of native Irishmen in the Church. He did all he could to encourage the repression of the living descendants of those saints he admired so much.

Matthew Arnold's famous lectures on the Celts in Oxford in the 1860s excited English interest in the subject. But while Arnold heaped praise on the Celtic sensibility, he disapproved of the delay even for 'a single hour' of the anglicisation of Wales, even if he did confess to a 'a moment's distress to one's imagination when one hears that the last Cornish peasant who spoke the old tongue of Cornwall is dead'.[5] The Celts were wonderfully sensuous, he insisted, but they belonged strictly to the past and his 'distress' at the death of Cornish was not deep. 'The fusion of all the inhabitants of these islands into one homogenous English speaking whole . . . the swallowing up of separate provincial nationalities is a consummation toward which the natural course of things irresistibly tends,' he remarked. 'The sooner the Welsh language has disappeared as an instrument of the practical, political, social, life of Wales, the better.'[6]

More recent trumpeters of the Celts have also done much to water down what remains of Celtic culture in Britain, Ireland and France by fuelling a mania for holiday houses in what were once seen as inaccessible and undesirable locations. From the Outer Hebrides to Brittany, the extent of this massive shift in property ownership startled me. Within a generation it has turned much of the western coast of Britain into a new English lordship. More people share in the Celtic musical tradition now than at any stage in history. But as shows like *Riverdance* continue to notch up huge audiences from Mexico to China, the Celtic cultures are entering what looks like the last lap. Talk of a Celtic revival has only masked this decline. It has even assisted it, by drowning out the sound of the community's death rattle. As I found out in environments as different as Brittany and Patagonia, a growth in the number of outsiders learning Breton or Welsh does not compensate for the loss of those who were brought up in these languages and immersed from the start. The learners and buyers-in import a new agenda. This is very visible in Northern Ireland, where the revival of Irish culture is fuelled by the politics of separatism. In consequence, the revival is limited to only one of the two sides of the community.

Nova Scotia in the twentieth century has practically gone the way of Cornwall in the eighteenth. When I visited the island of Cape Breton, Celtic music appeared to be booming but the language was virtually finished. I found much the same story, with variations, all over the Celtic lands. An energetic programme by the assemblies of Wales and Scotland and by the governments of France and Ireland might save rural communities in Brittany, the west of Ireland and the Scottish islands from becoming totally absorbed into the anglophone (or francophone) mass. But no one is holding their breath. There is no hope of such an initiative from the centralising government of France. Not much more can be expected from the new devolved authorities in Scotland or Wales, which, though they flirt with the notion of a Celtic identity, know full well that their power resides with the anglophone urban majority. The new elites there want only a Celtic garnish, such as bilingual airport greetings and other attention-seeking decorative devices that advertise their independence from London.

The eighteenth-century Cornish writer Nicholas Boson of Newlyn likened the fate of Cornish to a creature that had been pushed to the edge of the cliff. 'Our Cornish tongue hath been so long on the wane that we can hardly hope to see it increase again, for as the English confined it to this narrow country first, so it presseth on still, leaving it no place but about the cliff & sea.'[7] This prophetic remark was appropriate to all the Celtic cultures I encountered. Like Cornish, they have been pushed further and further west to the point where they hover 'about the cliff & sea', with little, it seems, to stop them from disappearing finally and for ever over the edge.

Celtic revivals were always the work of outsiders. They reflected the English and French societies' need for contrasting otherness and had little connection to the actual life and beliefs of those societies we call Celtic. The compilers of the early *Vitae Sancti* in the eighth and ninth centuries are usually cited as the sponsors of the first Celtic revival. Like later revivalists, they were often outsiders, working at a distance in time from the objects of their cult. Like modern writers on Celtic spirituality, they embellished and projected.

It is not the sixth-century British writer Gildas that we have to thank for the image of Celtic saints as superhuman heroes, striding across landscapes, banishing reptiles and monsters and floating across water on leaves or stone altars. Nor are there many signs of magic and wizardry in St Patrick's *Confession*, an autobiographical fragment which, if original, predates his death around the year 461.

The image of the Celtic saints as miracle-workers springs from the writings of later chroniclers. Many of these early Celtic revivalists were monks who wanted to attribute the foundation of their monasteries to a saint from what was already seen as a lost golden age. After being virtually forgotten during the two centuries that followed his death, Patrick was rediscovered by a Celtic revival that started in the 690s. Under the revivalists' hand, the all too human missionary of the *Confession* mutated into a fantastic, serpent-expelling wizard. This is the Patrick we know today and who is celebrated on St Patrick's Day wherever the Irish have settled. But the Irish scholar Daniel Binchy noted the stark contrast between the earlier human Patrick of his own writings and the magnified creature that emerged from the first Celtic revival. There was a chasm, he wrote, 'between the real Patrick and the "conquering hero" of his late seventh-century biographers . . . who . . . pulverises his opponents often by a display of bigger and better magic than the local druids'.[8]

Columba, or Colum Cille, the sixth-century Irish missionary and abbot of Iona who died in 597, underwent a similar process. His image was transformed about a hundred years after his death by Adamnan, his kinsman and successor as abbot of Iona from 679 to 704. Adamnan's *Vita* is typical of the genre. A few dates and historical events were sprinkled into a mass of signs and wonders based mostly on the miracles contained in the Old and New Testaments. And so it was that Colum Cille, according to Adamnan, made stones float, raised people from the dead, changed water into wine, expelled a devil from a milk pail and drove a monster from a stream.[9] Devoid of what we would now call facts, and wholly different in tone from the *Confession*, the aim of this 'life', the Celtic writer Ian Bradley has said, was 'to assert Iona's primacy over the far-flung Columban monastic *paruchia* and promote its close links with the ruling house of Dal Riata, the Irish colony in Argyllshire'.[10]

Adamnan was an Irish churchman and he was writing about an Irish saint. But the first Celtic revival was not limited to the Irish. It embraced the Anglo-Saxons, too, in spite of the enmity between the Germanic tribes and the Britons whom they drove into the north and west during the fifth and sixth centuries. Once the invading Angles converted to the faith of their victims, lines of communication sprang up between the incomers and the indigenous people. Lindisfarne, Christian centre of the kingdom of Northumbria, had strong contacts with Irish Iona, for example, which supplied its first bishops. The evangelisation of Northumbria in the 630s was the work of Irishmen, and when the Northumbrian historian Bede, a monk at Wearmouth who died in 735, wrote *The Ecclesiastical History of the English People*, he exalted the Irish founders of the Northumbrian Church, headed by Aidan, as well as lauding the achievements of Columba and Ninian in Whithorn in Scotland. Bede was one of the first Englishmen to romanticise the Irish and Ireland as a land of saints and scholars. It was a land that abounded in 'milk and honey',[11] he said, whose piety and spirituality contrasted favourably with what he saw as the more pedestrian qualities of the eighth-century English.

The second Celtic revival followed the Norman Conquest of 1066. The Norman bishops of Welsh and Scottish sees turned into assiduous collectors of Celtic *Vitae,* partly to advance the antiquity, prestige and claims of their cathedrals and partly also because, having conquered the Anglo-Saxons, it suited them to trumpet the merits of those whom the Anglo-Saxons themselves had conquered. The Norman bishops of St Davids and of Llandaff in Wales promoted the cult of St David, of St Samson and other Celtic saints, while the Norman bishops of Glasgow did the same for St Mungo. The pattern was replicated by the Anglo-Norman conquerors of Ireland in the 1170s: a Norman adventurer named John De Courcy in the 1180s conveniently discovered the bodies of all three of Ireland's leading saints, Brigit, Patrick and Columba, and had them ceremonially reburied in the cathedral of Down, which De Courcy renamed Downpatrick (Dún Pádraig). De Courcy had been in the country only six years but had realised the value of placing the relics of three Celtic saints to further his plans to become the prince of an autonomous Norman state in Ulster.

The Anglo-Normans also discovered Arthur, the Celtic British hero who had kept the Anglo-Saxons at bay. Legends of such a hero had lingered in Wales, where he was not always recalled in a flattering light – a fact ascribed by some to the Church's jealousy of a layman as hero. But in the twelfth century the story snaked back into England, where its anti-Saxon slant ensured a favourable reception among the Anglo-Norman elite.

The great conduit was an inventive historian and storyteller, Geoffrey of Monmouth, who created the modern Arthur in two popular works of the 1130s, the *Prophecies of Merlin* and *History of the Kings of Britain*. The name Arthur had been little known in England before Geoffrey's time. There was no mention of anyone called Arthur in Gildas's *The Ruin and Conquest of Britain*, written in the 540s, which mentioned only a great battle in the year of Gildas's birth (around AD 500) between the Germanic invaders and the Britons at a place called Mons Badonicus. Later writers, however, began to credit this British victory to a certain Arthur, and Nennius, writing in the ninth century, briefly mentioned a figure called Arthur as the enemy of the Saxons at Mount Badon in his *History of the Britons*.[12] Geoffrey made no mention of Nennius in his own account, however. He mysteriously claimed that he obtained his material from an old tome supplied by the Archdeacon of Oxford – the first of many Celtic revivalists to locate his single source in a precious chronicle that had unfortunately since crumbled away, or been lost.

More responsible contemporary historians despised Geoffrey's stories about Arthur, Uther Pendragon, Merlin and Avalon. William of Newburgh, writing in the 1190s, thought them a disgraceful work of scholarship. They were 'a laughable web of fiction', he wrote. 'He has taken the deceitful predictions of a certain Merlin which he has very greatly augmented on his own account and . . . published them as though they were authentic prophecies.' Geoffrey, he pronounced, was guilty of 'wanton and shameless lying'.[13] Alas for William of Newburgh. His own meticulously researched history book was soon forgotten while Geoffrey of Monmouth's legends coursed round England, inspiring Henry II to name his grandson Arthur, and to order a search for Arthur's grave at Glastonbury Abbey. As the sixteenth-century antiquary William Camden put it: 'When Henry 2, King of England, had learned from the songs of the British bards that Arthur the most noble heroe of the Britains, whose courage had so often shattered the Saxons, was bury'd at Glassenbury between two Pyramids, he order'd search to be made for the body.'[14] Geoffrey's works spread into Wales, too, where they were enthusiastically received, and proceeded to burn a trail through the courts of Europe as far as Poland and Cyprus. They were medieval best-sellers. As one historian remarked in the 1950s: 'Thanks chiefly to Geoffrey of Monmouth, Merlin was revered for his magic powers from Sicily to Ireland and the prophecies concocted for him in 1135 were still taken seriously enough in Germany nearly 500 years later as to be published in 1608.'[15]

The Reformation saw yet another Celtic revival. This might seem paradoxical, as the Protestants destroyed as many of the physical and architectural props of the cult of the Celtic saints as they could get hold of. They demolished the shrines to those half-remembered missionaries that the Norman bishops had erected so assiduously, pulled down the statues and forbade pilgrimages to wells linked to saints' healing powers. But the Protestant relationship to the Celts was complicated. Faced with Catholic taunts of 'Where was your Church before Luther?' Protestant writers turned to the pre-Saxon, Celtic Church for aid in the battle against Rome. John Bale, the aggressively Protestant Bishop of Ossory in Ireland under Edward VI, was most interested in ancient British writers like Gildas and sympathised passionately with his account of British Christians fighting a desperate battle for survival against the pagan hordes from Germany.

To Bale, and to other English Protestants then and since, it was clear from Gildas that the early British Church had anticipated most of the doctrines of the Reformation and that the corruption of the medieval Church could therefore be laid at the feet of the Anglo-Saxons. 'In Englande was there afore their [the Saxons'] commyng a Christianitie, but it was all without masses,' Bale wrote in the *Actes of the English Votaries* of 1560: 'The Britaynes in those dayes hadde none other Gods servyce but the Gospell.' The halcyon period, Bale said, ended with the arrival in England in 597 of Augustine – no longer a saint but an emissary of papal darkness. 'Thus did that carnall Synagoge (then called the Englysh churche) which came from Rome with Augustine, mooste cruelly persecute . . . the christen churche of the Britaines.'[16]

Bale, John Jewel, Elizabethan Bishop of Salisbury, Matthew Parker, Elizabeth I's first Archbishop of Canterbury, and Richard Davies, Bishop of

St Davids, pored over the surviving accounts of the British Church that had existed before the Roman mission of St Augustine. In Ireland, James Usher, Protestant Archbishop of Armagh, did likewise, reviving interest in St Patrick and the other early saints as spiritual forefathers of the Protestant Church of Ireland. In reality, the Church of Ireland was the church of the Protestant English settlers and of the English Pale, as the strip of land around Dublin on the eastern seaboard was known. But Usher, a true Celtic revivalist, used the Celts to project a very different image of his Church as old, organic and part of the seamless tapestry of Irish history. The essence of his message, contained in *The Religion Professed by the Ancient Irish* of 1631, was that 'the religion professed by the ancient bishops, priests, monks and other Christians in this land was for substance the very same with that which now by publike authoritie is maintained therein'.[17]

It was the Protestant apologists who first described the ancient Britons as Celts. The word was drawn from classical descriptions of the barbarian tribes inhabiting central Europe and Gaul and would have been foreign to Bede and the Norman ecclesiastics. It did not enter European consciousness until the rediscovery of Greek and Roman classical writers during the Renaissance. The widespread printing of classical works from the 1490s onwards awoke the interest of the new book-buying public to the existence of the 'Celtae' who flitted across the pages of Roman accounts of contemporary Europe. Julius Caesar mentioned them in *The Gallic War,* for example. The opening page declared Gaul to be divided into three parts, 'one of which the Belgae inhabit, the Aquitani another, the third a people who in their own tongue are called "Celts" but in ours "Gauls"'.[18] Another source was Tacitus.

Inconveniently, no classical writer linked the 'Celtae' of Gaul to Britain, let alone Ireland. However, Caesar said of the people of Kent that 'their way of life is much the same as that of the Gauls',[19] and he drew attention to the existence of a druidic cult in both lands, which he thought had begun in Gaul and been transferred to Britain. Likewise, Tacitus described the language of the Britons as 'not much different'[20] to that of the Gauls. Confusingly, he claimed the inhabitants of Caledonia were of Germanic origin, which serves as a reminder of the fact that Greek and Roman writers used the terms 'German' and 'Celt' almost interchangeably. The truth was that none of these accounts added up to much beyond a thumbnail sketch. The classical writers were centripetal. Rome was all-important and what interested them was the struggle between the great politicians at the centre. The rest of the cast were but faint shadows.

It was the writers of the Reformation era who worried away over the Celtae, floating theories and drawing links. The Scottish humanist George Buchanan, tutor to the first British king, James VI and I, was the driving force in Celtic studies in his *History of Scotland*, published in 1582. Most Protestant writers from Bale to Ussher had been interested only in proving that the ancient Britons anticipated their own religious opinions. Reflecting a more scientific interest in the study of language, Buchanan made much of the fact that Tacitus – while not actually identifying the ancient Britons as 'Celtae' – had remarked on the similarity between the Gaulish and British languages. Buchanan drew an explicit conclusion from this: if the Gauls were 'Celtae', then the ancient Britons were, too.

Buchanan reinforced this claim by citing examples of similar root word forms found in place names that ranged from Roman Dacia to Scotland, such as *dun* for fort, and *dur* for water. There was a Dundee in Scotland, he remarked, a Dunelmum in Roman Durham and the Roman for Lyon in France was Lugdunum. The Celtae, he concluded, had originally spoken one tongue in Britain and Ireland, which later on dissolved into different speeches, 'for if anyone of either of these nations hears a person speaking British he still recognises the sound of the language and understands many of the words'.[21]

Buchanan was a pioneer in claiming the ancient Britons and Gauls as Celts on the basis of their language. But as an anglophone historian of Scotland, he naturally did not choose to dwell for too long on the issue. It took a much later Welsh scholar, Edward Lhuyd, Keeper of the Ashmolean Museum in Oxford, to draw up a more elaborate study of the Celtic languages, using tables to illustrate the common root of many words used by the Scots, Welsh, Irish and Cornish in his *Archaeologia Britannica* of 1707.

Lhuyd both advanced interest in the various languages and popularised the term 'Celt'. The Celt, or Kelt, began to displace the increasingly confusing term 'Briton', which since the union of the English and Scottish crowns in 1603 had taken on a new life and a new meaning. 'Briton' was, in fact, becoming confused with the word 'English', for in the new state of Britain England was the dominant element. As Thomas Habington wrote in *The Epistle of Gildas, The Most Ancient British Author*, in 1638, England was the furnace in which the British crown had been forged. 'Hath not the force of the English furnace melted all their crownes into one mighty streame of gold,' he asked, 'and like the rod of Moses devoured all the rods of the magicians'.[22]

Celt and Briton, therefore, went their separate ways. Well into the eighteenth century they were still interchangeable, but Celt slowly gained the upper hand as the term applying to the non-English peoples of Britain. When the clerical writer Henry Rowlands, author of *Mona Antiqua Restaurata* (in 1723), paid tribute to the *Archaeologia,* he used both. Rowlands reminded his readers that Lhuyd had demonstrated the links between the branches of 'this language, call it Celtic or British, or what you will', which had split into 'severall different languages, as the Welsh and Cornish, Highland-Scotch, Bretoon and Irish now do, tho all proceding from one common Head or Fountain viz the antient Celtish or British Tongue'.[23]

Growing interest in the peoples who inhabited Britain's remote edge dovetailed with the Romantic movement – the reaction that set in from the mid-eighteenth century onwards to classical antiquity and the cult of reasonableness and utility. Responding to Jean-Jacques Rousseau's call that people should be more 'natural', look more critically at society and its forms and cultivate 'feeling', the public began investing cultures formerly dismissed as primitive and worthless with different qualities. They were still primitive, but now it appeared they also had sensibility, spontaneity and feeling. The Romantic sensibility had a great impact on art. Cliffs, storms, waterfalls, bolts of lightning and other signs of nature's dramatic impact took over as themes from studies of ordered fields and plains. Smoothness and order gave way to jaggedness, and peace to violence. The mountain, once a nuisance and dreaded as the home of savage rebels, became an object of veneration. Druids, those shamans glimpsed in the writings of Tacitus and Julius Caesar, were another popular subject, painted robed and awaiting doom at the hands of Roman armies on the edges of cliffs, their hands flung up to the angry sky.

The fact that 'the druids remain obscure' because 'they attempted to keep secret all things concerned with their activities'[24] made interest in them all the greater. A general fascination with druids converged with the rise of archae-ology. Were the Iron Age stone circles at Stonehenge, at Carnac in Brittany, in Cornwall and on the island of Lewis disused temples of the druids mentioned by Caesar and Tacitus? The writers of the eighteenth century were not to know that the stones predated the Romans and their druid enemies by millennia. The Irish writer John Toland linked the stone circles from Orkney to St Buryan in Cornwall to the druids in his *Critical History of the Celtic Religion* in 1718. At the same time the antiquarians wanted to hunt down the druids' ancient headquarters, which Tacitus had located on the island of 'Mona'. Taking his cue from Caesar, who positioned Mona between Ireland and Britain in his *Gallic War,*[25] the Scottish historian and archbishop James Spottiswoode in his *History of the Church of Scotland,* written in the 1620s, identified 'Mona' with the Isle of Man. Determined to claim the druids as actors in an early Scottish Protestant drama, Spottiswoode claimed the Scottish king Cratilinth had expelled the druids in 277 in 'one of his first works to purge the kingdom of heathenish superstition'.[26] By the 1700s the Welsh had relocated Mona on Ynys Môn, or Anglesey. 'I may take it for granted', Rowlands wrote loftily in the 1720s, 'that it is the generally received Account among all sorts of people in Wales who pretend to anything of Antiquity that the Isle of Mona, or Anglesey, was antiently the Seat of the British druids.'[27]

Toland, an Ulster convert to Protestantism – like Spottiswoode – rejoiced in their destruction, seeing them as a species of early papist. 'The History of the Druids in short is the complete history of Priestcraft,' Toland wrote. 'No heathen Priesthood ever came up to the perfection of the druidical, which was far more exquisite than any other such system, as having been much better calculated to beget ignorance.'[28]

But druidism had lost such negative, papist and anti-Christian connotations by the late 1740s. English society was less worried by 'priestcraft' by then and ceased to recognise an analogy between druids and the Catholic clergy. Instead, a fashion developed for druidic societies, at which gentlemen dined, dressed up and performed vaguely Masonic rituals under the excuse of carrying out charitable works. The Druidical Society of Anglesey, formed in 1772, under an 'archdruid' and a 'sub-druid', was essentially a social club. It drew the local gentry and clergy together for small-scale charitable and agricultural activities. In 1794, for example, it awarded five guineas to the farmer with the best-kept hedge on Anglesey.[29] The members did not don the long robes, togas and torques that have since become *de rigueur* at the opening ceremonies of a Welsh eisteddfod. The Anglesey society wore dark blue uniforms, embossed with yellow buttons with druids' heads on them.

The Romantics yearned to hear the authentic voice of the descendants of the druids and the Celts. In 1760 an ambitious Scotsman, James Macpherson, tapped this appetite with the publication of a Gaelic epic. Stirred into action by an article in the *Scots Magazine* of 1756, which lamented the prevailing ignorance of the Irish language, Macpherson compiled a 70-page epic, entitled *Fragments of Ancient Poetry Collected in the Highlands of Scotland and Translated from the Gaelic or Erse Language.* It was an instant sensation and Macpherson followed it with two more poetic epics, *Fingal* and *Temora* in 1762 and 1763. Where did it all come from? It seems to have been the story of Geoffrey of Monmouth over again. Geoffrey had obtained his material on Arthur from a mysterious tome in the keeping of the Archdeacon of Oxford, which, of course, was never seen again. Macpherson's epic was allegedly based on the 1,200-year-old manuscript of a Gaelic bard called Ossian, which – similarly – was never produced.

Ossian, as the collection of works came to be known, enjoyed the same huge success as Geoffrey of Monmouth's Arthurian legends. Like Geoffrey's works, being rubbished by the critics proved no bar to popularity. Walter Scott loathed Macpherson's *Ossian* for the same reason that William of Newburgh had loathed Geoffrey of Monmouth's tales of Arthur. It was 'an absolute tissue of forgeries ... absolutely drivelling',[30] he said. Horace Walpole affected total boredom. 'It tires me to death to read how many ways a warrior is like the moon, or the sun, or a rock, or a lion, or the ocean,' he wrote to George Montague in 1761. 'I cannot believe it genuine – I cannot believe a regular poem of six books has been preserved, uncorrupted, by oral tradition from times before Christianity was introduced into the island.'[31] This was a very fair point, but the critics' scepticism did not suppress the public appetite for *Ossian*, which was republished almost annually until 1800 and went on to triumph in Europe as well. The catcalls did not deter imitators in Wales and Ireland from unearthing their own epics either. Edward Jones took up the cudgel for Wales, with his *Musical and Poetical Relicks of the Welsh Bards* in 1784, while in Ireland, Charlotte Brooke produced *Reliques of Irish Poetry* in 1789. These works played to the same Romantic English audience as *Ossian*. 'Our Irish bards,' Brooke announced breathlessly, 'exhibit a glow of cultivated genius – a spirit of elevated heroism, sentiments of pure honour'.[32] *Our* bards? The phrase was revealing. Brooke was in the tradition of the Anglo-Norman bishops – a complete outsider to the world she admired. The unmarried daughter of the Protestant Bishop of Elphin was Irish to the extent that she lived there. The Brookes were descendants of Jacobean planters in Donegal. But England's imagination was stirred. 'There emerged many brilliant images – now an awe-inspiring group of white-robed priests offering human sacrifice, now a chorus of bards chanting potent curses against a Roman or British tyrant, now a valiant Celtic hero, dying, usually in vain, in the eternal struggle for liberty.'[33]

In December 1865 and in February and May 1866 the Oxford Professor of Poetry since 1857, Matthew Arnold, delivered four lectures on 'The Study of Celtic Literature'. They were inspired by Lady Charlotte Guest's translation of the Welsh legends, known as the *Mabinogion*, and the Count of Villemarque's popular 1839 book, *Barzaz Breiz*, a pioneering collection of Breton poetry. Arnold owed most to another French writer, Ernest Renan, whose essay in 1854, 'Sur la Poésie des races celtiques', had anticipated many of Arnold's own conclusions. Renan had drawn two principal observations in his essay. One was that the Celts, taken as a whole, were essentially feminine, and the other was that a direct correspondence existed between their poetical, dreamy, feminine character and their marginalisation as nations. Artistic success, it seemed, had bred political failure.

Arnold relayed all of this to his English audience, not, now, with the Bretons in mind, but the Irish, the Welsh and the Scottish Highlanders. Defining the Celts as melancholy, he, too, posited a relationship between the Celts' moral and spiritual qualities and their apparent lack of political or economic success. Their poetic nature had doomed them, though only on the material plain, for it was 'a consoling thought that nations disinherited of political success may yet leave their mark on the world's progress'. Arnold was a Celtic revivalist *par excellence*, for his real interest lay not in the Celtic cultures themselves, but in what they could do for England. Arnold's Celts had one central function, which was to counterbalance the dull materialism of the English middle class, now unmistakably the dominant force in society. Arnold was revolted by the potential impact of the massed ranks of middle-class English tradesmen and shopkeepers on high culture. 'We in England have come to that point when the continued advance and greatness of our nation is threatened by one cause,' he mused. 'Far more than by the helplessness of an aristocracy whose day is fast coming to an end, far more than by the rawness of a lower class whose day is only just beginning, we are imperilled by what I call the Philistinism of our middle class.'[34]

Again, a fantasy version of the Celts was created to serve other people's purposes, in effect to supply a deficiency that some English intellectuals felt in their own society. Arnold found middle-class England prosaic and summoned forth the Celts to be sensuous and sensual, lovers of bright colours, and of company and pleasure. At the same time they had to remain ineffectual, for Arnold was not interested in investing real live Celts with political power. That was not for them. 'For ages and ages the world has slipped ever more and more out of the Celts' grasp,' he said. '"They went forth to war," Ossian says most truly, "but they always fell".'[35] While the Teutonic English built their factories and their railways and kept the reins of government firmly in their own hands, the Celts would gladden their spirits with song. 'The Germanic genius has steadiness as its main basis with commonness and humdrum for its defect . . . the Celtic genius, sentiment as its basis, with love of beauty, charm and spirituality for its excellence, inef-fectualness and self-will for its defect'.[36]

Arnold's Celtic lectures cast a long shadow over the late nineteenth century. When Arthur O'Shaughnessy wrote in his collection of poems *Music and Moonlight*:

> We are the music makers
>   We are the dreamers of dreams
> We are the movers and shakers
>   Of the world for ever, it seems[37]

his lines lauded the *fin-de-siècle* poet as a social outcast. But his words also reflected an increasingly powerful image of the Celts as Pan-like figures, spinning their dreams and playing their music, eternal elves of the west. Fairies and elves did, of course, form part of the traditional belief system of people in Cornwall, Ireland, the Isle of Man and Scotland (and were part of English folk culture, too). But after Arnold, the Celts and the fairies fused in the English imagination into a single race of beings, ghostly inhabitants of a twilight zone.

Arnold's ideas influenced the school of romantic Anglo-Irish writers that grew up around W. B. Yeats, the author in 1893 of *Celtic Twilight*. They were also felt in the Gaelic League in the 1890s, which sought to revive the Irish language and invested the Celtic Gaels with the assumption of auto-matic moral and spiritual superiority over the base and material English. Arnold's ideas also helped to form the thought of one of the Gaelic League's most famous students, Patrick Pearse, the nationalist hero of the 1916 Rising. Pearse gave a lecture in 1897 on 'The Intellectual Future of the Gael' that was almost pure Arnold. In it, he declared: 'The Gael, like all Celts, is distinguished by an intense and passionate love for nature. The Gael is the high priest of nature . . . He revels in imagination. He loves to gaze on what is beautiful, to listen to sweet and rapturous sounds.'[38] Many of Pearse's admirers saw the rising he led in Dublin as the realisation of a thor-oughly Celtic philosophy of heroism and sacrifice.

The revival of the 1890s boosted the idea of a Celtic commonwealth that would unite Ireland, Scotland and Wales. The decades before the First World War marked the high point of such Celtic societies as the Gaelic League, An Commun Gaidhealach in Scotland and sister movements in Brittany and the Isle of Man. It was the age of Celtic congresses, the first of which was held in 1867 in St Brieuc in Brittany. Weakened by the carnage of the war (though not in Ireland), the Celtic revival faded in Scotland, Wales and Brittany in the 1920s. Language revival and dressing up in togas was not an answer to the questions of mass unemployment and industrial decline. Wales and Scotland turned away from Celtic nationalism to socialism, a movement that paid scant regard to Celtic claims to nationhood and made the argument about the Celts' moral and spiritual values look anachronistic.

The Celtic societies lost their vigour, their dream of creating a common-wealth of Celtic states faded and public interest fell away. When the first Celtic Congress was held in Dublin in 1900, people lined the streets to cheer the self-selected representatives in their adopted nationalist dresses. By the 1920s there was far less interest in such events and Ireland was recovering from the civil war that followed the granting of independence to the 26 counties in the south. The Celtic nationalists had to face the fact that three or four decades of cultural activism had done little to reverse a trend towards anglicisation that had, in fact, accelerated in the early twentieth century. The 1930s and 1940s were a lean time for the infant Welsh, Breton and Scottish nationalist parties, marked by derisory results in the elections they contested. Irish independence had not delivered the Gaelic state that the Celtic activists had dreamed of either. Even there, where the government was committed to promoting Gaelic culture, the arrival of the cinema was helping English to penetrate Irish-speaking rural strongholds.

Against this unfavourable background, another Celtic revival was born. It arose in the 1960s as part of a wave of anti-establishment sentiment that engulfed American student campuses and saw the birth of both the hippies and the anti-Vietnam war movement. In Europe it revealed itself in the violent student protests in Paris, the uprising in Czechoslovakia, and in the upsurge in militant nationalist activity in the Italian Tyrol, in the Basque Country of Spain and in Northern Ireland. There was no real violence in Scotland and Wales, but both witnessed a sudden upturn in the fortunes of small nationalist parties which for the first time successfully challenged the old dominion of the Labour and Conservative parties and swung national attention towards the suddenly much-talked about 'Celtic fringe'.

This wide-ranging rejection of the political and social post-war order was youth-based and had a strong musical component. A revival of folk music in the early 1960s, which in Ireland quickly became the new musical estab-lishment, fed a renewed interest in Celtic languages. This, in turn, helped inspire the growth in popularity of Irish, Welsh, Breton and Gaelic-language schooling. In Ireland, people began to discard English-sounding names, to assume Irish names and to use traditional Irish spelling. It was a process that had clear parallels with the trend among African-Americans towards casting off 'white' Christian names and adopting African and Islamic ones, the most famous example being the re-baptism of the US boxer Cassius Clay in 1964 as Muhammad Ali.

A few decades into the latest and most recent Celtic revival, the actual gains, however, are hard to locate. There is the relentless marketing of supposedly Celtic music, books, designs, spirituality, medicine and the application of the word Celtic to an increasing number of aspects of human activity. But outside Northern Ireland, where it could be argued that Celtic revivalism has partly rolled back English culture and language and reintroduced Irish as a means of communication, the latest Celtic revival has done no more than any of its predecessors to hold back the advance of English. As primarily English-inspired phenomena, the revivals have tended mainly to reinforce an image of Celtic societies as peripheral. They are quaint, rural, fairy-like, not quite real and something that the inhabitants of the 'real' world, can escape to when they feel like it, for rest and recreation.

We have become so attuned to English cultural supremacy that it stretches the mind to imagine any other outcome that does not feature England and the English language in the centre and the Celts hovering on the edge and in the corner. The English conquest now seems not only absolute, but predestined, so that it is easy to forget that it was once just one of several competing languages and cultures on these islands. It is equally easy to forget that the fortunes of English varied greatly over the centuries, and that English often was forced on to the defensive, especially in Ireland.

The twists and turns of fortune that displaced the Celtic languages and set English on its way to supremacy, not only in England but throughout the world, began with the invasions of the fifth and sixth centuries, which brought the Germanic Angles and Saxons into the south-east of Britain. Why the Germanic tongue of the Angles should have become established in Britain is a mystery, for another invading Germanic tribe, the Franks, did not achieve the same result. The Franks turned Gaul into France, but the Gauls imposed their Latinised language on the Germanic Franks, not the other way round. In Britain it was the opposite. There, the Germanic language had such success that within a short time little remained of the older British tongue except place names. The Germanic transformation of Britain's cultural landscape was almost complete. A huge natural disaster may have played its part, perhaps a plague that emptied the land for the incomers. Either way, they moved relentlessly north and west, pushing the Britons into the corners and into what we now call Wales, Cumberland, Somerset, Devon and Cornwall.

The legend of Arthur, the hero who resisted the invaders, suggests that the Britons held up this advance. But if the Angles lost battles on the way, they won the war, consolidating an Angle-land that eventually included the British redoubts of Cumberland, Somerset and Devon. With the exception of the Britons who migrated to what had been Roman Armorica to create Little Britain, or Brittany, the Britons found themselves confined even more narrowly to Cornwall and Wales. No longer sharing a land border, the British language began to diverge into two tongues – Welsh and Cornish. And with the conquest of Cornwall in the ninth century, England took on the rough contours that have lasted until today.

The Norman Conquest checked the advance of English, as both English and the British languages (Welsh and Cornish), were then thrown into an inferior position. But English won in the end. Absorbing a great deal of Norman French, it re-emerged in the fourteenth century as the language of kings and parliaments and began its conquest of the British Isles and Ireland in earnest. But by the end of Elizabeth I's reign the conquest was still far from complete. English was still struggling in Ireland, where it had been on the retreat ever since the Black Death ravaged the English settler colonies. There a confident and aggressive Gaelic society swallowed up the English settlers planted in their midst, so that, as the authorities complained, people of Saxon descent progressively threw off their English language, names and clothing.

But Ireland was a special case. In Cornwall, the weakest branch among the Celtic languages succumbed rapidly. In 1549 the Cornish rebelled against the introduction of the first English Prayer Book. As the historian Mark Stoyle points out in his study of early modern Cornwall, *West Britons,* the Cornish revolt was not entirely a rebellion against the English language, for the centre of the revolt lay in the anglophone east of the county, not in the Cornish-speaking west.[39] But it remains fair to conclude that the roots of the rebellion lay partly in the fact that for at least half of the Cornish people, the new English service book was incomprehensible. As the rebels put it famously: 'We the Cornyshe men (wherof certen of us understande no Englysh) utterly refuse thys newe Englysh.'[40] Only half a century later a rebellion citing those grounds was inconceivable.

At the same time, English was advancing rapidly in Scotland against Gaelic, pushing north and west and anglicising the old Gaelic-speaking county of Galloway, once a bridgehead between the Gaels of Ulster and their kinsmen in north-west Scotland. This anglicisation of Galloway began a process of breaking up the Celtic-speaking peoples into a series of disconnected pools that were geographically isolated from each other.

Even in Ireland the Gaelic resurgence was eventually checked. While Galloway was anglicised peacefully, James I broke the backbone of Irish Gaelic resistance to English rule in nearby Ulster by force, expropriating land and 'planting' it with a mixture of Scottish, English and Manx settlers who formed an English-speaking wedge in the heart of the province. Half a century later in the south, the Cromwellian conquest and destruction of the old landed families in the 1650s opened the door to lasting penetration by the English language.

By then the Celtic societies were locked into the defensive position they have maintained to this day. But the Celts remained numerically very significant. Until the Irish famine of the 1840s decimated the peasantry, the population of Ireland was little less than half that of England, and at least half of those were Gaelic-speakers. When the Welsh evangelical Thomas Charles rode from Clonmel to Waterford in 1807 he noted: 'All speaking Irish and many Irish only',[41] and that in a region that had been subjected to English influence for centuries. In 1835 the Scottish evangelical Christopher Anderson thought plans to convert Ireland to Protestantism useless unless the missionaries first learned fluent Irish. 'The Irish speak Irish still and to an extent ten times greater than in the days of Henry VIII,' he remarked. 'The language has increased, of course, with the natural increase of the people'.[42]

As late as 1879, when the *Journal of the Royal Statistical Society* published an article on the 'The Celtic Languages of the British Isles', non-English-speakers still dominated a large part of Ireland and the British Isles, even if they did inhabit mostly mountainous and thinly populated land. The geographical line in Scotland that separated the Lowlands from the Highlands remained a linguistic and cultural frontier and half of Scotland's landmass lay north of it. Wales still spoke Welsh, an obstinate little lump in the middle of Britain that had defied centuries of effort by English clergymen, judges and politicians to coerce its inhabitants into surrendering their identity. About 900,000 of the country's 1.15 million, or about 80 per cent of the population, still used the language. Even on the tiny island of Man, Manx was spoken by about 14,000 people, which was about half the island's population, while Irish was still spoken by more than 900,000 people, concentrated in the west. Adding to this the roughly 2 million Breton-speakers makes a figure of around 3.5 million people in Britain, Ireland and France who spoke one of the old Celtic languages in the last quarter of the nineteenth century.

But from the 1870s the decline accelerated. Today 400,000 people in Wales speak Welsh, or 18 per cent of the population, down from 977,000 in 1911, the high-water mark of the Welsh-speaking community. There are about 250,000 who speak Brittany's Breton but they are nearly all elderly and make up less than 10 per cent of Brittany's population. There are about 60,000 Scottish Gaelic-speakers, half living in the cities and half living on the islands of Skye and Harris, Lewis and Barra on the Outer Hebrides, the Highland line having long since vanished as a linguistic frontier. Together they make up not much more than 1 per cent of Scotland's population. A few hundred people have learned revived Cornish and Manx. The Republic of Ireland boasts over a million Irish speakers but this high figure is politicised, reflecting the identification of the language with patriotism and its compulsory status in schools. It is not an accurate barometer of the number of people who actually use Irish as a living language. That number is probably not much higher than the figure for Gaelic-speakers in Scotland. Even in the Gaeltacht, the areas set aside by the Irish government as Irish-speaking regions, the proportion of the local population who used Irish daily in 1996 was estimated at less than 50 per cent.[43] Altogether, the number of speakers of non-English or non-French languages in what until recently were thought of as Celtic lands reaches no more than 800,000. Of that figure, more than a quarter are Bretons who are almost all aged over 60. The anticipated extinction of Breton as a community language over the next two decades, which almost everyone in Brittany expects as a matter of course, will cut the 800,000 figure to half a million and throw Welsh into even greater prominence.

The overall picture is of a weak dam, already full of holes, that has quite suddenly collapsed, leaving the floodwater to wash over the already waterlogged land behind it. Not everyone alerted to this great change believes it matters all that much. Several hundred languages die every decade in Australia, New Guinea and Latin America, and the pace quickens as the world's 6 billion humans consolidate into a club of 'winning' cultures, of which 2.4 billion speak one of the top eight languages – Mandarin, English, Spanish, Bengali, Hindi, Portuguese, Russian and Japanese, each of which has more than 120 million speakers.

Most experts on 'language death' believe that about 90 per cent of the world's 6,700 or so languages face imminent extinction through a combination of assimilation, physical domination, natural disasters and 'language suicide'.[44] Hardly any of the 250 Aboriginal languages in Australia are likely to survive long, while Daniel Nettle and Suzanne Romaine's recent study of the world's dying languages, *Vanishing Voices*, has pointed out that 51 of the 79 native languages in the United States already have fewer than 10 speakers.[45] Many are vanishing undocumented and without any of the government grants, schools and 'gaeltachts' that have been set up to prop up the Celtic languages of Britain and Ireland. It is certainly Eurocentric to concentrate on the plight of the peoples of the edge of north-west Europe.

Some critics believe too much effort is being concentrated on Europe's failing cultures, and that just as failing schools must close in the end, it may be time to turn off the life-support machine for Europe's dying languages. Instead of pumping resources into maintaining the culture of a few tens of thousands of rural Europeans, they say, we should focus on dynamic, evolving dialects now emerging among immigrant communities in the US and in some inner-city areas in Europe.

Such advocates could cite some of the pioneers of Celtic studies in defence of their views. Edward Lhuyd did not set much store on the continued use of Cornish. 'For my part I am not very solicitous about keeping up the Cornish language,' he wrote, 'since it is not very necessary to the people who know very well how to speak English.' Lhuyd laboured to collect the last fragments of spoken Cornish solely for posterity because he considered that 'to preserve something of an Old Tongue in some printed book is without doubt a thing very pleasing to Scholars and Gentlemen and very necessary to our Antiquaries'.[46]

Lhuyd need not have worried about his antiquarians. The Celts have never been so well provided for in terms of books and dictionaries, museums, exhibitions, interpretive centres, language schools, language videos and 'taster' days during which people are introduced to Celtic cultures. What would have surprised Lhuyd is the shrinkage at the core, not merely in Cornwall, but in his own Wales. All the Celtic revivals of the past and present have been predicated on the existence, somewhere, of people for whom these languages, traditions and beliefs actually mean something. As they finally disappear and the Celtic sea, having retreated into disconnected pools, reduces to puddles after which there may be nothing, we enter a new territory.

PART ONE

CHAPTER ONE

The Scottish Highlands
'The Ald Scottis toung'

We are dealing with a people who love their own tongue and feel its power and pathos.
(Free Church statement to the Royal Inquiry into the Crofters, 1884)

Some flyers I found in the Sabhal Mòr Ostaig, the Gaelic college on the island of Skye, announced that on 14 July a Gaelic service would be held in the old cemetery just outside Broadford village. And so, on the day, I joined a small column of tourists and language enthusiasts trussed up in wind-cheaters walking across a boggy moor, past trees bent almost double by the wind, towards the sea.

The windswept cemetery, overlooking the isle of Raasay, birthplace of the great twentieth-century Gaelic poet Sorley Maclean, adjoined a large, overhanging rock. The preacher who took the service said that the apostle of Skye, Mulruabh, the 'bald, red-headed one' in Gaelic, might well have preached from that same rock after landing from Ireland in the sixth century. Today people think of Skye today as quintessentially Scottish. It has something to do with the mountains, the presence of golden eagles, and the fact that many older people speak Gaelic and are, or were, famous for their Presbyterian piety. Then again, the landscape bears many marks of the terrible land war known as the Highland Clearances. Dr Johnson came here on his Highland journey and encountered the Jacobite heroine Flora Macdonald, saviour of the doomed Bonnie Prince Charlie. Skye seems as Scottish as they come.

But Scotland belonged to the future when Mulruabh lived here. In his time, the north of the country was inhabited by the Celtic people known as Picti, or Picts, while the south-west was held by Celtic Britons, related to the modern Welsh. The Irish tribe known as Scoti was only beginning to fashion the lordship of Dalriada in what is now Argyllshire, from which Scotland emerged.

On my way up to Skye I stopped off at the hill fort of Dunadd, the crag that rises out of a great bog, encircled by the River Add near Kilmartin. The numerous cairns, rock carvings and standing stones that dot the landscape come as a forceful reminder that this land was inhabited long before the Scoti came from Ireland, for they were several thousand years old by the time this hill fort was built.

Dunadd is believed to have been the capital of Dalriada, a place of coronations, assemblies and other great ceremonies. When the seventh-century abbot of Iona Adamnan described his great predecessor, Columba, or Colum Cille, addressing people in the 570s from the 'caput regionis', the capital of the region, Dunadd may well have been what he referred to. The first written inscriptions around here recall the fact that the Scoti were linguistically and culturally part of Ireland. A seventh- or eighth-century cross at Barnakil, about a mile from Dunadd, reads 'XRI Reiton', or 'In the name of Christ, Reiton'. A stone inscribed at Poltalloch reads 'Cronan', a common Irish name from the ninth century, and is written in ogham script, the early Irish system of writing.

The Scoti absorbed and subsumed the Picti in the 840s under Kenneth mac Alpin. Possibly the two peoples came together to better resist the incursions of the Vikings, who were harassing them both with increasing frequency. But the memory of saints like Mulruabh in Skye outlived and overcame these political and cultural conflicts. The people of Skye held on to the cult of the bald, red-headed Irishman long after the Picts had vanished and as those who had become the Scots spread their Irish speech across the whole of modern Scotland, outside the south-east.

By the ninth century, Viking raiders posed the greatest challenge to the Scots. They overran the north-west and ransacked Columba's foundation on Iona, an ecclesiastical centre for the Gaels on both sides of the water. The Norse left a strong imprint on north-west Scotland, especially on Na Hearadh and Leodhas (Harris and Lewis in English), where place names such as Horgabost and Roghadal are of Norse origin. The islands' most famous cultural artefacts, the twelfth-century chess pieces found on Lewis in the nineteenth century, are of Norse design.

But although the Norse influence in the islands of north-west Scotland lasted until the 1260s, theirs was not the last word. The language and culture of the Gaels was clearly evangelistic, confident and outward looking, for it overcame and absorbed that of the Norse. Norse culture posed no long-term threat to the Celtic, Gaelic culture of Scotland. The real danger would come from the south, from the Northumbrian Angles who settled the Lower

Tweed and the Teviot in the seventh and eighth centuries, and from the English and Anglo-Normans who penetrated the whole of lowland Scotland between the eleventh and the thirteenth century. It was the 'Inglis' speech and culture, not that of the north, which would overwhelm the Gaels.

The cult of Mulruabh went on. It was unaffected by the spread of the 'Inglis' vine through lowland Scotland in the early Middle Ages and its slow penetration of the north-east over the next two centuries. It survived the rise of the Lordship of the Isles, as the semi-independent half-Gaelic, half-Norse kingdom centred on Iona was known, and the suppression of the lordship by the centralising Scottish king in 1493. It survived the religious cataclysm of the Reformation that swept lowland Scotland in 1560, when the kingdom formally accepted a church reformed on Calvinist lines under the firebrand preacher John Knox

From then on, the cult of saints was suppressed in Scotland. The purge was far more vigorous than it was in England, for while saints lingered on in bowdlerised form in the Anglican Book of Common Prayer, Knox's *First Book of Discipline* roundly pronounced all feasts of Christ, saints and apostles as popish inventions. As the Kirk Assembly complained in 1595, people did not always live up to these exacting standards, and there was frequent 'keeping of festival days and bonfires, pilgrimages, singing of carols at Yule',[1] which shows that traces of Catholicism survived the religious earthquake in the Lowlands for decades. Nevertheless, the rigour of the Scottish Reformation was proverbial, drawing both contempt and admiration south of the border. As Margaret Todd wrote in *The Culture of Protestantism in Early Modern Scotland*, the reformed Kirk wrought a 'profound cultural change that has given us a Scotland characterised (and caricatured) by abstemious self-restraint, sober but affective piety, unrelenting sabbatarianism, highly rigorous and visible social discipline, and a militant conviction of the rightness of the Calvinist cause'. Furthermore, 'It has given us a people determined to claim their own ground as an elect nation distinct from a pitiably half-reformed neighbour infected by popish ceremony and corrupted by sin undisciplined.'[2]

But Knox's religious revolution in the anglophone Lowlands had little immediate impact in the north-west. There, the collapse of the Catholic Church did not lead to its replacement by an efficient successor. The Reformation was an anglophone, indeed an anglophile, affair that exacerbated an existing divide between the English-speaking south and the Gaelic-speaking north and west. In the Highlands, the cult of saints did not cease but decayed into an amiable muddle. With no priests to provide reminders of what these ceremonies were about, saints' days lost their meaning and even the very names of the saints became blurred.

By the time the reformed Church of Scotland began to evangelise the north-west Highlands and the islands, an unchurched people was perform-ing a mass of corrupted rituals, known mainly to us through the condem-nations they inspired from the church authorities. We have only a tantalising description of the parishioners of Craignish, near the old hill fort of Dunadd, who were described by the disapproving Synod of Argyll in 1650 as 'goeing sun-gates about the church before they go into the kirk for divyne service'.[3]

A century after the Reformation claimed urban Scotland, the Gaelic north was still – in Protestant eyes – in the dark in matters of faith. John Carswell, the 'father of the printed literature of the Scottish Gael' who trans-lated the reformed church service in 1567, said that the people of Argyll and the isles remained infatuated with the heroes of the old Irish mythological cycles to the detriment of religion. In 1655 fires were regularly lit on hill-sides at midsummer on the old feast day of St John, drawing a complaint from the presbytery of Dingwall that people were routinely 'burneing torches . . . and fyres in thair townes' on the day.[4] Not long before, the pres-bytery of Inverness was still discovering images of old Celtic saints concealed in the town, ordering the public burning of 'one idolatrous Image called St Finane'[5] at the market cross in December 1643.

The memory of Mulruabh, which now boiled down to 'Mourie', contin-ued to haunt the imagination of the people of Applecross parish on the mainland opposite Skye, for in 1656 the Dingwall presbytery charged them with enacting 'abominable and heathenish practizes', including the sacrifice of bulls, and the only marginally less objectionable custom of ritually stick-ing their heads through a round stone 'at a certain tyme upon the 25 of August'. Besides this, they were guilty of making 'frequent approaches to some ruinous chappells and circulateing of them . . . and withall their adorn-ing of wells, and other superstitious monuments and stones'.[6]

Semi-Catholic, and even semi-pagan, cult practices lingered in northern Scotland until the end of the seventeenth century; in 1678 Robert Mackenzie, minister of Gairloch, complained that bulls were still being sacrificed there on 25 August in 'ane heathenish manner',[7] while Martin Martin found the people of Lewis in 1695 still celebrating an obscure cult of a god or saint, now called 'Shony', at Hallowtide, marked by hurling a cup of ale into the sea after which there was dancing and singing. On the distant island of Hiort, or St Kilda, the reformed religion was virtually unknown.

Martin found that the islanders still treasured a cross in their church and invoked the old saints in their oaths and prayers.

In the eighteenth century we hear no more of Mulruabh. After the failed Jacobite risings of 1715 and 1745, the British government tamed the Highlands once and for all. The clan system was dismantled and the removal of the more obstructive Jacobite gentry opened the way for the reformed Church to convert the Highlands. With the placement of a more numerous and settled ministry, such obviously un-Protestant practices as the sacrifice of bulls, the lighting of holy fires and pilgrimages to wells succumbed to ministerial denunciations. But it was a long time before all the old cults, let alone such practices as wakes and wedding dances, were rooted out. Popular culture in eighteenth-century Skye still differed markedly from that of the Calvinist Lowlands and was still as much Irish as Scottish. People still built 'healing stones' into their houses to ward off evil, while witches remained feared and the gifts of prophecy and 'seeing' were prized. Dr Johnson found these beliefs on the wane when he visited Skye, though he said it had not been long since people had stopped believing in a local sprite, or 'sturdy fairy' named 'Browny, who if he was fed and kindly treated would, as they said, also do a great deal of work'.[8] Only thirty years previously, Johnson said, people had put out milk every Saturday for another being from the spirit world, 'the old man with the long beard'; the practice had been stamped out by a minister who was still living in Johnson's time.

The highland Scots, like the Irish, were a dancing people, for in 1759 Lewis presbytery ordered the demolition of a house in Shawbost given over to 'fooling, dancing and other sports' that was 'frequented by a vast number of people of both sexes and a fiddler [who] resort to the same on the Saturday nights, where there is music, dancing, drinking of spirituous liquors, loose carriage, cursing and swearing'.[9]

The reformed Church struggled for several more generations against wakes, wailers at funerals, pipers' laments and dancing and drinking for several days at weddings. The reformed Church had long opposed funeral wailing. In 1642 the Synod of Argyll inveighed against the habit of 'poore women to howle their dead unto the graves . . . a thing unseemly to be used in any Christian kirk'.[10] Ministers were ordered to preach on how 'offensive to God and scandalouse to others the lyke practice and carriage must be' and punish offenders. The Church also greatly disliked 'penny weddings' – weddings of the poor, so named for the subscription paid by attenders towards the costs of the revelry. In 1675 the church authorities in Moray ordered 'that all piping, fiddling and dancing without doors ... be restrained and discharged' along with all 'obscene, lascivious and promiscuous dancing within doors'.[11] The campaign against wakes included a ban on the attendance of all who were not immediate relatives of the deceased, and a plea to those who did attend to avoid 'all light and lascivious exercises, sports ... fiddling and dancing, and that any present at such occasions behave themselves gravely, christianly, civilly ... spending the time in reading the scriptures'.[12] Duller Presbyterian weddings gradually replaced the old frolics but it proved a drawn-out war, for although dancing at weddings disappeared from Duirnish by 1840, a report noted that it was not that many years since 'from 80 to 100 persons used to assemble and to pass at least two days in feasting and dancing'.[13]

In 1797 a Presbyterian minister touring the Highlands shortly before the evangelical revival described the land in the same terms as Anglican clerics used for rural Ireland. He was profoundly shocked by the 'popish mode of blessing' still common in the Highlands, such as 'By my soul, by my faith, by Mary it is so, and the like'. When admonished, 'some of them told me such expressions were very common, even with their ministers . . . I begged of the Low Country people who then heard me that they would embrace every opportunity of pointing out [to] the natives the great impropriety of such expressions.'[14]

Within a generation the minister's hopes were realised and such impropriety was indeed on the way out. As the reformed Church faltered in the urban and increasingly industrial Lowlands, Presbyterianism made its great breakthrough among the Gaelic Highlanders, virtually snapping cultural bonds that had linked them to Ireland since the era of lordship of Dalriada. The Highlands, outside tiny Catholic enclaves in South Uist and Barra, took on the contours they have since preserved – a region marked by a strong tradition of sabbatarianism and a puritanical distaste for instrumental music and dancing, which have only recently regained popular acceptance.

Presbyterianism conquered the highland Gaels using the same tools as the Methodists employed in Wales. It took up the language. Unlike the Anglican Church in Ireland, the Church of Scotland had never entirely neglected the need to teach and preach in Gaelic. But for two centuries after the Reformation, the Protestant Church failed to convert the Highlands. Carswell's Gaelic translation of the Reformed Church's book of worship, the *Book of Common Order*, was never distributed. As a result his 'vision of a Protestant church spanning the Gaelic people of the two countries'[15] on either side of the Irish Sea remained unrealised. There was not a single

Gaelic book printed in Scotland after Carswell until 1631, when a Geneva catechism was published. However, the seventeenth and eighteenth centuries saw fitful initiatives to convert the Highlanders using bursaries to plant Gaelic-speaking ministers in Highland parishes.

The reformed Church produced a few visionaries, such as Robert Kirk, who translated the Bible into Gaelic in 1688 and then set off for the 'vast great wilderness'[16] of London to have it published. The 'Glorious Revolution' against James II, which in Scotland saw the Protestant episcopacy displaced by Presbyterianism, disrupted the works, for Kirk was an Episcopalian, but by the time of his early death at the age of 48 in 1692, some 3,000 bibles, 1,000 New Testaments and 3,000 catechisms had been printed. However, the ministers' lack of enthusiasm meant that only 1,700 of the 3,000 available bibles were distributed to parishes,[17] while the illiteracy of the mass of the population and the use of the Irish script in the bibles meant they were little used. But after Kirk's death, his close ally James Kirkwood lobbied strenuously for libraries and Gaelic bibles in the Highlands, and his campaign received backing from the newly founded Anglican missionary organisation, the Society for the Promotion of Christian Knowledge. The SPCK settled a school on St Kilda in 1711 and was maintaining 25 schools in the highlands by 1714; this rose to 48 by 1719, 109 in 1732 and 323 in 1795.

The SPCK, whose Scottish sister society was incorporated under Queen Anne in 1709, built libraries and schools in the Highlands to anglicise the population. It was not interested in realising Kirk's and Kirkwood's dreams. Rules for SPCK teachers set out in *The Account of the Age, Constitution and Management of the Society* in 1720 enjoined them to teach writing and basic arithmetic 'but not any Latin or Irish'. The society boasted that it was thanks to their schools 'that barbarity and the Irish language in that place by their means are almost rooted out'.[18] An act of the society in 1753 stipulated that scholars were forbidden 'either in the schoolhouse or when playing about the doors thereof to speak Erse, under pain of being chastised'.[19] The ban on Gaelic was relaxed in the 1760s, but in 1790 a society preacher was still insisting it was their goal 'that in process of time Britons from North to South may speak the same language',[20] while SPCK schools were flogging pupils for using Gaelic a decade later. The policy distressed Dr Johnson. He thought Scottish Gaelic very inferior to Irish or Welsh, but his humanity revolted at what the SPCK schools were up to. 'Their language is attacked on every side,' he complained. 'Schools are erected in which English only is taught and there were lately some who thought it reasonable to refuse them a version of the holy scriptures, that they might have no monument of their mother-tongue.'[21] Kirkwood's efforts to bind literacy to the mother tongue in the Highlands had come to nothing.

While the reformed religion spoke only English, Gaels continued to view ministers as the emissaries of an alien, conquering race, much as the Irish viewed the Anglican ministers settled in their midst under Elizabeth I. The Gaels had to wait for the evangelical revival for a true change of heart, and it was this, rather than the efforts of bodies like the SPCK, which wrought the great religious change in the Highlands. The Scottish evangelicals, like the Calvinist Methodists in Wales, were not much interested in statecraft, in furthering the Whigs' unionist political agenda, or in ensuring that everyone in Britain spoke the same language. Like their Welsh counterparts, they had little intrinsic interest in local languages or cultures. What they did have was a pragmatic willingness to champion them for evangelical purposes. To preach and teach in English to a people whose only language was Gaelic struck them as an almost blasphemous contradiction of one of the most basic biblical injunctions. Evangelical organisations, such as the Gaelic Schools Society, founded in 1811, took a contrary line to that of the SPCK in education, setting up peripatetic schools in the Highlands whose job was to instruct people in the scriptures in their native language. The evangelical teachers, unsurprisingly, were far more popular than their SPCK counterparts and by 1822 the GSS managed 44 schools, teaching 2,623 pupils.[22]

The GSS teachers were not Gaelic nationalists. As a report in 1866 outlined, they were convinced that literacy in Gaelic would act as a spur to learning better English, 'so that in practice, the Gaelic schools, instead of interfering with the operations of the English ones, have generally been . . . their pioneers and feeders'.[23]

The GSS, with its allies in the Ladies' Gaelic School Association, founded in 1840, created a literate population. Without a reading people, the evangelical revival would never have taken place. Evangelicalism conquered the Highlands and displaced the remnants of Catholic survivalism when men and women were able to read bibles in their own home and when cheap Gaelic bibles became available for the first time. The Gaelic bible underpinned the authority of the fraternity of religious laymen known simply as the 'Men' who brought the evangelical Reformation into the dispersed villages of the Highlands and islands. The 'Men' did not form an official structure within the Church. But they were a recognised, distinct phenomenon for all that, whose poverty and familiarity with rural Gaelic society made a people who had never before felt at home with the Reformation suddenly feel very at home indeed.

Evangelicalism in the Highlands, again like Methodism in Wales, tapped and absorbed religious energies that had lain dormant since the extinction of the old Catholic Church and its inherited Celtic traditions. Like the Church of Mulruabh's day, it spoke their language and was spiritually demanding. The 'Men' appropriated some of the space once occupied by the Celtic saints. Miracles were not attributed to them, but some were credited with the supernatural powers of 'seeing' and of prophecy. Malcolm Maclean (Callum mhic Callum) of Lewis had a reputation as a prophet and was revered as a saint for his childlike simplicity and purity of life. The 'Men', just like the Celtic saints, pushed hard doctrines with a soft voice and were often remembered for great personal sweetness. Malcolm Morrison, of Bernera, on Lewis, was said to have 'carried a bird in his heart' as he dispensed evangelical teachings over tea from his hearth, where a large kettle was always bubbling in the corner. Donald Maclay had a great power over children. These craggy patriarchs were not men of terror. 'He spoke with such kindliness', it was recalled, 'that a little girl who once heard him tugged at her mother and said "You must ask that man to stay at our house"'.

The 'Men' helped to put down the fiddles and the dances, and to destroy the Gaels' lingering suspicion of Presbyterianism as a Lowland, Sassenach religion. They introduced people to rigorous sabbatarianism. Penny weddings and Saturday night dances went the way of earlier sacrifices of bulls to 'Mourie'. This account from Strathnaver in the 1800s reflects the way many early nineteenth-century Gaelic-speaking communities began to spend their Sunday:

The household is up early, for many of them are seven or eight miles from the church. After breakfast and family worship, they are ready to start. At last the leading Christians leave their houses; all the rest assemble around them and a portion of scripture being named, religious conversation begins. The younger people are silent; but they listen with deep interest while one venerable man after another speaks from a full heart about the love of Christ . . . When half-way to church, they sit down to rest and after singing a few verses to one of their pleasant airs, prayer is offered up for the outpouring of the spirit and for a blessing on the words they are about to hear. At last the groups unite, and 800 people assemble in the house of God . . . When the service is over, the several groups return each to their own hamlets, and after taking the necessary food, they meet in the house of one of the leading men. He begins with prayer and praise; he then makes the people repeat all they remember of the sermon.[24]

The evangelical movement in the highlands, like the evangelical revivals in England and Wales, split the church it was intended to revive. The great issue in the Kirk concerned patronage in relation to church livings. Scotland's Presbyterians had always despised the Church of England's subordination to civil power, and the reintroduction of private patronage to livings in Scotland by Act of the British parliament in 1712, shortly after the union of the English and Scottish parliaments, rankled from the start. While lay patrons did not press candidates on hostile parishes, and while the latitudinarian party known as the Moderates controlled the Church's machinery, the quarrel did not come to a head. But when the evangelicals became the dominant force in the Kirk's general assembly in the early eighteenth century, patronage became a burning issue.

The crisis approached its peak in 1834, when 287 families in the presbytery of Auchterarder opposed the appointment by the Earl of Kinnoul of Robert Young as their minister. The Scottish courts ruled in the Earl's favour, as did the House of Lords. Other cases then piled up. When another patron imposed a minister on Marnock, in Strathbogie, the evangelical parishioners voted with their feet. On 21 January 1841, 'In a body the parishioners rose, and gathering up the bibles . . . they silently retired. The deep emotion that prevailed among them was visible in the tears which might be seen trickling down many an old man's cheek.'[25]

In 1842 the evangelical-dominated general assembly retaliated by adopting a 'Claim, Declaration, and Protest' against the intrusion of ministers who had not been selected by congregations. Shortly afterwards, 465 ministers met in Edinburgh and issued the Tory Prime Minister, Robert Peel, with an ultimatum. Desist, they said, or we will secede. The last days of the undivided Church of Scotland were passed in an atmosphere of high drama, for 'the Disruption', as it became known, had caught the nation's imagination. Religious or not, people were fascinated, even awestruck, by the unlikely prospect of the ministers of the national church voluntarily surrendering all the emoluments and privileges of establishment. The final day came. David Welsh, the last moderator of the undivided Church, held divine service on 18 May 1843 in the High Church in Edinburgh in the presence of the crown's representative, the Lord High Commissioner, the Marquis of Bute, the Lord Provost of the city, the Lord Advocate and many dignitaries. They then proceeded to St Andrew's church for the general assembly. To a vast crowd, which had gathered around the building since about 4 a.m., Welsh read out the document of protest, signed by 203 ministers and elders, 'amid the unbroken silence of the vast multitude'. According to the *Annals of the Free Church of Scotland*.

The reading ended, Dr Welsh laid the document on the clerk's table, bowed with courtly grace to the High Commissioner, lifted his hat and left the building.

Slowly and steadily, seat after seat became empty of occupants; longer and longer grew the procession that wound its way to Tanfield Hall [the seceders' headquarters] on the north side of the city, evoking the ringing cheers of the dense throng that crowded the windows, the balconies and even the roofs of the houses that were on the line of march.'[26]

An Act of Separation, formalising 'the Disruption' and the creation of what now became the Free Church of Scotland, was signed by 474 ministers on 23 May.

The events of May 1843 in Edinburgh had a tremendous impact on the Highlands, not because the new Free Church thought of itself as a specifically Gaelic, Highland church, but because Gaelic-speaking highlanders formed a large part of its members. Thanks partly to the influence of the 'Men', the highlanders overwhelmingly quit the old Kirk. The Church had only recently won over the Highlands and islands and they had little sentimental attachment to it. Many of the seceding ministers were Gaelic-speakers, like Mr Mackenzie, of Farr, who recalled his departure thus: 'On the 11th of June [1843] I preached for the last time in the Established Church which I had occupied for twenty-eight years, taking for a text in the Gaelic, Micah II and 10: "Arise ye, and depart, for this is not your rest"'. Dr Ross of Lockbroom, seen as the finest Gaelic scholar of his day, left and took the whole parish with him.

The first Sabbath after the Disruption, Dr Ross, then in very infirm health, attended the church as a hearer. After the sermon by the Revd Mr Grant, Dr Ross rose in his seat and, with tears running from his eyes, praised the Lord for the testimony to the honour of Christ given by the Disruption party. He then exhorted the people to leave the state church, which almost to a man they then did, and to this day [1867] have never returned.[27]

Urged on by the 'Men', the Gaelic Highlands and islands turned their backs on the state church and started afresh, often worshipping at first in barns, tents or in the open air.

The Disruption and the Free Church have come in for harsh criticism especially from the political left in recent years. Apart from inflicting a peculiarly censorious and dour version of Christianity on the population, they are charged with imbuing them with ultra-Calvinist pessimism and political passivity, and with encouraging them to dwell on trivial points of doctrine while their communities were being laid waste by the landlords.

There is something in the charge. Few highland ministers emulated the Catholic clergy of Ireland, who commandeered the Repeal movement in the 1830s and 1840s and the land campaigns several decades on. The Catholic clergy in agitated Irish counties like Tipperary led the agrarian militants from the front, which cannot be said for most Disruption clergy or their successors. Evangelical Presbyterianism counselled submission and acceptance of misfortune. But it was a faith chosen quite voluntarily by the people and if it failed to make them rebels against injustice, it certainly lent them dignity.

The Free Church was without doubt a people's church, charged with a fiery spirit of asceticism that would have gladdened the heart of Patrick, or of Columba and the other Celtic saints. When A. N. Somerville, Moderator of the Free Church in 1887, toured the Highland and islands in that year, he returned in euphoria after witnessing at first hand the fervour of popular religion there. They were dedicated to religion, and 'whether the meetings were held at midday in the afternoon, or evening, in moonlight or dark, whether in sunshine, rain, snow or tempest, the people assembled in large numbers'.[28] On Harris he had been amazed by the sight of congregations arriving in 12 boats for a service that he was about to hold, 'the people singing and praying on their voyage, to and fro'. He had seen nothing like it, and 'comparing them with other people which I have seen, there is no such appetite to listen to the gospel as is to be found among our Highland people'. Somerville viewed the fruits of the evangelical conquest of the Highlands from the inside, of course. Less religious observers were more inclined to condemn the suppression of song and dance and what they saw as ministerial tyranny. By the 1880s the people of St Kilda had long put aside their crucifix in church and semi-Catholic usages. They were an entirely Free Church community. When Robert Connell visited the island in the mid-1880s, he voiced disgust not only by the islanders' 'Gaelic gibberish' but also their 'fantastical sacerdotalism',[29] one consequence of which was eight hours spent in church each Sunday, singing 'like a pack of hyenas'. Connell blamed the evangelical campaign on the island, which began in the 1820s, for the disappearance of games, sports, amusements and secular songs, and for draining people's energies into hours spent in prayer and listening to sermons. Yet he was not a friendly observer. The St Kildans, he wrote, 'like Celts in general, whether at home or abroad ... seem utterly incapable of any sustained mental interest'.[30]

The Gaelic culture that the Free Church helped to survive has not endured on Skye. The society that Dr Johnson encountered has vanished, as has the world that Màiri Mhór, 'poetess of the Clearances', knew a century later. It has not quite gone the way of Mull, the island Sorley Maclean considered 'intolerable for a Gael' on account of the 'terrible imprint of the clearances on it'.[31] Skye is not a pleasure garden for southern exiles and retirees. Both landscape and climate are too harsh for that. A size-able percentage of the population still speaks Gaelic, and the fortunes of the language have been boosted by the erection of an impressive Gaelic college, the Sabhal Mòr Ostaig, in the south of the island, under the patronage of Sir Iain Noble.

But the island has the air of a place in flux. The language heard casually on the roads of Broadford and Portree, the two largest settlements, is almost invariably English and the erection of bilingual road signs does not dispel the impression that the island's culture is merging with that of the anglophone mainland. At the church service I attended in Broadford, standing beside the rock from which Mulruabh may have preached, virtually everyone attend-ing was like me – a cultural tourist. The sound of us all struggling to sing a psalm in Gaelic, following the example of the precentor, was painful. The precentor had a dark expression on his face, as if assisting in the execution of this task was proving a slightly embarrassing charade. At the end, we all trudged away without a word, puzzled, perhaps, by a desultory sense of pointlessness. A disappointed Canadian, called Sine, descended from one of the many Highland emigrant communities in Ontario, said she learned Gaelic as an adult with a view to hearing it in its natural setting. But her cultural pilgrimage to Skye had not yielded much fruit, for the island that only half a century ago had been almost entirely Gaelic-speaking was now home to a growing number of 'incomers' with only a limited knowledge of the older culture of the island. She was off to the Catholic outpost of South Uist in hope of better things.

I spent a week in the Sabhal Mòr Ostaig, taking an introductory course in the Gaelic language. We learned basic words, listened to CDs of the new Gaelic singers who had brought the old laments and songs to life and watched videos put out by the Gaelic-speaking arm of the BBC, BBC Alba, compered by a cheery, doll-faced woman who spoke in – and about – Gaelic with a presenter's typically relentless optimism. The videos included instal-ments of a soap show, featuring a family who were not rural people from Lewis and Skye but city folk, bustling around the metropolis and talking in Gaelic to all and sundry, from estate agents to railway ticket inspectors. The programme was clearly challenging assumptions about Gaelic as rural and 'old'. It aimed to cut the automatic associations in many people's minds linking the language and its culture to grandmothers, churches and remote Highland villages. The campaign to immerse visitors to the college totally in the Gaelic culture continued after classes with ceilidhs and organised songs.

The college has undoubtedly created in the Sleat area of Skye what never existed before: a concentrated, Gaelic-speaking intelligentsia, a kind of Gaelic bourgeoisie, comprising teachers, lecturers and other staff. But the college's patron, Iain Noble, is not under the illusion that the foundation has single-handedly reversed a cultural shift that has been going on for decades.

He told me he was bitter about the steady depopulation of the Highlands that had drained the life out of the glens. In 1820, he said, Skye had a population of about 24,000, while the Faroe Islands, ruled by Denmark, had about 7,000. Today, the population of Skye is closer to 7,000, while the Faroes have about 40,000 inhabitants. 'If the Faroes had had the misfortune to be British, they would be uninhabited by now,' he said. Much of this trend he attributed to a centuries-old policy of suppression of the Gaelic culture, which he believed had undermined the will of rural communities to live. 'Nobody wants to be part of a dying civilisation,' he said. By the time he bought land in Skye in the early 1970s, emigration was fast carrying off the young, Sleat had few inhabitants under 50 and the six schools of the area had shrunk to one. The college has since turned round the economy in southern Skye, with more than 100 people on the direct payroll. But it was not enough to revive an island, let alone an archipelago. 'The new Scottish parliament has done nothing so far,' he added. 'They are talking of a new Act for Gaelic but the chances of Gaelic surviving at all are slim unless the language is given first-language status in the islands, meaning education on Skye and the other islands all being in Gaelic. Then the children of the incomers would be assimilated.'

Noble excited a media controversy in Scotland, where the leftish political establishment is wary of its mild, mainstream nationalism being confused with racism. A public attack on the growing number of incomers to the Hebridean islands, which Noble said was smothering the local culture, drew comparisons with the former British Prime Minister Margaret Thatcher's controversial remarks about immigrants to Britain swamping local people. The furore highlighted the potential pitfalls of addressing the whole topic of immigration, and the difficulty cultural activists now face in trying to balance concern for the survival of local languages with the free movement of people. But he told me he was unrepentant about the fuss. 'Europe is a casket of jewels and we have to maintain them all,' he insisted. 'You cannot stop the inflow, but you can assimilate them by giving Gaelic first-language status. Of course, it would take money, but the British government owes the Gaels a good deal. It set about trying to exterminate Gaelic, and that was wrong by any standards.'

It may be too late to fence off Skye from anglophone Britain in that manner. The anglicisation process is fairly advanced, and not only on Skye. Inside the Sabhal Mòr Ostaig, it felt natural to hum the Gaelic songs we learned in class, but when I finished my brief course and re-emerged into Skye, I felt as if I had left a bubble. The world of the 'Men', and of Màiri Mhór and of the crofters she championed, has departed.

It was time to put more water between the mainland and myself. The boat to Uibhist a Tuath, or North Uist, left from the little northern port of Uig. I slept the night before the crossing in a remote bed and breakfast, tucked behind the headland above the port. The elderly couple who ran it addressed me in English, though when they closed the kitchen door, I could overhear them conversing to each other in Gaelic. They seemed part of an older order on Skye that had, perhaps, submitted rather too patiently to its fate. For my part, I was impatient to leave. This island had become too silent and too empty for my liking. It was hard to imagine that the British author-ities had been sufficiently nervous about crofter agitation against the land-lords to send a gunboat here in the 1880s. It was even less easy to imagine when it had been populous enough to supply the British empire (so the boast ran in the 1860s) with four colonial governors, a Governor-General of India, a Lord Chief Baron of England, a judge of the supreme court in Scotland, at least 21 generals and 10,000 foot soldiers. Now all was silence and wind whipping through the long grass of empty moors.

In the rural settlement of the Uists, North and South, I heard Gaelic used routinely for the first time. Here it did not survive in a bubble but had remained the ordinary means of communication in shops and post offices. The Gulf Stream insulates these north-western islands from the freezing weather they would normally be exposed to at such a latitude, but it does not shelter them from the high winds sweeping in from the Atlantic and blowing unimpeded across the flattish landscape. This is an almost treeless world, and as I cycled from the north to south across a sequence of small bridges in Benbecula in the middle, the sight of flocks of wild geese flying in V-formation across the vast sky, the huge expanse of coarse, tufted grass ringed in the distance by mountains, and the churning lochs in the fore-ground recalled Iceland, or the Arctic tundra, more than any landscape in

Britain. Cairns and standing stones dotted plentifully round these islands and in neighbouring Harris and Lewis recall a time when a warm climate enabled a large population to flourish amid woodlands of birch and oak.

The Uists straddle a religious frontier. The north island is Protestant, while the south island and neighbouring Barra, are Catholic. They are mementoes of the Catholic Scotland that disappeared under the Calvinist avalanche in 1560. This is not a harsh religious frontier. There are no echoes of the strife-ridden confessional dividing line between Catholics and Protestants in County Antrim or County Armagh, in Northern Ireland, where angry flags and defiant slogans proclaim the approaching crossing point. A single shrine to the Virgin Mary, standing like a white sentinel beside the main road, is the only humble advertisement to visitors that they have left behind Knox's Scotland. A little further on I encountered the more imposing statue of Our Lady of the Isles. Hugely impressive from a distance, it was less so close up. The building blocks of the statue have been piled crudely on top of each other, while the planted boxes beside the base had been left to wither. A profusion of wire fences and humming electric pylons around the site rendered the whole arrangement desolate. The statue is not, of course, a miraculous survival from the vanished pre-Reformation Scotland, but was erected in the 1950s with a view to throwing a benign haze over the nearby British military base.

The old religion did not 'carry on' in South Uist. Here as everywhere in the Highlands, organised religion virtually collapsed after the Reformation, but while Protestant missionaries slowly claimed most of the Highlands and islands, Irish Catholic missionaries snatched this corner for themselves. They might have taken more. Had Rome invested in more missionaries, the Counter-Reformation might have converted much of the Highlands, and kept alive the links that bound the west of Scotland to Gaelic Ulster. As it was, the seventeenth-century Plantation of Ulster with English and Scottish Protestants disrupted the connections, while the bulk of the Highlands was abandoned to the Protestants almost by default. In 1669 Cardinal Giulio Rospigliosi reported that the islanders' faith remained up for grabs. When a priest visited them, he said, they 'show much greater affection and venera-tion for him than for the [Protestant] preachers. They sign their foreheads with the sign of the holy cross. They invoke the saints, recite litanies and use holy water.'[32] The links between the region and Ireland were obvious enough to the Pope for him to turn to the Archbishop of Armagh to supply labourers in this neglected vineyard. Priests from Lowland Scotland were seen as of no potential help whatever. In the 1670s Rome was advised 'to send thither some Irish priests or religious since the people of these islands understand nothing but Gaelic and they can hope for spiritual assistance from none but the Irish, since the Scots speak a corrupt form of English'.[33]

A small mission conducted by Irish Franciscans in the 1620s and 1630s provided a taste of what might have been achieved. The three men reported that they had reconciled thousands of islanders to Rome, though the campaign lapsed after the missionaries gave up, complaining of hardship. There was no new Catholic mission until the 1650s, when Francis White and Dermot Duggan baptised people in their eighties on Barra and South Uist, where Duggan died in 1657. By then the Catholic character of the people of South Uist and Barra was assured and even the small community of local Protestants, Rome was informed, had absorbed Catholic practices, 'making the sign of the cross, the invocation of saints and sprinkling them-selves with holy water'.[34]

The Catholic outpost of the western isles has no defiant or outgoing quality. It is low-key, discreet, largely private – the curving contours of Our Lady of the Isles providing the community's only extravagant gesture of faith. This is also still a poor land. The houses are for the most part neither traditional nor cute, but grey, modern bungalows, whose sometimes neg-lected appearance points to the low income of many inhabitants. The Uists have largely escaped the attention of incomers, who are put off by the distance, climate and lack of urban centres. Their isolation has preserved their Gaelic culture, though the flip side of this is the desultory air of South Uist's tiny 'capital', Lochboisdale. The teenagers I met were dismissive of their prospects, and of the desirability of remaining on the island. One I met in the island's museum laughed scornfully at the idea. 'Stay? Are you crazy?' she barked. She had her heart set on a film school course in Glasgow or London and was not swayed by talk of a Gaelic revival. 'People opt for Gaelic in school because the standard is so low you literally *can't* fail,' she announced. She wanted to talk about her career. 'I'm going to direct films one day,' she kept repeating.

I took a boat from the Uists to An Tairbeart (Tarbut), and travelled north-wards from there north to Steornabhagh (Stornoway), the only town of any size on the isles. The island of Na Hearadh (Harris) has long been more popular with outsiders than the Uists, or Lewis. In the nineteenth century, it became famous for tweed clothing. The industry has now declined, as the fashion for heavy jackets faded. Tourism has filled some of the gap, and Harris's white sand beaches feature heavily in Scottish tourist advertise-ments, but it has not compensated for the loss of the clothing manufacture.

Like Skye, the island looks emptier than it should. Many communities were swept away in the nineteenth-century clearances but the more recent decline in fishing, crofting and weaving has proved just as deadly. In the communities that remain, more and more houses are passing into the ownership of outsiders who spend only part of the summer there. Harris has exactly the same problem I would encounter on the west coast of Ireland, in west Wales, along the coast of Cornwall and throughout Brittany. Improvements in transport, and cheap flights, have transformed what were once long journeys into potential weekend trips. City workers on high incomes now find it quite practical to buy property hundreds of miles away with a view to making brief flying visits. House prices in what remain poor areas rise sharply under this stimulation, leaving local people priced out of their communities. Villages are prettified through this investment, as the outsiders are often far more interested in preserving historic architecture than the locals. But it is a mummified preservation and the external bloom conceals inward decay, for a high proportion of summer homes depresses the need for local schools, churches and shops, few of which are patronised by these part-time residents.

Slowly, there is a language shift, too, as Gaelic gives way to English. Bill and Chris Lawson have observed the shift in their own village of Taobh Tuath, or Northton. 'Many homes here are now owned by Scots, Italians, French, Swedes,' Bill told me in the local community centre. 'The language of the village is now English, not Gaelic. It happened over about 15 years. The young people cannot get jobs, so they leave.' The Lawsons detected some irony in the fact that Gaelic was receding just as it had become chic for the first time. 'Gaelic is no longer a language that's looked down on,' Bill said. 'That's all changed. It's a lot more respectable now, but a lot less used as well!'

The institutions that underpinned the traditional culture have disappeared or drastically scaled back their activity in the village. The school closed 20 years ago. The church holds a service once every four weeks on a Wednesday. The islands still have a reputation for strict sabbatarianism, but according to Lawson, that refers simply to the fact that everything closes. 'Hardly anyone goes to church now,' he said. 'Many of those who might like to go are just too old to get out of the house.' The depressing statistics – no school, not much of a church, few people aged under 50, 15 of the 50 houses in the village lying empty – explain the futility of expecting a cultural renaissance here. As Lawson put it: 'If you don't have any people, you can't have a language.'

The future of Harris is tied now to its success as a tourist destination. Salvation no longer lies in kelp but white sand. Harris tweed has gone under.

The industry boomed in the 1840s under the patronage of the island's improving landlords, the Earl and Countess of Dunmore, who sent local women to the mainland to improve and perfect traditional weaving techniques. The investment paid off. A royal visit to Stornoway in 1902 boosted the industry further. The cloth was valued at £8,000 in 1903 and at £20,000 in 1905. By the 1960s the centre of gravity had long shifted north to Lewis, and the industry maintained some 2,000 registered wool producers in the Hebrides, while another thousand or so worked in the mills. Weaving had become an indispensable source of income to struggling crofters, and was helping to sustain rural communities such as Shawbost and Carloway on Lewis's western coast. A historian of Harris tweed wrote with satisfaction in the late 1960s: 'The industry is just about the only successful amalgamation of cottage industry and modern factory in today's industrial milieu.'[35]

The weaving was more than a business, for it sustained a way of life. It was a communal enterprise, bringing women together for companionship, mutual support and song. They met at each other's homes for the 'waulking' of the cloth. The woven material was too dense and hard for use. 'Waulking' involved softening it up by wetting, rubbing, banging and stretching it on the ground, or at long tables. There was a festive flavour to these finishing sessions, and women knew a repertoire of 'waulking' songs designed to be sung rhythmically to the sound and action of banging and stretching the cloth. This tradition of singing while working the cloth was an old one, for Boswell recalled Johnson's fascination when he encountered a group of women in Skye. They 'kneel upon the ground and rub it [the material] with both their hands singing an Erse song all the time,' Boswell said. 'He [Johnson] was asking questions while they were performing that operation and amongst their loud wild howl his voice was heard in the room above.'[36]

But the loud, wild howls are now mainly for the stage or recording studio. Professional musicians have ensured the survival of waulking songs and at the Sabhal Mòr Ostaig I attended a session put on for people to learn them. But the raw, untutored noise that Johnson heard has vanished and all people can do now is record them, for the industry and the way of life that spawned the songs has itself disappeared. There are few weavers left working at home in the Hebrides and most are elderly. Large-scale fishing has also gone, thanks to foreign fleets fishing out the seas. Some local fishermen survive on catches of prawns and scallops but this is a smaller business, which in no way compensates for the decline in mackerel, herring and cod catches. Agriculture never really paid. It was always marginal in this climate and terrain and produced nothing for export. Even the island's local dairy has almost gone. Most milk now comes from Dingwall by boat from the mainland. No one seriously anticipates a revival of the island economy through the land. It is the outsiders – the incomers – who voice nostalgia about the sight of people working the soil, though they have no intention of doing it themselves. The locals have little nostalgia for those days. 'You can't expect people to work the land when they are all old,' Bill Lawson mused. 'No one makes lazybeds[37] now, or cuts their own fuel from the peat. Why should they? It was back-breaking labour.'

I drove north, leaving the white sand beaches of Harris for the bleaker, flatter landscape of Lewis, heading first to the northern tip called the Butt of Lewis. Extremities always attract people and although Lewis is not the most northerly point in Scotland (the Orkney and Shetland islands lie well to the north), the Butt of Lewis looks like the end of the world – Scotland's own *finis terrae*, or Finistère. Beyond the lighthouse and the black crags, surmounted by gangs of cormorants insouciantly braving the high wind and freezing spray from the crashing of great waves, lies the ocean. The vast stretch of churning salt water reaches from here to Iceland and beyond that to the Americas. It is thoroughly inhospitable-looking terrain, yet the north of the island is surprisingly well populated, with none of Harris's air of emptiness. It benefits from its proximity to the town of Stornoway, a regional hub boasting its own airport, university college, supermarkets and radio and television centres.

The Hebrides are contracting into Stornoway. Over the past four or five decades, the town has grown at the same pace that the rural community has shrunk. It has sprouted suburbs, absorbing what were once separate villages. On arriving there I was struck by the number of young people, a much rarer sight elsewhere. After leaving school, groups of teenagers cruise down the streets wearing the regulation, US-style baseball caps that are a routine feature of youth culture everywhere in Britain. It came as a slight surprise to see such a faithful portrayal of youth fashion and behaviour, seemingly transplanted from urban Scotland or England to this distant island setting. But as Roddy Murray, director of the town's arts centre, explained to me, Stornoway was never a Gaelic stronghold.

Murray grew up a few miles from the town, in an area that has since merged into the suburbs. In his childhood, he said, there were many looms in villages and few cars; most children wore clothes knitted by their parents or relatives. He remembered people from the northern village of Ness who had never even been to the town. 'In my father's generation only a handful went away to university. Everybody else stayed behind and worked the croft, cutting peat and growing potatoes. And of course, they spoke

Gaelic.' Murray attributed the English conquest to television. 'What TV did was to bring a new member into the living room who spoke only English,' he said. Murray and his older siblings speak fluent Gaelic, while his younger brother – a child of the television age – speaks only English. The age of the television has sliced right through a family, leaving different cultures on either side. But Murray was not full of regret for the old ways. 'In my childhood you couldn't even run on Sundays,' he said. 'Church services lasted for three hours; even the cooking had to be done on Saturday night. Now I go cycling on Sundays, which wasn't even contemplated when I was a kid. My parents were not that religious – it was simple peer pressure.'

If the Gaelic language and the culture it nurtures is to survive on the western isles, it will have to keep a firm foothold in Stornoway. I often heard Gaelic used by older people, women especially, but not once by the gangs of teenagers in the Coffee Pot, which the young haunt in the afternoons. The men who came to work on the island before the 1970s were immersed in the language whether they liked it not. The temporary foreign workers I encountered in the town, many employed in a local salmon factory, were scarcely aware it even existed. A group of young Australians said the only phrase they had learned in Gaelic meant 'Feel my breasts'. Apparently it is a trick that old-timers in the factory play on newcomers – to teach them to mouth this phrase and then explain the meaning to a chorus of derisive laughter. That seemed to be the high-water mark of these Australians' exposure to the culture.

The recipe that will preserve something of the older culture, while blending in the new, is elusive. In Harris the cry is 'We need jobs'. In Stornoway there are jobs, but many demand skills that suit trained professional immigrants more than locals. Their presence accelerates the island's integration into the mainland. It was easier to maintain a distinct identity among a small population before the recent technological revolution. As Murray put it: 'When I grew up, hardly anybody had a car, or a television. Many didn't have telephones. The average person here now gets up, gets into a car, sits behind a computer all day, goes home, eats a microwaved dinner and settles down to watch *EastEnders*. Lewis is now part of a global village.'

The traditional culture had folded in on itself at a time when its popularity with middle-class professionals has never been higher. Stornoway is one of the three centres of a new Gaelic 'establishment' (the other two being Glasgow and Inverness), comprising the arts community, the Gaelic-speaking media (press, television and radio), and development bodies such as Commun na Gaidhlig and the Highlands and Islands Development Board (HIDB). It pays to be a professional Celt in a way that it never did. Not since the Scottish crown suppressed the Lordship of the Isles in 1493 has Gaelic society been buttressed with such structural support.

The 1970s and 1980s saw a proliferation in government organisations in which familiarity with Gaelic culture and language was not merely tolerated, but insisted on. Much of the impetus followed the local government reforms of 1974, which made the Gaelic-speaking western isles a single unitary authority for the first time. The HIDB, set up by the Labour government in the 1970s, was soon nudged into taking a far more pro-active stance on language and culture as well as economic issues. At the same time, a new enthusiasm to set up local co-operatives and Gaelic-speaking streams in schools fed the perceived need for a Gaelic umbrella agency that would span both public and private development initiatives: from this the Gaelic Development Organisation was born. Whereas the emphasis in the 1960s and 1970s had been on economics and on setting up co-operatives, the GDO's thrust was cultural, concentrating on education and broadcasting. In the media field, increasing Gaelic radio proved more attainable financially, for whilst Scotland's two main television broadcasters, Grampian and Scottish Television, appeared receptive to pressure, the results have been smaller. The target of two hours of television broadcasting in Gaelic a day has yet to be attained.

The campaign to establish Gaelic-medium education began in Glasgow, the Highland emigrants' traditional capital, and in Inverness, the largest town in the Highlands. There are now about 60 primary schools with Gaelic-medium instruction, while Glasgow has one purely Gaelic-medium school. On the western isles about 35 per cent of children now have Gaelic-medium education. So there is growth, but not enough to guarantee the survival of the culture. It is hard, perhaps too late, to reverse a centuries-old policy of anglicisation that long predates the union of the English and Scottish crowns. The story of the creation of the Scottish kingdom is interwoven with and inseparable from the story of its rulers' campaign to turn it into an English-speaking state. The policy trails back as far as the reign of Malcolm Canmore in the 1070s and his Saxon Queen, Margaret, who encouraged the immigration of merchants and ecclesiastics from the south and under whose heirs 'Inglis' conquered first the court and infant burghs and then the rest of the Lowlands. Margaret's sons continued to plant Scotland with Norman, Flemish and English incomers, much as the English crown encouraged the Flemish and English to settle medieval Pembrokeshire, transforming the south of that county into a 'Little England' inside Wales. But the Scottish crown did more than plant the odd county. As the medievalist Maurice Powicke wrote, by the twelfth century 'the ruling class in Scotland was almost exclusively recruited from the Norman element, to which the Breton and Flemish should be added'.[38] The Scottish king became increasingly alienated from the Gaelic culture of the majority of his people, 'regarded', Powicke wrote, 'as a Frenchified lord, surrounded by aliens, in a court given to foreign ways of life'.[39] The veneer of English or Anglo-Norman abbots, priors, bishops, knights and baronets may have been spread thin but its influence on Lowland Scottish culture was absolutely decisive. Gaelic was eclipsed in the Lowlands outside Galloway, leaving little but place names.

The presence of two large language communities established the dichotomy of Highlander and Lowlander as alienated, opposing cultures, the one representing civility, the other, barbarism. The court, towns and the universities of Edinburgh, Glasgow, Aberdeen and St Andrews lay within the anglophone world, and one result was the stigmatisation of the other language and culture as inferior and even foreign. Just as the descendants of the Anglo-Saxon invaders of Britain saw the ancient Britons as aliens or 'Welsh', the anglophone Lowlanders came to see the new, English tongue as 'Scottis', while the older language became known as 'Erse', or Irish. In 1578 Bishop John Leslie of Ross defended Gaelic as 'the ald Scottis toung' and praised the highlanders for having 'keipt the institutiounis of thair eldaris sa constantlie, that nocht onlie mair than 2 thowsand yeirs they have keipet the toung hail uncorupte bot lykewyse the maner of cleithing and leiving'.[40] But his was an increasingly lone voice. The historian John Mair in his *History of Greater Britain, As Well as England and Scotland* of 1521 struck a typical note when he said Scotland was split into two, one half comprising 'wild Scots' who 'delight in the chase and a life of indolence . . . and follow their own savage and worthless chief in all evil courses sooner than they will pursue an honest industry'.[41] Archbishop Spottiswoode was more temperate in his *History of the Church and State of Scotland* when he discussed the differences, but he took it as read that Scotland was essentially a land of two languages and cultures. 'The Low-Countrey man calls the High-landers Irish not so much for their ancient descent as for their language. . . and for their wayes of living,' he wrote. 'On the other side the High-lander calles the Low-countrey men Saxons, not so much for their descent (although many of them are come from the Southern people . . . a progenie of the Saxons) as for the language, which differeth only by dialect for the language of the South'.[42] As Charles Withers wrote in *Gaelic Scotland: The Transformation of a*

Culture Region: 'Gaelic forms and value systems no longer carried with them any sense of a lost Scottishness . . . Gaelic had become the language and in wider terms the symbol of a geographical region.'[43]

The Scottish crown did not passively accept the continuing existence of a separate culture in the north. When James I and VI convoked an assembly of clansmen on Iona in 1609, the resulting statutes urged highland landowners to submit at least one child for schooling in English, a policy backed strongly by the Privy Council in 1616, which demanded that 'the vulgar Inglische toung be universallie plantit and the Irische language . . . abolisheit and removeit'.[44] While verbal declarations meant little in practice, they set in stone official attitudes to the Gaelic language that the highlanders would eventually internalise. It was universally associated with 'barbarity and ignorance' and seen as an obstacle to the formation of a unified British state. Daniel Defoe echoed a commonplace when he lauded the arrival of 'Reformation and Virtue' in the Highlands in the 1750s, and voiced the hope 'that in a few years, Ignorance, Popery and the Irish language will be utterly extirpated; and in their stead, Virtue, Industry and Loyalty will take their place'.[45]

The SPCK schools continued the work of integrating the Highlands and islands into a Protestant, English-speaking kingdom and by the time the evangelicals modified that hostility to the Gaels, hatred had become self-hatred and the Scottish Gaels – like their Irish counterparts – could not now be persuaded of the worth of their own culture.

Many people remained bitterly opposed to the policy of the Gaelic Schools Society, which they saw as 'fruitless attempts to preserve that on which the hand of death is already irremovably fixed,' John Maculloch wrote in a published letter to Walter Scott in 1824. He was delighted to report that 'a traveller in the Highlands now meets English in some shape almost everywhere, and chiefly among the children'. It was to Gaelic that Scotland was 'indebted for the long series of misrule, rebellion, rapine and disorder in which it was involved before the final termination of Highland independence'.[46] He could hardly wait for the day when Gaelic, Welsh and Breton would follow Cornish to extinction, as these tongues had rendered their speakers 'a minority of foreigners in their own country'.[47]

When Patrick Butler toured the SPCK schools in the Highlands in 1825, he found parents opposed to any change of heart by the authorities on Gaelic. 'There seems to be in the minds of the people . . . a very general prejudice against using the Gaelic as a school language,'[48] he wrote. As in Ireland, many parents who barely spoke a word of English supported the systematic punishment of their children for failure to use English. These punishments were public and often deeply humiliating. Of a teacher in Glenurquart parish school, it was recalled:

> He made it his duty after the opening prayer to hand to the boys a roughly carved piece of wood . . . the boy transferred it to the first pupil who was heard speaking in Gaelic. That offender got rid of it by delivering it to the next, who in his turn placed it in the hand of the next again . . . At the close of the day it was called for by Mr Kerr. The child who happened to possess it was severely flogged.[49]

These kinds of punishments did not die out as the century progressed. Donald Masson told the Gaelic Society of Inverness in 1889 that when he was a child, hatred of Gaelic had been inculcated in children by the cruellest methods possible.

'It was an iron rule that under certain stress of nature we should thus address the supreme head of the school – "Please, master, shall I get out?"' he recalled:

> If asked in Gaelic, no notice was taken of the agonised request. It must be spoken in English. You can fancy what happened, as happened often. The poor, shy, self-conscious boy would long defer the awkward attempt to utter the sounds he could neither remember nor coordinate. But nature in such cases would have a strong pull on a fellow. And so the attempt must be made. Very slowly and painfully embarrassed in more ways than one wee kiltie edges his way up the master's desk, pulls his forelock and makes his doubly painful bow. Pleasche, Meash – pleasch-h-h, Mheaschter-r . . .

By that stage, Masson said, the boy might well have already urinated in his clothes. A boy unable to speak good English would be 'mimicked and grossly caricatured', he added. 'To crown it all he was almost daily made to wear the fool's cap, a huge erection of goatskins with the hair outwards and the tail hanging down behind'. The passage of the years had not dulled his indignation. 'To this day my blood boils when I recall the cruel and grossly absurd "teaching" of which he was the helpless victim.'[50] Yet Masson sadly drew the same conclusion as Patrick Butler, namely that the teachers' *Kulturkampf* enjoyed most parents' support. 'The parents in many cases, even those who themselves knew little or no English, were dead against the teaching of Gaelic; they wished their children to learn English that they might get on in the world.'[51]

The pace of anglicisation speeded up in the schools after the government's educational reforms in 1872, when the church schools were taken into the state system, for parliament laid down no provision for teaching in Gaelic. Although this omission was modified in 1878, schooling was now essentially once again all in English. The difference from the eighteenth century was that by this stage virtually all children attended schools, which gave these institutions a far more pervasive influence over society than the SPCK schools had enjoyed.

Gaelic lobbyists seemed often to miss the significance of the school question. Societies dedicated to 'the fostering of a Celtic spirit among the Highlanders' proliferated in the late nineteenth century, many in Glasgow, which had a Gaelic-speaking population of at least 20,000 in the early 1800s, concentrated in the Gorbals. Some societies concentrated on ensuring that the Highlanders' religious needs were catered for through the provision of Gaelic chapels, of which there were four in Glasgow by 1851. Others were concerned with the folkloric aspect of Highland dress and on reviving Jacobite songs. The Gaelic Society dated back to 1782 and had been established to revoke the ban on Highland dress instituted after the 1745 rising. After setting itself the task of promoting 'the language, poetry, music and dress of Caledonia', it spawned numerous local branches in the following century, such as the Gaelic Society of London and the Gaelic Society of Inverness. The 1860s saw the formation of numerous societies dedicated to representing the interests and culture of the western islands, such as the Glasgow Islay Society, founded in 1862, the Glasgow Skye Association, founded in 1865 and the Mull Association, founded a year later. In the 1870s Celtic debating societies were set up in Inverness, Oban, Tobermory, Greenock, Glasgow and Aberdeen among other places, while the 1880s saw the emergence of more militant groups, led by the Skye Vigilance Committee.

The debating societies were largely the inspiration of John Stuart Blackie, the charismatic Professor of Greek at Edinburgh and champion of the Gaels, whose lecture in Inverness in October 1874 on the need for a Celtic university chair was instrumental in the establishment of such a chair in Edinburgh University. But the optimistic slogan: 'Blackie! Celtic Chair! Success!' disguised a weakness in some of the societies: there were too many of them and most drew their members from the top, not the base, of society. They did not have a mass membership and were easily elated by prestigious events. They overlooked the degree and speed with which traditional Gaelic culture was unravelling in the countryside, thanks partly to the schools.

Some did realise the deadly significance of the schools. Addressing the Gaelic Society of Inverness in 1873, the Reverend Archibald Farquarson castigated Highland schools that taught Gaelic-speakers in English as 'schools of Antichrist'.[52] The Free Church Moderator A. N. Somerville noted the impact of the state schools when he toured the Highlands in 1887. 'It is plain that under the new system of school teaching in the Highlands, Gaelic is rapidly ebbing throughout the country,'[53] he said, adding that if the trend continued, ministers would have to switch to English to retain a following. Blackie himself sometimes contributed to a slight muddle-headedness about what was going wrong. 'Only let the Highlanders see to it that the Gaelic bible be read and Gaelic songs be sung regularly in all the Highland schools and everything else will follow,'[54] he told an audience in Inverness in July 1880. He warned against the Highlanders allowing their 'souls to be sucked out of them' by 'Saxon schoolmasters' but offered no practical advice as to how this might be avoided.

The Church offered no counsel at all. Whether or not the clergy resented the state takeover of church schools, they did not resent the forcible imposition of English. The Free Church assured the government in 1884 as part of the parliamentary inquiry into the plight of crofters that they would do nothing to hinder the anglicisation of the population. 'Any disposition to hinder the acquisition of English or keep the people shut up in Gaelic would be lamentably foolish,' the Church said in its statement, though it added: 'We are dealing with a people who love their own tongue and feel its power and pathos.'[55]

The upper- and middle-class members of the Celtic and Gaelic societies could not contemplate direct action. The more radical, pro-Irish, agitators found their influence counterbalanced by titled patrons who were keener on confining activities to displays of tartan kilts, recitals of Jacobite airs and historical lectures. There was little to link the bulk of the middle-class societies to the peasants and crofters whose culture they claimed to preserve. They became less and less political with time. The seventeenth assembly of the Gaelic Society of Inverness in 1889, held in the town's Music Hall, was indicative of a change in mood. A reporter noted: 'The platform as usual presented a background of Highland weapons and armour, relieved by shrubs, heather and tartans, amid which might here and there be seen stag's heads and wild birds and animals, the whole harmonising into an exceedingly tasteful and appropriate picture.'[56] The proceedings were dominated at first by Misses Kate and Clare Fraser who were reported to have sung 'Turn ye to me' with 'scientific accuracy', while 'the greatest treat of the evening' was the piano duet of Mrs Mackenzie and Mr Davis. Their rendition of old Jacobite songs, so the society recorded, constituted 'a musical revelation'.[57] By the end of the century the old missionary zeal had evaporated and the membership increasingly spoke no Gaelic. Sir Hector Munro, who took the chair in 1899, told the assembly that while he knew nothing of Gaelic, he had been assured its study made for 'a delightful pastime'.[58] 'Indeed, he was told by those who knew Gaelic that nothing impressed them more than its antiquity and purity.' The society ceased its activities during the First World War and when it recommenced afterwards, it no longer entertained serious hopes of reversing the Highlands' cultural and linguistic meltdown. Expectations of a Celtic revival in the Highlands had by then been dashed by the blight of depopulation.

The sight of a land drained of the people who lived there for generations is always depressing and has lent that atmosphere of melancholy to the Highlands that so many poets of the eighteenth and nineteenth centuries explored. The recollection of their lamentation impregnates the modern appreciation of the landscape, just as the memory of the Famine affects our view of the west coast of Ireland. On the road from An Tarbert to Stornoway, a small tower of stones beside the road commemorates one of the many episodes in the long struggle over land that the people eventually lost, when a group of local people forced their way into land that had been 'cleared' for a deer park and were arrested.

Ireland has commemorated the Famine with an impressive monument in Dublin, depicting a group of stick-thin figures dressed in ragged clothes. The air of motion is deeply disturbing, for we do not know to where these figures are walking, only that their destiny is terrifying. They may be walking to a soup kitchen, a workhouse or to a 'coffin ship' that will transport them to America. The Highland Clearances have no similar landmark in the Scottish capital, not only because the Clearances were more drawn out than the Famine and resulted in infinitely fewer deaths, but because the displacement of Highland people from their land was usually the work of Scottish, not English, landlords. The Skye poetess Màiri Mhór laid all the blame for what happened on the English, but as Sorley Maclean – no anglophile – remarked: 'She attacked the English for their doings in Skye, though it was very plain that not one clearance had been made in Skye by anyone who had not a name as Gaelic as her own.'[59]

The Clearances were the result of the changes that followed the Jacobite defeat in 1745 and the disbanding of the clans. While Highland society was organised on clan lines, the clan chiefs had an interest in keeping as many people on their land as possible. But when chiefs simply became landlords, priorities changed. They no longer needed an army of adult males to fight other clans, and the receipt of money became more important than receipt of homage. Dr Johnson remarked on the change in the 1770s. 'The Chiefs, divested of their prerogatives,' he said, 'necessarily turned their thoughts to the improvement of their revenues, and expect more rent.'[60] He added that tenants were being expelled and replaced with better payers. The new tenant, paying more, treated with the chief on equal terms 'and considers him not as a Chief but as a trafficker in land. Thus the estate, perhaps, is improved, but the Clan is broken.'

The transition from chief to capitalist landlord is embodied with great clarity in Roderick MacNeill, of Barra, who told the parish priest in 1825 that he saw his sole interest as improving his property and raising rents. The tenants were 'of little or no importance to me, whatever may be their value to you', he said, 'and if I don't on my arrival find them heart and hand engaged in fishing, I pledge you my honour they shall tramp and the land shall be this ensuing spring occupied by strangers'.[61]

The process of pushing people off the land that disturbed Dr Johnson even in the 1770s gathered pace after the Napoleonic wars. While the struggle continued with France, and Britain laboured under a blockade, Highland landowners earned huge profits from the sale of kelp – seaweed burned to ash to make rich fertiliser. As long as the war continued, they had a strong incentive to keep tenants on their estates, though as close to the coast as possible, to perform the arduous labour of gathering and burning the seaweed. But after peace was declared in 1815, cheap foreign imports of fertiliser ruined the domestic kelp industry and landowners rushed to clear people from their estates to make way for sheep runs and deer parks. Many landowners persuaded themselves that the introduction of sheep would do everyone a favour. The *Edinburgh Review* in 1804 supported the change wholeheartedly. It foretold, quite inaccurately, that 'sheep husbandry would bring with it manufactures, and consequently, villages and towns . . . the Highlands instead of being thinly populated with an indolent and wretched race, would become the abode of industry and comfort'.[62]

The clearance of the estate of Elizabeth, Countess of Sutherland and Marchioness of Stafford, attracted special notoriety because of the legendary brutality of the chief estate manager, or 'factor', Patrick Sellar, who ended up in court charged with homicide. The first clearances began on the estate in 1802, but the case that attracted most opprobrium involved the clearance of Farr and Kildonan in March 1814. According to Donald Macleod, whose book, *Gloomy Memories of the Highlands,* embarrassed the Countess, Sellar burned people out of their houses. Told of the desperate position of the

90-year-old mother-in-law of a tenant called William Chisholm, Sellar was even reported to have said: 'Damn her the old witch, she has lived too long, let her burn.'[63]

Whether or not he used those words, Sellar undoubtedly loathed the Highland Gaels with a Lowlander's raw racial passion. 'Their obstinate adherence to the barbarous jargon of the times when Europe was possessed by savages', he declared, put them 'in a position not very far different from that betwixt the American colonists and the aborigines of that country'. They were the 'Aborigines of Britain', he sneered, whisky-smugglers all, with an inbuilt 'detestation to every introduction to industry or innovation on the ancient manners of the Gael'. The Sutherland estate was wrong even in allowing them to have their own clergy, he declared. They should have been placed under Lowland Scottish clergy 'with a passion for industry in them',[64] and though he did not say so, with a passion for English, too.

Neither Sellar nor the Countess was moved by the pleas of the tenants that they should be left undisturbed while their sons and brothers fought in Britain's war with France. They were just an irritant, getting in the way of rent. 'The people of the Lower Class in general appear so unwilling to come into any plans for bettering the general condition,' the Countess grumbled in June 1809. 'I am glad to hear that about 60 have emigrated . . . I hope, however, that a number of the better disposed sort will remain, as we can well spare all the idle ones.'[65] The Sutherland clearances did not stop with Sellar's trial for homicide, unsurprisingly, as he was acquitted of the charges. To cap it all, the tenants who survived the Countess's 'improvements' were ordered to subscribe to a pompous monument to her consort when he died in 1833, expressing their heartfelt gratitude for everything they had experienced. By then the whole county had been transformed and a land

> where the martial notes of the bagpipes sounded and reverberated from mountain to glen . . . [was] converted to a solitary wilderness where the voice of man praying to God is not to be heard, where you can set a compass with twenty miles of a radius upon it and go round with it full stretched and not find one acre of land within the circumference which has come under the plough for the last thirty years.[66]

The Sutherland estate clearances set the precedent for other estate landlords, in the Uists, on Skye, on Rum, Muck and Islay, on Raasay, on Mull and elsewhere. Of the minister of Morvern, John MacLeod, it was said: 'His latter years were spent in pathetic loneliness. He had seen his parish almost emptied of its people. Heath and glen had been turned into sheep walks and the cottages . . . unroofed. He thus found himself the sole remaining link between past and present – the one man . . . who remembered the old days [and] the traditions of the people'.[67]

The irony of the clearances was that they devastated the Highlands at exactly the time when the Romantic movement was extolling the virtues of the Highlanders to urban Britain. Old Mrs Chisholm was being hustled out of her burning cottage at the same time as Walter Scott was enthralling the reading public with tales of poetic, gallant Gaels in *Waverley* and *Rob Roy*. Highland society was being decimated just as the poetic image of the Highlander became synonymous with Scotland as a whole, and just as every Scotsman became an honorary Highlander. As Dugald Coghill put it in his book, *The Elusive Gael*: 'Soon the vulgar imagination was so completely occupied by plaids . . . that by most Englishmen, Scotsmen and Highlanders were regarded as synonymous words'. As Coghill added, this concept received striking confirmation during George IV's visit to Edinburgh in 1822, when the King 'thought that he could not give a more striking proof of his respect for the usages which had prevailed in Scotland before the Union than by disguising himself in what before the Union was considered by nine Scotsmen out of ten as the dress of a thief.'[68]

Much has been made of the more absurd aspects of the King's visit, which Scott choreographed as a gathering of the Highland clans with the King posing as a clan chief. Critics have ridiculed his eccentric appearance at the royal levee in Holyroodhouse, where the probably unpleasing sight of the King's swollen legs was concealed under the kilt by flesh-coloured stockings, which were then edited out of the portrait of the occasion. It was, of course, a theatrical and unreal occasion – a parade of dead and dying clans (bulked out by middle-class townie members of Gaelic societies) in a city that had always aimed to destroy everything those clans stood for. Scott's biographer, J. G. Lockhart, recalled the peculiar atmosphere. 'Every height and precipice [was] occupied by military of the regular army, or by detachments of these more picturesque irregulars from beyond the Grampians – lines of tents, flags and artillery . . . and the old black castle and its rock, wreathed in the smoke of repeated salvoes, while a huge banner-royal, such as had not waved there since 1745, floated and flapped over all.' Lockhart also recorded an unforgettable glimpse of Scott, the master of ceremonies, 'seated in an open carriage in the Highland dress, armed and accoutred . . . heroically . . . and evidently in a most bardish state of excitement'.[69]

Scotland's modern, left-wing and puritanical nationalist establishment does not remember the occasion gladly and has heaped obloquy on Scott as a Tory royalist, distracting the people from their social problems with a deceitful parade of Highland flummery. The political commentator Andrew Marr delivered a typical dig in *The Battle for Scotland*. Scott was a man who 'despite his deep and complex understanding of his country's history . . . turned his early Jacobite rebelliousness into a gooey pastiche first of itself and then of all Scotland . . . Scott's promotion of the Highland cult enabled him to reconcile conservative loyalty to the fat Unionist lecher George IV with moist-eyed Scottish nationalism.'[70] Many modern historians take a similar line. They savage Scott for selling the Union to an otherwise 'radical' Scotland and for kick-starting the royal cult of the Highlands that gathered tremendous pace under George's niece, Victoria. She spent much of her life in the Highlands at her Balmoral castle, releasing on to a curious public long accounts of her travels there with Prince Albert and Lady Jane Ely, entitled *Leaves from a Journal of Our Life in the Highlands*. Published in 1868 and followed with *More Leaves* in 1883, the 'leaves' contained numerous romantic paeans to the Highlanders, centring on their chivalry, their nobility and, above all, their loyalty. In the Highlands, Victoria felt like a primitive queen, not a dull constitutional monarch. 'There was such devoted loyalty to the family of my ancestors,' she wrote excitedly, 'for Stuart blood is in my veins and I am *now* their representative, and the people are as devoted and loyal to me as they were to that unhappy race.'[71]

While Scott may be found guilty of starting a sentimental Victorian cult of the Highlands summed up neatly as 'Balmorality', he cannot be accused of insincerity. This intense, romantic and conservative patriot was not, in fact, a slavish admirer of the Union. On the contrary, he felt keenly that it was undermining Scotland's identity and that the nation desperately needed to jolt its slumbering imagination. His books formed part of this campaign of awakening and the royal visit in 1822 was another. 'By such efforts,' he wrote in the introduction to his *Minstrelsy of the Scottish Border*, 'I may contribute somewhat to the history of my native country, the peculiar features of whose manners and character are daily melting and dissolving into those of her sister.'[72]

Scott was not a mercenary truckler with Scotland's ancient emblems, cynically distracting the nation from its 'real' problems with historical pageants. When Whig opponents smirked at his patriotic orations, Lockhart recalled that Scott literally wept with frustration. 'Scott broke out on them that it was no laughing matter. "Little by little, whatever your wishes may be, you will destroy and undermine, until nothing of what makes Scotland shall remain." And with that he turned away from them . . . tears running down his cheeks.'[73] Scott was well aware he lacked an intimate knowledge of Gaelic culture and was humble about it. On a visit to Staffa he recalled his embarrassment when the head boatman made a speech to him. 'As it was in Gaelic, I could only receive it as a silly beauty does a fine-spun compliment, bow, and say nothing.'[74] It was not Scott's fault that the reading public the world over devoured his novels and rapidly assumed that all the Scots wore kilts. Nor was it his fault that while he publicised a romantic image of the Highlanders, less romantic landowners were forcing the objects of his literary cult off their land. The British public warmed to Scott because the world he glamorised was no longer a threat. While Gaelic-speaking Highlanders comprised half the population of Scotland, as they did in the 1520s, according to the historian John Mair, fear outweighed curiosity.[75] By the time Scott's works became famous, the industrialisation of the Lowlands and the quantum expansion of Glasgow had brought about great change. The one-in-two had become the one-in-ten. The average lowland Scot no longer dreaded Highlanders, but Irish immigrants.

The memory of the Sutherland evictions lingered in the Highlands for decades. When a new round of evictions took place in the more militant climate of the 1870s and 1880s, it was not difficult for crofter supporters to find old people in their eighties who recalled the misery they had witnessed 60 years before. Grace Macdonald, then 88, told John Mackay in 1884 she still remembered Sellar's men throwing a live cat into a flaming croft, one of 20 houses she saw burned. Bell Cooper, aged 82, said: 'For some days after the people were turned out, one could scarcely hear a word, with the lowing of cattle and the screaming of children . . . Sellar burnt everything he could lay his hands on . . . I shall never forget that awful day.'[76] In Nova Scotia, the land to which many expelled tenants were sent, Mackay found local people who prized the memory of Big Jane, 'Sìne Mhòr', who had resisted the eviction of her octogenarian father from his home with a wild fury. They remembered that she 'took hold of the summons in her teeth . . . and though she was thrown down on the ground by the constables who held her fast, she tore it in pieces with her teeth'.[77]

In *Gloomy Memories*, Macleod accused the local clergy, the same clergy Sellar disliked, of assisting the Sutherland clearances by telling the people it was the will of God. But in the decades that followed the crofters became less isolated and dependent on the clergy for their interpretation of events. Even by the 1850s, the mood was very different. When the Sutherland estate tried to dispossess crofters at Coigach in 1852, women spearheaded a campaign of violent resistance, holding demonstrations, destroying summonses and on one occasion stripping the clothes off the officer serving an eviction notice.[78] In the 1860s societies such as the Skye Vigilance Committee began monitoring events and co-ordinating action by local people in tandem with a press campaign waged by radical journalists in Glasgow and beyond. The extension of the franchise meant that the British parliament was no longer the preserve of the landed and the very rich. Above all, there was the example of Ireland. There, the Home Rulers under Charles Stewart Parnell were openly encouraging an economic war by the peasants against the landlords through the organisation of the Land League, founded in 1879. The League's precise aims were vague. Some wanted peasant proprietorship, while others had a more revolutionary agenda. Either formula threatened the landlord class with annihilation. The success of the Land League kindled hopes – and fears – that the turmoil in Ireland might fan agitation on both sides of the water, reuniting the Gaels and surmounting the religious divide that had proved so useful to the English overlords of both communities. The new pan-Gaelic, pan-Celtic sentiment was incarnated in John Murdock, a radical journalist from Islay who hoped the Highland Gaels might become the cornerstone of a new Scottish nationalism. Murdock's newspaper, *The Highlander*, launched in the mid-1870s, was aimed at 'sinking the differences between the different members of the great Celtic family . . . after the ages and generations during which they have been perpetuating follies and wickednesses against each other at the bidding of their common political enemies'.[79]

The mid-1870s and first half of the 1880s saw this pan-Gaelic feeling reach its high point, symbolised by Parnell's appearance at a rally for the crofters in Glasgow City Hall in Easter 1881. The following year saw the establishment in Inverness of a Scottish land league, called the Highland Land Law Reform Association, under John Mackay. Modelled on its Irish counterpart, its foundation raised the distinct possibility that Queen Victoria might be disabused of her cherished image of the Highlanders as united in devotion to the dynasty. On 17 April 1882 the attempted eviction of crofters from Ben Lee in Skye sparked a scuffle with the police that achieved media notoriety as the 'Battle of the Braes'. As the trouble spread on Skye, the authorities sent a gunboat, the *Jackal*, to Glendale to ensure the arrest of three resisting crofters. The trial of the 'Glendale martyrs', as they were nicknamed, did the landlord cause no good and they spent only two months in jail. The military were back in Skye in October 1884, when HMS *Assistance* and two gunboats carrying 350 marines were deployed, following new disturbances in Uig.[80]

The fallout from the Highland agitation was the election of five pro-crofter candidates in the general election of 1885, two Land Leaguers and three pro-crofter independents. The success in Argyll of Donald MacFarlane, a pro-Irish Catholic and a supporter of Irish Home Rule, seemed a particular portent of the coming fusion of agitated Gaels. But the radical tide ceased to flow when the startled government acted to stop the Irish virus from infecting all Scotland. In 1886 the Liberal Prime Minister William Gladstone put into practice the recommendations of an earlier Royal Commission into the crofters. The Crofters' Holdings Act of 1886 gave crofters security of tenure and set up a commission to arbitrate disputed rents, most of which were later reduced by about 30 per cent. The belated attempt to pacify the Highlands had no immediate result. Lewis remained especially turbulent. The eviction of crofters from Bernera in 1874 had caused a riot, which brought the Matheson family, landlords of Lewis since the mid-1840s, unwelcome publicity. There was more trouble there in November 1887, when people from the Lochs area of Lewis moved into the newly established deer park to slaughter the game. The affray was serious enough for a gunboat to be sent to Stornoway, while the police charged 16 men, including the radical local schoolmaster Donald MacRae, with riot and trespass.

The monument on the main road from Tarbert to Stornoway commemorates that chapter in the Highland land war. But the trouble in Lewis marked the end, rather than the beginning, of an era. The Crofters Act slowly reduced the heat in the struggle and talk of a pan-Celtic front faded. Parnell had never been very interested, in spite of his star appearance in Glasgow in 1881. The Irish Land Leaguers and Home Rulers were unwilling to share their crown of martyrdom with the Scots, Welsh or anyone else. Under Parnell and John Redmond, who took the helm of the parliamentary party after Parnell's disgrace, they defended their conviction that Ireland was a special case, and not a symptom of a wider Celtic malaise. They feared to endorse the slogan of the young Welsh firebrand David Lloyd George of 'Home Rule all round', suspecting it might lead to home rule for nobody.

The Scots also drew back from pressing the Gaelic connection. When the Irish Land Leaguer Michael Davitt toured the Highlands in 1887, the *Oban Times* welcomed the 'harbinger of a bright day for the sea-divided Gael',[81] but this was, in fact, a last gasp. The land question was losing its central place in the Highlands, while the Liberal Party's embrace of Irish Home Rule split opinion in Scotland as a whole. Murdock's *Highlander* closed in 1882, unregretted, said the *Celtic Magazine*, 'in consequence of its extreme views and its general mismanagement'. MacFarlane lost his seat in 1886. The various Gaelic societies gradually turned away from politics. The plight of the

Highland Gaels did not ignite a nationalist movement along Irish lines.
Instead, nationalism slumbered, repelled more than galvanised by the subsequent course of events in Ireland.

When nationalism returned in Scotland as a popular force – far stronger
than before – in the 1960s it was in urban, Lowland guise. The great by-
election victory of 1967 that propelled the Scottish National Party into
prominence did not take place in one of the old Land Leaguers' seats of 1885
but in Hamilton, a town of coal- and steelworkers on the outskirts of
Glasgow. The SNP won the western isles in the general election of 1970,
but although some early twentieth-century fathers of modern nationalism,
such as the Hon. Ruaraidh Erskine, dreamed of a re-Gaelicised Scotland,
the party never thought of itself as a Gaelic movement. It did not help that
Erskine insisted that Alba needed reconverting to Roman Catholicism as
well as to the Gaelic language, and that he believed 'every great evil which
Alba labours under owes its existence to the continuance of Protestantism'.[82]
This kind of talk did not commend itself to most nationalists in Edinburgh
and Glasgow, who, unlike their counterparts in Dublin, did not even superficially align their separatist instincts with the cause and culture of the Gaels,
let alone with Catholicism.

In the 1920s, Scottish patriotism often adopted an anti-Irish, anti-
Catholic tone, reflecting many people's morbid concern about the large
Irish immigrant population in Glasgow. Those of Irish descent were 'a
completely separate race of alien origin', Lord Scone, MP for Perth,
declared in 1932, and their presence was 'bitterly resented by tens of thousands of the Scottish working class'.[83] Ireland was no longer the beacon of
hope. The Scottish nationalists were more interested in the precedent of
Northern Ireland, a Protestant British enclave carved out in 1921, with its
own parliament at Stormont. Since the 1960s the SNP has gone out of its
way to forget that episode and woo Catholics of Irish descent. But it has not
become philo-Gaelic or philo-Catholic. The Scottish Kirk remains an
object of nationalist veneration as the torchbearer of nationality through the
dark centuries of unionism. The influential journalist and writer Neal
Ascherson is closer to the instincts of most nationalists than was Erskine in
giving the Calvinist tradition a cautious thumbs-up. To Ascherson, Knox
and the Calvinist patriarchs rescued Scotland's separate identity when they
saved it from Anglicanism and for that reason even the die-hard utterly
unreasonable fundamentalists of the seventeenth century known as
Covenanters get an endorsement. 'They ensured it was a nation whose
identity would be preserved by its religious distinctness,' he wrote. 'If

Presbyterianism had failed, Scotland today would be little more than an item of British regional geography.'[84]

It would not, in any case, now make practical political sense for Scottish nationalism to lay stress on Gaels or Gaelic. Unlike the situation in Wales, there are too few votes to be gained in championing the Gaelic language for it to be worth it. Instead, they champion the resurrection of the Stuart state that did its best to wipe out that language. Modern Scottish nationalism tacks between those who see Gaelic as *the* Scottish language and others who believe that title belongs to Lowland English or 'Lallans', the language of Robert Burns, the country's most popular poet. Some of the stalwarts of modern nationalism have ridden both horses simultaneously. Hugh MacDiarmid, the acerbic and xenophobic communist poet, changed his name to mark his own contribution towards the business of healing the Lowland–Highland divide – he was born Christopher Murray Grieve. MacDiarmid's best-known work, *A Drunk Man Looks at the Thistle*, was written in Lallans, but at the same time he described himself as a 'purely Celtic poet' filled with a 'a bardic concern for Celtic history and the continuity of Celtic civilisation'.[85] His great goal, he wrote, was to 'get rid of the English ascendancy and work for the establishment of workers' republics in Scotland, Ireland, Wales and Cornwall, and indeed make a sort of Celtic union of Socialist Soviet republics in the British Isles'.[86]

MacDiarmid's splenetic anglophobia (it was for him not a hobby 'but my very life') never commended itself to the Highlands and islands. His was a borderer's obsessive loathing for the all-similar neighbour down the road, on the other side of a near frontier. The Gaelic scholar Malcolm Chapman spied a wrong note in MacDiarmid's attack on the 'false Highland/Lowland distinction'. It was 'purely wishful', he wrote. 'His plea obscures the fact that this false distinction has been the very substance of Scottish disunity, and the dominant political dividing line in Scotland since the time of Malcolm Canmore'.[87]

The Gaels were always one step removed from the hothouse nationalism of the Lowlands with its flags, battles and medieval heroes. In the early middle ages, the Celts of the west and north in the Lordship of the Isles allied often with England against a common enemy, the Scottish crown. As one writer put it in 1909: 'Their king was the Lord of the Isles, or any Macbeth or MacWilliam, their ally was England, their cause was the retention of their ancient institutions . . . [and] they were not to be successful; they had little education, scarcely a true Celtic town, and they had no horses fit for cavalry use.'[88] The wars that stir Scottish patriotic passions today, glamorised in the popular Hollywood film *Braveheart* (1995), had nothing to do with them and they took place in the English-speaking south. The leaders of the war of independence from the England of Edward I in the 1290s – Robert Bruce, William Wallace, James Douglas, Andrew Moray, Christoper Seton and Robert Wishart, Bishop of Glasgow – were all of Anglo-Norman or Flemish descent.

Something of that emotional distance remains. The people of the western isles I met seemed only mildly interested in the politics of Scottish nationalism and in the workings of the parliament in Edinburgh that Britain's Labour Prime Minister Tony Blair set up after the Labour landslide of 1997. They wait to see if the gossamer-thin Gaelic culture, which a century ago covered much of north-west Scotland and has now shrunk back across the Minch to the Isles, will fare better under Holyrood than Westminster. But they are not natural flag-wavers. Some have only half an eye on events in Edinburgh, as they try to breathe new life into the ties linking Gaelic Scotland and Ireland, ties that predate the rise of a Scottish state and the Reformation.

It was not a British sovereign or a Scottish minister but Mary Robinson, president of Ireland, who came to Iona to open the museum dedicated to Colum Cille in 1997. When I visited the veteran Gaelic activist John Angus Mackay, president of the Gaelic Broadcasting Committee, in Stornoway, his gift to me was a copy of a beautifully illustrated volume entitled *An Leabhar Mór, The Great Book of Gaelic*. This book, containing a selection of Gaelic poetry from the last 1,500 years from both sides of the water, is just such a cultural collaboration. It recalls the illuminated gospels known as the *Book of Kells*, today one of the best-known emblems of Ireland, but which most likely originated in the Scottish-Irish monastery of Iona.

In his office, Mackay unfolded a modern map of Ireland and Scotland drawn up for the Columba Initiative, a joint Scottish–Irish project that fosters the Gaelic heritage of both countries. The map was drawn from a very different perspective from the ones I remembered from my school classroom, in which everything tumbled down towards London, and Scotland and Ireland lay on the fringe. Instead, this map showed the land of Columba, the Tìr Cholm Cille, with the Irish Sea in the middle and Scotland, the Isle of Man and Ireland forming an arc around it. This was the world as Colum Cille, or Mulruabh, might have imagined it, in which the Irish Sea was the 'inland sea', serving as a channel of communication between lands sharing a similar culture and language.

Staring at the map of Tìr Cholm Cille – land of Columba – on which Glasgow was Glaschù and Dumfries was Dun Phris, I wondered if enough people remained to recreate anything meaningful of this. Leaving aside the Manx and Irish, the 250,000 Gaelic-speakers in Scotland registered in the census of 1881 have dwindled to 80,000 today. Of those 80,000, only 23,000 live in the western isles, but it is hard to see much more than a museum culture surviving without them, for this is the only slice of the old land of Alba where it remains a community language. But school lists are ominously down in the Outer Hebrides. Newspapers have projected that there might be only 800 school-age children by 2016 in the western isles,[89] which if true would render the whole Gaelic education project virtually redundant.

There is no sign of a great economic revival there, merely a remorseless decline in the number of young people and an increasing number of summer residents whose interest in local culture is minimal. But John Angus Mackay declined to be pessimistic, or echo the thousands of grim lines written by Gaelic poets from the 1740s till now. 'There is just no point regretting change, you have to shape it,' he said. He recalled the gleaming outline of the Sabhal Mòr Ostaig on Skye as an example of what people can do if they put their minds to it. 'If you had been to Sleat before that', he recalled, ' I remember when there was nothing there but an old barn.' It was hard going, he admitted, as the Highlanders were 'a fiercely uncompetitive people'. They 'don't like putting their heads above the parapet'.

Is it worth saving the language and culture of 1 per cent of the modern population of Scotland? Not everyone thinks so. Jonathon Keats, writing in the influential British magazine *Prospect* in 2003, argued that Gaelic, along with Manx, belonged in the dustbin of history. He urged that more attention be focused on vital new languages, such as Spanglish, an English–Spanish hybrid spoken by millions of Latino immigrants in urban North America.[90] I was not won over. One does not have to subscribe to Victorian racist apologetics for Gaels and Highlandism, which attributed superior moral values to 'the Highland race', to see that the Gaelic language remains the key to understanding a large part of Scotland's history, literature, culture and geography. Part of Scotland's persona and identity are locked away in Gaelic and will become unknowable without it. Even if it is true, as *The Great Book of Gaelic* declared, that there are now fewer Gaelic poets in the whole of Scotland than there were on the single island of Tiree in 1900,[91] that sense of cultural exhaustion does not apply to music. Though far less publicised than its Irish counterpart, Gaelic music flourishes in Scotland, communicating elements of the culture behind it to a much wider and younger audience than could ever have been reached by the printed word. Alyth McCormack, a Lewis singer from the group Shine, is part of a musical renaissance that has profited from the decline in the Presbyterian religion, with its disapproval of instrumental music; Shine performs to large audiences at the annual Celtic music festival in Glasgow, as well as at festivals in Nova Scotia and all over the world. When I met her in Inverness, she expressed no doubt that Gaelic music had a future as well as a past in Scotland. When she grew up in Lewis, she recalled, there was still a lingering suspicion of music as 'an instrument of the devil', and while few people at school held those views, there was not much interest in Gaelic music. Now, she added: 'The energy of Gaelic music is something people want to be part of. It's got much more of a platform, people have more respect.' There has also been more cross-fertilisation, as Scottish and Irish musicians exchange and borrow ideas. Here, at any rate, the Columba Initiative was being put into spontaneous practice, without any official grants or NGOs becoming involved. The Gaelic musicians will always be in the minority in Scotland, but McCormack maintained this did not matter. 'It's living and breathing,' she said, and that is enough.

CHAPTER TWO

Connemara

'A vague reverence for the Gaelic'

The instructor of the nations, the preacher of the gospel of nature-worship, hero-worship, God-worship — such Mr Chairman is the destiny of the Gael.
(Patrick Pearse, *The Intellectual Future of the Gael*, 1897)

'English', my new companion remarked, 'is a language for dogs. Everyone says that here.' To demonstrate the point, he shouted: 'Hey, you, *dog!*' at an amiable-looking animal dozing on the porch just outside the door. The dog got up wearily and slunk out of the door in the direction of the herb garden, with a sorrowful backward glance.

I was in a small white cottage in Connemara, a few miles west of An Spidéal (Spiddal), in the heart of the Connacht Gaeltacht. This is the Irish-speaking region, west of Gaillimh, or Galway, where Ireland's native language is maintained with government support as the first language of schools, local government, business and the airwaves. My host was not a real local boy. An independent film-maker, with a passionate commitment to the Irish language, he was one of many city children to move to the Gaeltacht not simply for the 'lifestyle', and for the clean air and fine views, but as a conscious, cultural choice. 'Blow-ins', the locals call them in English. They do not always look on them kindly. They fear that they will either make no effort at all to learn the Irish language or, like my host, have a zeal for Irish and a holy hatred for all things English that they find excessive. When I repeated my canine anecdote to one of these locals, she laughed and shouted: 'Hold it, just hold it right *there*. Who on earth said that?' 'He's not from the area,' I began, but got no further. 'I knew it!' the woman cut in triumphantly, snapping her fingers. 'A blow-in! And I bet he's from Dublin.'

The family who ran the bed and breakfast I was staying in were similarly bemused. A Connacht family born and bred and Irish-speakers, they had recently returned from a holiday in England's Lake District. The idea of

Irish people vacationing in England struck me as peculiar. Most Dubliners of my acquaintance had been quick to communicate a strong aversion to virtually everything English, and conversation about English matters often proved a risky affair in the Irish capital, winding its way back to a long list of crimes, starting with Henry II's invasion of Ireland in the twelfth century and proceeding through the great Famine of the 1840s to the execution of Patrick Pearse, leader of the Easter Rising in 1916.

The anglophobia of many Dubliners seemed to stem partly from a fear of being mistaken for their dreaded neighbours. The Irish, especially abroad, often meet a degree of incomprehension from foreigners when they hear that their guests speak English, but definitely are not English. I heard many conversations to this effect, centring on some 'eejit' (slang for a fool) who had failed to take note of my interlocutor's nationality and mistook him or her for a 'Brit'.

Those problems simply do not occur with the people of the Gaeltacht, who are never likely to be taken for anyone else except perhaps their Gaelic-speaking Scottish highland cousins. They seem more secure in their culture than Ireland's anglophone majority, which helps to explain why my hosts were so relaxed about their unashamed enjoyment of their English sojourn, and why the most concentratedly Irish-speaking part of Ireland – the most Celtic portion of the land – is the least inclined to nationalism and flag-waving.

The Anglo-Irish, descendants of the English conquerors, promoted a holy horror of England in order to justify their own outrageous supremacy. The Anglo-Irish writer and critic Cyril Connolly recalled the obsession with point-scoring in his childhood before the First World War, when he spent long holidays with relatives in Clontarf, near Dublin. 'Being English', he discovered,

> meant possessing a combination of snobbery, stupidity, and lack of humour and was a deadly insult. There were many stories of social triumphs at the expense of parvenu England – especially against unpopular viceroys . . . The Anglo-Irish were a superior people. Better born but less snobbish; cleverer than the English . . . poorer no doubt but with a poverty that brought into relief their natural aristocracy.

As an adult, Connolly saw through this fake, self-serving nationalism. It dawned on him 'that the England I hated, the oppressor of the Celt and Gael, was made manifest in my grandfather who owned a thousand acres of suburban Dublin'. He concluded that 'the Anglo-Irish were themselves a possessor class whose resentment against England was based on the fear that she might not always allow them to go on possessing'.[1]

The sentiments of the Anglo-Irish are easily dissected. With no language of their own, or even a distinct literary culture until William Butler Yeats spearheaded the English-speaking revival in the 1890s, they had to fall back on character traits. They were partly responsible for a certain film and stage stereotype of the Irish as characterised mainly by an almost oppressive feistiness. It was their last bequest before they vanished from the stage – attributing to an entire people the traits they had assumed for their own self-defence. Anglophone Ireland has maintained this identity, half conscious that without a language as a badge of difference, religion alone will no longer do, and character has to step into the breach. It lives on in the modern cult of Dublin as the capital of 'craic', or fun, an image flogged relentlessly by the city's tourist literature. If anything, the stereotype has hardened in recent years thanks to Hollywood, which has taken to the image of Irish 'rebel hearts'. Hollywood movies are densely sprinkled with Ryans, Murphies, Finnegans and Flanagans (think Regan in *Alien*, or Connor in *Terminator*) whose heroic cussedness dovetails with an older cinematic image of the Irish as cute rural folk living an almost elf-like existence.

It is an anglophone affair. Cross the Shannon and push west into Galway and you cross a cultural frontier. The Iberian contours and cupolas of the cathedral of Our Lady and St Nicholas (a building loathed by Dublin's architectural snobs) mark the gateway to a different culture, less delineated by 'character' and more by culture. The west of Ireland has always faced south, towards Italy, Spain and the Mediterranean. Until Ireland's English governors, the Lord Deputies, bridged the River Shannon in the mid-sixteenth century, road travel from the east to the west of the country was hazardous and Galway flourished as an autonomous city state, more accessible by sea than land. Commercial links to Spain and Portugal were far stronger than ties to Dublin.

The Reformation in the 1560s and the Cromwellian invasion in the 1650s successively severed Galway's bonds to southern Europe. But the centralisation of Irish government in Dublin under British rule, a policy continued after Irish independence in 1922, never entirely reorientated Connacht to the east. Deprived of their old contacts with the world of the Mediterranean, the people of Connacht turned west, towards America. There is a grain of truth in tourist-friendly descriptions of various points on the Irish west coast as the 'last parish before America', for America is closer than Dublin (or London) to many people in Connacht in family terms. When Yeats's colleague, the writer John Millington Synge, visited the Aran islands at the turn of the twentieth century, he was struck by the deep, personal attachment these Gaelic-speakers felt to the United States, which was then at war with Spain over Cuba. 'The conflict with Spain is causing a great deal of excitement,' he noted. 'Nearly all the families have relations who have had to cross the Atlantic, and all eat from the flour and bacon that is bought from the United States, so they have a vague fear that "if anything happened to America", their own island would cease to be inhabitable.'[2]

When the people of Great Blasket Island, off Dingle, gave up the unequal struggle to live on their windswept outpost in the 1950s, they departed for the state of Massachusetts, not for Dublin or London. The sense of familiarity with America lives on. I met many people in the Connacht Gaeltacht who spoke of San Francisco, Boston or New York as if it were a neighbouring town, but who had rarely, if ever, visited their own national capital.

Anglophone Ireland and Irish-speaking Ireland are no longer equal in size and power. There are eight portions of the Gaeltacht, in County Donegal in Ulster, in counties Mayo and Galway in Connacht, in Kerry and Cork in Munster and in counties Waterford and Meath in Leinster. But together they make up a minute proportion of the landmass of the Republic of Ireland. Only in Donegal, Mayo and Galway does the Gaeltacht make up a significant proportion of the county's area.

The decline in the language has been relentless for several centuries, but was astonishing for the speed it gathered from the mid-nineteenth century onwards, defying the efforts of the language revival activists who began their work in the latter half of the century. Ireland is unique in Europe as the only country where a successful nationalist movement failed to engender a successful language revival. The Celtic nationalist societies that flourished at the end of the nineteenth century looked to Ireland as the Celtic motherland. But they were disappointed in their expectation that Ireland's freedom from foreign rule would trigger a revival of the culture and language of the Gaels who inhabited Ireland before the Anglo-Norman conquest of the 1170s. Today Ireland continues to inspire the same mixed feelings. The 'Celtic Tiger' economy draws unalloyed admiration from nationalists in Scotland, Wales, Cornwall and French Brittany. At the same time, the country's stubbornly anglophone character carries a health warning, inviting them to beware of the perils of over-concentration on legislative independence.

The Gaeltacht is not the only repository of Irish speech. The number of urban speakers has increased markedly since the 1960s thanks to the growing popularity of Irish-medium schooling, which, like Welsh-medium schooling, has a reputation of providing better education than English schools. But the Gaeltacht is still vitally important as the only area where Ireland's older language is consistently spoken, and where it is still connected to the land. There has always been something slightly taut and artificial about the urban *Gaelgeoir*, or learner. The language is hard to slot into the urban landscape of Dublin, a city moulded by centuries of Protestant English rule. Language bureaucrats have gone round each and every alleyway, bestowing Irish versions of street names honouring dukes and viceroys, but the translations have a laboured air, for the likes of Belvedere Place, Rutland Place North and Chancery Place were never designed to be rendered into Irish.

In Marks & Spencer, on Grafton Street, the city's pedestrianised retail showcase, a tape-recorded greeting in Irish thanks the patrons of the store at closing time. There are similar greetings on the planes of the national carrier Aer Lingus. Likewise the buses: each double-decker heading to the city centre bears the words 'An Lár' on the headboard, which is Irish for 'the centre'. There is no lack of reminders that Irish is the first language of the state. The bus signs and streets signs point towards a date hazily planted in the future when everyone will have returned to *an teanga*, the tongue, as language enthusiasts called it. Yet, more than 80 years after the last British troops marched out of Dublin Castle, the goal is not in sight. A visitor not actually *looking* for Irish would be far more likely to overhear words spoken in Albanian, Romanian, Polish or Yoruba than in Irish. The Celtic Tiger has sparked sustained immigration to Ireland for the first time since the Ulster Plantation of the seventeenth century. North of the city centre, new communities have sprung up who do not share even a vestigial sentimental commitment to the language. It is one reason why the Gaeltacht, tiny and watered down with holiday-home owners as it is, remains so important to the country's cultural integrity. It is the wellspring of Irish culture and identity into which the rest of the population can periodically dip and, if they are so inclined, be reminded of what came before.

A few miles west of An Spidéal, the village capital of the Gaillimh Gaeltacht, stands a long low building that some see as holding the key to the future survival of the Irish language. It is the centre for TG4, the Irish-language television station that since its inception in the late 1990s has captured the public imagination with innovative, youth-centred programmes. The official prominence of Irish since independence has always guaranteed the language a place in public-service broadcasting on the state network, RTE. But it was only in the late 1990s that the idea for a separate, or autonomous, station achieved fruition. At the station in An Spidéal I found no one over the age of 30. There was not a suit, a tie, a navy-blue dress or even an Aran sweater in sight. The staff moved round in casual, student-like gear. Several of them have no background in the media. One had worked as a primary-school teacher while another had worked in a bar in Germany. The newsroom was a hotch-potch of accents and dialects in Irish, with Ulster shading into Munster, and there was no great regard for linguistic purity.

The scriptwriters were preparing for the autumn run of the station's flag-ship soap opera, *Ros na Rún*, which, set amid the blazing heather of Connemara, has developed a penchant for risky storylines. The small screen has given rural, Irish-speaking Connacht a crash course in such themes as homosexual relationships and murder. *Ros na Rún* is one of the big guns in TG4's arsenal as it takes aim at the traditional image of Irish as old, rural and respectable. A measure of its success is its familiarity among thousands of viewers who would never normally watch an Irish-language television station. 'It's caused a radical reappraisal of the language,' the deputy direc-tor, Pádraic Ó Ciardha, explained in Dublin. 'When I was a teenager Irish was almost a cause of shame. For the 95 per cent who didn't speak it, it was just something to endure. We have surprised people. We have shown it can be young and attractive, and risk-taking.'

Sport has provided the other great string to TG4's bow. The station scored a coup by buying the rights to televise club matches of Ireland's national sport: hurling. They also tapped an unsatisfied public appetite for past games, by buying up the television archives and showing the matches again. They televised women's Gaelic football too, which the mainstream networks had neglected, and found a big audience there. The station drew 170,000 viewers to an All Ireland Ladies' Gaelic Football championship. This may not sound much when weighed against 19 million viewers in Britain of the soap, *Coronation Street*, but it represents a healthy proportion of Ireland's 1.2 million televised homes. Ó Ciardha said that when he saw pub crowds watching televised sports matches in Irish in the old Protestant bastion of south Dublin he knew they had finally made it, for when they had cracked 'Dublin 4', the exclusive south Dublin postcode that stands for everything fashionable and metropolitan, they were 'in'.

TG4 is run on a shoestring. Its funding is paltry in comparison to the money that the British government pours annually into its Welsh-language counterpart, S4C, on air since 1982. Total funding in 2003 reached about 30 million euros, compared to the 110 to 115 million euros received by S4C, which does not include about 550 hours of no-cost programmes supplied by the BBC, worth around another 40 million euros. The task TG4 faces in trying to turn round entrenched public attitudes cannot be overestimated.

From the start, the movement to return Ireland to its Gaelic and Celtic roots was dogged by sectarianism and by an association with moral puritanism which, in today's transformed religious and moral environment, is difficult to shake off.

Nineteenth-century Irish nationalism was little concerned with Celtic or Gaelic themes. Daniel O'Connell, named the 'Liberator' for his success in 1829 in overturning the ban since 1691 on Catholic representation in parliament, was the public face of Irish nationalism for several decades until his death in 1847. A lawyer and a superb populist agitator, O'Connell seized the advocacy of Catholic rights from the decorous and polite committees of lords and viscounts who had dominated the various Catholic associations since the eighteenth century, finding his power base among the Catholic priests and the emerging middle classes. His decision in the 1830s to conduct a single-issue campaign – the repeal of the Act of Union of 1800, which abolished the Irish parliament – was both a failure and masterstroke. It was a failure because the British government was unmoved by the 'monster meetings' for repeal that O'Connell summoned in the 1840s, and at the same time a masterstroke, for the simplicity of the cause stirred the national imagination.

O'Connell was part of a Europe-wide phenomenon. The Repeal movement in Ireland had much in common with the nationalist stirrings in Italy, Tsarist Poland, Austrian Bohemia and Moravia, Croatia and among the Austrian Serbs. All over Europe, radical lawyers, journalists and their pushy, middle-class supporters were disinterring ancient and half-forgotten Diets and assemblies, which for centuries had slumbered quietly in the corners of empires, serving mainly as meeting places and watering holes for the gentry. Bodies with no national or representative character whatever suddenly became invested with a new democratic, national significance. The Irish parliament was one. For centuries it had functioned as the lifeless rubber stamp of Ireland's English rulers, forbidden even to initiate legislation without first sending the heads of the bills to England for approval. Only in its last decades, in the mid- to late eighteenth century, did it have a late flowering as a soapbox for the discontented Protestant gentry, making use of England's moment of weakness following the American war to demand and obtain legislative freedom in 1782 under Henry Grattan.

The memory of 'Grattan's parliament' cast a spell over succeeding generations, but there had been a large element of sham to it. The progressive Protestant 'patriots' who flourished under Grattan were never in the same position as the 'patriots' in America. They talked the same talk about rights and tyranny but could not walk the same walk, for while the American Congress rested on the shoulders of several million farmers with whom they shared the Protestant religion and a political language, their counterparts in Dublin scarcely knew the nation they claimed to represent. Many of the Irish lived almost like Russian serfs and were divided from their rulers by language and religion.

Those contradictions were exposed when Ireland erupted in 1798 in a rebellion over which the radical Protestants rapidly lost control. It took the British army several weeks to defeat the insurgents and rescue the terrified landowners, who never again pretended to be in the same position as the American colonists. Shaken to the core, they meekly accepted the Union of 1800 and remained overwhelmingly, even fanatically, pro-unionist to the end. But the contribution of the Protestant radicals of the 1770s and 1780s shaped the nationalist discourse of Ireland throughout the following century. It was the Catholics like O'Connell who took up the fallen banner of the fight against tyranny and garlanded the memory of that most corrupt and unrepresentative institution, the old Irish parliament on College Green.

Catholic nationalism in the nineteenth century was imprisoned by the agenda of the old Protestant gentry. It was very faithful to Grattan's causes and quite indifferent to reviving the Gaelic, pre-Plantation, culture. It accepted and popularised the Anglo-Irish gentry's contempt for the Gaelic world. It was a curious development, in the context of Europe's 'springtime of the nations' in the 1840s, when political radicalism was accompanied everywhere by campaigns to resurrect moribund peasant dialects as 'national' languages. This was no easy business in the Habsburg empire, where, in Bohemia and Croatia, the Slavic tongue had long been expelled from urban society. Slovene was virtually reinvented. It was the same in the Baltic lands, where German had been the language of town life since the Middle Ages. But collective willpower asserted itself, and the ancient peasant languages were sorted out, hacked about and reassembled. Like so many Frankensteins, they got up and actually walked. Unlike Frankenstein, they improved their appearance with time. Country conquered town and German lost its supremacy in Buda, Riga, Zagreb and Prague, as did Swedish in Helsinki.

But in Ireland, the old language and culture continued to wither long after political nationalism had won the nation. The language of Dublin conquered the countryside. This is usually presented as inevitable, but it was nothing of the sort, for although Irish had been in retreat since the 1650s, when the Cromwellian confiscations destroyed the old gentry, Irish was still the language of half the population in O'Connell's time and could conceivably have been rescued, just as Finnish, Latvian, Croat, Slovene and the others were rescued.

Just how Gaelic Ireland was in the 1800s is often forgotten, for the presence and vigour of the Irish language was widely ignored by those with the power to write. When the Welsh Nonconformist minister Thomas Charles, founder of the Welsh circulating schools, visited Ireland in 1807 at the request of the evangelical Hibernian Society, he remarked that Protestantism had failed because the established Church never preached to the people in their own tongue. Even in the old English stronghold of Kilkenny he found that 'Irish is generally spoken, though English is understood',[3] while in Clonmel, 'all the county spoke Irish . . . they spoke Irish in the streets'. On the road from Clonmel to Waterford, Dr Charles found 'all speaking Irish and many Irish only', and when he continued from Cork to Limerick he noted: 'Irish spoken throughout – all Catholics.' Further west, in Tuam, he added: 'All speak Irish and are Catholics. Schools everywhere teach English – none learn Irish.'

Charles's perspective is especially interesting because it starkly contradicts the reports of many English visitors who from the 1750s onwards usually said almost all the Irish spoke English. It suggests that most of these visitors simply did not hear Irish. To them it was a background buzz that could be screened out. Charles, as a Welsh-speaker and champion of the Celtic languages (he was equally appalled by the forced anglicisation of the Scottish Highlands), heard a different Ireland. He was angry about the lack of provision of books in the native tongue. 'Religion cannot be diffused in general among the Irish without Bibles in their own language and schools to teach them to read Irish . . . we have not met with anyone who could read Irish. There are no elementary books in the language.'[4]

The fact that evangelicals continued to put their faith in a greater provision of religious literature in Irish shows that Irish was still a 'people's language', as they had no a priori commitment to Irish. The evangelical author of *Ireland, But Still Without the Ministry of the Word in Her Own Native Language*, published in Edinburgh in 1835, declared that the spread of Protestantism in Ireland depended on Protestants embracing Irish. 'The native Irish speak Irish still to an extent ten times greater than in the days of Henry VIII,' the writer remarked. 'The language has increased, of course, with the natural increase of the people.'[5] Evangelical bishops agreed. Power de la Poer Trench, last Protestant Archbishop of Tuam, learned some Irish after his conversion to evangelicalism in the 1820s, not from any antiquarian interest but in order to communicate more effectively with Connacht people.

That Irish remained so strong in the 1830s attests to the strength of popular attachment, as the language had been relentlessly pushed to the margins since the Anglo-Norman conquest over six centuries before. The Reformation was conducted almost exclusively in English, which, as Dr Charles remarked, helps to explain its failure. The reformed Church of Ireland translated the key texts into the Irish tongue. William Daniel, Archbishop of Cashel, translated the New Testament in 1603 and the Book of Common Prayer in 1608. But there was no repeat in Ireland of the successful triangular partnership in Wales between Elizabeth I, Archbishop Whitgift of Canterbury and William Morgan, which saw the Bible not only translated but published and distributed. In Ireland, unlike in Wales, the English or Scottish settlers outnumbered the native converts among the Protestants, and the incomers had no desire to see the conquered Irish obtaining preferment in a Church they intended to monopolise. The Irish Bible and the Prayer Book remained a dead letter, ignored by the imported clergy. Elizabeth I founded Trinity College in Dublin in 1592 as a Protestant alternative to the continental Catholic seminaries. But, although Irish formed a part of the college curriculum, the provision was forgotten.

There were a few famous exceptions among the Irish Anglicans. William Bedell, English-born Provost of Trinity and Bishop of Kilmore from 1629 to 1642, learned Irish as an adult and used it in his diocese. Charles I was delighted. 'His Majesty likes wondrous well the Irish lecture begun by Mr Bedell,'[6] he was told. But at home the settler gentry sabotaged Bedell's scheme to promote native converts to parishes in Ulster. They had his convert protégé, Murtagh King, jailed for trying to take up a living. Nor was Bedell backed by his archbishop, the learned but bigoted James Ussher. No settler himself, Usher sided with the 'New English' settlers, as the more recent imigrants were called to distinguish them from the Catholic 'Old English' stock. Usher was an early champion of Celtic studies, writing extensively about Patrick and the saints of the Irish Church and reviving interest in them. In *A Discourse of the Religion Anciently Professed by the Irish and the British*, published in Dublin in 1631, he described Ireland as 'the iland of saints' and recalled 'that innumerable company of Saints whose memory was reverenced here'.[7] But as the book went on to show, Ussher's interest was to prove that the long-dead Celtic saints anticipated the views of sixteenth-century Protestants. As can be seen from his dealings with Bedell and King, he had no interest in the living material.

After the royalist Restoration of 1660 the Church of Ireland took a renewed interest in the 'natives' and their culture, and the Church's assembly, the Convocation, passed resolutions urging fresh translations of books and Irish-speaking missions. William King, Archbishop of Dublin from 1703 to 1729, championed such moves, lending support to John Richardson, the Rector of Belturbet, in County Cavan, the great agitator for this work. But these short-lived initiatives went against the grain of the Church of Ireland and Richardson and King had few successors. As church incomes rose in the eighteenth century, competition for bishoprics and deaneries attracted an increasing number of imported Englishmen who took a dim view of encouraging the natives to speak a language associated with sedition and popery. The generation that followed Archbishop King saw the collapse of schemes to evangelise the Irish in the Irish language, as well as the rise of bodies such as the Society for the Promotion of English Protestant Schools in Ireland whose title explains its missionary outlook.

Daniel O'Connell straddled two worlds: the old Irish and new English. The family estate lay in Derrynane, deep in the heart of west County Kerry, then as now the stronghold of Gaelic culture. The O'Connells belonged to the tiny class of Catholic gentry who had survived the Cromwellian land settlement and the imposition of penal laws after the Williamite Revolution of 1688, which parted most Catholic proprietors from their land in the following decades. Daniel Corkery described the world of these remote, almost hidden, families, like the O'Connells of Kerry and the Martins of Connemara, in *Hidden Ireland: A Study of Gaelic Munster in the Eighteenth Century*. Vestiges of an older, patriarchal Gaelic culture survived in these homes well into the eighteenth century, though the culture was enfeebled. 'At the same time, they were all slowly becoming less Gaelic,' he wrote. 'The old lord, the chief, would die and his heir would be less learned, that is to say, less Gaelic than himself.'[8]

This was the childhood of O'Connell, who in the tradition of great Gaelic families, was fostered out in early childhood: in his case, to a herdsman. Irish was certainly his first language and his early years steeped him in the lore and traditions of the Gaels. Yet as an adult he turned his back on it. While his compatriots in central and eastern Europe were trying to recover the culture that their forebears had discarded, O'Connell regarded his own childhood world with coolness, even contempt. He was not a Romantic but a very pragmatic Whig, with a whiggish disdain for old glory and abstract ideas. 'He swam in the mainstream of British parliamentary radicalism,'[9] one biographer, G. Ó Tuathaigh, has noted. Unmoved by the rhetoric of the

1798 Rebellion that had attracted a certain kind of disaffected Protestant, he remained faithful like any good Whig to limited monarchy and constitutional reform.

O'Connell spoke to his tenants at Derrynane in Irish, as 'not three of the forty present could deliver his thoughts in any other language'.[10] He spoke Irish at rallies. But he did it to be understood, or fool the police, not from concern for the language. He explicitly supported its suppression.

> 'I am sufficiently utilitarian not to regret its gradual abandonment,' he said in 1833. 'A diversity of tongues is of no benefit; it was first imposed on mankind as a curse, at the building of Babel. It would be of vast advantage to mankind if all the inhabitants of the earth spoke the same language. Therefore, although the Irish language is connected with many recollections that twine round the hearts of Irishmen, yet the superiority of the English tongue, as the medium of all modern communication, is so great that I can witness without a sigh the gradual disuse of Irish.'[11]

There was a sphinx-like quality to O'Connell. The Gaels' champion (Protestant Ulster loathed him) quietly put to sleep the language and culture of his followers. What no amount of imported Protestant ministers or charity schools had destroyed, Ireland's hero lovingly helped to strangle, for as Tuathaigh said: 'O'Connell's lack of understanding of, or sympathy for, the concept of Gaelic Ireland, effectively deemed its irrelevance'.

O'Connell was the real father of the modern Irish state. His suspicion of the English as a people, but not as a culture, found its expression in the post-independence Free State, with its bewigged judges and its civil service modelled closely on Britain's. The Free State proved its descent from O'Connell in its conviction that the great difference between Ireland and England lay not in language or culture but religion, for this had been the one point on which O'Connell had not been prepared to compromise. The Catholic bishops had been deeply suspicious of the Protestant radicals and freethinkers behind the 1798 Rebellion but had repaid O'Connell's devotion by blessing his movement for the repeal of the Union. The association of Repeal with the Church gained O'Connell an army of unpaid volunteers but did little good to the Irish language. It put most Irish Protestants in the opposite camp, while the Catholic Church was no friend to the language until the 1890s, by which time it was too late. Throughout Europe, it was the Protestants who had defended the local peasant languages against the imperial tongue. Such was certainly the case in Bohemia, the Baltic states and Hungary. In Britain, it was the Protestants who brought the Welsh

Bible to Wales and the Manx Bible to the Isle of Man, ensuring the survival of both tongues – for a while. It was an article of faith among Protestants that the gospel must be preached in the tongue of the people, not locked up in Latin, the tongue of the clergy. Only in Ireland, where the Protestant Church was purely a settler church, did the Protestant clergy jettison this great principle.

But the Irish Catholic Church did not shelter the indigenous culture either. In Brittany, the Catholic Church defended Breton as a 'language of faith', believing that it shielded the Bretons from French atheism. But the Irish Catholics felt no such need to distance themselves from English. O'Connell's contemporaries in the Catholic Church, such as James Doyle, the influential Bishop of Kildare, and Paul Cullen, Archbishop of Armagh and then Dublin, did not give Gaels, Celts or the Irish language much thought. Determined to impose a devotional revolution on the Irish Church's idiosyncratic traditions, theirs was a centralising agenda that left little space for anything particularly Irish. The spirit of those reforming bishops pervades the parish churches of Ireland today, most of which look as if they were assembled from a kit, with the same design of altars, crucifixes and statues.

Archbishop Cullen's great obsession was with the introduction of the National School system by the Whigs in the 1830s. His great worry was that Protestant ideas might seep into Catholic Ireland through the lessons in religious instruction. He was not the slightest bit concerned about the language of the schoolroom. Once reassured of their doctrinal purity, he was a strong supporter of the new schools. John MacHale, the combative Archbishop of Tuam from 1834 to 1881, took a different view, fighting a rearguard action against the introduction of national schools into Connacht. But he was widely criticised for impeding people's access to education, and for thus inadvertently letting Protestant missionaries get a foot in the door. In any case, his own motives were very confused and Cullen dismissed them as absurd. Having toured the new schools in the early 1830s, Cullen confined himself to undermining the position of the Protestants on the new board of education.

Until the end of the nineteenth century, the Catholic Church was one of the great engines that transformed the Irish-speaking peasants into an anglophone nation. Irish was not taught for decades at the seminary of Maynooth, in County Kildare, opened in 1797 to provide an alternative to the continental seminaries closed by Napoleon's armies. Of the other seminaries, only St Jarlath's in Tuam taught Irish in the 1860s. The O'Connellite politicians and the Catholic clergy ensured that the nationalist discourse in Ireland would be in English. The new journalism was also in English. Nationalist newspapers had a yen for Celtic script and fonts, but they satisfied a burgeoning interest for folk tales in English. In spite of occasional columns in support of Irish, the nationalist press did not use it. The arrival of popular newspapers instead 'fixed' English as the language of Irish ideas and debate. When the *Tuam News* experimented with placing job advertisements in Irish as well as English in the 1890s, the idea was mocked and did not last.[12]

O'Connell had died half a century earlier. Quite fittingly, he expired on his way to Rome. He died in the middle of the Famine that completed what the Church, schools and O'Connell had started, namely the total abandonment of Irish. English was already associated positively with religion, politics, business, progress and modernity. Now Irish became negatively hitched to hunger, misery and a slow death. The transition from one language to another was so rapid that by the 1860s the civilisation that Thomas Charles had encountered had almost vanished. Instead, the Irish were increasingly seen as foot soldiers in the army of the English-speakers who were helping to spread English over the world.

The writer Oscar Wilde's father, Sir William Wilde, was shocked at the speed with which the Famine liquidated the rich, rural culture he had known. Leprechauns and banshees had disappeared along with the old language, he lamented in 1852. 'The old forms and customs, too, are becoming obliterated; the festivals are unobserved and the rustic festivities neglected or forgotten; the bowlings, the cakes and the prinkums (peasant balls) do not often take place when starvation and pestilence stalk over a country.'[13] They had disappeared along with waits, 'wren-boys' (they were, perhaps, no loss), mummers and May-boys. Wilde did not blame the Famine on its own for this cultural meltdown. He blamed the reforming Catholic clergy for making Ireland more 'Protestant' by suppressing the pilgrimages to holy wells that had once formed such a large part of devotional life. Wilde was right to blame the Church, for the clergy certainly spared no effort in crushing these lingering traces of old Celtic traditions. The Cullenite agenda, proclaimed at the Synod of Thurles in 1851, was a clericalist manifesto, aimed at stamping out any lingering, semi-pagan remnants and bringing Ireland fully into line with modern continental devotional patterns. Now that Catholics no longer had to practise their religion in secret, or resort to open-air 'mass rocks', the church reformers wanted religious activity returned to church buildings where it could be directly managed by the priests. Unsupervised trips to holy wells and saints' days' 'pattens' at shrines, which degenerated into carnivals after nightfall, were strongly discouraged.

A decade later, in the mid-1860s, Wilde remarked that the future of the Irish was now yoked to the English language. 'The manifest destiny of the Celt is being fulfilled,' he told the Dublin YMCA in 1864. 'Ocean steamers, each capable of holding 10,000 persons, are sending these hardy pioneers to help . . . in founding the great empires of Australia, America and Canada; to spread the English language and to carry Irish hardihood, bravery and poetry throughout the world.'[14]

The decades of the mid-nineteenth century, which in the rest of Europe saw the revival of 'lost' languages, was in Ireland a time of cultural and linguistic suicide. It was a process in which the Irish themselves, clergy and lay politicians alike, were deeply complicit, even if the English authorities were ultimately responsible. Irish schoolteachers, Irish newspapers, Irish clergy of all denominations and Irish nationalist politicians all took part. By the time a new generation decided the revival of nationalism without a language was futile, it was too late to reverse the shift.

About 20 miles west of An Spidéal, on a finger of land that protrudes from the honeycombed coastline of the bay, lies the village of Ros Muc. Village is not, perhaps, the right word, for it suggests a snug, densely packed settlement such as can be seen in England, Germany, the Low Countries and France, huddled around an ancient church, or encircling a green. The Celtic lands do not have many villages of this type. They form no part of their history. The villages of the Gaeltacht are sprawling settlements, strung out along a main road, each house spaced a fair way from the next. The Gaeltacht boasts little that is both man-made *and* old, for few people here treasure old barns and thatched roofs as the English and Germans do. The past here carries a whiff of ancient poverty and is something to be forgotten and replaced. On the Aran islands, there are thatched farms or homes with stonework that dates back a century. But they are few, and often belong to the Irish heritage organisation, Dúchas. Around Ros Muc, houses, churches and shops all appear to have received a thorough recent makeover and the area has little of the architectural charm of Cornwall, or of west County Cork. If it did, it would have attracted many more holiday-home owners, who would take more interest than the locals do in dry stone walls and open fireplaces.

The Gaeltacht remains home to second-generation peasant farmers. Having only recently escaped from bondage to the soil, they regard the soil with a suspicion bordering on enmity, as an opponent to be wrestled into submission, expelled from the house and banished, as far as is practicable, even from the garden. The children of those who worked the land in Connacht do not coo and moon over uneven stone floors, exposed brickwork, wooden beams, or gardens that are a riot of flowers. They leave that to the east-coast 'blow-ins', who have imbibed a love of the old, the dusty and the uneven from the Anglo-Irish and the English. The homes of modern Gaels are shrines to modern living – unthinkingly minimalist in taste. They have central heating, carpets made of artificial fibre, double-glazed windows and a lot of walnut-effect furniture as shiny as a mirror. The central principle on which these homes appear to operate is the efficient expulsion of dirt, hence the watertight windows, vinyl floors and polished wooden veneers. The windows of these fortresses of cleanliness usually yield a view of a mathematically rectangular 'garden', where the grass is crew-cut short and a few brightly coloured flowers crouch in a small bed by the wall, or an 'easy-care' rockery comprising heathers, hebes and dwarf conifers. Stone walls have been largely demolished in favour of walls of a low, smooth-topped concrete variety. Vegetable gardens are rarely seen, for the people of the Gaeltacht have been liberated from working the land too recently to feel much nostalgia about the joy of growing their own food. 'The old people here really like *buying* their carrots,' one disappointed 'blow-in' told me.

An exception to all this shiny modernity is the cottage in Ros Muc that once belonged to Patrick Pearse, hero of the 1916 Uprising. Ringed by trees, sitting snugly atop a hillock overlooking a glassy lake, whitewashed and thatched (even the adjacent public lavatory for visitors nestles under thatch), its status as a Dúchas heritage site suggests to visitors that this is a national shrine. Which it is, for if O'Connell was the father of modern Irish nationalism, Pearse was its patron saint. The buses with 'An Lár' written on the headboards, the recorded greetings in Irish on Aer Lingus planes and the laboriously translated street signs proclaim the Irish state's loyalty to Pearse's ideal of an Ireland that was not only free but Irish-speaking too.

The legacy of Pearse affects far more than buses and street signs. It is in the letter writers to the *Irish Times* who end their correspondence with the Irish sign-off, 'Is Mise' (I am). It is in the Irish titles used for all state corporations, such as Radio Telefís Éireann (RTE) and Córas Iompar Éireann (the bus corporation, CIE). It is in the Irish titles given to the chief office holders of state, who are never publicly addressed as Prime Minister or deputy premier, but by the Irish forms 'Taoiseach' and 'Tánaiste'. It is there in the bizarre, antique-sounding names of the political parties, Fine Gael and Fianna Fáil, literally 'Sons of the Gael' and 'Warriors of Destiny'. It is in the compulsory use of Irish in schools and the insistence on Irish qualifications for state-sector jobs. It is there in the whole, grand official cult of Irish by the state and in the vague but discernible squeamishness about the use of English, even though it is the vernacular tongue of more than nine-tenths of the population.

Pearse was not the only man responsible for this official cult of Irish and the Gael. But he was by far the most influential. Douglas Hyde led the language revival movement in Ireland for decades, but no personality cult has grown up in his memory, and reverential visitors do not traipse around his summer cottage as if in a cathedral, as they do round Pearse's home in Ros Muc. Even the front of Pearse's father's funeral stonemasonry shop in Dublin has been preserved, while the street running past it, and the nearby railway station, have been renamed Pearse.

Pearse's school in the south Dublin suburb of Rathfarnham has also been preserved as a museum. Guardians usher visitors past bookcases filled with Irish tomes into rooms filled with profile portraits of a severe, self-important-looking man with spectacles perching on his nose. Upstairs, visitors are shown a film of his life, a piece of hagiography that resembles that old *vitae* written by the disciples of the saints. Like those old *vitae*, the film leaves out the questionable aspects. It does not touch on the issue of his sexuality or his attitude to children or question his curious addiction to violence. Pearse cherished a strong belief in the cleansing virtue of spilt blood, which was partly Christian, but partly pagan too, and in divided Ulster many young men have committed acts of startling brutality against their neighbours inspired by Pearse's homilies. The school at St Enda's is, perhaps, a more telling monument to Pearse than the cottage in Ros Muc, for the school was the principal theatre for his activity for most of his adult life. This is where he tried to mould the sons of English-speaking shopkeepers and civil servants into heroes worthy of the Fionn or Fenian cycle of tales of mythical heroes.

Pearse, son of an Irish mother and an English immigrant father, was not the initiator of but a co-worker in the movement for an Irish-speaking, Irish-thinking Ireland. It was a mood that seized the country after the fall of O'Connell's successor at the helm of Irish nationalism. The ruin of Charles Stewart Parnell, triggered by the publicisation in 1890 of his affair with a married woman, Kitty O'Shea, had many of the elements of a Greek tragedy. Within weeks the master of his universe had become a reviled figure, caught in a pincer action by the English Liberals, the Irish Catholic hierarchy and his own lieutenants, all of whom had their own reasons for wishing his downfall. With him died all serious hope of achieving Irish Home Rule and the Irish parliamentary party split into factions. But Parnell's sudden fall from grace did not destroy Irish nationalism: its energies were diverted from politics to cultural projects. The literary revival, the movement to revive the country's old Gaelic sports and the drive to rescue the Irish language from extinction all gathered pace at the same time as the Parnellite implosion. Augusta Gregory, Yeats's great friend and ally in the literary movement, looked back on the 1890s as the decade when a subtle change of tempo in Irish cultural life took place. There was 'a setting free of the imagination' around the year 1896, she wrote later. Like Yeats, Lady Gregory was a child of the Protestant Ascendancy who had discovered Celtic nationalism as an adult. Many other sons and daughters of the 'big house' also swapped a potential existence revolving around hunts and vice-regal balls for the world of Celtic nationalism at that time, while some, like Yeats's friend Maud Gonne and Constance Gore-Booth became extreme opponents of their parents' values.

A kind of popular revolt against English sports began even before the fall of Parnell, partly thanks to Thomas Croke, Catholic Archbishop of Cashel and, like MacHale of Tuam, a combative opponent of British influence. In 1884 Croke and Parnell both became patrons of the new Gaelic Athletic Association, which set itself the task of reawakening interest in neglected traditional sports, above all hurling. There was a great deal of internecine warfare on the governing board between the clerical faction and the militants of the Irish Republican Brotherhood, none of which disrupted the GAA's success over the next few years in displacing football as the country's number one popular sport.

The language revival also predated Parnell's collapse. The Society for the Preservation of the Irish Language started in 1876 under the patronage of MacHale and Isaac Butt, Parnell's predecessor as the head of the Home Rule movement and, like him, a Protestant. The language movement enjoyed some early successes. A memorial sent to the government in 1878, citing the information in the 1851 census, claimed that 1.5 million people, about 23 per cent of the island's population, still spoke Irish as a first language, and demanded its inclusion in the school curriculum. A long list of clerical signatures, including those of three archbishops and 12 bishops, hinted at the future close alliance between Gaelic revivalists and the Catholic Church, in contrast to the indifference of most bishops in the past. The education commissioners were impressed enough to concede optional status to Irish, on a par with Greek, Latin and French. It was not much, but it was a start. By 1890 about 40 national schools taught Irish classes, while the following decade saw the start of the successful campaign for Irish to be made compulsory in matriculation from the new National University, which opened in Dublin in 1908.

The early years were not easy ones. The east-coast towns contained plenty of enthusiasts but the objects of the revival – the Irish-speaking peasants in the west – remained aloof in the early years. The anglophone learners were puzzled to find their heroes were bored by the learners' anglophobia. 'It is curious that there exists (that is in the mouths of the people) so few war songs and patriotic chants,' Hyde wrote in 1885 with disappointment of the Connemara peasants, 'and that very little hatred of the Sassenach is displayed in them. The very name of the colour green is not understood as having any political significance . . .'[15]

Denis Heraghty of Letterkenny, in Donegal, complained in 1886 to the society that the parents in his area all wanted their children to learn English. He noted 'an infatuated notion which prevails among parents that Irish is not, as it were, fashionable, an idea which prevents them from imparting a knowledge of the language, however rudimentary, to their children'.[16] Bishop MacCormac of Achonry was also sceptical. 'People are apathetic about the preservation of our ancient language,' he declared, also in 1886. 'They see that Shakespeare's tongue is the one in use in America and the Colonies.'[17] And the movement had to deal with the phenomenon of emigration, which was physically removing Irish-speakers from the land at a much faster pace than the society could teach new learners. In its report for 1892, the society noted this dilemma. 'Whilst interest in the language, literature and folklore of the country is increasing, the Irish-speaking population is diminishing, owing to emigration and other causes,' it said.[18]

The language society's successor, the Gaelic League had more of an impact. It was founded in 1893 and until 1915 was led by Douglas Hyde, son of a Church of Ireland rector and descendant of an Elizabethan planter family from Berkshire. Like Pearse, Yeats, Lady Gregory, Maud Gonne and Constance Gore-Booth, Hyde was a convert from the Protestant Ascendancy to Gaelic nationalism. Born in 1860 in Castlerea, County Roscommon, Hyde caught the dying embers of the Gaelic culture that had collapsed after the Famine, learning Irish from a local keeper of bogs and a milkmaid. He was a youthful supporter of Parnell's nationalism, composing dull poems in Irish on the themes of England's misrule. One such ode from 1878 ran:

I hate your law, I hate your rule
I hate your people and your weak Queen
London for all its grandeur, its pomp and fame
Deserves from God the most severe chastisement
Like ancient Rome or great Babylon.[19]

The plodding, puritanical quality of this very teenage 'curse' says a lot about the character of the young Hyde, whose diary reveals a regular Victorian prig, self-absorbed and almost devoid of filial or fraternal feeling. Marriage, however, altered him, and his political ardour cooled. The teenage foe of the English queen left republicanism behind as an adult. It was the salvation of the Irish language, not the quest for political independence, that now absorbed him. Further, Hyde became convinced that only a politically bipartisan, interdenominational movement had any hope of achieving his goals. He set out his stall in November 1892 at the Irish Literary Society in Leinster Hall in Dublin in an address entitled 'The Necessity of de-Anglicising the Irish People'. The Gaelic League was born the following July.

Hyde was aware that the language movement in Ireland had come late in the day. 'The Gaelic people is making its last stand for its native language', he told the Irish Literary Society in London that year. 'If something be not done . . . and done quickly, our noble, ancient, flexible, cultivated, musicful speech, the speech of our fathers and our great men, of our scholars, martyrs, priests, patriots, the speech of Red Hugh, Owen Roe . . . must soon be as extinct as Cornish.'[20] As the title of his address in Leinster Hall made clear, he did not support a half-way house, but the total de-anglicisation of Ireland, a rewinding of the cultural clock by 500 years. Alarmed by the prospect of the imminent extinction of Irish, he felt impelled to take dramatic action.

This was partly because he believed the anglicisation of Ireland had been deeply counterproductive, making the Irish far more anglophobic than they might have been. Ireland 'continues to apparently hate the English and at the same time continues to imitate them', he remarked, 'hence it continues to clamour for recognition and a distinct nationality and at the same time throws away with both hands what would make it so'.[21] Because the masses had refused to embrace an English identity, their only option was to 'become the other, cultivate what they have rejected and build up an Irish nation on Irish lines', he said. 'In a word, we must strive to cultivate everything that is most racial, most smacking of the soil, most Irish, because in spite of a little admixture of Saxon blood in the north-east corner, this island is and ever will remain Celtic to the core.'

Veneration of the soil, which Hyde encouraged, became an integral part of the Gaelic movement, along with a rejection of urban culture as degenerate. Hyde was not, however, responsible for the movement's strong association with Catholicism. The son of an Anglican clergyman naturally hoped the Gaelic movement would link the Orange and Green traditions. 'The

Irish language, thank God, is neither Protestant nor Catholic,' he told a meeting in Carnegie Hall in New York in 1905, 'it is neither a Unionist nor a Separatist'. He claimed as the League's 'crowning glory' that 'for the first time in Ireland within my recollection, Catholic and Protestant, Unionist and Nationalist, landlord and tenant, priest and parson, come together'.[22] This was not an accurate description of the true state of affairs. By then, most Protestants were backing away from the Gaelic revival, alarmed by the dominant role of the Catholic clergy, whose support was proving instrumental in bringing the League to parishes up and down the land.

Many Catholic priests relished the talk about soil and the Gaelic race, propagating an Irish, Gaelic version of the British cult of Teutonic and Saxon lineage. Father Patrick Forde told a clerical audience at Maynooth seminary in December 1899 that to speak to an Irishman in English and Irish was a contrasting moral experience. 'Use the former and you might never imagine he knew a word about Christianity. Speak to him in Irish and you are at once in the presence of a mind incredibly, almost reproachfully edifying, of a soul full of affectionate devotion and docility.' He added that the Irish language was 'charged with religious life'.

Forde claimed that the use of Irish inoculated speakers against atheistic thoughts. 'No one could speak it [Irish] from infancy without feeling himself so moulded that to him active living faith was the very breath of daily existence,' he said, 'while the development of an infidel mind was not only impossible in himself but inconceivable and incredible in others.'[23] Father John O'Reilly warned the Maynooth Union in June 1900 that the converse was equally true. English morally contaminated its speakers. 'The character of an English mind ought to be fairly understood in Ireland', he said. 'It is a fleshly spirit, bent towards earth, a mind unmannerly, vulgar, insolent, bigoted, a mind whose belly is its God . . . a mind to which real Christian virtue is incredible.'[24]

The League's progress was slow at first. In 1897 there were only 43 branches. But by 1902 there were 227 and by 1904 there were 600, with about 50,000 members. By 1906 the League had set up teacher-training colleges, including one in Belfast, and had penetrated the far west. On his visits to the Aran islands, Synge observed how the Gaelic League had put down roots, especially among women. On Sunday afternoons, he noted, 'bands of girls – of all ages, from five to twenty-five, begin to troop down to the schoolhouse in their reddest Sunday petticoats. It is remarkable that these young women are willing to spend their one afternoon of freedom in laborious studies of orthography for no reason but a vague reverence for the

Gaelic.' Their elders, he added, were not so enthusiastic. 'In the older generation that did not come under the influence of the recent language movement, I do not see any particular affection for Gaelic. Whenever they are able, they speak English to their children, to render them more capable of making their way in life.'

He added: 'The women are the great conservative force in this matter of the language. They learn a little English at school and from their parents but they rarely have occasion to speak with anyone who is not a native of the islands, so their knowledge of the foreign tongue remains rudimentary.'[25]

For many Irish people, attendance at the Gaelic League meetings (like joining the GAA) was a social occasion. As one observer wrote: 'In the flat dullness of an Irish village, or still worse, an Irish country town, a Gaelic League class is to the ranks of those who avail of it an unexpected source of light and gaiety.'[26]

The Gaelic movement attracted the young Dubliner Patrick Pearse in his teens. He began learning Irish at the age of 14 in 1893, the year that the League was founded, joined up in 1896 and two years later was on the executive committee. Pearse was as much an outsider to Gaelic Ireland as Yeats and Hyde, indeed more so, as his father was not of Anglo-Irish planter stock, but an English immigrant who had moved to Dublin to pursue his funerary business. Hyde's enthusiasms had set him on a collision course with his father, who wanted him to enter the Church of Ireland. Pearse's Gaelic interests caused no such domestic rupture, as his father had embraced both Home Rule and Catholicism. Pearse's biographer, Ruth Dudley Edwards, suggests that the Gaelic League's cult of celibacy and tone of puritanism made it congenial to him. Certainly, he shunned close contact with women outside his family. 'Anything coarse disgusted him,'[27] she quotes Mary Hayden, a colleague in the League, as recalling. Unsurprisingly, Pearse shared the Catholic clergy's squeamishness over the moral tone of the literary revival. He approved of the clerical attack on Synge's *Playboy of the Western World*, a play that caused uproar in Dublin's Abbey Theatre by taking aim at the League's cult of the Irish peasants as people of uniform piety; instead – to the fury of devout Catholic nationalists – he painted them as earthy and sensual.

Pearse also showed himself a disciple of Matthew Arnold in his conviction that the Gaels were distinguished by their otherworldliness and unique relationship to nature. The Gael was not destined to be martial like the German, or commercial like the Englishman, he said. 'A destiny more glorious awaits him,' he told his audience in a talk on 'The Intellectual Future of the Gael' in

October 1897. This was 'to become the saviour of idealism . . . the instructor of the nations, the preacher of the gospel of nature-worship, hero-worship, God-worship – such, Mr Chairman, is the destiny of the Gael'.

Pearse defined and defended this hero worship as 'a soul-lifting and ennobling thing', which corresponded to the Celts' mystical union with nature. They were 'distinguished by an intense and passionate love for nature. The Gael is the high priest of nature,' he said. Ireland's destiny was to become a mecca for those in search of spiritual enlightenment. 'Thither as to a sacred soil, the home of their fathers, the fountain-head of their Christianity, students are floating from east and west,' he said, 'and south – from America, from Australia and India, from Egypt and Asia Minor – and last, though not least, from England.'[28]

The school that Pearse ran from 1908 until 1916 was the great laboratory where all these ideas about hero worship and Irish Ireland could be put into practice. The students were not bullied into using Irish, for St Enda's practised a gradualist approach. The smallest children used Irish admixed with a little English. Irish was infused drop by drop until the senior school was fully bilingual. The goal was not to coerce Irishness but to encourage pupils to take Irish for granted – to see it as natural. 'You need not praise the Irish language – simply speak it,' Pearse said. 'You need not denounce English games – play Irish ones.'

Hero worship was promoted through pageants, in which the boys dressed up and acted out the parts of Cuchulain and other ancient heroes of Irish mythology. 'I shall remember long the march of the boys round the field in their heroic gear,' Pearse wrote enthusiastically after one parade, 'with their spears, their swords, their hounds, their horses; the sun shining on comely fair heads and straight, sturdy bare limbs; the buoyant sense of youth and life and strength that was there'.[29]

There was an old-fashioned, very English, quality to Pearse, for all his Celtic nationalism. With his severe heartiness, his religiosity, his childlike idealism and the cult of his own virginity, he belongs absolutely to the world of gaslight, Gladstone, Cardinal Newman and Queen Victoria. His sensibility was Victorian, so much so that it is hard to picture him in the faster world of the 1920s. It comes as a shock to recall that he was a close contemporary of a man like James Joyce, who to our eyes is 'modern', not least in his frankness about sexuality. Even in its own time, some people may have seen something comic about St Enda's, with its portly, bespectacled headmaster fussing over his beloved boys as they wriggled in and out of their 'heroic' togas, clanking shields and trailing their spears behind them. If so, the mockers misunderstood their man, for the older and more portly he became, the more his spirit hurried on to the strange destiny he had prepared for it, increasingly obsessed by half-Christian, half-pagan notions of redemption through blood sacrifice.

Pearse never tired of trying to imbue his charges with their heroic destiny. It was not prosperity, in the form of throbbing mills or busy harbours, that would make Ireland happy, he assured the school in 1913, but sacrifice, sacrifice, sacrifice. 'I know that Ireland will not be happy again until she recollects that old proud gesture of hers,' he said, 'and that laughing gesture of a young man that is going into battle or climbing to a gibbet'.[30] But who would climb to the gibbet? On one level, Pearse hoped it would be one of his boys. He was struck by a dream he had of a St Enda's boy, 'standing alone upon a platform above a mighty sea of people: and I understood that he was about to die there for some august cause, Ireland or another. He looked extraordinarily proud and joyous; lifting his head with a smile of amusement: I remember noticing the bare white throat and the hair on his forehead stirred by the wind . . . and I felt an inexplicable exhilaration as I looked on him.'[31] In lines such as these, Pearse came as close as he ever would to touching on the deeper recesses of his thoughts about his charges.

But he finally concluded that the beautiful boy with the bare white throat who would die for Ireland was himself. On 21 March 1916, the feast day of St Enda, Pearse informed the school that its work was done. 'It had taken the blood of the son of God to redeem the world,' he said. 'It would take the blood of the sons of Ireland to redeem Ireland.'[32] A few weeks later, on Easter Monday, surrounded by some of his beloved 'boys', Pearse was leading a doomed rebellion against British rule from within the General Post Office in Dublin, with Maud Gonne's estranged husband, Sean MacBride, beside him. Pearse had long been a member of the underground Irish Republican Brotherhood and was declared president of the rebels' provisional republican government. It fell to him to sign the proclamation of Ireland's independence and, not much later, to sign the surrender to British troops on 29 April. While Britain was at war with Germany the outcome of the revolt was not in doubt. He was shot in Kilmainham jail on the night of 2 to 3 May. He went to his death entirely confident: 'The memory of my deed and of my name/A splendid thing which shall not pass away,' he wrote just before his death. Pearse had achieved the crucifixion he longed for.

His predictions concerning the galvanising power of his own shed blood proved entirely accurate. Though the 1916 Rising was at first unpopular among the Dubliners, many of whom had relatives at the front in Belgium, the execution of the rebels swung public opinion dramatically in their favour. As Yeats brooded in his famous poem, 'Easter 1916':

> I write it out in a verse
> MacDonagh and MacBride
> And Connolly and Pearse
> Now and in time to be,
> Wherever green is worn,
> Are changed, changed utterly:
> A terrible beauty is born.

As Yeats recorded, the Ireland of the past several decades, the Ireland of the Irish parliamentary party, of constitutional politics and the old Irish regiments, had been knocked away. In its place came an Ireland that was tailored more to Pearse's way of thinking, the Ireland of abstention from the British parliament, of total independence, Sinn Féin, and – if need be – of armed struggle.

The spokesman of the older Ireland had some trouble acknowledging that the events of 1916 had changed the landscape. The *Freeman's Journal*, the venerable organ of the parliamentary nationalists, opposed the candidates of Sinn Féin right up to the general election of December 1918, which in Ireland was fought almost solely on the issue of abstention. The Sinn Féin party was British Prime Minister 'Lloyd George's best asset in Ireland', it snorted on 15 November.

But the clergy had defected overwhelmingly. Bishop Hallinan of Limerick was an outspoken supporter of Sinn Féin. The Irish, he said in October 1918, had a 'duty to shake the dust of the House of Commons off their feet, bid goodbye to it for ever, return to their own country and there take counsel with the leaders of Sinn Féin'.[33] Archbishop Walsh of Dublin also committed himself to their cause, attacking the parliamentary party in a letter to the *Freeman's Journal* just before the election[34] and publicly voting for Sinn Fein on 14 December. At Sinn Féin conferences up and down the country, priests took a leading role. At a meeting at Lisnaskea, in south County Fermanagh, most speakers were priests. Another big Sinn Fein assembly, held in Tralee, County Kerry, had a similar clerical tone. Indeed, the clergy who attended claimed they 'had all the priests with them', except for the Dean.[35]

The 1918 election was a Sinn Féin landslide. The Republicans took 73 seats to a mere six for the old Nationalists, while the Unionists cleaned up the Protestant seats in north-east Ulster. The winners soon constituted themselves as an independent parliament. It became clear that the Sinn Féin victory had marked the triumph of the spirit that Pearse had fostered. It was an election victory not merely for Sinn Féin but for the Gaelic League, the GAA and all the other societies that had sought a more self-consciously Gaelic Ireland. There was no social revolution, for the hard-line national-ists came from the middle class, as did their opponents. But there was a real cultural revolution and for at least a decade afterwards, many wondered if English-speaking Ireland would survive it.

The Gaelic militants hoped it would not. 'We assert that the national person of Ireland is the Gael and that all belonging to the Irish state must be identified with and informed by the spirit of the Gael,' the passionately anti-British *Catholic Bulletin* wrote on 9 November 1919.[36] Archbishop Gilmartin of Tuam similarly took it almost for granted that the new Ireland would dump the language of the English colonists. 'When the nation was shackled by the fetters of slavery she began, one might say, to lose the power of speech,' he said at Tourmakeady, County Mayo. 'But now that the Irish nation is becoming daily more conscious of her resurrection, her tongue ought to be loose and ought to find expression . . . in the language of her birth and ancient glories.'[37]

Government bodies were immediately renamed with Irish titles to signal the break with the past. The Sinn Féin assembly that met on 7 January 1919 styled itself Dáil Éireann and its sessions were bilingual. It did not take its cue from Grattan's parliament, which O'Connell had fought to revive, but from the republic that Pearse had proclaimed in Easter 1916 in the Dublin General Post Office. When the Dáil proclaimed Ireland a republic on 21 January, the declaration of independence was read out in Irish, as was its 'Message to the Free Nations of the World'.

The armed struggle against British rule that engulfed Ireland in 1920 and 1921 intensified the conviction of Sinn Féin supporters that they were ushering in a new Gaelic cultural order. The new/old Ireland would not only be Irish-speaking, but rural, governed on the principles (as far as they could be discerned) of the pre-Norman High Kings. The Dáil was to act like an assembly of the High King, the Sinn Féin propagandist Aodh de Blácam predicted, in *What Sinn Féin Stands For*, in 1921. 'In the Dáil will sit the good, the wise and the brave – men chosen not for their expertness in economic matters, nor for their learning or technical skill, but for character, for Kingliness.'[38] To De Blácam, Sinn Féin sought a revolution not in order to accelerate the future but to recover the past. 'We only welcome revolution because, by cancelling capitalism, it frees us to get back to that order of old,' he said.[39]

But the old order, whatever it was, was not recovered. Contrary to Archbishop Gilmartin's expectations, the 'old tongue' was not loosened by independence and statehood. The provision of Irish street signs and official titles, and the insistence on compulsory Irish in schools and the civil service, gave the new state a Gaelic veneer. But the country remained resolutely anglophone, and indeed became more so with every passing year. The revolutionary rhetoric about Gaelic culture was not translated into practice. It was disrupted first by the civil war that broke out between republicans and supporters of the 1921 Anglo-Irish Treaty, which demanded an oath of allegiance from parliamentary deputies to the British crown. Pro-Treaty forces won easily and drove the republican leader, Éamon de Valera, into the political wilderness for several years. The victorious party continued to promote the use of Irish in schools and government, but the mood of 1918 was not recovered. Government institutions took up their Irish titles, but carried on much as before independence. As one southern Protestant recalled with relief:

> The Oireachtas [legislature] and the civil service were shaped on lines familiar to those bred in the British tradition, showing few traces of the romantic return to Gaelic ways foreshadowed in some Sinn Fein writings of the revolutionary era ... The new legal system ... was closely modelled on the old. The barristers even retained their wigs. The Church of Ireland and Trinity College continued to function as before.[40]

Independence revealed that the Irish people's apparent commitment to Gaelic renewal was more of a fashion than many had realised. The number of branches of the Gaelic League shrank in the 1920s, as people decided it was no longer necessary to stress a Gaelic identity now that political independence had been won.

The result was that strangely schizophrenic official culture that has lasted until today – officially Irish, but English in practice. The biographer of the popular writer Brian O'Nolan (Flann O'Brien) remarked tellingly that enthusiasm for Gaelic waned as soon as it became necessary to have a knowledge of the language to obtain a position. 'The language began to be seen as the preserve of the careerist and the job hunter,' he wrote. 'Civil servants thirsting for promotion made sure to use the Irish forms of their names and so did many employees of the new state broadcasting service. Politicians were wont to begin their speeches with two sentences of pidgin

Irish and then to continue, "And now for the benefit of those who don't know their native language, I will continue my address in English".[41]

O'Nolan, who became a much-loved columnist in the *Irish Times* under the Irish pen-name 'Myles na Gopaleen', was a case in point. After growing up in an Irish-speaking home, he might have been expected to become a Gaelic stalwart after independence. Instead, he increasingly abandoned the language of his childhood. His 1941 comic satire, *An Beal Bacht* (*The Poor Mouth*), though written in Irish, wickedly sent up the entire Gaelic revival and its cult of the countryside. He despised the quality of the 'official' Irish publications. 'The Government-sponsored "Gum" publishing house maintains a downpour of essays, poems, plays, in Gaelic; scarcely a soul buys or reads them because they are chiefly composed of embarrassing dreeder and prawnshuck,'[42] he wrote in 1957. He described 90 per cent of these works as 'worthless'. He did not even think much of Hyde, claiming the patriarch of the Gaelic League had spoken Irish 'inaccurately and badly'.[43] O'Nolan ridiculed a certain type of east-coast, urban Gaelic enthusiast. They were men who had 'nuns' faces, wear bicycle clips continuously, talk in Irish only about *ceist na teangan* (the language question) and have undue confidence in Irish dancing as a general national prophylactic,' he snorted.[44] O'Nolan's friend, Niall Sheridan, also castigated the direction that the language movement was taking. 'All those who cherish Irish for the culture it enshrined are being gradually antagonised by the methods of the revivalists', he warned in 1938 in *Ireland Today*. 'The intolerance and bigotry displayed by its leaders have alienated all those to whom language is not a trade.'[45]

The alienation of many Irish intellectuals dealt the Gaelic movement a deadly blow. Elsewhere in Europe the writers and the poets had championed the old/new language and crowned its revival. Yeats, patron of the literary revival at the turn of the century, ceased to enthuse about the 'Celtic twilight' and Ireland's uniquely Celtic character. In 1897 Yeats had helped Maude Gonne to organise the violent nationalist boycott of Queen Victoria's jubilee celebration, when the windows of shops carrying union flags had been smashed and the British empire symbolically buried in a coffin. But he became prouder of his Protestant roots in middle and old age, writing admiringly of the Coole Park home of his friend Lady Gregory in 1914: 'A long continuity of culture like that at Coole could not have arisen and never has arisen in a single Catholic family in Ireland since the Middle Ages.'[46]

Yeats never liked the Catholic clergy, especially since the Primate, Cardinal Logue, that 'dull, pious old man',[47] had denounced his play *The Countess Cathleen* in 1899. The clerical tone of the Free State drew out his contempt and roused him to a majestic defence of the Protestant Ascendancy's cultural contribution to Ireland in 1925, during the parliamentary debate of an Act proposing to outlaw divorce. Yeats, then a senator in the upper house, lectured his colleagues with hauteur. 'We against whom you have done this thing are no petty people,' he said. 'We are one of the great stocks of Europe ... We have created most of the literature of this country.'[48] It was bombast, for Yeats represented a fading strand and the 'great stock' was on its last legs, depleted by a low birth rate, intermarriage with Catholics and emigration. The Protestant intellectuals were, in fact, dying off. Synge died tragically young in 1909. Lady Gregory died in 1932 and within a decade the house at Coole that Yeats eulogised had been all too symbolically razed. Yeats cut a lonely profile from then until his death in 1939. But cantankerous Protestants like Yeats did not give way to submissive Catholics, ready to serenade the Church and the Gaelic League. Men like Joyce and Sean O'Casey were, if anything, even less hesitant about attacking the new Gaelic establishment. O'Casey's 1926 play, *The Plough and the Stars,* dealt blasphemously in the eyes of nationalists with the subject of Pearse and the Easter Rising, generating as much turmoil in the theatre audience as Synge's *Playboy of the Western World* had done almost 20 years earlier.

The more the Catholic Church patronised all things Gaelic, the more the writers kept a distance. The outlawing of divorce and the introduction of literary censorship in the 1920s created the conditions for a cold war between the Irish Church and the Irish intelligentsia that lasted decades. The intelligentsia proved a mutinous and fickle partner for the new state, determined not to be force-fed opinions by the clergy. Censorship, like British rule in its last decades, overshadowed life just enough to excite anger while wholly lacking the means to terrify. To fall under the censor's ban became a badge of honour, an entry ticket to an exclusive club and a sign that a writer had 'made it'.

The Church battled on behalf of the Gaelic revival in the 1920s, but as Bishop Hoare of Ardagh admitted in 1926, professions of support were one thing; learning and speaking Irish another. 'The people of Longford were very determined to learn the Irish language,' the *Catholic Bulletin* of August 1926 reported the Bishop as telling the Longford *feis*. But he added: 'It is not an easy task. All those who have tried it and succeeded acknowledge it to be rather difficult ... he [the bishop] hoped they would all do their best to carry all the objects of the *feis* – learn the language again, become a child again, a scholar and master of their own language.'[49]

The true believers in the Gaelic League, the nationalist clergy, the republican widows and the supporters of De Valera were aware about a decade after independence that the world's first independent Celtic state had not turned out quite as expected. Irish periodicals in the early 1930s regularly carried articles on 'The ruin of the Gaeltacht', which complained that industrialisation and urbanisation were eroding what remained of the rural, Irish-speaking heartland. 'Machinedom is proving more deadly than alien landlords,' a clerical writer complained in 1932, signing off with the prayer that 'Gaeldom may yet prevail over the flashy glitter of American-Yiddish progress'.[50] On the other side of the denominational fence, the Protestant *Church of Ireland Gazette* took quiet pleasure in the Gaelic League's apparent failure. 'After eight years [of government pressure] the whole country is as English-speaking as ever,'[51] it proclaimed cheerily in 1931.

Margaret Gibbons, writing about the state of the Galway Gaeltacht in 1932, said the Catholic Church had done everything conceivable to promote Irish culture – while mysteriously failing to achieve its goal. 'The Lord Bishop of this diocese is a fluent Irish speaker; an annual *feis* is held under his auspices. The diocesan college is staffed with native-speaking priests, so is every parish in the diocesan Gaeltacht without exception . . . confession, sermons, prayers – all are exclusively conducted in Irish in the Gaeltacht districts . . . It is difficult to see what more the diocesan church *could* do.'[52] Yet the writer concluded that the Gaeltacht was failing. Irish had been made the language of the school room, but little attention had been paid to its use at home. This was the more important arena, as most pupils left school at the age of 14 or 15.[53]

The Gaelic project had started too late. The national revivals in central Europe and the Baltic lands had all begun in the early to mid-nineteenth century, when technology was in its infancy and the fate of cultures and tongues could still be determined by the effort of a small elite of clergy, intellectuals and benign magnates. But the Gaelic movement had coincided with the rise of mass-circulation newspapers and tourism and had been forced to compete with the advent of cinema. Archbishop Gilmartin complained at the Galway *feis* in May 1937 of a wave of cultural penetration that was undoing the achievements of the war of independence. 'While we have got rid of foreign political domination, we have not unfortunately got rid of foreign influences,' he said. 'We are, in fact, in much more danger of succumbing to foreign influences under modern conditions than when we stood with our back to the Atlantic Ocean, fighting for political and religious freedom.'[54]

The feeling that they were under cultural siege in their own country gave a strange flavour to the life of the urban *Gaelgeoir*. Their lot was not dissimilar to that of the southern Protestants who kept their union flags furled in the attic and discreetly celebrated British royal events. Like the Irish Protestants, the new Gaels felt not quite at home in their homeland, for they saw the outside world as hostile to their values. At its worst, life could take on the grim, claustrophobic quality evoked in Hugo Hamilton's memoir *The Speckled People* published in 2003. Hamilton's Dublin *Gaelgeoir* father in the 1950s banned English from the family home and maintained a little Gaelic universe within its four walls by sheer terror. Hamilton described a family that was isolated not only from the world but from Ireland. They might as well have been members of some obscure religious sect; in fact, Hamilton's account resembles nothing so much as the English writer Jeanette Winterson's recollection of childhood in a fundamentalist Christian household, *Oranges Are Not the Only Fruit* (1985).

Because the Gaelic ideal remained unrealised in Ireland, the Gaeltacht had a different future from the one the government had mapped out in the 1920s. The officials had seen the Gaeltacht as a wellspring, from which a polluted Ireland could draw pure water. At the same time, they had envisaged everyone moving in the same direction, towards a Gaelic future. In this scheme of things, the people of the Gaeltacht were simply ahead of the mass, as they had already reached the goal towards which everyone else was striving. But as Ireland remained an anglophone society, the Gaeltacht assumed a different role, as a kind of reservation, or cultural museum, where a precarious older way of life could be artificially maintained.

The Gaelic enthusiasts' fading hopes were reflected in the decision to radically redraw the borders of the Gaeltacht. In the first years of independence, a government commission had set aside a large proportion of County Galway for the Gaeltacht; this was then subdivided into two zones, an inner zone, the 'Fíor-Ghaeltacht', in which 80 per cent of the population spoke Irish, and an outer zone, the 'Breac-Ghaeltacht', in which about 25 per cent used Irish. The optimistic assumption was that the whole area would become Irish-speaking, reflecting a trend throughout the country. Instead, the Gaeltacht was drastically cut back in 1956, reducing the population from over 100,000 to less than 29,000. The 1956 census revealed that much of the 'outer zone' had become less Irish-speaking than ever. As a study of the area noted, decades of state-sponsored Irish had achieved little by the early 1980s. 'As a language maintenance policy, the policy of the state in the Gaeltacht would appear to have been largely successful . . . but considered as a language-revival policy, the results were much more questionable.'[55]

The community that lives near Pearse's whitewashed cottage faces new threats today. For all the enthusiasm generated by TG4 and Irish radio, the media cannot alone shoulder a culture that has been battling adverse forces for centuries. Massive economic interests pull in the opposite direction, steadily drawing the rural community in County Galway towards Galway city and converting the eastern fringe of the Gaeltacht into a suburb. The Gaeltacht's Celtic culture is falling victim to the demands of the Celtic Tiger, which has fuelled Galway's expansion from sleepy county town to Atlantic seaboard metropolis. The city grows out and up all the time, enticing thousands of immigrants, drawn by the relaxed lifestyle, the setting astride the River Corrib and easy access to Connemara. The city and the local university promote Irish culture, but economics dictate that visitors are far more likely to overhear Polish, Slovak and other Eastern European languages than Irish, as the hundreds of restaurants and cafés have sucked in a large foreign seasonal labour force.

A few decades ago Bearna (Barna), on the eastern flank of the Gaeltacht, was mainly Irish-speaking. Now English is the normal language of shops and pub. 'Bearna is gone,' said Mairéad Mhic Fhionnlaoich, of the Údarás na Gaeltachta, the government board in charge of the Gaeltacht's development.

The Údarás is in an unenviable position. It must avoid trying to 'put things in a jar to preserve them', as Mhic Fhionnlaoich said, but cannot encourage indiscriminate development, which merely entices English-speaking professionals. There were errors in the 1980s and 1990s, when the Údarás invited in multinational companies to counteract the high local unemployment. Many of the beneficiaries of the job-creation schemes were outsiders, leaving local jobless levels untouched, and after a few years many of the firms pulled out and reinvested elsewhere. Now the Údarás concentrates on small-scale, light technology, such as the media, information technology and even call centres. But Galway city beckons. 'There is always a trend for the young to go and live in Galway,' Mhic Fhionnlaoich said. 'Some will come back, but there is a good social life there. There is not much for young people to do in the Gaeltacht.' Mhic Fhionnlaoich said the number of Irish-speakers in the Gaillimh Gaeltacht had dropped in a decade. 'Only about 50 per cent of the people here use it on a daily basis,' she said. 'There is a vocabulary shrinkage going on. A lot of the richness has gone.'

It is a complaint I heard from many Irish-speakers, that the vocabulary of the community was shrinking, diminishing the culture as a whole. Meta Ní Mháille runs Pléaráca, a woman's group in Ros Muc that promotes social activities in Irish through workshops in quilting, painting, theatre, IT and creative writing. She was optimistic about the number of young families returning to raise families but still worried about the long-term prospects of her culture. 'You increasingly get parents speaking Irish and the children speaking back in English,' she said. 'My own two-year-old grandson has more English than Irish even though both his parents speak Irish. The language of the playground is no longer Irish. It's the television. It's cool to speak English.' Ni Mháille said the west of Ireland had altered out of all recognition since the time when Pearse sojourned in Ros Muc, but it was nothing to what would happen in the future. 'This area is changing drastically. But by 2010, the way of life as we now know it will be totally gone, and with it a lot of the culture and what kept it alive.'

At a pub in Ros Muc, about a mile from Pearse's cottage, I observed this cultural tilt for myself. A small crowd, mainly male teenagers, was watching a televised football match. The commentator bellowed from the screen about great kicks and missed goals in English and the youthful audience in the pub discussed the match in English, too. When I raised this with the manager of a nearby café, he was not surprised. 'My kids talk Irish to me and my wife, but as soon as I'm out of the room I can hear them switching over to English,' he said. 'They watch TG4 but they don't listen to the Irish radio. It's just not a medium for the young.' This man suggested that the decline in Irish had run in tandem with a decline in community values. 'People don't visit each other like they used to,' he lamented, recalling the days 'when we had the only TV set in the whole area, and fellows would walk miles across the bogs just to watch *High Chaparral* at our place'.

I moved south from Connacht to the Munster Gaeltacht in Kerry, O'Connell's home county. In Dún Chaoin (Dunquin), in the heart of the Kerry Gaeltacht, I met Micheál de Mordha, director of the Blasket Centre, a spare, single-storey building dedicated to passing on the story of the people of the hump-shaped Great Blasket Island lying opposite the centre. De Mordha told me he had also noticed a steady erosion of community values in his part of Gaelic Munster. The son of a small farmer, he did not even speak English until he was 12. That would be almost inconceivable today. 'Life then revolved around farms,' he recalled. 'It was poor enough, though we lacked for nothing. We carried on the oral tradition – people talking by the roadsides, and visiting. The small farm was the cornerstone of society. That whole culture has broken up, and there are lots of second-home owners here now.'

De Mordha had also observed the language shift between the generations that so many Connemara people had described to me. 'In my age group – in our fifties, we talk Irish,' he said. 'I'd feel a fish out of water talking English. We'd feel foolish. I spoke Irish to my children at home but they picked up English on the television, from the pop groups and so on, so they are bilingual. At school we didn't speak a word of English. But now the kids all use English. When they move on to university, they get interested in Irish again.'

The story of the Blasket islanders encapsulates something of what went wrong for Gaelic culture in post-independence Ireland, which ought to have been the Promised Land – and wasn't. This tiny, entirely Irish-speaking community produced a school of writers in the late nineteenth/early twentieth century, of whom Tomás Ó Críomhtháin, Muiris O Súilleabháin and Peig Sayers remain widely read today. When Victorian Britain discovered the Blasket islanders, it came into contact with a culture that was almost self-contained. A Protestant missionary, Mrs A. M. Thompson, left a description of her meeting with them in the early 1840s, which reads like contemporary missionary accounts of first encounters with tribes in Africa. 'When I got into the new schoolroom, the women and children in great numbers crowded in and squatted themselves on the floor round me,' she recalled, 'chewing seaweed incessantly, a large supply of which was in every woman's pocket and lap, and of which they pressed the long strings into their mouths with their thumbs in a most savage manner, and spat about unceremoniously at will; they touched my dress, turned me round and round to look at every separate article, laughed with admiration at my shoes and gloves, kissed and stroked my old silk gown, repeating "Bragh!" "Bragh!" "nice", "nice!"'[56]

Antiquarians followed the missionaries, among them the English Celtic scholar, Robin Flower, who regularly visited the island, fascinated by the language and rich deposit of oral folklore. The visitors encouraged a new self-consciousness. Three well-received books, Ó Críomhtháin's *The Islandman* (1929), O Súilleabháin's *Twenty Years A-Growing* (1933) and Sayers's *Peig* (1956) emerged from this effort to make the islanders aware of their precious heritage. But it was impossible to maintain an equal relationship for long between the Western world and an island with a population of less than 200.

Sayers was not carried off to London and exhibited in a cage like a seventeenth-century dwarf, but experienced the next-worst fate: in her own lifetime she was turned into a national treasure. The great irony of the affair was that Peig exerted a highly negative influence on the culture she loved, after her dictated tales became compulsory reading matter for generations of Irish schoolchildren. A born raconteuse, her books worked less well. As Cole Moreton, a recent writer on the Blasket islanders, wrote, Peig had a vast repertoire of tales, ranging from the Fenian cycle to the romantic and supernatural.

> Some of her stories were funny, some savage, some wise, some earthy; but very few made it on to the pages of her autobiography. The words were dictated to her son, then edited by the wife of a Dublin school inspector, and both collaborators sanitised the text a little in turn so that it was homely and pious, a book fit to be taken up as a set text in Irish schools. The image of Peig's broad face smiling out from beneath a head-scarf, hands clasped in her lap, became familiar to generations of children who were bored rigid by this holy peasant woman that had been forced upon them. They grew up loathing Peig . . . without hearing the stories as they had been intended.[57]

Today, mere mention of the word 'Peig' is enough to make many people over 30 roll their eyes and giggle, as they recall being force-fed trite stories whose editors and translators had rendered them so much more respectable and less interesting than they were in the telling.

Increasing contact with the world made possible the production of memoirs such as *Twenty Years A-Growing,* but then cut the ground from under the feet of the culture that produced them. It was a literary school with one sweet season of life in it. Photographs taken in the 1930s illustrate the gulf that already yawned between the generation of islanders born in the mid-nineteenth century, before the outsiders arrived, and their children. The older generation of women is pictured in headscarves, shawls and long dresses, the garb of virtually all peasant peoples from the Atlantic to the Urals. But the daughters of these women look more like their grandchil-dren. They stare at the lens, dressed in short, pleated skirts, in heeled shoes and with their hair cut in the same fashionable bob as women wore in London and New York. The photographs tell how the gap separating Great Blasket Island from the anglophone world had closed, and with it the readi-ness to continue a way of life rooted in fickle soil and sea.

The island's population peaked at about 200 in 1916, the year of the Easter Rising in far-off Dublin, thanks mainly to a boom built on exports of mackerel to the US. It plummeted after independence, when the US imposed tariffs on mackerel imports, hitting the islanders' main source of income. By 1930 only 121 islanders remained, and by 1938 just 106. The only school closed in the 1940s and by 1953, when a mere 22 islanders remained, their evacuation was a 'when', not an 'if'. The death of a young man who fell ill and could not be taken to a doctor because of the rough seas brought matters to a head. On 17 November 1953 the last four families were brought to the mainland for rehousing, on the boat, the *St Lawrence O'Toole*. It was a strange end to the story of Great Blasket Island. In many ways it resembled the end of the St Kildans in Scotland, who were evacuated from their island in 1930. But the Gaelic-speakers of St Kilda were citizens of a centralised British state, governed from far-away London, whose officials certainly did not see the preservation of the Gaelic way of life on remote Scottish crags as an essential part of their remit. The Blasket islanders were citizens of a state that saw the preservation of a rural Gaelic way of life as its *raison d'être*. Was not the very fibre of their existence precisely what the Saorstát Eireann, as the Irish Free State was called in Irish, had come into being to uphold? They had been honoured with a visit by the country's leader, De Valera, who addressed them in their own language. Yet they had reached exactly the same end as their Scottish counterparts.

The departure of the islanders did not even have the benefit of reinforcing the embattled Gaelic culture of the mainland. Peig Sayers's descendants live in Hartford, in Connecticut. According to Micheál de Mordha, only two islanders now live in Dún Chaoin. Most of the US emigrants were concentrated in the Irish-American stronghold of Springfield, Massachusetts. 'The language survived for a while in the US,' said de Mordha, 'but they didn't pass it on. From the 1950s it began to die out.' Irish is now less likely to be heard in Springfield than Spanish, for the area has a large Puerto Rican population.

There are, of course, more keys to a country's identity than the written or spoken word. The movement to revive Gaelic sports that Archbishop Croke encouraged in the 1880s has never faltered. While the Gaelic League fizzled out after independence, the GAA entered into a golden inheritance. Along with the Catholic Church, the farmers and De Valera's party, Fianna Fáil, it became one of the supporting pillars of the new state. Unlike the Gaelic League, the GAA never tried to be apolitical or to provide a common ground for unionists and nationalists. From the start it was the cultural and sporting face of militant, anti-British republicanism. Braving Croke's disapproval, the hard men of the Irish Republican Brotherhood, the forerunners of the Irish Republican Army, took over the GAA executive in 1889. Coups and counter-coups followed but none of these internal struggles sapped the GAA's Gaelic, anti-English tone. It was uncompromising in its Irish-Ireland values and members of the Royal Irish Constabulary and the British armed forces were barred from participation. No one was allowed a foot in both camps. They could play football, rugby and cricket and the other 'garrison' sports, or hurling, the ancient Irish sport that in some ways resembles hockey. The GAA waged war on football and rugby with astonishing success in the 1890s, the decade Lady Gregory recalled as having witnessed a marked change in the nation's culture. The sporting taste of the country was revolutionised in a generation. Within two decades, support for football, rugby or cricket had become the mark of the Protestant, the unionist, or the 'west Briton', as upper-class, pro-British Irish people were disparagingly nicknamed. Gaelic games and nationalism became so intertwined that the confrontation between the British military and the republican rebels after the 1918 election inevitably spelled serious consequences for sport. The most notorious of these occurred on the 'Bloody Sunday' of 21 November 1920, when auxiliary policemen, enraged by the execution by republicans of 14 soldiers that morning, burst on to the GAA pitch at Croke Park in Dublin in the middle of a match and opened fire, killing 12 people including the Tipperary team player Michael Hogan. Like the disastrous Amritsar massacre the year before in India, 'Bloody Sunday' was a defining moment in the history of the nationalist movement in Ireland. There could be no return to the *status quo ante* after it, only victory or defeat. The GAA was part of that equation and when the Anglo-Irish Treaty of 1921 conceded Irish independence, the GAA entered into its inheritance. In just over a year, it went from being a banned organisation to part of the new establishment.

The GAA museum, housed in the munificent Croke Park stadium which was rebuilt in 1995, pays tribute to the power this organisation has enjoyed since independence. The photographs on the walls highlight the close ties linking the GAA to the political class, the Catholic Church and the Irish language. They show bishops and politicians, De Valera among them, attending GAA matches in front of vast crowds. A short video clip shows the captain of a victorious team celebrating his win with a rehearsed speech in Irish. Support for the GAA remains interwoven with commitment to the Irish language and the opening of the captain's speech is always delivered in Irish. Meetings of the Ulster council of the GAA are held exclusively in Irish, a reminder of the intimate links between the GAA and all-Ireland nationalism in the divided north. The GAA is not just a sporting organisation, as a continuing controversy over the ban on contact between GAA members and the British police and army in Northern Ireland underlines. Even a recent upsurge of popular interest in football has not dented the popular commitment to hurling. You only have to see the crowds streaming from Croke Park after a match to see that, or drive through Ireland before a cup final between Leinster, Munster, Ulster or Connacht, when villages are decked in so much bunting you might think the nation was giving thanks for the end of a great war.

Back in Dublin, in a pub on the regenerated north side of the River Liffey, the music was in full swing. This was not a musicians' session, but an evening for people to get up and sing their own ballads. None of the songs came from the contemporary British or US charts. In fact, none was a recent composition, the newest being 'The Old Triangle', a song composed in the 1950s by the writer Brendan Behan. Some were old nationalist favourites, like 'Fields of Athenry', which has become almost an alternative national anthem. Others I had not heard, and several were in Irish. I had left my glasses at home by accident and, standing in the dense crowd, wreathed in a blue fog of cigarette smoke, could barely make out the precise nature of a box being passed along a line of people, into which some were slipping money. I thought it was for the lifeboat crews, for the simple reason that it resembled the lifeboat boxes standing on countless British pub counters, awaiting the loose change of friendly drinkers. But as I felt in my pocket for some coins, my companion nudged me and hissed for me to be quiet. 'It's for the north,' he whispered. 'I wouldn't talk aloud right now in your accent.' Days later, only yards away, I found myself sitting in the open-plan foyer of a plush new hotel, the whole building a shrine to the successes of the Tiger economy. A foyer of exposed brickwork led visitors' eyes to a bar behind which row upon row of bottles were lit up in soft blue light. Vaguely Celtic or Norse decorations of wood and metal and rope hung from the ceiling and walls. In the centre of the floor a band played traditional pipe music to an audience composed of American tourists sipping wine and gin-and-tonic, who applauded quietly when the music was over.

Irish traditional music wears a Janus face. On one side, it is deeply linked to militant nationalism and to the armed struggle against the British link in the north of the island. On the other side, it is the blandest, most acceptable of Irish exports, a suitable accompaniment to the sweet liqueurs of the 'Celtic Dew' variety that Ireland exports in vast quantities and which foreigners consume under the delusion they are drinking some ancient beverage. In fact, these creamy confections date back to the 1970s. The latter type of music, like the sticky drinks, has a homogenised, manufactured flavour. It is almost inescapable in Dublin, oozing out of hotel lifts and shopping malls. There are stacks of CDs of this stuff in the music shops and supermarkets, instantly recognisable from the twirling 'Celtic' script on the front, the frequent use of the colour green and a cover photograph dwelling on 'typical' Irish scenes, such as a rolling green meadow, a cow or a quaint-looking old man holding a fiddle. The back covers of these CDs usually feature a few lines of Celtic musings, words that – very dimly – reflect Matthew Arnold's thoughts on the Celts as a mystical race imbued with a higher spirituality than the rest.

The world now recognises a definitive Celtic 'sound'. It is as familiar as the bagpipe, though Ireland's calling card is a combination of pipe, fiddle or harp, often accompanied by a plaintive-sounding woman singing, or hard-shoe dancing. This is a universally familiar brand, and to most foreigners, Americans especially, it is the sound of Ireland and the sound of the Celts. What gave it a truly international profile was the phenomenal success of *Riverdance*, a musical spectacular that started out as a seven-minute 'filler' slot between the big acts in the 1994 Eurovision Song Contest in Dublin and went on to be one of the world's largest-grossing shows, seen by millions in dozens of countries by 2003, when it was still far from running out of steam.

Traditional Irish musicians pull long faces at the mention of *Riverdance*, many of them seeing it as an over-commercial exploitation of traditional sounds. But it continues to spawn an infinite number of spin-offs. An evening spent in the tourist-orientated Temple Bar area of Dublin yields many opportunities to watch sub-*Riverdance* performances. Taking place in pubs – with none of the real article's enormous budget – they feature tired-looking women clattering round a stage that is often too small. Come what may, a large foreign audience will be there, gamely applauding what they believe is a genuine Celtic musical experience. Foreigners lap up this synthetic Irishness. At one pipe and fiddle session I attended in the village of Oughterard, in Connemara, I soon realised that almost the entire audience was foreign – in this case German or Dutch. The younger local crowd I discovered in another pub down the road – at a karaoke session, singing along to Madonna.

The road to *Riverdance*, with its vast audience figures and multimillion-dollar takings, has been a long and winding one. Less than half a century ago, Irish folk music was small-scale and rooted in local areas. Fiddle players were identified by their regional styles. The musicians saw themselves as heirs to the bardic tradition of the Gaelic great homes and as descendants of the seventeenth-century harpists. There was not much of a commercial scene and they did not play often in pubs, where the presence of musicians was often viewed as not respectable.

Traditional Gaelic music had much the same status in post-independence Ireland as the Irish language. It was part of an officially venerated Gaelic patrimony. De Valera himself, who incarnated the values of the new state, spoke of his vision of an Ireland in which 'comely maidens danced at the crossroads'. But like the language, music suffered, rather than benefited, from close association with the state. The popular imagination associated it with rural life, poverty, backwardness and the Famine. The Catholic Church, all powerful in the 1920s and 1930s, was a dubious ally, for the clergy patronised only the most sanitised forms of dancing at cultural events, such as the local *feis*. At the same time, the Church waged a relentless war against the holding of private dances, which they stigmatised as bacchanalian orgies and dens of Satan, as a result of which they were largely outlawed by the 1935 Public Dancehall Act.

The great change came in the 1960s, with a boom inspired by the American folk explosion and the sight of college students rediscovering their popular roots in country music. In Ireland, the Clancy Brothers and Tommy Makem ballad singers, achieved a breakthrough to popular exposure. Seán O'Riada represented another strand of the musical revival. A classically trained pianist and composer, he was one of the first from such a background to engage with traditional music, uncovering much of the half-forgotten music of traditional harpists and radically rearranging it for a band, as the harpists had been soloists.

In 1961 O'Riada formed an ensemble, the Musicians of Coolin, Ceoltóiri Cualann, the nucleus of which went on to form The Chieftains, who are still playing and are perhaps Ireland's most famous traditional group. The fiftieth anniversary of the Easter Rising in 1966 was a milestone in the Celtic music revival, for De Valera commissioned two films for the year, *Mise Eire* (I am Ireland) and *Saoirse* (Freedom) and O'Riada was asked to do the soundtracks. When the films were shown at countless schools and public events, the tracks were hugely popular, disseminating traditional tunes to a wider audience. As one musician told me: 'Suddenly, old musicians were playing to large audiences of people from Dublin with long hair.' He said it made an odd combination – self-consciously cool audiences with studiedly uncool musicians. 'The Chieftains didn't exactly look bohemian,' he said. 'They looked like seven bank clerks.'

The Irish music scene today is flourishing as never before. Unlike its shyer Highland Scottish sister, which has far less prominence in its own land, traditional music is now Ireland's signature tune and it caters for a vast market, running from die-hard republicans to visitors reaching for 'something Celtic'. It runs the gamut from the homogenised Celtic pulp produced for a foreign market to traditional or regional sounds created by and for a very discerning audience. Irish music, in fact, reaches a far wider audience than the Irish language ever could at home and abroad. Ask the average foreigner why they think of Ireland as 'Celtic' and music will loom large among the reasons.

But whether there is anything particularly Celtic about Irish traditional music is a moot point. One insider in the Dublin music industry gave me a very iconoclastic response. 'There is no such thing as Celtic music,' he insisted. 'People wouldn't thank me for saying this but many "traditional" Irish tunes come from England. As for the jigs and reels, we often don't know where the tunes came from. Some might have come from France.' He added:

Most people think step-dances in Kerry are quintessentially Irish. In fact, they come from eighteenth-century quadrilles. They came from the 'Big House'. The servants copied what they saw and speeded it up. Talk of a pure unbroken Celtic tradition is bullshit. Then take the concertina. People think it's the quintessential instrument of Clare, but it's only a hundred years old and it came to us from Germany. As for the harp, that was a late nineteenth-century revival. It was a drawing-room revival, a Romantic revival.

Turning to the instruments, my friend asserted that the only real unbroken musical tradition in Ireland was the tradition of dancing and singing. The actual dances and the instruments were revivals, or imports. Perhaps it was because of this that he took such a relaxed view of the *Riverdance* phenomenon and its numerous spin-offs. 'About 71 million people have seen it, which is a damn sight more people than have seen any other folk-related music from Ireland', he said. 'It makes me gag, but I don't get upset about it personally. The traditional music scene is confident now, and it's almost self-policing. No one says "this is right", or "this is wrong". There is no orthodoxy.'

Before I left Dublin, I returned to Munster and caught a small fishing boat from the tip of south-west Kerry to Skellig Michael, a remote, rain-lashed crag that juts out of the ocean like a large, blackened tooth. To reach Skellig Michael, the boat takes visitors past a smaller crag, which was covered in hundreds of thousands of gannets. It was an incredible sight, though it reeked at a distance of a hundred yards. Alighting at Skellig Michael I found the little jetty and the winding set of stairs carved into rock that Victorian engineers had installed for the lighthouse they built. But it was a steep and slightly perilous ascent to the tiny plateau near the top of the crag, where –

wind-buffeted and covered in a fine mist of spray – I wandered round the nest of beehive-shaped huts Irish monks built here about a millennium and a half ago. Skellig Michael reaches back to the dawn of Christian Ireland, and to that Celtic Church whose legendary spirituality is still a potent attraction to many modern Christians. The antiquity of these partly restored huts filled me with awe. From today's vantage point, the Ireland of the twelfth-century Anglo-Norman adventurers seems impossibly distant – an Ireland glimpsed through a glass darkly. Yet Skellig Michael was many centuries old by the time that the Normans set sail for Wexford. We can only speculate on how the monks lived there. Presumably fish and the sea birds nesting in such vast numbers on the nearby crag made up most of their diet, augmented by the offerings made by pilgrims who sailed here in the summer months. But it is impossible to recreate much of the world of those monks on their storm-lashed crag. We cannot enter their thoughts and hopes. The veil has descended between us and them.

The Gaelic nationalists of the Ireland of the late nineteenth and early twentieth century thought they could re-enter that world. They thought they could recreate the Celtic Ireland of round towers and monasteries on crags by sheer force of willpower. But they were defeated. Though the British were expelled in 1921, the culture and the language they had sowed and re-sowed over seven centuries proved sturdy enough to see off the Gaelic challenge. De Valera saw the people of the Gaeltacht as promise-keepers, holding the fort for an Irish Ireland that would encompass everyone. When he visited Great Blasket Island in July 1947, he addressed the local people as trustees of the future, as well as the past. 'People of the island, you are keeping the language safe for our country', he said, 'until such time as it will be heard on the lips of every man, woman and child, from this place to Dublin.'[58]

Half a century after the Blasket islanders left their home, the promise remains unfulfilled. The Gaeltacht has assumed a role different from the one that was expected and it faces a daunting future. Diluted by the immigration of non-Irish speakers and suffering a shrinkage of the vocabulary, it is uncertain if the Gaeltacht can maintain the slender rope bridge that connects the world of Skellig Michael to modern Ireland, where well over 90 per cent of the population belongs firmly to the anglophone culture. Most of what is called 'Celtic culture' is just junk, a marketing device replaying to visitors the comforting images that they themselves have constructed. Before I left the Republic, I took a last look at a group of women clump-ing rather lifelessly round a wooden stage in Temple Bar, performing their ten-thousandth 'Celtic' dance for the entertainment of half-interested tourists. I visited the *Book of Kells*, the ancient illuminated gospels whose history links Iona in Scotland to Kells in Ireland, an artistic record of the Gaelic culture that once straddled the Irish Sea, embracing both countries. To see the book meant joining a long line of tourists processing slowly past a few pages of the opened gospels, beautifully lit up behind glass. It was a bit like a trip to see the Crown Jewels in the Tower of London. The crowd *oohed* and *aahed* appreciatively as they moved through the darkened chamber, while taped 'Celtic' music provided a background mood. *The Book of Kells*, perhaps the finest surviving artefact of the Celtic Church, is a good earner for Trinity College, the Protestant university set up by Elizabeth I that has spent most of its existence trying to stamp out Ireland's native language and culture. *The Book of Kells* is an apt symbol of the Celtic culture of Ireland, in fact. It is a neatly packaged 'experience', designed for the benefit of fee-paying foreign visitors, sandwiched between the Viking Dublin 'experience' down the road and a visit to the themed pubs for later on.

CHAPTER THREE

Belfast
'The liveliest Gaeltacht in Ireland'

The Ulster Protestants are mainly Gaelic in blood. Their ethos is that of the Scottish Protestants. They have the same traits of character as Catholic Gaels, but inverted.
(Aodh de Blácam, 'Some Thoughts on Partition', 1934)

I left the Republic of Ireland, but not Ireland. Driving north I crossed the international frontier established in 1921 by the descendants of the great Jacobean plantation in Ulster who – unlike the Old English settlers in Leinster and Munster – never exchanged their former identity for an Irish one.

In the largest town forged out of the plantation, Belfast, I found a bed and breakfast. The atmosphere of this place reminded me I was now in another country. It was neither English nor Irish, but something else. Religion dominated everything. On awaking my eye made contact with a stern biblical phrase above the wash-basin, carved on a long piece of varnished wood. The word of the Christian Bible is not often found on the walls of English (or Irish) homes and when it is, the English prefer comforting and ecumenical phrases of the 'Be Still and Know' variety, or the chintzy folk wisdom of the 'Nun's Prayer' ('Lord make me thoughtful but not moody. . .').

But Ulster Protestants are not interested in the prayers of nuns and positively relish the most challenging bits of the Bible, and the walls of this house were covered with sentences of God at his most finger-wagging. 'Remember the Lord in the days of your youth,' one enjoined. There was another similar phrase on the landing. As I darted past, a third biblical exhortation met me in the bathroom (unavoidable, as it hung by the shaving mirror). On the ground floor injunctions hung like bats from chains in the corner of the breakfast room, the television room and the hallway. In case I escaped them, the table in the sun lounge by the main door had been planted with flyers advertising church service times and bible societies.

The house fairly hummed with evangelical activity. On the evening that I arrived from Dublin I found the hallway filled with visitors whose Spanish conversation, black hair, almond eyes and olive skins suggested Central or Latin American origin. They stayed late; when I dozed off I could still hear them singing down below. The food served at breakfast the following morning was tasteless and undercooked, but my hosts served it with the broad grins and knowing smiles of those who have higher things to concentrate on than cooking sausages and eggs. I felt they were making a point, that they were not here to dwell on *food*. What did fried bread matter, compared to the bread of life? I asked the woman in charge what the name of her house meant, thinking it might be Portuguese, or Greek, for 'sunny view' or 'the herons', or some other such bland suburban commonplace. An evangelical opportunity had clearly presented itself, for she drew herself up with a smile and practically shouted: 'It means. . .*THE LORD WILL COME QUICKLY, and it's in HEBREW!*'

I was staying in east Belfast off the Ormeau Park that divides the Protestant east from the Catholic, nationalist Lower Ormeau Road. In Belfast, marked changes in atmosphere can be measured by the yard. A tense confrontation zone strewn with angry murals and slogans may give way minutes later to leafy avenues where children play in the streets undisturbed. For all its proximity to a religious and political 'front line', my road felt calm and relaxed. The street was lined with solid Victorian churches, all open for business. In England most would now have been converted into 'loft' apartments, art centres, coffee shops or – if it was an inner-city area with an immigrant population – mosques for the growing Muslim community. But Ulster has not turned its back on organised Christianity and has few immigrants. It is proudly behind the times. Only when an area changes hands, when it 'turns', as they say, from the static Protestant community to the growing Catholic side, are churches to be found with broken windows and wild buddleia sprouting through the roof.

Up the road, I found the Martyrs' Memorial Church, the church of the Reverend Ian Paisley, the most famous of Ulster's political clerics and since the early 1960s the unbending defender of its Calvinist inheritance. Paisley's Protestantism is rooted in the religious traditions of John Knox's Scotland and of the seventeenth-century Covenanters who faced death at the hands of Charles II's officials rather than renounce a jot of their fundamentalist beliefs. In Wigtown, in County Galloway, I had visited the site where two Margarets, Margaret Lachlane and Margaret Wilson, had been drowned in 1685 in the Bladnock river for their adherence to Covenanting principles. 'Murdered for owning Christ supreame', as Lachlane's tombstone read in the churchyard. 'Within the sea tyd to a stake, she suffered for Christ Jesus sake.' The Paisleys honour the Covenanters and Paisley's daughter, Rhona, wrote in her autobiography of family holidays spent in south-west Scotland hunting for their graves on the moors. Paisleyite Protestantism is biblical but not evangelical in the contemporary sense of the word. It spurns the ecstatic atmosphere, the emotionalism and emphasis on receiving the gifts of the Holy Spirit, such as speaking in tongues. I knew my bed and breakfast hosts and their Latin American friends would not have found a spiritual home at the Martyrs' Memorial Church. The Metropolitan Tabernacle, a huge modern church in the northern suburbs, where the worship is charismatic and has an American Midwestern flavour, would be more to their liking.

As it was June, here and there I caught the distant sound of banging drums and whistling flutes carried in the wind. Local Protestants were preparing the grand parades of the Orange Order in July and August when they would march in the uniform of black bowler hat and orange sash to celebrate the relief of the Protestant city of Derry in 1689 from the besieging Catholic army of James II.

Before the start of the violent bombing campaign in 1969, invariably known as the 'troubles', the Orange Order dominated the Northern Irish state in harness with the Unionist Party, much as the Catholic Church, the GAA and the Fianna Fáil party ruled the larger south. In 1934, the Northern Ireland Prime Minister, James Craig, Lord Craigavon, thought nothing of saying that he valued his membership of the County Down Orange Order more than his post as Prime Minister. 'I have always said I am an Orangeman first and a politician and Member of this Parliament afterwards,'[1] he said. Church of Ireland bishops and politicians attended Orange marches as a matter of course, their annual performance serving to remind the Catholics that in this small corner of Ireland at least, the gains secured by the relief of Derry had not been undone.

The Order now has only a fraction of its old clout. Catholics do not fear it any longer, while middle-class Protestants hold aloof, repelled by the atmosphere of sectarian confrontation that accompanies the disputed parades. The Order lost face in the 1990s over the struggle to maintain its annual march to the hamlet of Drumcree from the centre of Portadown. This most hotly disputed parade of them all brought to the surface all the changes, both political and demographic, that had overtaken Northern Ireland since the 1960s. An Orange march had taken place here for generations, running from the centre of the mostly Protestant town to the small country church in Drumcree. But in the 1970s and 1980s the Garvaghy Road, along which the march passed, 'turned' both denominationally and politically. The empty fields were ploughed up for housing estates that quickly became overwhelmingly Catholic and thus nationalist. The Orangemen found they were walking in enemy territory. In the 1990s the local residents became increasingly vocal in their opposition to the annual Orange march through their midst and determined to block its passage. From 1995, the police and British army simply stopped the parade from reaching the church at Drumcree by sealing the Garvaghy Road, citing fears of a potential bloodbath. The thwarted marchers accused the paramilitaries of the IRA and their political allies in Sinn Féin of masterminding the whole affair but when I spoke to people on the Garvaghy Road it was clear the blockade enjoyed solid local support. Their mood could have been summed in the old Spanish civil war slogan 'No pasaran!' – they shall not pass. They were just not going to let the Orange Order pass through the area any more.

The marchers did not give way easily. For several years in the 1990s the Drumcree march became an annual media pantomime, affording television stations the world over a chance to turn the housing estate and nearby fields into a Hollywood-style film set. Film crews descended for weeks on Portadown with huge container lorries and metal cranes on which search-lights were mounted, waiting for the Garvaghy Road residents, the Orangemen and the police of the Royal Ulster Constabulary to act out their appointed parts. Local families living on the 'front line' did a roaring trade from renting out their homes to foreign crews. But by 2003 this grotesque soap opera had run out of steam, largely because it had filtered through to the Order that they were not going to get down the disputed road now or at any time soon. They had lost, and the disappointed media, cheated of the longed-for bust-up, gradually drifted away.

The retreat from Drumcree is symbolic of a wider withdrawal. North of Belfast city centre stands one of the grandest Orange lodges of all – a huge pile of stonework crowned by a statue of William III, the Protestant saviour of Derry in 1689. The building symbolises much of what has happened to the Order since those great days. It looks battered and besieged. Many stones and missiles have clearly been thrown at it, as the lower floors have been covered in protective wire mesh behind which the windows are dirty and shuttered. The building has been as good as abandoned.

The Ulster Protestants have spent so much energy in grimly defending their British image that it comes almost as a surprise to recall that many of them are as Celtic as anyone else on the island. The Sinn Féin writer Aodh de Blácam addressed this concealed aspect of Ulster Protestant culture in the 1930s. 'The Ulster Protestants are mainly Gaelic in blood,' he mused in an essay entitled, 'Some Thoughts on Partition', in 1934. 'Their ethos is that of the Scottish Protestants. They have the same traits of character as Catholic Gaels, but inverted. An Orange procession is utterly unEnglish. It is like a parody of a Catholic procession.'[2]

The Scottish ethos that De Blácam referred to relates to geography. North-east Ulster is closer to south-west Scotland than, say, to Dublin. A narrow strip of water, about 12 miles wide, separates Antrim from Ayrshire and on either side the population feels this proximity. As a recent Irish Presbyterian leader put it, his churches' roots 'lie across that narrow strip of water and go through Glasgow and Edinburgh to Geneva . . . Dundalk seems a long way away, never mind Dublin.'[3]

The Ulster plantation was a Scottish, not an English, settlement, carved out by a Scottish monarch to break the back of Gaelic resistance to colonisation in its heartland. It was Scotland's first great colonial enterprise, though modern, left-leaning Scotland does not care to acknowledge it, insisting that it was itself colonised. There were many English settlers in the Jacobean plantation, but they were not the preponderant element, except in Derry which they renamed Londonderry, and County Fermanagh. The most Protestant part of north-east Ulster, County Antrim and the north of County Down, were almost wholly settled by Scottish settlers from Ayrshire, shipped over by two Ayrshire adventurers, James Hamilton and Hugh Montgomery. Andrew Stuart, minister at Donaghadee in County Down and one of the earliest historians of the colony, wrote in 1670 that the Scots felt far more at home in this land than the English. The English could not cope, he said, 'being a great deal more tenderly bred'. He added: 'The marshiness and fogginess of this island was still found unwholesome to English bodies . . . so that we have seen multitudes of them die.'[4] James knew his Scottish settlers. 'The king had a natural love to have Ireland planted with Scots,' Stuart said, 'as being, beside their loyalty, of a middle temper between the English tender and the Irish rude breeding, and a great deal more like to adventure to plant Ulster than the English'.[5] The Scots had to live under Anglican bishops in Ireland, but the King smoothed that difficulty away, too, by appointing Scotsmen as bishops in Raphoe and Down, and they knew better than to try to force the Anglican church discipline or the English liturgy on Scottish congregations.

Scottish immigration preceded the plantation of Ulster by James I. Scottish people had been drifting to and fro across the narrow strip of water for centuries. The Catholic villages of north Antrim and the Protestant villages of south-west Ayrshire are one stock. As Pádraig Ó Snodaigh recalled in his book, *Hidden Ulster* (1998), the Ulster plantation was a movement within a single cultural continuum, bringing the descendants of the Irish tribes that originally settled Dalriada back to the land of their ancestors. As Ó Snodaigh also recalled, many Scottish settlers in seventeenth-century Ulster would have been Gaelic-speakers, as parts of Galloway and Ayrshire were still Gaelic-speaking lands at the time. The Protestant authorities in Ireland acknowledged this fact, for Bishop King of Derry employed Scottish Highland ministers to preach to Gaelic congregations as late as the 1690s in Inishowen, in County Donegal. The Presbyterian Church in Ireland in the eighteenth century continued to produce Gaelic preachers. William Nelson, a notable Presbyterian minister, preached in Irish in Newry, County Down, in the 1800s, while Presbyterian Belfast was the centre of societies such as the Belfast Harp Society, established in 1791 to revive ancient Irish poetry and music, and the Ulster Gaelic Society, formed in 1830.

The city was for generations largely Scottish in its ethnicity and character. It was instinctively egalitarian, hostile to the Church of England, cool towards the crown and devoted to the concept of liberty. It gave the British cause for concern in 1798 when Ireland erupted in revolt, for it was a notorious hotbed of republicanism and support for the United Irishmen, the underground revolutionary movement behind the revolt. The Belfast radicals became disenchanted by the direction that the revolt took in the south, where there were well-reported sectarian massacres of Protestants. Belfast abandoned its radical, Scottish traditions only slowly. It remained a dissenting city well into the nineteenth century, and many Belfast Presbyterians thought they had more in common with the disenfranchised Catholics than with the Anglicans of the establishment. They donated freely to the building of Catholic churches and the Catholics repaid this benevolence by ignoring their Church's ban on close religious contacts with 'heretics'. William Crolly, Catholic Archbishop of Armagh in the 1830s, often attended Presbyterian dinners and even the installation of Presbyterian ministers, where he was effusive in his affection, declaring once that if he found a single illiberal Catholic in his diocese, he would 'send him for his cure to inhale the liberal atmosphere of Belfast'.[6]

Although the mood changed in the middle years of the century, Ulster Protestants played a significant role in the Celtic revival of the 1840s. A Belfast man, Edward Bunting, published *The Ancient Music of Ireland* in 1840. Another Belfast man, Samuel Ferguson, born in 1810, translated Irish epics and greatly stimulated interest in the subject. Much later in the century Francis Bigger, a Presbyterian solicitor, became a keen patron of the Gaelic revival, naming his Antrim Road home, Ardrigh, meaning 'High King', and receiving Hyde and other founders of the Gaelic League.

But as the Ulster historian Jonathan Bardon has written in his magisterial *History of Ulster*, though northern Protestants helped launch the Gaelic revival, they did not carry their community with them. 'Bigger and his friends . . . were utterly unrepresentative of the mass of Ulster Protestants who were repelled by these new interpretations of cultural identity.'[7] Bardon added that the Ulster Unionist Convention of 1892 was the last to witness the display of the Irish slogan of 1798, 'Erin go Bragh' (Ireland For Ever).[8]

Massive industrial expansion in Belfast in the decades after Crolly's death in 1849 killed off the 'liberal atmosphere' that he admired. The rural masses, Catholic and Protestant, who poured into the factories brought the sectarian tensions of Armagh and the rural counties to the city. Belfast was too small to resist wider changes in the religious climate in Ireland, which was becoming increasingly polarised. By the 1870s it had become unthinkable for a Catholic archbishop to attend the installation of a Presbyterian minister. The riots that erupted in Belfast in 1886 as parliament debated Gladstone's ill-fated Home Rule Bill, and that claimed between 31 and 50 lives,[9] buried what remained of Belfast's reputation as a radical and religiously tolerant city.[10]

People today on both sides of the sectarian divide are fond of recalling a more comfortable era with their neighbours before 'the troubles' of the 1960s began. The reality is that Belfast has experienced bouts of violence and great religious and political tension since 1886. Bloodshed returned on the eve of partition, when there were 121 deaths from sectarian riots in Belfast in 1921 alone,[11] and there was more violence in 1935, during the silver jubilee celebrations of George V. The violence that returned – redoubled in strength – in 1969 was shocking partly because it followed one of the longest intervals of peace the residents of Belfast had ever known.

The withdrawal of the descendants of the Scottish settlers from their Gaelic roots and their adoption of a British identity has taken generations. It proceeded in tandem with the rise of Parnell and the Home Rule movement. The closer came the prospect of a Catholic-dominated Irish parliament in Dublin, the more the northern Protestants shrugged off anything with an Irish, Gaelic or Celtic dimension. The mood change was clear in 1875, when one observer wrote: 'All things Celtic are regarded by our educated classes as of questionable tone and an idea exists that it is not expedient to encourage anything tending to foster Irish sentiment.'[12]

Although Hyde's Gaelic League numbered prominent supporters in the north, like Bigger, and one of its first branches was situated in the ultra-Protestant Shankill area of west Belfast,[13] it could not compete with the growing tendency to exalt the Ulster Scots as a distinctive race. This Ulster patriotism was encouraged by books such as *The Scots in Ulster* by John Harrison in the 1880s and by Hanna's *The Scotch-Irish* in 1902, which proclaimed the Ulster Protestants to be a distinct cultural and ethnic society and enthroned Presbyterianism as *the* religious identity of Ulster Protestantism.[14] The cultivation of Britishness was accentuated by partition, in part a reaction to the way the Free State stressed its Gaelic, as well as its Catholic, identity.

'The Troubles' of 1969 onwards have widened the chasm between Catholics and Protestants in Northern Ireland, and between the northern Protestants and the rest of Ireland. Most formerly mixed wards in Belfast now belong to one side or the other. When I visited a Presbyterian minister and his wife in east Belfast I found they had no social contacts with Catholics. They worked and lived in their own community. They were not hostile to the other side, but incurious. Likewise, few people I met in Dublin had met, or wanted to get to know, any Ulster Protestants. When politicians or ordinary people spoke of needing to help 'our people' in the north, they meant Catholics, not people in general. It is so obvious that it provokes little discussion.

There is little interest now among Protestants in their Celtic heritage. Belfast is famous for murals, loyalist and nationalist, whose bright colours and urgent slogans demarcate territory and remind those on either side of their values and identity. Some Protestant murals appeal hazily to a half-forgotten Gaelic identity. Cuchulain, hero of the Fenian cycle, and praised for defending Ulster against Queen Maeve of the south, appears on walls as a kind of proto-Orangeman, his role in taking on the southerners exerting an obvious appeal. Protestants have also adopted another Gaelic emblem, the 'Red Hand', which was once the symbol of the Gaelic lords of Ulster who were expropriated under James I to make way for the Jacobean plantation. That is as far as the engagement with the Gaelic past goes. The Protestants do not use the Celtic script, which is seen as 'Catholic' and thus republican, and have little interest in the Gaelic language, largely because it is so central to Catholic republican culture, its public display a sign of the local political power of Sinn Féin.

Interest among the Protestant Celts of the north in Celtic culture is confined mainly to progressive clergymen, one or two of whom hold

Irish-language services. Protestant ministers in the north have never let the Catholic claim to sole ownership of the Celtic Church pass unchallenged. Since Archbishop Usher's era in the seventeenth century, they have written scholarly books on the Celtic saints and to mark the 1,500th anniversary of Patrick's mission in 1932, the Protestants duly put up their own monument at the village of Saul to rival that of the Catholics. But these are affairs of bishops, ministers and intellectuals. As a people, they do not identify themselves as members of the Celtic family. They found their identity long ago in Protestantism. Many, perhaps most, may be agnostic or even atheistic now, but they remain Protestant agnostics and atheists for all that.

It is quite different on the other side of the city, where I met Máirtín Ó Muilleoir. He was getting ready for a republican commemoration. A bustling, youthful-looking man, he was enjoying life as editor of the *Andersonstown News* which sprang right out of the 'Troubles' and is now one of Belfast's most successful newspapers. As we hurried through the newsroom he stopped to chat with his staff. The remarks were beyond me for they were all delivered in Irish. The language may have virtually died in Ulster a century ago, but it is enjoying a remarkable resurgence among the Catholic community today.

The partition of the 1920s, the discrimination that Catholics suffered under the Unionist administration, the civil rights movement of the 1960s and the armed struggle of the 1970s and 1980s have hardened the Catholic identity in Northern Ireland. As in the other 'debatable lands' of Europe, such as Kosovo, Cyprus, Corsica or the Basque Country, even place names are charged with political significance. What 'Ulster' is to Protestants and 'Northern Ireland' to British civil servants is what 'the Six Counties' or 'the north of Ireland' is to most Catholics.

The evolution of the Catholic identity has, like that of the Protestants, taken decades. Partition surprised them and initially the community was disorientated. They did not accept a British identity because they found themselves on the wrong side of the new border. Their schools, their churches and the GAA all reminded them that they remained Irish, and if anything, separation heightened their Irish consciousness. At the same time they had to accept that 'the south' was now a different country, not least because many were conscious of a certain feeling of rejection by the southerners, as if they were an embarrassing reminder of the dirty compromise of partition. In his 1996 autobiography *Angela's Ashes* the Irish–American writer Frank McCourt touched on this new discomfort. McCourt's father Malachy was a staunch IRA supporter with a repertoire of nationalist songs such as 'Kevin Barry' and 'Men of Wexford' always tripping from his lips. But his ardent nationalism cut little ice with the southerners among whom he made his home, and when he tried to get a job in Limerick he was stonewalled. 'Bosses and foremen always show him respect and say they're ready to hire him, but when he opens his mouth and they hear the North of Ireland accent, they take a Limerickman instead.'[15] The Belfast Catholic writer Fionnuala O'Connor touched on this feeling of reserve in her book *In Search of a State: Catholics in Northern Ireland*. 'The Northern accent brings discomfort [to southerners],' a Belfast IRA supporter told her. 'A Catholic Northerner more so. If it's a Unionist, they'll fall back: "We don't really dislike you." But to come into contact with Northern nationalists means confronting the realities of the situation.'[16]

The institution of a welfare state in Britain after the Second World War imposed new complexities, for even the bitterest opponents of British rule had to reconcile patriotic sentiments with a hunger to share in the benefits of free health and education. A teacher born in the hard-line republican area of Crossmaglen, close to the border, told O'Connor: 'The National Health Service, free education, the Eleven-Plus ... getting a grammar school education, which would have been unavailable in the South – this conflict set up all sorts of tensions and unspoken contradictions. If you brought it up, there was a sense that you were a sort of traitor ... the way they managed was they didn't think about it.'[17]

Catholic Belfast of the 1950s was a small, introverted world, whose suffocating atmosphere was brought vividly to life by Brian Moore in his classic novel, *The Lonely Passion of Judith Hearne* (1955). Moore portrayed a world in which Catholics dealt with partition by sealing themselves off from the surrounding world. When the lonely spinster in the book goes to the cinema with her hoped-for beau, they automatically signify their non-participation in the state they live in by refusing to join the popular applause for the British sovereign. 'The news then, men diving, jumping, horses racing, planes zooming, cars roaring around corners, dividing into sections with all doing all at once. The Items. First: the Queen. A few claps. More. The house applauding, louder and louder. Miss Hearne and Mr Madden sat with their hands in their laps. No handclaps for her, a foreign queen. Let them give back the Six Counties and then we'll clap. Irish people, a disgrace, applauding like that. But Protestants, what can you expect, Scots Protestants, black-hearted all.'[18] Judith Hearne's fictional world, the Ulster of the 1950s when Unionists ran the provincial assembly at Stormont and the respectable life of the Catholic bourgeoisie revolved around the Church, disappeared as if it had never existed in the 1960s. There was no violence at all in Judith Hearne's world, even if there was a good deal of hatred for the black-hearted Protestants and their British allies. A decade later, violence and Northern Irish Catholicism were seen, at least by outsiders, as linked intimately. Yet the paramilitary activity that flew suddenly on to the television screens in the late 1960s was also not entirely new.

The IRA did not see themselves as new. They viewed themselves only as the most recent foot soldiers in a long war to expel English and British rule from Ireland that dated back to the Jacobean Plantation of Ulster, if not to the Norman conquest of Ireland in the eleventh century. Although the IRA cultivated the memory of the Protestant radicals who inspired the 1798 rebellion, such as Wolfe Tone, popular support for the IRA rested on a much older tradition of Gaelic resistance to English colonisation. Appeals to the tradition of progressive Protestantism and merely verbal condemnations of sectarianism never concealed the obvious fact that the IRA had no cross-denominational appeal. Most militant movements solicit a token membership from the 'other' side to advance their credentials, but the IRA never even had that. It was always entirely Catholic in its membership and support, and it has been regarded with near-universal dread on the Protestant side as the successor to the secret Catholic societies that periodically sought to uproot Protestant settlers from the 1600s onwards.

The IRA faded away in the south after De Valera's ascent to power in Dublin in 1932 reconciled most of the losers in the civil war to the Free State. But the existence of the border and the Orange state in the north kept it alive in vestigial form and it periodically flickered into activity and reminded the world of its existence throughout the 1930s. In 1937 the IRA protested against George VI's visit to Northern Ireland by attacking customs posts, and in 1939 they took their campaign to the British mainland, killing five people in a single blast in Coventry.[19] Violence sputtered on throughout the war years. An RUC constable was shot dead in April 1942 and two more were killed that September.[20] The morale of the paramilitaries sank after Nazi Germany's defeat in 1945, as the union between Britain and Northern Ireland now looked stronger than ever, but violence in the north resumed in 1956 and 1957 and fizzled on until 1962. There was a gap of only a few years between the last IRA violence in the early 1960s and the formation of a new, more successful terrorist organisation in late 1969.

The sustained violence between the two communities and between Catholic republicans and the state that lasted from 1969 until the IRA ceasefire of 1994 changed the Catholic community as much as the Protestants. It was during those years that Belfast took on its present contours, with a Catholic-republican west separated from a Protestant and unionist east by a series of walls known as peace lines. While Protestants who had once accepted both Irish and British identities increasingly stressed a purely British one, Catholics – who had not felt 'British' to start with – took their rejection of the British state further. The revival of the Irish language was part of politically charged cultural awakening.

The reformed, 'Provisional', IRA emerged in 1969 as a defence force in the Catholic ghettos of west Belfast, where people feared imminent attack by the Protestant paramilitaries. But the armed insurrection that gathered momentum that summer had a cultural dimension. Repelling the Protestant gunmen, the RUC or the British army was not enough. The revival of a specifically Gaelic identity was a by-product of violence. Richard English's recent book on the conflict, *Armed Struggle,* cites an article in *Republican News* in May 1971, which stressed that people were under an obligation to 'learn Irish, speak Irish, be Irish'. It went on: 'Sinn Féin members have a duty to encourage the use of Irish among themselves and the public at large.' Founding members of the Provisional IRA like Sean MacStíofáin, originally John Stephenson, according to English, 'had a vision of a united Gaelic-speaking Ireland; having taken the trouble to learn Gaelic himself, he no doubt thought everyone else could and should'.[21]

Republicanism in Northern Ireland has come to cultivate a strongly Gaelic image since the start of the 'troubles' and republican murals draw on the Celtic script and the Irish language for inspiration. Sinn Féin as a matter of course has an Irish name. Irish names have been bestowed on republican political campaigns. Many streets still bear the word 'saoirse' on them, which means 'freedom', and refers to the demand for the freedom of republicans interned in British jails.

Ó Muilleoir is typical of a generation of Catholic nationalists whose attitudes were shaped by the experience of growing up in west Belfast at a time when the military confrontation between the British and the IRA was at its height. Like many of his peers, Ó Muilleoir was radicalised by his university years at the former Protestant bastion of Queen's. 'We weren't exactly grateful,' he laughed. 'We were aware of the torture of detainees. We had gun battles on the streets. We all became politicised and nationalists and for some of us the Irish language was a natural part of our politicisation.' He learned Irish at night school as an 18-year-old, when most of his British or American counterparts were spending their free time in clubs and bars. His sisters also learned it. 'It became popular in our social circles,' he said. 'It was a peaceful way of saying to the government: "We owe you no allegiance".'

West Belfast, or as Ó Muilleoir thinks of it, Béal Feirste, bears the scars of those years of armed conflict. In the centre lies Milltown cemetery, the scene of many burials of republican gunmen but also of ordinary civilians caught up, like the Protestants on the other side, in a whirlwind not of their making. The massive Celtic crosses flung up in the cemetery in the nine-teenth century are a reminder that wealth in Victorian Belfast flowed into Catholic hands, as well as into the vaults of the Protestants. But it is the more modern graves that command attention, inscribed with the angry legend 'Murdered for his faith'. Some are the graves of Catholics killed in the tit-for-tat killings that increasingly characterised the last, vicious years of 'the struggle', as the paramilitaries took indiscriminate revenge for any losses suffered on their own side.

Belfast today is a changed city from those years, not long ago, when barbed wire, patrols, searchlights and curfews were the stuff of daily life. It is vastly richer than it was, too, though the wealth rests partly on the huge state sector, which is almost Eastern European in its size and influence. 'We might as well be living in another country from the one we were raised in,' the columnist Malachi O'Doherty wrote recently in the *Belfast Telegraph*.[22] He had bitter-sweet recollections of the time when children shared beds, when clothes were stitched and restitched to last longer, when today's meal usually comprised yesterday's leftovers, when holidays were spent with relatives in Donegal and when central heating was not even thought of. 'When my mother got her first fridge she put a chair in front of it so she could sit staring at it for an hour,' he said. 'Now we want ciabatta bread with olives or sun-dried tomatoes. People that I played in the streets with now buy art from galleries and play golf.' He finished by 'wondering where this middle class came from, and particularly this Catholic middle class'.

There always was a Catholic middle class in Belfast, and the pompous tombs with their Celtic revival motifs in Milltown cemetery are its legacy. But the modern middle class that Malachi O'Doherty half saluted and half lamented sprang from the massive expansion in higher education under-taken by Harold Wilson's Labour government in Britain after the 1964 elec-tion victory and from the growth of the bureaucracy, which has ballooned since the 'troubles'. The Stormont government functioned with a tiny bureaucracy, which numbered about 12,000 people in the 1960s. After Britain assumed direct rule of the province at the height of the 'troubles' in 1972, the state sector grew steadily. Thomas Hennessy's *History of Northern*

Ireland claims that more than 50,000 Catholics worked in the public sector in Northern Ireland by the early 1990s, or 28 per cent of all economically active Catholics in employment. 'By the early 1990s therefore just over 1 in 4 employed Catholics were employed in the public sector.' [23]

The back-to-back housing that was a feature of working-class areas like the Falls and Shankill Roads has disappeared as densely packed streets are razed to make way for modern estates, mixing private and socially owned housing. Belfast looks almost prosperous, richer than at any time since partition left it becalmed like Vienna in Austria, a swollen head attached to a shrunken body. Media comparisons of Belfast with Barcelona can be put aside. The more authentic comparisons are with Liverpool, Glasgow and Manchester, semi-ruined relics of the industrial revolution that have seen dramatic urban renewal as a result of local authorities wooing professionals back to city centres through the mass conversion of derelict industrial sites into fashionable apartments. The banks of the River Lagan in Belfast are lined with these developments, towers of glass and metal that sit oddly beside the still-sullen housing estates beneath them.

The more old-fashioned Protestants take little pride in the shiny new Belfast. With a religion in which pessimism traditionally plays a large role, they cannot be expected to revel in the cult of conspicuous consumption, or in the erection of towers of metal and glass. Some suspect they are losing out, and that the makeover of the city forms part of some concealed plot to do them out of their inheritance.

The Catholics are indeed getting the upper hand in Belfast. With a higher birth rate and a lower rate of departure for the suburbs, they can expect to dominate the proceedings in the fabulously opulent City Hall, with its 'Indian Durbar' domes, fronted by a vast statue of Queen Victoria. The election of the first Sinn Féin Lord Mayor of Belfast in 2002 was a watershed event. Unionist politicians sulked during his year-long reign, but Alex McCaskey trod cautiously, even attending the annual service of commemoration of the Battle of the Somme in Flanders, at which thousands of mainly Protestant Ulstermen lost their lives.

Belfast was almost entirely Protestant in the eighteenth century and in 1800 Catholics made up only 10 per cent of the town's 19,000 inhabitants. There was almost no significant Catholic population until the industrial explosion of the nineteenth century catapulted the city's population to 349,000 by the 1890s. The number of Catholics climbed throughout the century, though as a proportion of the population they actually fell between the 1860s and 1900s from one-third to one-quarter, as Catholic Irish immigration was exceeded by immigration from Protestant parts of Ulster and from Scotland.[24] It is only during the last 30 years that Catholics in Belfast have risen again from a third to around half of the population, a phenomenon aided by Belfast's overall numerical decline.

The gradual cessation of violence since 1994 has not slowed the Gaelic revival in the north. It has given it renewed impetus, and the revival has found expression in the movement to set up a gaeltacht in west Belfast. In one sense, a gaeltacht already exists there. There are several streets now to which people have moved because of a conscious desire to create an Irish-speaking community. Belfast Irish-speakers now also have their own newspaper, *Là,* which started as a weekly in the mid-1980s and went daily in April 2003 in recognition of the fact that it had more than 3,000 regular readers. Concubhar Ò Liathain, *Là*'s deputy editor, told me that a gaeltacht was emerging in the north that had a very different character and energy from its state-backed southern counterpart. 'This was a gaeltacht that was unrecognised – it grew up in *opposition* to the state,' he said. 'To my mind that's why it's the liveliest in Ireland. We see it as growing. Unlike in the South, we don't get any advantages in housing for speaking Gaelic.' O Liathain leads a life in Belfast that does not involve much use of English, thanks to the proliferation of Irish-speaking pubs, schools, clubs and community centres. 'I use Irish about 80 per cent of the time,' he says.

'It's like putting on another pair of gloves,' *Là*'s editor, Ciaran Ò Pronntaigh added. 'It feels comfortable. You have a sense of access to music, and history that you don't get from translation.' As with many northern nationalists and republicans, there is an air of superiority in his discussion of the Republic. 'They had the ball but they lost it,' he says, of the whole Irish-Ireland movement since the 1920s. 'Because they made Irish compulsory, they thought that was all they needed.'

Half-way down the Falls Road, a former Protestant church, a relic of the time when even the Falls was a mixed area, has been turned into an Irish cultural centre, the Cultúrlann Mc Adam Ó Fiaich, named after a Presbyterian businessman, Roibeard Mc Adam, who supported the Gaelic revival in nineteenth-century Belfast and Tomás Ó Fiaich, the nationalistic Catholic Primate of Ireland in the 1980s. The Cultúrlann is a far cry from the image of the Falls as an impoverished war zone, all barricades and barbed wire. The food is modern and tasty and includes a wide range of specialist coffees. There is no problem here about talking English but the menus and the ethos of the place are Irish.

Upstairs, local charities and NGOs make use of the converted loft, among them Pobal, set up in 1998 to lobby on behalf of Ulster's growing Irish-speaking community. Its chief executive, Janet Muller, told me she had learned Irish as an adult in the 1980s and now used it as her 'language of choice'. 'It is my daughter's mother tongue, now,' she added, proudly. 'It now feels like it's grafted on to us – it is an integral part of my relationship to her. It is the language of emotional life, and of my social life.' Like Martin O Muilleoir, Muller said west Belfast already had a gaeltacht. All they needed was formal recognition. 'I'd like a gaeltacht quarter, a place that would entice visitors and have purpose-built facilities and interpretive centres.'

It is an appealing idea, a celebration of diversity that might attract outsiders, rather than repel them, as the old ghetto murals certainly do. A formal gaeltacht might invite some questions rather than bellow all the answers. Chinatowns are an old idea in the United States. London has also begun to acknowledge and commercialise its ethnic diversity with Chinese and Bangladeshi 'quarters' in Soho and Brick Lane.

But Belfast may have to wait a while for an officially approved – and subsidised – Béal Feirste. In the fractious north, additions to one side are invariably seen as subtractions from the other. 'In the 1970s there was a perception that anyone who wanted to speak Irish was a terrorist,' said Muller. 'It was no joke during the time of internment. You would never get any Irish-language funding unless it had a cross-community element. If not, it was seen as perpetuating divisions.' Muller declined to elaborate on her own religious background and made it clear she opposed what she called 'the assumption that we are all from Catholic backgrounds. It's an uncomfortable assumption, and the sooner we get away from that, the better.'

But you cannot escape the assumption. *Lá* has contributors among Unionist Protestants. There is a Presbyterian church in south-central Belfast that holds Irish-language services. A traditional musician in Dublin told me that his best fiddle-maker as a Belfast Protestant. But there are more than flickers of interest on the other side. Significantly, I was also told that the Belfast fiddle-maker had to keep his hobby secret from his friends and neighbours, because many working-class Protestants still see an interest in Irish music as tantamount to treason – a sell-out to the historic enemy. The boom in the Irish language, in Irish music and all things Celtic and Gaelic in the north is politically driven and linked to the Catholic and republican resurgence of the last 20 years. Its centre is in west Belfast, where more than 80 per cent of the population votes for Sinn Féin, as opposed to the more centrist Catholic alternative of the Social Democratic and Labour Party, SDLP.

The Gaelic movement is a continuation of the armed struggle of the late 1960s and 1970s by other means. Having failed to push the British out of the north, many people have simply decided to bring Ireland in. The slogan of the IRA, proclaimed on many walls, was that victory would come through the gun *and* the ballot box. But most people are disappointed with what the guns have achieved, including republicans. The weapons only brought a type of mayhem of which almost everyone eventually sickened. The nationalists in the north have discovered that culture is a more effective weapon than guns in the long run. And with little sign as yet of a cultural or political revival on the 'other' side, they appear to be winning.

CHAPTER FOUR

The Isle of Man
'An iceberg floating into southern latitudes'

Old salt, old rip old friend
Keltic that is, the Kelt emerging
If you will, but the Kelt a good deal
Leavened and corrupted by the Saxon
That is Tom Baynes – that is, myself, in fact
('Tom Baynes', by the Manx poet Thomas Edward Brown, 1830–97)

At the church at Kirk Braddan, outside Douglas, I bent down to look at the inscriptions on a group of ancient crosses that had once stood in the church-yard and had been brought inside the church for shelter. One, known as 'Thorlief's cross', bore the inscription: 'Thorlief built this cross for his son Fiac.' Thorlief was clearly a Viking. His son was clearly a Celt. One culture had merged, indeed mated, with another, creating a hybrid.

The short inscription on the cross said a lot about the origins of the Manx. Here, as in the Outer Hebrides, the Norse had come as raiders and conquer-ors only to be conquered in turn by sex. The Norse had added to the Manx strain just as they had added to the Hebridean strain, but in both cases the dominant element remained Celtic and Gaelic. Thorlief's children, like Fiac, had been given Celtic names and had spoken a Celtic language. So it was that the Manx absorbed the invaders and yet remained almost the same, a self-contained community of fishermen and farmers with a tongue that closely resembled that of the Scottish and Irish Gaels.

Reformation and Counter-Reformation drove a wedge between the Scottish and Irish Gaels. The ambition of Bishop Carswell, Gaelic translator of John Knox's service book, to create a Protestant Gaelic commonwealth including the two, was never realised. The ties between the Manx and the Irish decayed for the same reason. The island once had a strong cult of St Patrick. But from the sixteenth century onwards, the wells and holy places dedicated to Patrick were abandoned. The name lingered on in church dedications but no longer had much significance after the Manx ceased to believe in the intercession of saints. The Manx no longer looked to Ireland for lessons in how to approach God.

Only the language remained. For three centuries after the Reformation, the Manx communicated far more easily and readily with the Irish than with visiting Englishmen. To that extent, the Manx remained part of the Celtic world, not the English world. But then the language vanished. The generation of Manxmen and women who died in the mid-nineteenth century was replaced with astonishing speed by a generation that spoke English. This was English mixed with Manx at first, but soon it was English only. At the same time the Methodist revival swept through the island, removing earthy Celtic customs that had survived the Reformation virtually untouched and which continued to remind the Manx of their kinship with the Gaels. Out went the songs, the dances, the night services in churches at Christmas and the belief in fairies. The Methodists rolled over traditional Manx culture much as Knox's reformers had rolled over traditional Gaelic culture in Scotland, torching everything as they went. They created a new people, sober, teetotal, God-fearing and British, displaying pictures of Queen Victoria and maps of the empire on their walls. And they spoke English.

The church in Kirk Braddan recalls the long existence of the old Man. But outside it, there is barely a trace of the island's Gaelic culture. The Victorian tombstones in the churchyard bear the same sentimental inscriptions as their English counterparts. Even the oldest is in English, recording the remains of Patrick Thompson, 'Minister of God's Word 40 years, Vicar of Kirk Braddan, deceased 24th April anno. 1689'. Yet the Reverend Thompson must have preached, taught, thought and dreamed in Manx, for when Thomas Wilson was enthroned as Bishop of Sodor and Man more than a decade after Thompson's death, the island's vicar-general was a total stranger to English.

It was my second visit to the island. Months earlier I had landed at its tiny airport on a Manx Airways flight and hurried off to Hango Hill for a nationalist celebration. It was a freezing 2 January, a red-letter day in the calendar of any self-respecting Manx patriot, and a vicious, blustery wind was blowing in from the Irish Sea, catching behind my collar and pouring freezing droplets down my neck. I arrived at the ceremony by taxi and half an hour early. Disconcertingly, no one had preceded me and I paced up and down the beach in the wind waiting for others, worrying that it had been cancelled. But then people showed up in dribs and drabs, about 50 in all, Manx patriots who had come to hear the annual eulogy in Manx and

English to the man they see as a symbol of the Isle of Man's freedom and national identity.

William Christian, nicknamed 'Illiam Dhone' (William the Black, in Manx), was an unlikely hero. Born in 1608, he was executed as a traitor in 1663 under Charles II for having surrendered the island to the parliamentarians in 1651. Not that much is known about Illiam Dhone, though an impressive full-length portrait stands in the island's museum. It is far from clear that he felt much interest in Manx nationality or Manx liberty. What is clear is that he wanted a quiet life for himself and his island, and, in 1651, he handed over the island to Cromwell both to keep his post and save Man from bloodshed. It was all quite rational and not the stuff of martyrs. Yet the Manx see him as their quiet hero, and although the ceremony on Hango Hill is a recent invention, it builds on an older tradition, for the folk ballads composed in Christian's honour date back centuries.

The speaker delivering the eulogy at the place of Christian's execution on Hango Hill seemed to struggle to find anything new to say. He admitted that many people saw Illiam Dhone as a chancer, adding that the thrust of the commemoration was not really to discuss Christian's morals but to address the contemporary political situation on the Isle of Man. The wind blew away most of the words and I could only catch a few phrases about 'colonialism . . . globalisation . . . London . . . multinationals . . . the need to shake off the victim mentality of being a colonial underling . . . .' The rest of the words were lost in a terrific gust that shot in off the roiling sea, hurling spray in all our faces. Another man then staggered up the hill in a raincoat to lay a wreath on top of a Manx flag and the little crowd took up the Manx national anthem, but it had to be cut short. The weather was unbearable. It was time to adjourn to the pub. Before we broke up, a man handed round the latest news sheet from the nationalist organisation Mec Vannin. I scanned a short article on Illiam Dhone, which described him as 'a symbol of resistance to English oppression' and went on to complain about the euro and the danger of the European super-state. 'We are an independent nation and strong enough to seize our own destiny . . . let us not forget Illiam Dhone. Let us not betray his memory . . . Rise up Man!'[1]

The last event of the day was a church service in Manx at the village of Malew, where Christian lies buried. The crowd had whittled itself down to a few dozen now. A woman vicar delivered an oration in English, comparing Illiam Dhone's deeds to those of Christ, though why his shrewd pragmatism in surrendering the island to Cromwell rendered him Christ-like was beyond me. I had not come to the service to listen to this nonsense but to hear the ancient language used in the liturgy. The curious sermon over, the parish priest moved sonorously into the Manx Gaelic. 'Ayr ain, t'ayns niau; Casherick dy row dt'Ennym' – 'Our Father who art in Heaven, hallowed be Thy name'. The congregation followed, haltingly. As they did, I tried to cast my mind back to a time when these words would have been said lustily and unthinkingly by thousands, every Sunday in all the churches of the island. The congregations of those churches would have emerged into the light of day to hear the same words shouted on the quaysides, where the fishwives sat gutting their herrings in the narrow, stinking streets of the fishing ports, and up high in the whitewashed farmhouses of the interior. We ended with the grace: 'Grayse nyn jiarn Yeesey Creest, as graih Yee, as sheshagt ghergoil y Spirrid Noo, dy row marin ooiley er son dy bragh.' Then it was over. We came out of the church and journeyed back from the Celtic past to the English present.

The Isle of Man once lay at the centre of the Celtic lands, almost equally distant from three others. From the top of Snaefell mountain in the middle on a clear day you can see all three. Ireland lies 27 miles to the west and Scotland 21 miles to the north. Wales alone is relatively far away, at 45 miles' distance. The Irish, Scots and Welsh have all at some point dominated the Manx, infusing the island with their own culture while never absolutely subduing its spirit.

Ireland exercised the greatest influence. From there, the Manx received a language and their faith. Whether or not Patrick actually visited in person in the 440s, as legends maintain, the early Church in Man was heavily indebted to him. There are more religious sites on the Isle of Man dedicated to Patrick than to any other single saint, and they include two churches and 13 wells. For centuries Manx sailors invoked Patrick's blessing at sea and maintained the tradition of giving the dying a draught of water from one of the wells named after him.[2] The tally of Patrician sites does not give a full picture of Manx Christianity's debt to Ireland, for that would have to include the churches named after other Irish saints like Bride, or Bridget, and St Maughold.

If the Manx Church was an Irish enterprise, the Manx language was more of a joint Celtic enterprise. It was more Gaelic than Norse, but while the western half of the island took its Gaelic from Ireland the other side reflected Man's proximity to Scotland. According to William Camden's *Britannia* of 1586, the isle was 'divided into two parts, south and north, the inhabitants of this speak like the Scots, and those of the others like the Irish'.[3] John Speed in 1627 also noted divisions among the Manx in speech, though he pointed more to Norse survivals. 'The common sort of people both in their language and manners come nighest unto the Irish,' he wrote, 'although they somewhat rellish and savour of the qualities of the Norwegians.'[4] Bishop Wilson in the seventeenth century declared the people spoke both Irish and Scottish Gaelic. They used 'Erse, or a dialect of that spoken in the Highlands of Scotland, with a mixture of some words of Greek, Latin or Welsh', he said.[5]

Though the Irish played a crucial role in forming Manx culture and religion, they never ruled the island. The Welsh and Scots exercised a more obvious dominion. From the 520s to around 913 the Manx were subject to Welsh princes. After the long interlude of Icelandic and Norse rule until 1265 the lordship fell to Scotland and then to a succession of English families, one of which, the Stanley Earls of Derby, held the lordship for three centuries. When the Stanleys died out in 1735 it passed back to Scotland in the shape of the Earls of Atholl, who held the lordship until the crown bought them out in the 1760s.

The island is now chiefly known as the home of an annual car race and as a tax haven. It is still a 'lordship', with a parliament, the Tynwald, the heir of the old Norse assembly. It is under the British crown but – peculiarly – outside Britain. The island has also transformed its economy over the past quarter-century by becoming host to offshore banks and international financial organisations. The financial sector is now the island's biggest and by far the richest employer.

The money that flows into the Manx government's coffers through the offshore finance sector has not made the island a second Monaco. Douglas is no Monte Carlo, a playground for the rich and titled. It has none of the surface sheen of wealth one might expect from a tax haven. It is distinctly shabby, a down-at-heel town of seedy bed and breakfasts and long-stay hotels catering to an elderly crowd. Out of season it has the desolate air of so many declining British seaside resorts, long since deserted by the well-to-do and trying to survive on an ever-shorter 'season'. The seafront hotels are named after half-forgotten nineteenth-century royal personalities and statesmen, when not named with dreary predictability after the great Victoria. The Queen-Empress is commemorated everywhere. Douglas has its Victoria Street, Victoria Road, Victoria Crescent and its Empress Drive, besides its Albert Terrace, Brunswick Road, Windsor Terrace and Osborne Terrace. The names well suit a town and an island that was refashioned so radically in the Victorian era that it might as well have undergone a lobotomy. In Douglas the old, close-knit Gaelic-speaking fishing port has been buried under the monuments to a new culture and a new way of thinking, which is imperial, British and Protestant.

The Manx nationalists – the hardy group I encountered on Hango Hill – have successfully lobbied for some street names to be put up in Manx. The name of the Manx Museum in Douglas is now written also as *Thie Tashtee Vannin*. But there is nothing for these mementoes of the distant past to connect with. They simply fit the needs of the tourist industry, which in Man, as in Ireland and Scotland, is keen to market a vaguely 'Celtic' image to visitors. They mean almost nothing to the baseball-cap-wearing youths, any more than Gaelic street signs would mean to the average Londoner.

The Celtic nationalists, of course, do not see it that way. Like religious revivalists, they determinedly see victory round every corner. In his union office (he is an active trade unionist) I met Bernard Moffat, secretary-general of the Celtic League and president of Mec Vannin, the pressure group of which he was a founder in 1963. I told him that I had seen nothing on the Isle of Man that pointed to a real revival of the islanders' Gaelic identity, but Moffat said breezily that matters were going their way. 'If you look at the concepts that Mec Vannin advocated in the 1960s, like fiscal autonomy, its own postal service, own fishing protection vessels, they were regarded as potty back then, but now they're totally accepted.'

Was that what the Manx Celtic revival was all about – fiscal autonomy and fishing vessels? Manx nationalists, like their Irish, Scottish and Welsh counterparts, have always been split between champions of political independence and those who prioritise the struggle for the soul. For some Manx activists, like Moffat, the goals are socialism, a republic and legislative independence. He did not seem that interested in a distinct culture, nor did he speak Manx. In fact, he snorted at those who were 'steeped in some Celtic mist'. He shrugged when I raised the issue of Manx nationalists attacking the finance sector and the influx of English immigrants. They had a 'victim mentality', he mused. And he made short shrift of Mona Douglas, too, the mother of modern Manx nationalism.

Many people I spoke to had little time for Mona Douglas. She was without doubt enveloped in the 'Celtic mist' Moffat referred to which is now very unfashionable. Yet none of the modern nationalists who disparage her would probably even have been aware of a Manx identity if it had not been for her efforts. She dedicated herself to the cause of nurturing what remained of the island's Celtic culture and to countering its remorseless anglicisation. Douglas belonged to a phenomenon unique to the Isle of Man – a sisterhood of celibate women who spent their lives guarding the guttering flame of Man's Celtic identity. The fact that they largely failed does not undermine the worth of their struggle. Mona was the second in line, for before Mona there was Sophia.

Sophia Morrison was born in 1875, daughter of a prosperous fishing fleet owner in the western port of Peel. In 1917 at the age of 42 her life was cruelly cut short by stomach cancer. She died uncomplaining, but not before she had hooked Manx nationalism into a wider pan-Celtic movement centred on Ireland. Morrison took part in the first Pan-Celtic Congress, held in the Mansion House grounds in Dublin in August 1900, where representatives of the Celtic 'nations' marched in what they took for national costumes through the streets before large crowds, who saw it as a gesture of solidarity with Home Rule. The Manx let the side down, as they had no conceivable national dress to wear. The Welsh bards wore white, green and blue, the Irish donned green tunics, the Bretons had knicker-bockers and the Highlanders had tartan. 'Only the Manxmen wore the garb of denationalisation,' the magazine *Young Wales* complained.[6]

Morrison's family money enabled her to devote herself to writing, collecting folklore and promoting the Manx cause. She published a book, *Manx Fairy Tales* and – along with John Moore, Speaker in the House of Keys, founded the Manx Language Society, Yn Cheshaght Ghailckagh and a magazine, *Mannin*. Morrison was a kind of template for the new generation of independent women activists. A life like hers would have been inconceivable a generation earlier. As it was, almost the only serious obstruction she encountered in her work as a result of her sex was the sturdy refusal of the male Manx farmers to repeat the earthier of their folk songs in front of her.

Nineteenth-century Celtic folklorists like Morrison have come under sharp criticism for being middle-class amateurs, and for 'exploiting' the culture of the poor. Yet Morrison seems always to have been made welcome among the farm workers she visited. According to her Welsh friend, Alice Mallt Williams: 'In lonely farms far away among the mountains, in the houses of sea-faring folk in town or village, in lanes or fields, we met them, and at her greeting in the old language, eyes brightened, tongues were unloosed and they were their real Manx selves. She understood them because she was of them and proud of being so.'[7]

Then she died, after handing her baton to another unusual, slightly lonely woman. Morrison met Mona Douglas when the latter was only 10 years old in 1908 and later gave the isolated teenager – Douglas never appears to have had a conventional education – space to work in Yn Cheshaght Ghailckagh.

Douglas carried on Morrison's work. The language society promptly made Mona its new secretary. She saw herself as Sophia Morrison's spiritual heir. 'She was my heroine,'[8] she wrote of her mentor, to whom she composed an ardent poem 'Er Sooyl' (Away).

> We walked among the mists in eager quest
> Of fairy lore and talked with eyes aglow,
> Of all the old invisible powers that go
> About that sea-girt land we love the best
> Now you have passed out from these shadowed lands
> By unknown ways to seek the light of light.
>
> Still the pale winds whirl west across the sea
> And while gulls cry and rain beats on the sands
> But you are away among the strange delights
> Whereof the unquiet waves sing endlessly.[9]

Mona Douglas had to walk among the mists for many years after 1917, for she did not die young like her mentor, but survived until 1987, advocating the Manx language and the Celtic culture of the island to the end. 'There is no danger now-a-days that the Celtic nations will be swamped,' Morrison once said. 'They have all risen, like the phoenix, from their ashes.'[10] Mona Douglas lived to see those prophetic words disproved.

Shortly after Sophia Morrison's death, it became evident that the hopes raised by the Celtic congresses were not going to be realised. Ireland became independent, but as we have seen, independence did not lead smoothly to a Gaelic revival. The Irish Free State, engulfed in civil war in the early 1920s, did not assume the role the Celtic nationalists had anticipated, as harbinger of a Celtic renaissance. In Scotland and Wales, too, nationalism after the First World War retreated before the advance of socialism, which declared the whole business redundant and a diversion from class struggle.

By the end of Mona Douglas's life, her values appeared outmoded. The socialists and republicans in the ranks of the Manx nationalists openly sniggered at her belief in 'old, invisible powers' and fairy bridges and the fact that in old age she accepted a royal honour for her work. Language activists harped on her inability to converse properly in Manx and thought the stress on folklore misdirected. She was accused of making things up and of inventing a dance known as the 'dirk'. More cruelly, she was even charged with being a Nazi sympathiser, though there is no evidence that her long fight against English culture made her into an enthusiast for Hitler.

She was not a great writer of fiction. She wrote a novel about a young woman who returned home from America and became swept up in Celtic nationalism. It was awkwardly written and based on a fantasy of the Isle of Man that existed solely in Douglas's mind, a little world of clean-limbed, sexless young people who strode around exclaiming patriotic slogans, while communing with the spirits of the hills.

Sophia Morrison had handed her baton to Mona Douglas. But whom had Mona entrusted with continuing her work? Who still spoke Manx, for a start? The answer seemed to lie in Cregneash, on the southern tip of the island. The village was one of the last places where Manx was spoken and the cluster of whitewashed thatched cottages overlooking the sea recalls the aspect that the whole island must have worn before its Victorian makeover as a tourist resort.

In their thatched home in Cregneash, I met Philip and Ann Gorn. They spoke Manx. They were not only able to understand it, they spoke it all the time, not just to each other but to their children. In fact, it was Manx that brought the couple together and Mona Douglas who had introduced Ann to Manx culture. The Gorns believed that nationalism was less about parliaments and laws and more about culture. 'The way I express my Manxness is through my language,' Phil Gorn said. 'We're fed up with hearing English accents on Manx radio.' At primary school in the 1960s, Ann recalled, no one had even known what the names of the various towns and villages meant. It was as if a kind of amnesia had set in, blotting out all recollection of the past. But now even her parents had learned some Manx and at 72 her father had taken Manx O-Level.

But what was Manxness – was it a republic, a separate postal service, or performing a 'dirk' dance? Was it doggedly defying the trend by speaking a virtually extinct language at home? The Gorns were optimistic about the future of the tongue, citing the growth of interest in Manx in schools and on adult education courses. But it will never again be a community language as far as one can tell. The last native-born Manx-speaker, Ned Madrell, died in 1974. Today's Manx speakers are all learners.

Crackling recordings made in the 1950s and 1960s of the last Manx-speakers are all that link them to a vanished Gaelic culture, which withstood a millennium and a half of invasions before crumbling before the invasion of tourists. Brian Stowell, who learned Manx in 1953 and became the island's first Manx language officer in 1991, remembers tape-recording the last native speakers in the 1950s and the difficulties they had in persuading people to take part. 'Some people wouldn't let their relatives be recorded as they thought they were being made fun of,' he said. Morrison credited the nationalists with ridding the Manx of their feelings of shame about their language. But it seems she was wrong, for the last speakers had gone to their deaths still feeling foolish.

I set out to track down a Manx writer, hoping he or she could explain the Manx identity. Jennifer Kewley, author of a historical novel set in the island, *The Maid of Maughold*, turned out to be a Manx-speaker. She was far from strident, calling Manx-language education a luxury they might one day have to dispense with. 'We can afford lots of lovely things because of the finance sector,' she said, 'but if the finance sector buggers off we are going to be looking for handouts.' Kewley defined Manxness in terms of character traits. 'There is a steadfastness in them, a modesty in them, they appear slow but are actually perceptive . . . The Manx have survived by brinkmanship. We are little and if you are very little you have to develop strategies.' How do you know you have met a Manx person? I asked. 'When you meet one you just know,' she said. Modesty and steadfastness. When you meet one you know one. It was a small skeleton on which to drape a national identity. But without a living language, a cuisine, a costume or a religion to go on, it was unsurprising that the identity boiled down to a few character traits.

The Celtic nationalists have cornered the island's museums. The knowledge of history is theirs to shape and the thousands of children who pass through the island's museums can hardly emerge without at least a surface appreciation of their old Celtic roots. 'I am Mananan,' a loud tape-recorded voice shouted in the auditorium of the interactive museum in Peel. And there he was on the screen, a bearded and very Celtic figure garbed in a Tolkien-style wizard's cloak, hung with shamanic nicknacks. As the screen guide to the story of Man, the Celtic God-King Mananan ushered us through selected excerpts of history. I sat back in the dark and watched a nasty Norse invader grabbing a squawking Celtic girl. The actors were clean-cut and looked as if they worked in Man's booming finance sector when not starring in history videos.

The version of history presented on the screen, with the Norse in a negative role and the Celts as victims, did not surprise me, for Manx nationalists do not like to stress the Viking aspect to their history. They do not much like the flummery at the annual June open-air session of the Tynwald, where laws are promulgated with medieval pageantry. It is not just because the occasion reeks of loyalty and royalty but because the Tynwald recalls the strong Norse legacy. I thought back to the cross in Kirk Braddan church, inscribed with the words 'Thorlief built this cross for his son Fiac.' But many modern nationalists share the phobia about the Norse exhibited by the Celtic enthusiasts of the nineteenth century, who fretted over racial purity and saw the Norse as ersatz English-conquering Teutons. To acknowledge the Norse heritage seemed to lessen the strength of the links to the Celtic motherland of Ireland. Norseness got in the way.

I emerged from the museum into drizzle in Peel. This was Sophia Morrison's home town. In her lifetime, Peel was still a bastion of Manx language, resisting the tide of anglophone speech and manners seeping slowly westwards from Douglas. Morrison perfected her own knowledge of Manx from the Manx Bible, but there can be no doubt that she heard a more vernacular version of the language shouted in the lanes of her home town. It would have seemed incredible to her that the language should ever disappear entirely. Even in the early years of the twentieth century, her mentor, the German folklorist Carl Roder, chided her for concentrating on the language, saying the folklore, not the language, was in the greatest danger. 'I hope you will not entirely neglect collecting material, as suggested to you,' he told her in 1905. 'I think this is even more important than the language, at present, as the old people are dying fast, while the language is secure enough.'[11] The early stalwarts of Yn Cheshaght Ghailckagh took the same line. 'The Manx language society should by no means confine its energies to the promotion of an interest in the language,' A. W. Moore said in his presidential address in 1899, 'but extend them to the study of Manx literature, history, the collection of Manx music, ballads, carols, folklore, proverbs, place names . . . in a word to the preservation of everything that is defiantly Manx.'[12]

Morrison was sometimes complacent about the language because she worked in an age − the last, so it turned out − when knowledge of Manx was met with knowing smiles from the farmers and fishing folk she visited. She wrote in the 1903 annual report of Yn Cheshaght Ghailckagh: 'I have been more than ever convinced by experiences which I have had during the past summer when making walking tours in country districts. Everywhere did my travelling companion and myself find our little knowledge of the old tongue a sure key to the hearts of the people and hospitality was showered upon us.'[13] Morrison thought of her home town as the 'Celtic centre'[14] of Man and a little of the atmosphere she relished still survives, in comparison to Douglas. Like the village of Cregneash, parts of Peel recall an older way of life with their whitewashed fishermen's cottages.

The death of Manx was all the more surprising as it was not harried into the grave by hostile English landlords and clergymen. The Isle of Man did not follow the example of Ireland or the Scottish Highlands, where church and state combined to marginalise and repress Gaelic. The Manx authorities took a different, more positive, line.

Their relatively benign approach was a product of the island's religious condition. The Manx Gaels swiftly accepted the Reformation, so their language was never stigmatised like Scottish or Irish Gaelic as a language of rebellion and sedition. Camden's *Britannia* noted approvingly in 1586 that 'the people are wonderfully religious, and all of them zealously conformable to the Church of England'.[15] Bishop Wilson boasted in the eighteenth century that religious dissent on the island remained unknown: there were no Catholics at all, and only a family or two of Quakers.[16] The conformity of the Manx to England's religious changes encouraged the Anglican Church to take a different view of the islanders' culture from their attitude towards the Irish in particular. They felt no hostility to the use of Manx in religious services. All that retarded the advance of a distinctively Manx Protestant literature was a lack of competent scholars to translate works and – even more – of patrons with the money to have them published. In the sixteenth century the Manx clergy compiled home-made translations of Bible passages they needed for their services. According to Camden's *Britannia,* the clergy were 'generally natives and have had their whole education in the island . . . [and] read the scriptures to the people in the Manks language out of the English'.[17]

The Manx were lucky in their bishops. John Phillips, bishop from 1604 to 1635, spoke both Welsh and Manx and had the Bible translated for the first time, though he found no sponsor for its publication. The diocese of Sodor and Man was too poor to attract greedy pluralists – Archbishop William Laud had complained to Charles I of these 'church cormorants', who swallowed everything. It was too far from the royal court to attract even the kind of ambitious careerist who might make temporary use of a poor see in Wales as a stepping-stone. Bishops who came to Man came to stay.

For more than half a century, from 1698 to 1755, the see was in the hands of Thomas Wilson, who never contemplated promotion to a mainland see. When he came to the island, English was only spoken by the merchant families of the ports and by the small landed gentry class, who had long spoken English, and preferred it. In the sixteenth century Camden had noted: 'Their gentry . . . are more willing to discourse with one in English than in their own language . . . In all their carriage apparel and house keeping they imitate the English gentry.' According to Camden: 'not only the gentry but likewise such of the peasants as live in the towns or frequent the town markets do both understand and speak the English language'.[18] But outside the ports it was not used. Even the higher clergy were still Manx monoglots, for the Vicar-General, Samuel Wattleworth, who installed Wilson as bishop in Castletown on 11 April 1698, was so unfamiliar with English that the service had to be held in Latin.

After labouring for so many decades in the place, Wilson naturally learned to love both people and language. He encouraged the islanders to learn English, to better their prospects, but never disparaged or discouraged the native culture, as most of the Irish Protestant bishops did. His attitude was pragmatic. 'English is not understood by two-thirds at least of the island, though there is an English school in every parish,' he said.[19] At a time when the Manx had no moneyed patrons, the Bishop himself paid for the printing of a Manx catechism, *The Principles and Duties of Christianity*, to be published in 1707, and for 53 copies of St Matthew's gospel to be printed in 1748.

By the eighteenth century, Wilson's bishopric was a throwback. The Williamite Revolution of 1688 had forced the English church establishment to come to terms with religious toleration, but in the Isle of Man the Church sailed on regardless. Bishops could still enforce excommunications with medieval rigour, jailing culprits if necessary. Notoriously, Wilson had one woman, Katherine Kinrade, dragged through the sea by her hair for immorality, incurring opprobrium because she was mentally retarded. Wilson was unrepentant. Though not a conventional high churchman in terms of ritual, he was a disciple of Archbishop Laud in his belief that the church had an absolute right to wield the sword of discipline. By the end of his episcopate his regime was an anachronism. In England and even in Calvinist Scotland the Enlightenment had profoundly altered the religious climate by the 1740s.

The Isle of Man was also changing slowly in spite of Wilson. The Bishop's theocratic pretensions suffered a blow in 1722 when the island's hostile governor, Alexander Horne, jailed him briefly for refusal to pay a fine. The conflict came as a reminder that even on this isolated island the Anglican Church would not be permitted to uphold a semi-theocracy. England inevitably took a closer interest in the small island in the middle of the Irish Sea as the eighteenth century progressed. While the Bishop laboured to reform their souls, the Manxmen remained inveterate smugglers, trading on the island's status as an independent lordship under the dukes of Atholl to import goods tax free and then funnel them illegally into England. Deprived of customs revenue by the smugglers, the British government bought out the dukes' manorial rights in 1765 and united the lordship to the crown, after which the smuggling trade declined and many people emigrated.

Wilson's long reign until 1755 helped keep the Manx language and identity alive, because his determination to shield his flock from the influence of an increasingly secular and sceptical England isolated the Manx from all English currents. His death at the age of 91 caused no sudden break in the policy of the Anglican bishops on Manx language and culture. Mark Hildesley, bishop from 1755 to 1772, was another benign patriarch and as sensitive as his predecessor had been to the Manx. English continued slowly to advance on the island but the Bishop did not push it. There was no need to sing all the psalms in English in the liturgy, he told the clergy. Parts of the psalms were enough, 'full sufficient for ye case and comfort of ye minority who are supposed to understand it'.[20] He urged them to preach in Manx, and told the Archbishop of York in 1762 that the lack of Manx bibles was a scandal. It was 'a defect, I believe [that] . . . the major part of the people are unable to obtain any genuine knowledge of the genuine scriptures but what they receive from the off-hand translations produced by the minister'.[21]

Far from trying to put down Manx, Hildesley used his power to restore and promote it. It was 'a very ancient language, beyond doubt', he enthused to his clerical translator and ally Philip Moore in 1764, 'and could we get such a thing as an Erse dictionary, we should be capable of improving it, or rather restoring it'.[22] Two months later he exulted to Moore about a chance encounter with an old woman, being read parts of the Bible in Manx by her son. She had 'cried out with great exultation: "We have sat in darkness till now",'[23] Hildesley reported.

Hildesley persuaded the Church of England's voluntary society, the Society for the Propagation of Christian Knowledge, to subsidise the printing and distribution of Manx bibles and under his episcopate the SPCK supplied a growing amount of popular religious literature in Manx. A small edition of Manx Common Prayer books was produced in 1765 and a larger one in 1768. An edition of New Testaments appeared in 1767, while the rest of the Old Testament followed in sections over the next few years.[24] Genesis to Deuteronomy was printed in April 1770, the books of Joshua to Job in 1771 and the rest of the Old Testament in November 1772. 'It is impossible to describe the avidity with which these books which his lordship has enabled to get printed are sought,' Philip Moore assured the English public in an address in 1769, 'and with what joy and gratitude to their benefactors they are received.'[25]

The work was its own reward, Moore said. He was 'thankful to that good providence which has called me out in so glorious a cause as to be the instrument in making the mind of God more diffuse and intelligible to my countrymen and giving them the pure word of God in their own language, which I verily believe to be one of the most antient this day in the world, being manifestly a dialect of the antient Celtick, the language of all Asia Minor, and of Europe, for many centuries'.[26] Moore was struck by the similarity between Manx, Cornish, Welsh and Irish, which occurred to him after reading Borlase's *History of Cornwall*. 'The Welsh, the Irish, the Erse, and the Manks are all but different dialects of one and the same original language,' he mused.[27] By the 1790s the SPCK had distributed about 2,000 Old Testaments, 3,000 New Testaments, 6,500 copies of the Book of Common Prayer and 2,000 catechisms, a considerable achievement among a population of about 28,000, only a minority of whom could read.

In the 1790s, John Feltham, author of the *Tour through the Island of Mann,* crowed over what he claimed was the retreat of Manx, and its intellectual poverty. 'The enlightened Manksmen . . . must lament the barrenness of its literary field and the almost daily disuse of his mother tongue,' he wrote. But while pronouncing the obvious fact that English was 'indispensable' in courts of law, he had to admit through gritted teeth that English was still popular. 'In general, the lower class understand English and few are wholly ignorant of it; yet they are more ready at, and attached to, their Manks.'[28]

The weakness of the Manx revival, as Feltham said, was that it was tied totally to the Church. Almost everything published in Manx came at the behest of bishops and was connected to the Bible or Prayer Book. Manx established itself in print as a language of religious devotion but not as a language of secular literature, business or law. Even that seemed to be changing in the late eighteenth century, however, after the publication of the first Manx dictionaries and grammars and a translation of part of Milton's *Paradise Lost,* by John Christian, the Vicar of Marown.

Hildesley died in 1772, the last of the titans among the Manx bishops and the last to play the role of patron to Manx culture. Under Richard Richmond, his successor from 1773 to 1780 and George Mason, from 1780 to 1783, the Church lost both its drive and its authority. As the Anglican Church ceased to absorb popular religious energy, the way was left open for dissenting evangelicals under John Wesley, at first operating within the bosom of the Church but then outside it. The first Methodist mission was held in Douglas in 1776. Wesley himself reached the island the following year, touring Douglas, Peel and Ramsey and returning in 1781. Like the

Cornish and the Welsh, the Manx lost their reputation for submissive conformity to the Church of England.

Wesley was no friend to the non-English languages of Britain. He opposed the publication of religious literature in Manx[29] and urged the suppression of the remaining traces of the old Celtic religious culture, such as the 'Oie Voirrey', the traditional all-night Christmas Eve services, which were probably a relic of the Catholic celebration of Midnight Mass and had survived the Reformation as a celebration of song.[30] It was the start of a sustained and ultimately successful assault on the traditional culture of the island, which would in the end sweep away not only the often earthy 'Oie Voirrey' services but the whole spiritual pantheon that the Manx had inherited from the Irish and the Norse. The Methodists took aim at the Ny Shee – the 'ones', as the fairies were elusively called – at the Fynndderee, the Buggane, Glashtin and all the other fairies, trolls and goblins. They crumbled away as people were unable to resist the shrill call for a purely biblical religion and respectability. Such beliefs would have declined whatever the religious temper of the island, as the experience of Ireland under the reforming Catholic clergy of the nineteenth century showed. But the evangelicals were even more hostile to these beliefs, which is why they survived for much longer in Ireland than they did on the Isle of Man. Mona Douglas was certainly convinced that the Methodists were the greatest enemies of everything she cherished about the Manx. 'If there was one man in Manx history that has done more than anybody else to destroy the tradition of Manx music and dancing, it was John Wesley and his Methodists,' she said.[31]

If the evangelicals were sworn enemies of the Manx dances, songs and beliefs, their activities seemed of great potential benefit to the Manx language. They were pragmatically prepared to work with minority languages in the interest of reaching the widest potential audience. In Scotland the SPCK in particular acted as a battering ram for English culture. On the Isle of Man the 33 Sunday schools opened by 1818 by the evangelical Sunday School Society of London were Manx-medium establishments.[32] Another hopeful development was the formation in 1821 of the Manx Society for Promoting the Education of the Inhabitants of the Isle of Man through the Medium of their Own Language. As the *Manx Advertiser* stressed in December 1822, true Protestantism went hand in hand with the vernacular speech of the people. 'That every individual should be furnished with the means of reading the Holy Scripture in the language which he best understands appears to be an acknowledged principle among all Protestants,' it said.[33] The newspaper reported that in one year the society had printed 7,500 tracts in Manx.

It marked a new chapter in the history of the language, whose future looked assured. But an amazing reverse lay ahead. In spite of the popularity of the Manx religious tracts and the new editions of the Bible printed in 1810, 1815, 1819 and 1825, the language now entered on a dramatic decline that culminated in its virtual extinction within less than a century. Only four years after the establishment of the Manx Society in July 1825, Bishop George Murray wrote to the SPCK to inform them there was no longer a need for Manx bibles or prayer books.[34]

The engine of change was the Isle of Man Steam Packet Company, which opened the floodgate to mass tourism and shattered the insular culture within a generation. It was not the learned and English bishops of Man who made the Manx ashamed of their Gaelic culture but hordes of middle- and working-class English holiday-makers. Although a regular 'packet' had been sailing to Mann from Whitehaven since the 1760s, the service still only ran once every six weeks as late as 1821. There was no winter service at all until 1765 and the six-hour journey cost 10 shillings and sixpence.[35] The steamship changed everything. What had been an infrequent and uncomfortable journey became a pleasure trip lasting a few hours, especially after the construction of quays removed the need to disembark from the ships on to tenders that were rowed to land.

The first steamer to dock regularly in Douglas from 1819 was the *Henry Bell*. The Mona Isle Company was established a decade later, subsequently becoming the Isle of Man United Steam Packet Company (the United in the title was soon dropped). From then on the growth in communications was rapid. From August 1830 there were three sailings a week in the summer months and a minimum of one a week in midwinter, from December to February.

Holidays in the little Celtic island in the Irish Sea soon became the rage. By the 1840s there were 20,000 to 30,000 visitors a year, which was one visitor to every inhabitant. The numbers increased exponentially again after the opening of the Victoria Pier in Douglas in July 1871, after which bigger ships could dock. In 1883 the company carried 286,418 passengers.[36] In 1894 that figure had almost doubled, to 516,359. The numbers continued to climb. There were 711,514 passengers on Steam Packet ships in 1903 and after another huge surge in numbers, 1,152,048 in 1913.[37] By then a network of railways had snaked out over Man to facilitate the tourists' exploration of every nook and cranny of the island.

Manx shrivelled as the tourist industry grew. Manx seamen had always been affected by frequent contacts with the English. They were 'Kelts, a good deal leavened and corrupted by the Saxon,' as the Victorian poet, T. E. Brown, said. But as the economy shifted a gear, moving away from fishing and farming towards catering for English holiday-makers, the Manx became a great deal more leavened than they had been. A culture can survive constant interaction with English-speaking visitors without suffering any loss of self-esteem, as is shown by the situation in modern Greece and Spain where constant use of English in the workplace has not displaced the national language in the home. But the Manx followed the example of the Irish in deciding within a short time that English was not only useful but very superior to their own tongue. The Manx learned their English and jettisoned their Manx at the same time, abandoning an entire cultural package they now associated with backwardness and poverty. Newspapers, those reliable weathercocks of cultural trends, virtually ignored Manx from their start on the island in the early nineteenth century. The *Manx Mercury*, published from 1793 to 1801, and the *Manx Advertiser*, which came out for about 40 years until the 1840s, as well as the other newspapers, the *Manxman* and *Mona's Herald*, addressed their audience from the start in English alone.

The churches also deserted the language. The clergy had never championed Gaelic culture for its own sake, except for a few enthusiasts like Bishop Hildesley, but to communicate better, and once it became clear that the clergy could talk to people in English – and that the English tourists were in danger of missing out on their ministrations – they dropped Manx. 'It is now entirely discontinued in most of the churches,' an observer wrote in 1859. 'In the schools throughout the island the language has ceased to be taught and the introduction of the Government system of education has done much to displace the language. It is now rarely heard in conversation except among the peasantry. It is a doomed language, an iceberg floating into southern latitudes.'[38]

The language did not enter a long, gentle decline: it vanished quickly over the decades that witnessed the Isle of Man's transformation into a tourist resort. A survey of the use of Manx in parishes in 1874 by Henry Jenner found that only 12,350 of the island's population of 41,084 now spoke Manx, which was less than one-third of the total. The pockets where the language was spoken by at least half the population were also broken up. The two densest areas were the parish of Arbory, where it was used by 1,200 out of 1,350 and Jurby, where 600 of 788 local people used it.[39] But those two parishes lay at opposite ends of the island, separated by a solid wedge of anglophone territory. John Qualtrough of Arbory was the last clergyman to hold Manx services regularly and his death in 1879 marked the end of an era.[40] Addressing the new climate of active hostility towards the language on the part of the Manx people themselves, Jenner wrote: 'There is a decided feeling on the part of the people, especially the Manx speakers themselves, that the language is only an obstruction, and that the sooner it is removed the better.'[41]

By the 1890s, even those who most loved the island felt their alienation from the Gaelic culture. Hall Caine, the novelist, who published a sympathetic book *The Little Manx Nation* in 1891, mourned his inability to understand a language he felt certain he once understood as a child. 'I cannot speak it,' he wrote sadly, 'I cannot follow it when spoken, I have only a sort of nodding acquaintance with it out of door, and yet among my earliest recollections is that of a household where nothing but Manx was ever spoken except to me.'[42] The door was closing fast. Caine felt that the island had become too English and blamed the steamers chugging into the harbour day after day. By the 1890s there were two steamships a day from England, and it was wearing away what remained of the island's culture, he said. 'Our young Manxman is already feeling the English immigration on his character,' he wrote; 'he is not as good a man as his father was before him.'[43]

The remaining third of the population who clung to the language in 1874 were mostly elderly. That is clear, for most had died before the census of 1901, which recorded only 4,598 Manx speakers – less than 10 per cent of the population. The middle-class folklorists, nationalists and language enthusiasts like Sophia Morrison had no more success in stemming this decline in the Isle of Man than their counterparts did in Ireland. By 1911, after 12 years of work by the Manx Language Society, the number of speakers had slid down to 2,351, which was less than 5 per cent of the population and probably marked the point of no return. As ever, the tourist industry that had unthinkingly murdered the local culture was the last to acknowledge what was happening, let alone why. *The Isle of Man*, a travel handbook published in 1909 by Agnes Herbert and Donald Maxwell, absurdly claimed there were still lots of monoglots and that 'in Creignish and countless other parts there are still old people who can speak no tongue save the Manx'.[44] In fact, the language was almost dead and the last pockets of Manx monoglots had disappeared long before.

By 1921 Manx was effectively dead, as the census recorded only 896 surviving speakers, or just above 1 per cent of the population. The great irony was that Sophia Morrison's dream of awakening the Manx Celtic consciousness was finally honoured in that census year, when a Celtic Congress was held on the island. The delegates arrived to an island that had lost its Celtic attributes within living memory. The separate world that Bishop Wilson had ruled, whose culture had survived more or less intact until the beginning of the nineteenth century, was gone. The new port of Douglas, with its avenues and 'drives' named after imperial worthies, mirrored the values of the new generation of Manx people, who had become integrated into the mainland British way of life.

Mona Douglas had to carry the torch into the dark ages. 'Her vision was for a generation that could speak Manx, sing Manx, play Manx, dance Manx and above all, feel Manx and celebrate Manxness,' Fenella Bazin wrote in a tribute to her after her death.[45] But the goal was not remotely realised. Towards the end she must have felt that the spirit of the God-King Mananan had finally deserted them.

The population of the Isle of Man has now reached 76,000 and is rising. The immediate post-Second World War period was a lean time, coming after the decline of the tourist trade and before the boom in financial services in the 1960s. Since then the trend has been upward economically, even if the wealth that has poured into the island remains curiously invisible. There is virtually full employment and house prices are high. The wealth from the financial sector sustains the new emphasis on Manx culture and the nationalists grudgingly accept it. But there is a Faustian side to the bargain. The money from the financial services industry underpins the museums, the street signs in Manx, the festivals and the language teaching. At the same time, it draws waves of immigrants, further diluting what remains of the culture. The Manx face the same dilemma as the communities on the Outer Hebrides, in the Galway Gaeltacht, in west Wales and Cornwall. How far can they go, and how far will they be allowed to go, towards resisting the flow of English immigrants, second-home owners and pensioners without slipping into outright racism? The sheer number of immigrants to the Isle of Man means they face little pressure to adapt, and in a place where the local culture has already been diluted, a surge in incomers risks washing away whatever remains of older traditions. For every British immigrant who has learned Manx, at least 10 have not. As in Wales, many are refugees from English urban multiculturalism, searching for the all-white homogeneous Britain of the 1950s. These seekers after a vanished Britishness do not provide a happy hunting ground for Celtic activists to find supporters. A young Lancastrian couple I met in Douglas, with two children, knew nothing whatever about the Manx identity, the language, Sophia Morrison, Yn Cheshaght Ghailckagh, or the island's Celtic history, in spite of having lived there for several years. They told me quite simply that they had come to the island 'because it was white', and because they 'felt safe'. The Isle of Man is a magnet for such refugees and the Manx government will never try to limit the flow. It is too late now anyway, as recent British immigrants make up more than half the population.

The forces at play in Mona Douglas's 'sea-girt island' are those affecting all the peoples of the edge of Britain and France. The island is a microcosm of the whole. On the Isle of Man, a wave of British imperial culture washed over the local people, sweeping away the Gaelic culture that had grown up over the previous 1,500 years. As the British tide goes out, it ought to have left space for what was there before to return. But it has not, for what was there before has been squashed so effectively that it cannot regrow. It is not simply Manx that cannot regrow but the Manx-inspired English of a poet like T. E. Brown, whose work was described as 'a sort of escape-pipe for the mingled steam of English and Manx which was constantly generating in his own boiler'.[46] That sound cannot be generated any more, it can only be recreated in museum fashion, like the 'waulking' songs of the Outer Hebrides.

The Isle of Man is like Skye in that respect. The sprouting of bilingual street signs and museums disguises a vacuum. Working silently against the prospect of a local cultural revival is the constant inflow from multi-racial England of people many of whom have fled west precisely to avoid the challenge of diversity. They are not so much hostile as indifferent to – in fact unconscious of – the island's cultural heritage. They are like the man in his sixties I sat next to in the Manx Airways plane from London, who said he had emigrated for the golf and the 'quiet'. It is an almost ominous word, this longed-for 'quiet', and not one likely to awaken the spirit of the God-King Mananan.

PART TWO

CHAPTER FIVE

North Wales
'The dear old language of the country'

*In these latter days Celtic patriotism has leapt from the cold ashes of a dead
apathy into a vivid sentient, burning flame*
(J. J. Wallis Jones, in *The University College of Wales*, 1896)[1]

The sun arched low over Llanrhaeadr-ym-Mochnant. Above, a kite circled
on the air currents. Rooks cawed in the trees and swallows wheeled and
screamed over the rooftops. On a late summer's day William Morgan might
not have recognised much of the village he served as parish priest in the late
sixteenth century, but the church of St Dogfan has not changed wholly since
his time. It is very much an old Celtic church, squatting unobtrusively
beside one of the rushing streams that the Celts so often chose as a place of
worship. Vicar Morgan might have meditated beside that stream on a day
like this – still and peaceful, with a hint of autumn coolness – as he continued his mammoth task of translating the Bible into Welsh. A few miles away
lies the Rhaedr Pystil waterfall. I wondered if one of the 'seven wonders of
Wales', as it is called, had claimed Morgan's attention as he struggled to find
the right term in in a jumble of Welsh dialects for a particular phrase of the
Old Testament. Had he broken the tedious hours spent poring over manuscripts in a dark study, strewn with books, inkpots, tracts and letters from the
Archbishop of Canterbury, to stump off towards the Pystil, followed at a
distance by a gaggle of awestruck children and parishioners, half amused and
half honoured by the presence of such a scholar? Perhaps he never gave it a
thought, for Morgan lived before the Romantic movement made nature
worthy of such attention.

Llanrhaeadr-ym-Mochnant remains deeply Welsh even though it does
not lie deep inside Wales. Oswestry in England is 12 miles away. This is a
racial and linguistic border zone, where the territories of the Celts shade
into those of the Anglo-Saxons. Yet it has retained its Welshness and Welsh
services continue in St Dogfan's, while Welsh signs hang over shop

fronts and restaurants. English dominates casual talk in the post office and the pub, but on a Sunday morning Welsh is heard in the streets as the congregation leaves the Nonconformist chapel. Chapel culture is in decline, as it is everywhere in Wales, and several chapels have been converted into private homes but if Llanrhaeadr is losing its old identity the process is not complete.

Geography does not explain why it is not more anglicised. The village lies at the dead end of the Terat valley that ends at the waterfall. But lack of industry and a degree of physical isolation from the main thoroughfares leading to England do not tell the whole story. The border county of Radnorshire is almost entirely rural and no major transport routes run through it, but it has become effectively English. By the mid-1860s only a few old people spoke Welsh in the main town of Rhayader. It would have been ironic if Llanrhaeadr had followed the example of the villages of Radnorshire, for it was here that a whole culture was rescued from potential oblivion by the efforts of William Morgan.

The Welsh long ago abandoned the church that Morgan served. They grew to loathe 'the alien church', as they called it. It was 'anti-Welsh in its sentiment and it is utterly out of touch with the faith and hope of the Welsh people',[2] a Nonconformist minister wrote in 1907, adding: 'The Celtic church in its spirit lives today in the Nonconformity of Wales.' But they did not reject the memory of Morgan. In August 1892 a crowd attended the unveiling of a tercentenary monument to his 1588 translation of the Bible into Welsh in St Asaph, the cathedral town where he died in 1604. The stone monument that stands outside the cathedral was embellished with the words Morgan had chosen for the dedicatory preface to Elizabeth I: *Religio enim, nisis vulgari lingua educator, ignola latihabit* – 'for religion will lie hidden and unknown unless it is taught in the vulgar tongue'. The monument, paid for by people from Wales to Australia, included an effigy of the Bishop, but not him alone, for the Welsh Bible was a joint enterprise. Beside Morgan stand William Salesbury, Richard Davies, Thomas Huet, Gabriel Goodman, Richard Parry, John Davies and Archdeacon Prys.

William Salesbury and Richard Davies, Bishop of St Davids, were responsible for an earlier translation of the New Testament and the Book of Common Prayer in 1567. Huet, Precentor of St Davids cathedral, worked on the Book of Revelation. Prys worked on the Psalms, Goodman, Dean of Westminster, revised Morgan's proofs, while Bishop Parry was responsible for a subsequent edition of the Bible in the 1620s with the help of the Renaissance scholar John Davies.

The monument to Morgan and his colleagues was unveiled when Welsh pride had reached its apex and the work initiated by the future bishop in Llanrhaeadr seemed to have been fulfilled. Welsh Wales was seldom so confident of its future as in the 1890s. As the magazine *Young Wales* wrote in 1895: 'Our prestige as a nation was never so high and the recognition of our national individuality never so marked and thorough.'[3] The language Morgan helped rescue from obscurity, which in the 1840s was still treated by the English as a disagreeable patois, had undergone an astonishing revival. The 1890s marked the heyday of a Welsh press that was nationalist in politics and militantly Nonconformist in religion. The number of English-speakers was growing, especially in industrial South Wales, but so was the number of Welsh-speakers, so much so that in 1885 it was boasted that the million Welsh-speakers would number 3 million by 1985.

The creation of a university in Aberystwyth in 1885 confirmed the new dawn. The fact that its foundation was boycotted by most of the anglicised gentry turned the act of raising the subscription into a popular enterprise. Two colliery owners, David and Lewis Davies, contributed most of the £12,000 raised by 1872. But at 'University Sunday' collections in the chapels the people made the business of raising funds a patriotic crusade. 'The Celtic idealism of the Welsh people will be guided into the right paths,' predicted W. J. Wallis-Jones, describing the university's likely impact on society in *The University College of Wales* in 1896. The students 'will be taught how to use those peculiar gifts of the Celtic genius for the best interest of themselves and their native country'.[4] 'Few, I think, will deny that in these latter days Celtic patriotism has leapt from the cold ashes of a dead apathy into a vivid sentient, burning flame,'[5] he wrote.

Aberystwyth's mutation into a Celtic Athens was one of many hopeful developments. Resentment of landlords and of the payment of tithes to the Established Church was as almost as strong in Wales as in Ireland, but in 1892 the Liberal Prime Minister, William Gladstone, had agreed to a land commission to investigate the wrongs of landlordism. Sectarianism – the bane of the great nineteenth-century Nonconformist revival – was on the wane. In parliament, Cymru Fydd, 'the Wales that is to be', had since the late 1880s harnessed the energies of Welsh Liberalism to non-violent nationalism. Its founder, Tom Ellis, MP for Merioneth, was compared often to Parnell. After Ellis left Wales to become Chief Whip in 1892 the role of national hero devolved on his junior colleague, David Lloyd George, MP for Caernarfon, who was likened to the medieval champions of Welsh independence. He was a man, *Young Wales* declared in 1895, 'who believes with the soul's passion in the sacredness of Welsh nationalism'.[6] To the MP Llewelyn Williams, he was the most important Welshman to wield power in England since Llywelyn the Great, the thirteenth-century prince who united most of Wales under his rule. He was 'the statesman who redressed the wrongs of Wales', averred Williams, adding: 'Mention Mister Lloyd George and you not only get the whole audience cheering but when the clamour has died down, you hear isolated voices, thrilling with excitement and pride crying out *Cymru am byth*' (Wales for ever).[7]

In 1887 the Liberals bowed to their Welsh supporters by adopting disestablishment of the Church of England in Wales as party policy. Preoccupied with Ireland, Gladstone initially refused to support it. Wales and Ireland, he told parliament in 1871, had different histories and while Irish estrangement from the Established Church was ancient and bitter, the Welsh phenomenon stemmed from the intrusion of Englishmen into Welsh sees after the 1688 Revolution. 'So long as the sympathies of the nation were cultivated, the Church of Wales was perfectly acceptable to the people of Wales,'[8] he said.

But on 20 February 1891 the 'Grand Old Man' rose to announce he was now persuaded that it was impossible to resist the democratic claim of the Nonconformist majority. 'The people of England . . . will give and will insist on giving to Wales in respect of her reasonable demands the same just equitable and conclusive settlement which in the like circumstances I believe they would claim for themselves,'[9] he said. The Welsh repaid the great man's concession with a loyalty that approached adulation. To Ellis he was 'more Celtic than the Celts, more Cymric than the Welsh themselves'.[10]

The cause had gained over the previous 30 years as successive Nonconformist revivals battered Welsh allegiance to Morgan's Church into dust, leaving only a quarter of the population Anglicans. Disestablishment became a national cause and when Lloyd George made his first speech in England outside parliament as an MP in 1890 in the London Tabernacle, disestablishment was his topic. 'The Nonconformist chapels are crowded, but the churches of the Establishment are forsaken in every rural district in Wales,' he said.

> It is the same old story – it is not the people who do the work who receive the pay. In fact, it is a very old story! If you recollect, it was Elisha who cleansed Naaman's leprosy but Gehazi who secured the emoluments. It was Nonconformity that cleaned the moral leprosy which had afflicted Wales under the quack doctoring of the Established Church, but it is the Gehazi of the Establishment that is enjoying the emoluments![11]

As the young firebrand's tone showed, the change in the balance of power between the denominations in Wales had altered their political outlook. No longer cautiously conservative, the Nonconformists, especially the Calvinist Methodists, had become assertive. The bicentenary of St Bartholomew's Day in 1662, when the Puritan ministers had been expelled from their parish churches after the fall of the Commonwealth, turned into a rally of the Puritans' heirs. That the Puritans had not been much loved in Wales at the time was forgotten. Gladstone's disestablishment of the Church of Ireland in 1869 spurred on the Welsh. If Anglican supremacy could be overturned in Ireland, why not in Wales? In the 1870s, Liberalism and Nonconformity advanced together in Wales under the banner of disestablishment. As in Ireland, the revolt against the Established Church was part of a nationalist awakening. But in Wales disestablishment gained a grip on the popular imagination that it never had in Ireland. As *Young Wales* noted in 1895: 'Disestablishment . . . is as supremely important to Wales as Home Rule to Ireland.' The first bills to dismantle the 'alien church' in Wales predictably failed, but few Welsh observers in the 1890s doubted they would be denied their wishes for long.

William Morgan might have winced at the sight of a crowd composed mostly of dissenters unveiling a monument to the devoted sons of the Church of England, for a strange reversal had certainly taken place. In his time Wales had been won to the Church of England and Protestantism had revived and refashioned Welsh nationhood. That the cause of Welsh nationality should have come to be identified with the Church's enemies would have amazed the Vicar of Llanrhaeadr-ym-Mochnant in the 1580s.

The religious history of Morgan's homeland had followed that of neighbouring Ireland. Anglo-Normans conquered both lands in the twelfth and thirteenth centuries. The Irish rebelled in 1315. The Welsh followed in 1400, under Owain Glyn Dwr. For more than a decade much of north-west Wales was free from English rule, but at a cost. 'All the whole country was then but a forrest,' wrote the Tudor historian Sir John Wynn, 'and then waste of inhabitants and all overgrown with woods; for Owen Glyndwr's warres beginning in 1400 continued 15 years, which brought such desolation that green grass grew in the market place.'[12] As in Ireland, the suppression of the revolt was followed by the imposition of laws to separate the races and subjugate the natives. The Statutes of Kilkenny in Ireland in the 1360s had their counterpart in Wales in Henry IV's law of 1402, which forbade the Welsh to assemble, hold public office, or marry the English. As in Ireland, bards and rhymers were repressed. 'No wastrel, rhymer, minstrel or vagabond shall be in any way sustained in the land of Wales to make *kymorthas* [elegies],' the law said.

During the 1480s, the paths of Wales and Ireland diverged. The name of Henry Tudor meant nothing to the Irish but the Welsh imagination was inspired by the new claimant to the throne who was of Welsh ancestry. The Welsh had long cherished prophecies about Merlin and Arthur, the ancient British champion against the Saxons, who though defeated, was not killed and would return to avenge ancient wrongs. This lore had gained a strong following among the Norman aristocracy, too. It was the Norman Bishop of Lincoln who had encouraged Geoffrey of Monmouth to write his *Prophecies of Merlin* in the 1130s and it was to the Norman Earl of Gloucester that Geoffrey dedicated his hugely influential *History of the Kings of Britain*. The parvenu Norman barons wanted pedigrees, class and 'heritage'. The Welsh wanted a message of hope. Both despised the Anglo-Saxons. As one scholar of Geoffrey's work put it: 'The Anglo-Norman historians were interested in promulgating the view that their new possessions in England had a dignified and ancient past, reaching far beyond the Saxon plantation.'[13] As for the Welsh, the *Vita Edwardi Secundi* noted: 'From the sayings of the prophet Merlin they still hope to recover England.'[14]

Henry Tudor courted such associations. Born in Pembroke Castle, but exiled for 14 years to the Breton court, he was steeped in the Arthurian cult and the myths contained in Monmouth's *History* concerning the struggle between the red dragon of the Celts and the white dragon of the Anglo-Saxons. When he returned from Brittany to challenge Richard III his landing at Milford Haven in South Wales seemed like the fulfilment of prophecy. Henry obliged, promising to deliver the Welsh 'from such miserable servitudes as they have piteously long stood in',[15] and when his army mustered for victory on Bosworth Field, the red dragon was displayed among the banners.

The Welsh had exaggerated hopes of the future Henry VII. As one modern historian has written, the Welsh read rather more into Tudor's Welshness than he did himself. 'It was not a matter of the Tudors identifying with the Welsh, but rather of the Welsh identifying themselves with the Tudors.' Once established in London, the new King named his eldest son Arthur 'in honour of the British race',[16] and after Arthur's marriage to Catherine of Aragon in 1501, sent the couple to Ludlow, seat of the Council of the Marches, to give the Welsh a taste of royalty. But Henry VII was not the hoped-for Celtic tribune. He had his pedigree composed to link him to the Welsh hero Cadwalladr the Great but the business of being an English king came first. He gave favours to Welshmen but not to Wales. The old penal laws were scrapped but as in Ireland, such concessions were made in the interests of uniformity, a trend that accelerated under his son, Henry VIII.[17] In 1536 all court sessions were ordered to be held in English and it was laid down that 'no persons that use the Welsh language shall have any office or fees in England or Wales upon pain of forfeiting the same, unless they use the English language'. By the end of the 1530s the merger of Wales and England was completed by the creation of new counties and the allocation of seats for Welsh MPs in the English parliament.

The English Reformation broke over a church in Wales that had been heavily anglicised since Glyn Dwr's revolt. As in Ireland, the crown reacted to the rebellious sympathies of the native clergy by appointing English bishops. The Church in Wales was worse off than its Irish counterpart in this respect, as it had no ecclesiastical autonomy. The Irish had reformed their Church before the Norman invasion and established their own primatial see in Armagh. The English crown could impose English bishops on Irish sees but not abolish its separate identity. But attempts to establish a metropolitan see at St Davids had come to nothing and after the Norman Conquest the crown treated the four Welsh bishoprics at Llandaff, St Davids, St Asaph and Bangor as part of 'Ecclesia Anglicana'. As Gladstone later remarked, the term 'Church of England in Wales' was a misnomer. 'There is really no church in Wales,' he said in 1870. 'The Welsh sees are simply four sees held by the suffragans of the Archbishop of Canterbury.'[18] The pre-Reformation bishops were often English, or Europeans appointed by papal provision. The last pre-Reformation bishop of Llandaff was Catherine of Aragon's Spanish confessor. This was a full-time job that left the Bishop's distant Welsh diocese unguarded. His suffragans were of low quality. One of them, John Smart, was accused of selling holy orders in 1529.[19]

The Welsh religious houses appear to have been past their peak in the 1530s, which may shed light on popular indifference to their suppression. 'All that can be said with safety', the historian Glanmor Williams remarked of the Welsh religious houses, 'is that if the infrequency with which they appear in contemporary accounts is any guide, then they can hardly be said to have been making any profound impression on contemporary piety and devotion.'[20] The Welsh did not actively oppose the closure of the religious houses and the dismantling of the shrines in 1538. Even the introduction of the first English Prayer Book in 1549, which triggered a revolt in Cornwall, drew little response.

William Morgan's house still stands in the parish of Penmachno and on the morning I walked there from the nearby village, I fancied that the simple stone farmstead known as Ty Mawr, 'the big house', looked much as it might have done when Morgan was born there in 1545. Of course it does not, for the single-storey open-hearth farmhouse was rebuilt after Morgan's time into a storeyed house with chimneys. Nor would Morgan recognise the relative comfort of the furniture inside, for as one historian of the house remarked, most rural Welsh households of the time had no table, bedstead or chairs and even a house like Ty Mawr would not have displayed the oak dressers and grandfather clocks now thought so traditional, for they had not yet appeared on the scene.[21] The view outside has also changed, for the valley may well have been more populated in Morgan's childhood, when it lay on the drovers' road that led to the major cattle fairs of England.

Morgan's parents, John and Lowri, were probably tenant farmers of the Wynns of Gwydir, where William seems to have received his early education. Like many ambitious, intelligent Welsh people of his generation, he embraced full-blooded Protestantism at university, in his case St John's in Cambridge, to which he went up in 1565. Appointed to the vicarage of Llanbadarn Fawr in St Davids diocese in 1572, where he served under Bishop Richard Davies, he transferred to Welshpool in 1575 before moving to Llanrhaeadr-ym-Mochnant in 1578. By then the Protestant Reformation was starting to exert a profound impact on Welsh culture. Although Elizabeth I often imposed unpopular and unsuitable Englishmen as bishops in Ireland, she was more discerning when it came to Welsh sees. Hugh Jones, her first appointment to Llandaff in 1566, was the first Welsh bishop to occupy that see for 300 years while Morgan's first bishop, Richard Davies, appointed to St Asaph in 1560 and St Davids in 1561, was another significant choice. After seeing out Mary's reign in Calvinist Geneva, Davies was appointed as commissioner to visit the Welsh dioceses when Elizabeth came to the throne. The promotion of committed Protestants like Davies who were also patriotic Welshmen helped make the Reformation palatable to Welsh opinion.

The Queen did more than promote Welsh-speakers to key dioceses. In 1563 parliament ordered the translation of the Bible and Book of Common Prayer into Welsh from English, 'the which tongue is not understood by the greatest number of Her Majesty's most loving and obedient subjects inhabiting the country of Wales who are therefore utterly destituted of God's holy word'. The job was entrusted to the bishops of Bangor, St Asaph, St Davids, Llandaff and Hereford who were told to translate the books into 'the British or Welsh tongue' and ensure that copies were placed in all cathedrals and parish churches by 1 March 1566.

Only Davies was competent in Greek, Latin and Welsh, which is why William Salesbury was brought in. Another strong Protestant, Salesbury had been won to the reformed Church at Oxford, where he was a protégé of John Jewel, later Bishop of Salisbury. Salesbury's commitment to his native language was evident at Oxford, where alongside tracts against the papacy he compiled a Welsh-English dictionary and a guide to pronouncing 'the letters in the British tong (now com'enly called Walsh)'. A good friend of Davies's, he finished his work in 1567, based on Beza's Geneva Bible and the Greek New Testament. Bishop Davies's dedicatory preface to the Queen, *Epistol at y Cembru*, was artful propaganda, selling the reformed religion to the Welsh not as an English religious revolution but as a return to an older British order. Welsh opinion was flattered by the suggestion that the Anglo-Saxons had corrupted the faith of the ancient Britons. As Glanmor Williams put it: 'It met head on the criticism that the Reformation represented an alien, English creed' and held up Wales as a land where the British faith had been defended against Anglo-Saxon popery.

The translations of Salesbury and Davies did not meet with general approval, however, for they had used scholastic, sometimes incomprehensible, terms, which is why the cry went up in the 1570s for a new Welsh Bible and Prayer Book. Again the project benefited from the active support of the government, above all John Whitgift, former bishop of the border diocese of Hereford and since 1583 Archbishop of Canterbury. Whitgift became a key figure in the enterprise and may have financed the publication of the new Welsh Bible in 1588, when 800 to 1,000 copies were produced. Morgan was promoted for his contribution, moving to the bishopric of Llandaff in 1595 and to St Asaph in 1601, where he died three years later.

The Elizabethan Welsh reformers planted Protestantism among the Welsh with success. Rome's negligence helped them. The Catholic Church made less effort to retain the Welsh than the Irish and a combination of Catholic lethargy and Protestant activity condemned the old religion by the end of the century. Morgan's Bible rescued Welsh from probable oblivion. In Cornwall, which revolted against the English Prayer Book in 1549, the failure to have the scriptures or the liturgy translated into Cornish was the most important factor behind the decay of the language in the seventeenth century. In Wales the Vicar of Llanrhaeadr ensured a different outcome. As one nineteenth-century historian said, he 'found the Welsh vernacular a congeries of dialects and spellings, some of them deserving only of death, and he left it a language that has held its place with increasing estimation during a period of three hundred years.'[22]

The saviours of Welsh were not saints. As Chancellor of St Davids, Huet vandalised his country's cultural heritage. In 1571 he discovered a bundle of concealed 'masse books, hympnalls, Grailes, Antiphons and such like . . . [and] caused the said ungodly books to be canceld and torne in pieces in the Vestrie before his face.'[23] Bishop Davies was corrupt, alienating church leases to his family. This was common practice among Tudor bishops but it does not excuse him. They were a quarrelsome lot, each thinking he alone knew the precise word for whatever biblical phrase they were trying to translate. Salesbury eulogised Davies as 'a second Daniel' when he was translating the scriptures but they fell out later. Bishop Morgan was also disputatious, 'naturally inclined to contention and strife', it was said, with a tendency rather to 'prosecute vain and frivolous suits of law than to edify his parishioners'.[24] The people of Llanrhaeadr-ym-Mochnant may not have thought much of him after all.

But the translators deserved their monument in the nineteenth century. They were men of vision. As Morgan put it in his dedication to Elizabeth I: 'Faith indeed comes by hearing and hearing by the word of God: a word that until now has only barely sounded in the ears of our fellow-countrymen, as it is hidden in a foreign tongue.'[25] The men of the Irish Reformation tore up the Catholic Church without putting much in its place. Cashel Cathedral, ruined and roofless, is an appropriate monument to a Church that never became the people's church. In Wales, things of beauty were taken away but something new was put in their place. Morgan and his comrades brought the Church in Wales closer to the people, not further away, and as the language revived, they saw the hand of providence in recent history. 'One cannot at all believe God would have willed the preservation of this language in the face of so many disasters,' said John Davies, chief helper to Bishop Parry in his 1620 revision, 'had he not also ordained that his name should be called upon in this language.'[26]

In a side street off the centre of Llangeitho, a statue of Daniel Rowlands stands forlorn and neglected outside the chapel. The chapel did not appear closed when I passed but nothing outside the building pointed to signs of life within. There was no board advertising service times. A woman living nearby gave me a key with seeming reluctance and let me inside. A stack of hymn books lay at the front. Apparently a service was to take place at 5.30 that afternoon. 'Does anyone attend?' I asked the woman. 'Yes,' was the monosyllabic answer. My prompt departure was clearly sought. In fact, I had no desire to stay for what clearly was going to be a small gathering. Nothing about this desultory place suggested the past history of Llangeitho, when it had been a Methodist mecca – a place of pilgrimage with a popularity to rival that of any medieval Catholic shrine. All that remained was the statue of Rowlands, standing in the long grass, with the words, 'Heaven! Heaven! Heaven!' inscribed in Welsh on the base.

It is hard to believe it today, as they have been virtually forgotten, but Rowlands and his friend Howel Harris presided over a cultural revolution every bit as important as Morgan's. Nonconformity owed its rise in Wales to the decay of the energies that Davies, Morgan and Parry had helped to harness in the sixteenth century. The Stuarts in the seventeenth century felt the same residual affection for Scotland that the Tudors had felt for Wales, and one of the results of this was the promotion of Scottish candidates to Irish and Welsh sees. Under James I and Charles I a growing number of Welsh bishops were foreigners – a return to pre-Reformation practice. The reissue of the Welsh Prayer Book in 1621 and the Bible in 1630 showed a continuing commitment to Anglicanism with a Welsh face but the Stuart bishops of Llandaff – Godwin, Carleton, Field, Murray and Owen – were all English or Scottish men who naturally anglicised their dioceses.

Morgan's Welsh bibles saved the language from extinction as the translations 'fixed the language', so to speak. But it was only a partial dam against the spread of English. In the 1580s the Welsh Puritan John Penry claimed English was becoming the tongue of most market towns, and that in Pembrokeshire 'there is no great store of Welsh'.[27] Tudor commentators noted the allure of English and a contempt among the Welsh for their own tongue. 'Our own countrymen [are] . . . so attached to anything that is foreign and exotic,' John David Rhys wrote in *Cambrobritannicae Cymricaeae Linguae Institutiones*, 'and consequently so different from most other nations that if they have been but a short time out of the country they pretend to have forgotten their native language.'[28]

The Welsh bibles were expensive for ordinary people and not intended for private use. The 800 to 1,000 copies of Morgan's Bible were designed to match the number of parishes in Wales. The few leather-bound volumes left over, priced at £1 a piece, were out of reach for most people. Even the bibles that were distributed to parishes were not necessarily used much, for the Church in Wales, as in Ireland, was poor and lack of money prevented it from repairing material damage or paying for preachers. Babington, Bishop of Llandaff from 1591 to 1595, joked that he was only the bishop of 'aff'[29] and described his cathedral as a 'desolate and profane place'.[30] A poor church was by definition lumbered with a high proportion of absentee clergy who never preached. Of 134 clergy in St Asaph diocese in 1587, only three were resident. The Bishop of Bangor's visitation in 1623 showed that most parishes still had no resident clergy. Those who were resident were often low-grade pastors. At Diwygfylchi Edward Jones had turned his churchyard into a cornfield and put 'hives of bees in the church to be kept'. The Vicar of Aberdaron, Griffith Piers, was an alcoholic; once he had been too 'overseen by drink' even to bury a dead child.[31]

The popular *Candle for the Welshman*, written between 1615 and the 1630s, voiced the growing dissatisfaction of Welsh people with their religious condition. The author, Rhys Prichard, Vicar of Llandovery and Chancellor of St Davids cathedral, was a staunch royalist and loyal to his church. But the marrow of his religious poems, attacking dancing, smoking, drinking, the profane use of the Sabbath and lazy clergymen, echoed the complaints of puritan-minded people all over England and Wales. We have to be careful about the poems, as they were published after Prichard's death in 1644 and may have been doctored before publication to reflect the taste of a Puritan readership. But they clearly touched a raw nerve, as they were repeatedly republished after the Commonwealth was overthrown, running into 14 editions from 1658 to 1730.

The popularity of Prichard's censures did not mean the Welsh were ready to abandon the Church. During the Commonwealth, the Puritan advance was limited. The bulk of the converts were in the English-speaking pockets of the south, in the Gower peninsula, in Monmouthshire, and parts of Glamorganshire.

But although Morgan's Church survived the Cromwellian interlude, it frittered away its hold on the people after the Restoration when, as Gladstone said, the real problems began. There were a few notable bishops like William Lloyd, Bishop of St Asaph in the 1680s, who resisted anglicisation and demanded a knowledge of Welsh from his clergy. But Lloyd was not typical. Thomas Watson, appointed to St Davids in 1687 and deprived in 1699, was 'one of the worst men in all respects that I ever knew in holy order', Gilbert Burnet, Bishop of Salisbury and historian, said, 'passionate, covetous and false in the blackest instances, without any virtue or good qualities to balance his many bad ones'.[32] Edward Jones, Lloyd's successor in St Asaph from 1692, sold livings through his housekeeper, Mrs Burdett, who was little better than a pimp. When Griffith Williams wanted the living of Tremeirchion, 'he waited on Mrs Burdett at the Bishop's house at St Asaph who asked him what he would give to succeed at Tremeirchion, intimating to him that she had been offered 20 pounds for it.'[33] The Bishop was suspended in 1701 but not deprived. Watson and Jones were spotted and condemned.

The process of rot was so gentle that few noticed its slow advance. The incorporation of the Welsh dioceses into the Church in England meant Wales had no independent voice, and with no monarch to promote Welsh candidates the Whig-controlled machinery of government patronage led to an English takeover. As one Welsh church historian wrote of St Davids diocese in the eighteenth century: 'Nearly every remunerative post or benefice was held by Englishmen, usually absentees, who were careless and ignorant of the spiritual requirements of the parishes . . . the diocese was a mere stepping stone for Englishmen.'[34] In fact, 17 Englishmen were appointed to St Davids during the century, of whom 12 were translated to English sees.

In 1721, Erasmus Saunders described the ruined state of St Davids:

In some places we have churches without Chancels; in others we have some piece of a Church, that is, one End, or a Side Isle. In Some, not only the bells are taken away but the Towers are demolished . . . Did you, I say, see these general Desolations of our noble Cathedral and collegiate churches . . . it might well tempt you to think we had lain in the Road of the Turks and Saracens in some of their wild excursions.

The spiritual condition of the people was no better, he said. Services had ceased altogether in many places, or were held at no fixed times.

Devoid of instruction, the mass of people clung to a jumble of half-remembered Catholic practices and semi-pagan beliefs. Back in 1646, John Lewis of Glasrug in Cardigan, in *The Parliament Explained to Wales*, had complained of the way the Welsh continued to call upon saints in their prayers and blessings, as well as visiting holy wells. By the 1720s, Saunders indicated, little had changed. The nominally Protestant Welsh still prayed to the Virgin Mary and crossed themselves, 'with a short Ejaculation that thro' the Cross of Christ they may be safe', he wrote. 'At the Feast of the Nativity of Our Lord . . . they then come to church about Cock-crowing, and bring either candles or Torches with them, which they set to burn, every one upon the Grave of his departed Friend.' Holy wells linked to the cult of saints were frequented 'and there being not only churches and Chappels but Springs and fountains dedicated to those Saints, they do at certain times go and bath themselves in them and sometimes leave some small Oblations behind them'.[35]

The Welsh retained beliefs in fairies, apparitions, corpse candles and omens. The *History of the Principality of Wales* of 1695 remarked on the general faith in apparitions and premonitions of death such as corpse candles, 'which are so ordinary in these Counties that scarce any dye, either young or old, but this is seen before death'. Dwarves or elves, called knockers, were 'often heard and seen in the shape of men little statured, about half a yard long'.

Saunders blamed the appointment of Englishmen to Welsh bishoprics and vicarages for the Reformation's thwarted progress after almost two centuries of Protestantism. Making the case for a change in policy, he said the Welsh had 'by Experience learn'd the Inconveniences and Discouragements that attend a Conquer'd Language; yet as Christians from our brethren of the same Church and Faith we humbly hope there is that compassion owing to us to be allowed to serve God rationally, and this we can hardly be said to do when we must join in a Service unintelligible.'[36]

The religious revival that followed shortly after Saunders's lament for the state of the Church in St Davids burst the banks of the Established Church. In England a complacent and politicised Church experienced great difficulty in absorbing the energy generated by Wesley's revival, but it absorbed just enough to retain its place as the Church of the bulk of the population. In Wales and Cornwall it did not. There the great mass of the people, drawing perhaps on inarticulate feelings of hostility to the Anglican Church as a specifically English religion, simply threw off their allegiance to it, never to return.

This was not due to any design on the part of the dawn stars of the revival in Wales – or Cornwall. Griffith Jones, Rector of Llanddowror, started the first Welsh 'circulating schools' in 1730 with the support of the Anglican SPCK. Howel Harris and Daniel Rowlands were also devoted churchmen. Harris, born in Trefecca in 1714, remained an Anglican layman to the end of his life. Leaving Oxford in 1735 he returned to Wales, where he gained a reputation as a preacher. He met John Wesley's associate, George Whitefield, in Cardiff in 1739 and the religious societies he formed in Wales were modelled on the 'Methodist' societies that Wesley and Whitefield had established. Like the two Englishmen, Harris intended his societies to help the Established Church in its mission, not rival it. The first Methodist Association in Wales was held in Llandeusant in Carmarthen in 1743 while a second meeting on 6 April divided Wales into districts and established monthly and quarterly associations. Within a few years of the foundation of Harris's first association in the 1740s there were about 140 Calvinist Methodist societies in South Wales alone.

As Wesley discovered in Cornwall, attempts to revive the Church of England among the poor through public preaching encountered opposition, even if it was less fierce than later hagiographers of the movement made out. The local gentry and the clergy encouraged mobbing. At Newport, so Harris complained, 'the mob rushed upon us with the utmost rage and fury. They tore both the sleeves off my coat . . . while some pelted me with apples and dirt, others threw stones. I received one blow on my forehead.' At Monmouth, he added, 'The mob pelted us with apples, pears, stones and a dead dog.' He was attacked again at Bala. He was not put off in the slightest. At Swindon, in Wiltshire, he remarked that 'when they presented a gun to my forehead, my soul was happy'.[37] Like Wesley, Harris was a tireless traveller, telling one correspondent that he covered 150 miles in a week for nine weeks in a row, and talked to crowds twice to four times daily in public.

There simply was not room in such a small organisation for two such larger-than-life personalities as Harris and Rowlands, each with his own following. After a quarrel between the two erupted in 1751 Harris withdrew to a religious community at Trefecca called 'The Family'. Although he remained an Anglican until his death in 1773, the outlines of a distinct denomination began to appear. Denied the use of the parish churches, or unable to use them because they were too small, the revivalists became a separate denomination because they had no other choice. Rowlands's own experience was illuminating. For almost three decades he was the Church of England curate of Llangeitho until his bishop withdrew his licence for the crime of preaching outside his parish. As his own son held the living, he was left in the strange position of retaining a home in the parish rectory while being denied use of the parish church. It was a good example of how the Church in Wales committed suicide.

Rowlands died in 1790. By then the Methodists, or Calvinist Methodists as they were known, were heading for total separation from the Church, though they had to wait until 1811 for the formal split, when several men were ordained to administer communion and baptism.

From the start the Calvinist Methodists were distinctively and unapologetically Welsh. The old dissenters had spoken English in Wales. Theirs was a religion of the English borderlands and the anglicised pockets of the south coast. The Calvinist Methodists, by contrast, took nonconformity to the heart of Welsh-speaking North Wales. They did not merely accept Welshness but took pride in it. To Harris's biographer, John Bulmer, English was good enough for English preachers but was no language for a Welshman to preach in. 'When a Welshman preaches to an English congregation, he is like Samson when shorn of those mysterious locks on which depend his usual strength,' he said. 'When preaching in that language is required of them, they consider it as barren ground; and that their labours are not so successful as among the Welsh is but too evident to the most common observers.'

The preachers were the real successors of Bishop Morgan and made the Welsh scriptures part of the warp and woof of ordinary life. The Calvinist Methodist Peter Williams who joined the Church in 1746 did much to spread religious literature in Welsh, producing a print run of 3,600 copies of a Welsh family Bible in 1770 and further editions in 1779 and 1796. Thomas Charles was another dynamic convert who joined the Methodists in 1785. He re-founded the Welsh 'circulating schools' begun under Griffith Jones in the 1740s, which had lapsed after Jones's death in 1761. After nine years, in 1794 he employed some 20 teachers in five counties, each paid £10 a year. 'We move them from place to place all over the country,' he wrote, 'and teach all that will attend them, rich or poor, gratis . . . the only intention of these schools is to teach children to read their *own language* and to instruct them in the first principles of religion'.[38] Charles visited the schools himself, 'these little seminaries', as he called them, where he would catechise the children in public.

Charles of Bala was one of the indefatigable products of the religious revolution in Wales and like every true revolutionary, he could not bear to sit still. He set up a printing press in Bala to produce Welsh religious literature, but then complained to his London evangelical friends that a chronic shortage of Welsh bibles remained. The British and Foreign Bible Society was the fruit of his agitation. With its wealthy English backers, this society was able to satisfy the demand for Welsh bibles as never before. The cheap editions it produced enjoyed enormous popularity among the poor people who could now read, thanks partly to the 'circulating schools' and other charity schools. The cart that carried these popular editions of the Bible into the villages was received with euphoria. 'The Welsh peasants went out in crowds to meet it, welcomed it as the Israelites did the Ark of old, drew it into the town and eagerly bore off the copies as rapidly as they could be dispersed.'[39] The Bible now became part of the dowry of the average housewife. 'The Welsh bride in the humblest walks of life', it was said, 'does not feel that her little room has been completely furnished until she has lying on her chest of drawers a well-bound copy of Peter Williams' Bible.'

A characteristic of Calvinist Methodists was their lack of doctrine. Welsh nonconformity was more a moral than a doctrinal movement. Harris endorsed Whitefield's broad Calvinism over the Arminianism that Wesley preached but beyond that Welsh Methodists were remarkably unideological. They had no confession for decades until the *Rules of Discipline* were published in 1801 and a confession drawn up in 1823 in Aberystwyth and Bala. Of the 34 rules they then adopted, only six had an obvious connection with theology. Most were practical guides to good living. Welsh Methodists were not to consult wizards (Rule 22), trade in smuggled goods (Rule 15), swear (Rule 13), get drunk (Rule 11), default on payments (Rule 21), abuse family members or servants (Rule 26), wear flashy clothes (Rule 12), or agitate against the government (Rule 16).

Welsh Nonconformists in the nineteenth century gained a reputation for obsessive teetotalism. It would have surprised their predecessors. The Baptists who attended their quarterly meetings in Cardigan in 1774 brought along wine and port to drink,[40] and much of their early preaching took place at inns. The Welsh Methodist rule book did not enjoin abstinence. Rule 11 said only that members ought to be 'temperate and sober in eating and drinking, neither a glutton nor a drunkard'.[41]

Nothing in the rule book suggested the Nonconformists were to become a force for political Liberalism. Rule 16 was very conservative in tone, urging Methodists to 'conscientiously honour and obey the King and all that are put in authority under him, showing all fidelity in word and deed to the government we happily live under'.

Nonconformity was dominated by the thirst for *hwyl,* or spirit. The new preachers introduced a new style of emotive, extempore sermon that was quite foreign to the Anglican tradition of precise intellectual discourses. As the biographer of the Baptist preacher Christmas Evans put it: 'Great Welsh preaching is very often a kind of wild irregular chant, a jubilant refrain, recurring again and again. The people catch the power of it; shouts rise – prayers! "*Bendigedig!*" [Blessed, or synonymous with our Bless the Lord!] . . . they too, have caught the *hwyl.*'[42] The cult of reason, dear to the Broad-Churchmen who dominated the Established Church after the 1688 Revolution, was altogether thrown out. The new sermons were long, dramatic performances. Rowlands preached for six hours at a stretch. Harris's words had a tremendous force. It was said that 'multitudes of strong muscular men have been forced unconsciously by the thundering eloquence and awful earnestness of Howell Harris to scream and faint away'.[43] The early preachers caused a sensation with this oratory but their successors took it to extremes. A certain kind of preacher arose who routinely 'fumes, sweats and gnashes his teeth like a madman . . . more like a bedlamist than a preacher'.[44]

The Methodist preachers inspired an ecstatic following that the clergy of the Established Church never enjoyed. They were the film stars of their era and the quarterly associations of the ministers, attended by huge crowds, were the pop concerts of the day. Like the Wesleyans in Cornwall, the Calvinist Methodists in Wales channelled energies that had been suppressed since the Reformation. Imitating the language of Catholic fraternities they revived the term 'brothers' for their overseers. They also revived the Catholic practice of confession, and compiled written records of the progress of the souls of penitents. They revived the Catholic tradition of pilgrimage, not to holy wells for physical healing, but to places like Llangeitho to hear star preachers and find spiritual healing. People travelled 60 miles or more to hear Daniel Rowlands preach, starting out on a Saturday and travelling through the night. On one occasion a group of 45 people from Carmarthen walked a hundred miles to hear him. Harris described one such tumultuous pilgrimage in October 1742. 'Such a sight mine eyes never saw,' he wrote to Whitefield.

> By hundreds ye People went from one parish Church to another, 3 miles, singing and rejoicing in God and so having communicated of ye Lords Supper together, came so many miles again tonight and I was enabled with Power . . . To discourse in the highway till 8 o'clock to near 2000, I believe, and such was ye rejoicing in Christ and washing his Feet with ye Tears of a broken Heart as I believe your Eyes seldom saw.[45]

Religious ecstasy and fainting, until then more a Catholic than a Protestant phenomenon, was part of the Calvinist Methodist pattern from the start. In Pembrokeshire Harris told Whitefield he found 'many ravish'd with the Love of Christ in Singing that they faint away . . . the door is opening wider and wider every where, and fresh life given'. Rowlands himself fainted at his own services. 'Once . . . while dwelling on the sufferings of the Saviour for us,' an observer wrote, 'he seemed to have him before his eye and exclaimed "Oh, those emptied veins! Oh, that pallid countenance!" and then, overwhelmed by emotion, he fainted away.'[46]

Like Catholics and unlike most Anglicans, Welsh Methodists encouraged a belief in God's active intervention in the world through miracles. A man who stoned Harris's preaching house in Bala fell from his horse and died. A clergyman who preached against Methodists near Penmorfa in Caernarfonshire lost his speech. A woman who persecuted Methodists at Penrhyndeudraeth near Ffestiniog was boiled alive when a pot of water fell on her.[47]

The religious revolution astonished Welsh observers as much as English visitors. The Morris brothers of Anglesey were stalwarts of the Welsh intelligentsia. In 1751 Richard and Lewis founded the Honourable Society of the Cymmrodorion as an intellectual club for the London Welsh community. It was devoted to the pursuits then in vogue among antiquarian societies, of publishing ancient documents and poems, holding dinners and performing rituals borrowed vaguely from the Freemasons. The Morrises were, in short, in tune with Welsh life. But the change in the religious temper of Wales bemused them. 'This country, which some few years ago might be said not to have six persons within it of any other persuasion than that of the Church of England is now full of Methodists, or Independents or Presbyterians, or some other sect, the Lord knows what,' William complained to Richard in 1745.

Richard agreed and urged the Bishop of Bangor to promote more Welsh-speaking clergy in 1752, to see off 'the mad Methodists who have in a manner bewitched the major part of ye inhabitants'.[48] Lewis, the leading light in the Cymmrodorion, scorned the idea that the Welsh were especially religious, insisting the façade of religiosity masked nothing more than a desire for entertainment. He told his brother William: 'I am positive if Mahomet had any dareing fellows to preach him here, he would gain ground immediately, or any merry religion like that. And if Sadlers Wells and the playhouses could be brought in as branches of a new religion it would have an abundance of converts and would take extremely well.'

Not everyone was so dismissive. Iolo Morganwg, the Glamorgan antiquarian and founder of the modern eisteddfods, praised the Nonconformist contribution to the cultural revival in South Wales. Sunday schools and 'circulating schools' had built up the Welsh language. 'The Welsh language is greatly increasing in Glamorgan as is already to be seen,' he wrote in the 1780s, 'and this in great part through the Welsh schools . . . and also very largely through the Dissenters who are one and all Welsh readers.'[49]

Like the Elizabethan reformers of Morgan's generation, the men of the eighteenth-century revival took with one hand and gave with the other. There were no longer missals or statues to destroy but the Welsh evangelical preachers, like the evangelicals in the Scottish Highlands and in the Isle of Man, attacked popular customs that would now be considered benign. Charles of Bala boasted of putting down centuries-old traditions of entertainment. 'This revival of religion has put an end to all the merry meetings for dancing, singing with the harp and every kind of sinful mirth which used to be so prevalent amongst young people here,' he wrote in 1791. 'At a large fair, kept here a few days ago, the usual revelling, the sound of music, and vain singing, was not to be heard.' The use of the phrase 'sinful mirth' is illuminating, pointing to a horror at any amusement. It sowed the seeds of a priggish, censorious culture that later would be criticised for rank hypocrisy. Puritanism was at first the strength but later the Achilles' heel of the movement, and once the initial fervour wore off it became easy to stereotype Nonconformity as repressive. That was not clear in the 1790s, when bawdy songs in pubs were exchanged for holy songs in chapels and in the streets. The Bala of Thomas Charles was not short of excitement. He recalled the whole town crying almost as one, '"What must I do to be saved? and "God be merciful to me a sinner"'. And, about nine or ten o'clock at night, there was nothing to be heard from one end of the town to the other but the cries and groans of people in distress of soul . . . calling upon the name of the Lord.' Excitement was the keynote to Welsh preaching for several decades. In the 1840s it was still marked by 'a turbulent, manner of praising the Almighty, consisting of loud shouting, clapping of hands and sometimes of jumping'.[50]

The author of *The Welsh Looking-glass* in 1811 detected three reasons for the change in the religious climate. 'At a period not very far back,' he wrote, 'all the inhabitants of Wales were, to a man, Church people, with the exception of a very few dissenters called Independents. How then came it to pass that the country has been torn to pieces, and divided into multitudes of little sects and parties?'[51] The reasons he gave for the Nonconformist triumph were schools, popular literature and organisation. (Interestingly, language was not mentioned.) The Methodists had won 'by their unwearied and close attention to the education of the poor . . . in this way tens of thousands have been taught to feel their obligation to the Methodists for all the instructions they have revived'.[52] In the sphere of literature, he added: 'They alone have taken any pains to furnish the common people with religious tracts'. Their organisation resembled 'a well-oiled machine', compared to which the established clergy 'were like solitary bushes of low growth standing on the top of distant hills which never meet'.[53] Less than 40 years since Harris's death the Established Church in Wales had been routed.

The gentry observed the religious upheaval in Wales with a dispassionate eye. In the pioneer days they encouraged the pelting of preachers, but they adjusted to the Nonconformist takeover. As John Jones, author of the *The History of Wales* of 1824, noted: 'Had it not been for the almost heavenly industry of the ministers of these denominations, Christianity would have been lost in Wales, as the Established Church is but little frequented.'[54] The gentry recognised the Nonconformists for what they were – a progressive but anti-revolutionary force who taught people to read and combine for their own improvement, but did not encourage them to rise above their station. The circulating schools of Griffith Jones taught poor people to read the Bible and devotional tracts alone. The Nonconformists preached obedience to the law, sexual modesty and attacked drinking and gambling, which stopped people from working and added to the burden on the rates when the victims of vice finished up in the poorhouse. As Jones noted, the Nonconformists could hardly be accused of undermining the Church of England, as it had been 'little frequented' to start with and thus was of very little use in restraining the lower orders.

Splits and splinters were also to be part of the life of Welsh Nonconformity. Harris and Rowlands, as we have seen, quarrelled in 1751. There was another split in the ranks of the Methodists in the early 1770s, over Pelagianism, the belief that man can take his own first steps towards salvation without the operation of divine grace. Peter Williams was expelled in old age, charged with Sabellianism, an obscure third-century heresy concerning the character of the Holy Trinity. But these ruptures over nitpicking issues proved no bar to expansion. The evangelicals grew faster than ever as they divided into competing groups during the time of their final divorce from the Church of England. A great religious revival swept South Wales from 1807 to 1809 and the north from 1815 to 1820. By the 1840s the Calvinist Methodists probably had some 200,000 members, about equal to the Established Church, followed by around 175,000 Independents, 106,000 Baptists and 72,000 Wesleyans, out of a total population in Wales of about 900,000.

The tide in favour of Nonconformity continued for many years to come. In 1861 the Welsh Protestant historian, Thomas Rees, described the Welsh as 'now emphatically a nation of nonconformists. The bulk of a very small minority who make up the congregations of the Established Church are emigrants from England and some anglicised Welshmen.' As the figures suggested, the rise of Calvinist Methodism had encouraged other Nonconformists. Rivalry spurred them all on, lending Welsh towns the appearance they assumed until the 1960s, of streets dotted with grand neo-classical temples competing for attention within yards of each other.

The progress of Aberdare was typical. It had one Nonconformist chapel in the 1750s and 14 by 1840. The Baptists had been present in South Wales since the Commonwealth, when Puritan pockets established themselves in the Gower peninsula. Probably no more than a thousand strong at the start of the eighteenth century, the number of Nonconformists jumped to 10,000 by the close of the century, after breaking into North Wales on the coat tails of the Calvinist Methodists. By 1831 they had 231 chapels and by 1861 they had 506. They were still well behind the Calvinist Methodists, who had erected 937 chapels by then. The Wesleyans were last into the field, having little impact on Welsh-speaking Wales until 1800, when Owen Davies and John Hughes conducted a successful mission that brought them 400 societies by 1810 with 5,000 to 6,000 members and 533 chapels by 1861.

The emancipation of the Welsh from the Anglican Establishment was accompanied by an artistic liberation from Anglican norms and the development of a Nonconformist aesthetic. Early Welsh chapels in the 1740s had no architects and were simply long barns or rooms. But as Nonconformists gained confidence, congregations demanded trained architects and chapels became the vehicle for the development of a new Welsh national architecture. Disdaining Gothic as English and Anglican, they favoured classical styles on the model of St Paul's church in Covent Garden in London. They soon developed their own style. Round or round-headed windows became a feature of Welsh chapels, along with three-part windows at the front, known as 'trinity windows'. By the 1870s the rustic barns and long houses of the previous century had been abandoned for grandiose designs reflecting Nonconformity's coming of age as 'the religion of Wales'. Morriston Tabernacle in Newport built in 1872 at a cost of £18,000 to a design by John Humphrey was the most expensive chapel built so far. With a soaring spire and a portico of eight tremendous Corinthian columns, 'the cathedral of Welsh non-conformity' was an apt symbol for a nation reborn.

The religious revival sustained the revival of the Welsh language. The Welsh-language press depended on churches. Of 19 periodicals listed in 1892 almost all were linked closely to the Calvinist Methodists, the Independents or the Wesleyans, as were six of the 23 papers. The Nonconformist revolution could not keep English out of Wales, and did not seek to do so. But the Nonconformists saved Wales (as the Calvinists saved Scotland) from becoming a mere English region with no more identity than Mercia or Wessex. The Nonconformists knew that their language owed a debt to their churches. 'There cannot be any doubt that the pulpit of Wales has proved a great power in the perpetuation of the language,' Edward Roberts told an audience at Cardiff town hall in February 1886. 'Preaching still attracts the masses in our towns, villages and country districts,' he added, and 'no country of this size is swayed so largely by the pulpit, or enjoys such an amount of religious provision'.[55]

There were still fears that the language was eroding from within, partly because of the intrusion of English words for which Welsh had no equivalent. Even in 1841 in an essay on the character of the Welsh, William Jones raised the issue of the English monopoly on technological terms. They were universally English, he said, though 'mangled and made to sound as much like Welsh words'. Later, some pessimists began to predict the eventual extinction of the language. In the 1870s the Calvinist Methodist historian, William Williams, sounded a prophetic note. 'The English wave, having rolled over the border, is steadily progressing westwards,' he remarked, 'and it is generally anticipated that it will, by the by, have inundated the whole of Wales and completely have extinguished the dear old language of the country; we are afraid that this will come to pass, but it will not be just now, nor for many years to come.'[56]

But such gloom was not the norm at the end of the nineteenth century, when most Welsh-speakers marvelled at the comparative vigour of their cultural renaissance compared to that of the Irish and Scots. 'More than a million speak the Cymric language,' boasted the writer of the prize-winning essay 'On the Propriety of Maintaining the Cymric Language' at the Cardiff eisteddfod of 1898, 'compared to 50,000 Irish speakers and some 9 per cent of the Scots'. In 1885 Dan Isaac Davies made a famous prediction that by 1985 Wales's three-quarters of a million Welsh-speakers would have increased to 3 million. Often cited as an example of hubris, it was a rational calculation to make in the 1880s, for the number of Welsh-speakers had risen even in the industrialised south, in contrast to the experience of Ireland, Scotland and the Isle of Man, where industry hastened the decline of the native language. The ceremonial unveiling of the monument to Bishop Morgan in the 1890s was not a wake. The number of English monoglots in Wales had grown at the same time, but well into the 1890s most Welsh patriots thought their hardy culture would absorb all the incomers. 'The patriotism of the people has been aroused and awakened,' R. W. Jenkins wrote. 'Wales is springing forward in her religious, political and educational life. Not satisfied with the latent dormant past, she is awakening out of her long sleep and renewing her long lost youth . . . and she is not going to sleep again.'[57]

The religious revival transformed the political scene, for it was clear that the new Nonconformist majority would support whatever party took on the Anglican Tories. The 'well-oiled machine' of the sects empowered people, because it taught them to read, write and combine and gave them a great issue in the shape of disestablishment.

The popular agitation surrounding the repeal of the Test and Corporation Acts in 1828 and the Great Reform Bill of 1832 tempted ministers into assuming a political role. Dissenting clergy allied their flocks to the Whigs against the united front of the Church of England, the landlords and the Tory Party. Irish Catholics and Welsh Nonconformists abandoned their former claim to have no hostile design on the political order at much the same time. O'Connell scattered the decorous old aristocratic Catholic committees and united Catholic Ireland under 'Repeal'. Wales was less agitated than Ireland, where land hunger and discontent with the Union of 1800 fed each other. The Welsh had never had a national parliament and could hardly feel the same nostalgia as the Irish did for their old legislature. From the 1830s the Welsh fixed their gaze on getting rid of the Anglican Establishment instead. In January 1834 a Nonconformist meeting at Pontypool called openly for disestablishment and in February the Baptists at their quarterly meeting in Monmouthshire petitioned parliament that 'no specific form of religion be the subject of the government's exclusive recognition'.[58] Opposition to slavery was an additional factor. It stirred little interest in Ireland but in Wales opposition to the slave trade became as much a hallmark of the Nonconformist outlook as temperance, especially after the formation of the Liberation Society in 1844.

But disestablishment was the glue that united Welsh Nonconformists to the Whigs and the Liberals. It became the definitive issue from which dissent was treasonous. By the 1860s it was a political commonplace that 'there is no such creature as a Nonconformist Tory'.[59] The Liberal alliance tightened after the 1867 Reform Act widened the franchise, strengthening the middle-class radicals at the expense of the Whig dynasties. The Liberals tightened their grip on Wales during the century as support for the Tories waned. In 1831, the last parliament before the Reform Bill, the parties were evenly matched in Wales, with 16 Whigs to 15 Tories. In 1832 Wales returned 21 Liberals and Whigs and 11 Tories, while in 1868 the ratio was 23 and 10. By 1892 there were 31 Liberal MPs in Wales and only three Tories. Each extension of the franchise increased the number of Liberals at the Tories' expense.

The Welsh Nonconformists were heartened by Gladstone's decision to axe the Church of Ireland establishment in 1869, seeing it as a precedent. In some senses it was a diversion. The Irish wanted Home Rule but were given disestablishment as a sop. Unsurprisingly, it had no effect on Irish agitation, which continued much as before. The Welsh yearned for disestablishment and were far less interested in Home Rule, but were forced to endure the

Church of England until 1920. Disestablishment was a Liberal cause *par excellence*, but the party took too long to deliver it. The first motion on Welsh disestablishment in May 1870 won the support of only 45 MPs in all, and only seven Welsh MPs. In the 1880 election the Liberals won 29 of the 33 Welsh seats, and they repeated the performance in 1885, taking 30 of the 34 seats. But then half the new Welsh MPs were Nonconformists and when a new disestablishment motion followed in 1886, the margin of failure was narrower, the motion failing by 229 votes to 241. In 1887 the Liberals made Welsh disestablishment part of national policy at their conference in Nottingham and motions followed in 1889, 1891, 1892 and 1894. But the issue was dragged out and when Gladstone retired in March 1894, much of the party's enthusiasm for Celtic causes retired with him. Lord Rosebery, the new Liberal leader, seemed a throwback to the age of aristocratic Whigs. To the fury of Lloyd George, his first Queen's speech did not even mention disestablishment, though a new bill still made its appearance in 1895 and this time it actually passed the Commons, with a majority of 44. The general election and the Tory victory that intervened killed the issue. By the time the Liberals returned in 1906, they had an overwhelming majority and could govern without much reference to Irish or Welsh MPs and so both Welsh disestablishment and Irish Home Rule lost their urgency.

Frustrated over disestablishment, the Welsh – with the precedent of Ireland again in mind – began moving towards the notion of 'home rule all round' as the answer to all the discontents of the Celtic fringe, from the Highland crofters to the Irish peasants. When Tom Ellis, the great hope of the radicals among the Welsh MPs, established Cymru Fydd, 'the Wales that is to be', as a nationalist caucus among Welsh Liberal MPs, it seemed the Welsh might emulate the Irish by creating a totally independent, nationalist party.

Pressure for home rule in Wales strengthened in 1895 after a furore over the North Western Railway, which sacked a number of plate layers on the line from Chester to Holyhead because they could not speak English. The sackings generated so much anger that many people believed some form of home rule in Wales was now inevitable. 'Everything points to the probability that when Home Rule is granted, it will be on federal lines,' Lloyd George declared in a handbook on Cymru Fydd in 1895, adding that 'the claims of Wales will not be denied, because there will be nothing dangerous or unreasonable in them'.[60] The similarities between Wales and Ireland seemed much greater than their differences. The 'Irish Question', it was said, was now helping to make a 'Welsh question'. As the recent historian of Wales, John Davies, has written: 'There was talk of a coalition of radical Celts to resist the Toryism of England and Michael Davitt, the leader of the Irish Land League, received a warm welcome in such places as Blaenau Ffestiniog and Tonypandy.'[61]

The years 1895 and 1896 marked the high-water mark of Cymru Fydd. It was now under Lloyd George's leadership, and the MP for Caernarfon seemed ready to become the Parnell of Wales. But then the movement faltered. After Cymru Fydd united with the North Wales Liberal Federation, the obvious next stage was to unite with the Federation's southern sister, so forming an all-Welsh Liberal union. But petty jealousies, rivalry between north and south and the growing influence of the anglophone community in the south scuppered the plan and Lloyd George was humiliated at a meeting in Newport in 1895. As one of his biographers wrote: 'An all-Welsh union was "off". It was the beginning of an undeclared but unceasing war which raged between the Northman and the Southman for many a year. It was also the end of home rule for Wales.'[62]

The collapse of Cymru Fydd set the path for a parting of the ways between Wales and Ireland, for Cymru Fydd's decay coincided with the revival of the Irish Nationalist Party under John Redmond after the débâcle of Parnell's disgrace. Redmond was careful not to follow the path chosen by the Welsh nationalists that led into the Liberal Party. The Irish MPs remained entirely separate from the Liberals even if they often co-operated. The claims of Wales were denied, and increasingly by the Welsh themselves. The confident note sounded by Welsh nationalists in the 1890s gave way to uncertainty. Talk of a grand Celtic coalition faded in politics, and lost force in the field of culture.

In the 1880s and 1890s Welsh magazines carried numerous articles on Wales's 'Celtic spirit' and the 'Cymric spirit'. It was also a major theme of the eisteddfods, where speakers echoed Matthew Arnold's Oxford lectures of the 1860s on Celts and Teutons, contrasting the supposed virtues of the two races. 'As compared with the Teutonic genius, the Celtic is characterised by lightness and gaiety,' J. C. Parkinson, president of the 1885 eisteddfod, told the audience at Aberdare in August. 'The gloom of the future does not seem to depress the true Celt's spirit or hinder his enjoyment of the passing hour.'[63] Descriptions of the gay spirituality of the Celts (for which read Irish and Welsh) and the dull qualities of the Teutons (for which read English) were then part of the discourse of the Welsh and Irish media, as were poems on Celtic themes, like 'The Harp of Wales', printed in the magazine *Wales* in 1895.

Tune, tune the old, old harp anew
Dark daughter of the hills and dales
Strong sons of song with song renew
That broken heart, the harp of Wales.[64]

But in Wales, unlike Ireland, the vogue for Celtic themes began to decline at the turn of the twentieth century. Celtic nationalism 'as a powerful and possibly dominating factor in the development of the human race'[65] was no longer taken seriously. The Irish were partly responsible for growing Welsh boredom. Their leaders would not concede that Welsh or Highland Scottish grievances compared to their own. Redmond attacked Lloyd George's call for 'home rule all round' in the 1890s, saying it could delay Irish Home Rule. 'I am most strongly opposed to the substitution of home rule all round for home rule for Ireland,' he said, adding that 'ours is a special case and I believe Ireland ought to insist on the precedence Mr Gladstone gave to it'.[66] The Welsh became discouraged. 'A Gael holds a Cymro as much at arm's length as he would the alien Saxon,' was the moody comment of one Welsh commentator.[67]

The introduction of the state school system in the 1870s undermined local identities. The London-based educational establishment was as hostile to Welsh culture as it was to Gaelic culture in Scotland. The depth of this venom had been laid bare in the 1846 government inquiry into the state of Welsh education, whose inspectors attacked Welsh as a 'a vast drawback to Wales and a manifold barrier to moral progress and commercial prosperity'.[68] The inspectors intended their report to demonstrate the low level of knowledge among the Welsh poor. In Rowlands's old parish of Llangeitho, one inspector reported his interview with two 12-year-old boys, selected at random. 'Had heard of the Prophets but did not know their office or the names of any of them,' he reported. 'Christ was the son of Joseph and the Virgin Mary; wrought miracles; did not know what a miracle meant . . . There were twelve Apostles; did not know their names.' The report showed that while 99 per cent of Calvinist Methodist schools taught in Welsh, only 18 per cent of Anglican schools did. Even in Caernarfonshire, where most people spoke Welsh, only 18 per cent of Anglican Sunday schools used Welsh compared to 99 per cent of the Calvinist Methodist Sunday schools. In Glamorgan, 72 per cent of Calvinist Methodist Sunday schools were Welsh-medium compared to 4.3 per cent of Anglican schools.[69]

The report's commissioners, Henry Vaughan Johnson, R. R. W. Lingen and Jelinger Symons, admitted there was systematic persecution of the native language-speakers in anglophone schools. As in Scotland and Ireland, a wooden thong was passed among the boys who committed the offence of speaking their native language at school. 'My attention was attracted to a stick of wood suspended by a string round a boy's neck,' Johnson wrote of a school in Llandyrnog, in Denbighshire, 'and on the stick were the words "Welsh stick." This I was told was a stigma for speaking Welsh. But in fact his only alternative was to speak Welsh or say nothing. He did not understand English.'[70]

The hostile attitude shown towards Welsh in the 1840s transplanted itself into the state system after the 1870 Education Act. School logbooks contained numerous examples of teachers' hostility to the language. At Llanllyfni parish school in Caernarfonshire the logbook for 1872 showed the 'Welsh not' stick was in full force. 'Speaking Welsh in school punished' was a frequent comment. On 20 December the headmaster noted: 'The past week is memorable in the fact that Welsh has been transported from the premises in all Stds below Std III'.[71] Teachers who transported it back into the premises were disciplined and in 1885 the logbook recorded that Robert Williams had been 'sent home for speaking Welsh with his class after having been reprimanded twice during the same lesson'.[72] The 'Welsh not' became part of nationalist legend as a symbol of cultural imperialism and may not have been as widespread, or fearsome, as was once believed. Just as important was the positive promotion of English through prizes and conversational classes. The new national schools created a cultural space where English was for everyone and not, as before, 'for the gentry'.

The effect of the educational reforms was not immediately noticed. The slow infusion of English through the schools was counterbalanced by the continuing strength of Nonconformists where for one day a week the language of instruction was Welsh. But in the 1890s the confidence of the Nonconformist chapels began to stumble. They had overbuilt and there were now too many chapels. Merionethshire alone had 273 chapels and 34 churches by the turn of the twentieth century with a capacity for 75,000 people, though the population of the county was only 48,000. Wales by 1900 boasted 4,669 chapels, more than the total number of churches of all denominations in London, which had a population three times as large. The chapels sank into the red. 'Many of the churches are painfully small and correspondingly weak,'[73] a minister complained in 1912. He warned of the knock-on effect that debts would have on the quality of ministers, saying few men would want to enter the ministry on a salary of £60 a year.

Nonconformists traditionally kept their ministers poor. The preacher Christmas Evans once acidly informed a woman of his congregation, who assured him he would be rewarded in heaven for his services, that while that might well be true, his horse still needed feeding in the meantime. His biographer noted: 'The Welsh of that day seemed to think it was essential to the preservation of the purity of the gospel that their minister should be kept low.' The Welsh enjoyed controlling their ministers in a way they could never control the Anglican parsons, but once Evans's generation died in the mid-nineteenth century, the supply of charismatic preachers prepared to work for nothing dried up and chapels started to feel the negative effects of a low-paid ministry. Ministers at the end of the nineteenth century did not have the prestige of their predecessors. When John Elias died in 1841, aged 69, the whole of Anglesey turned out. 'As it passed by Beaumaris, the procession saw the flags of the vessels in the port lowered half-mast high: and as they passed through Beaumaris town and Bangor City all the shops were closed and all the blinds drawn before the windows. Every denomination . . . justified . . . the propriety of the text of the funeral oration, "Know ye not that a Prince and great man has fallen".'[74] Half a century later, no ministers had that princely aura.

Nonconformity relied on religious revivals to keep up the numbers. It was part of the price of a movement that set more store on *hwyl* than doctrine. But even in the mid-nineteenth century, it was noticeable that chapels often remained empty during times of peace and plenty and that they only filled up after the revivals that followed a cholera epidemic or a natural disaster. By the end of the century the revivals were over, not least because medical advances and improved hygiene had reduced the element of fear that drove people to church. A more educated population was less susceptible to fiery sermons, and an increasingly respectable audience was less keen than it had been on jumping up and down, clapping, fainting and crying. The old oratorical tricks that had once delighted congregations seemed dated.

Welsh preachers had always been keen, perhaps over-keen, on allegory. Christmas Evans once compared Jesus's enjoyment of heaven to the royal family strolling round Windsor Castle.[75] He was fond of mining analogies, too, and compared the work of a preacher to that of a miner taking his sledge in his hand 'to form bars of iron from the ore in its rough state'. The gospel, he said, was 'like a form or mould and sinners are to be melted, as it were, or cast into it'.[76] By the end of the century that type of analogy – so revolutionary in its day – no longer impressed people. The pulpit, in fact, was no longer seen as a suitable sphere of activity for an ambitious

Welshman. When Charles Williams retired as Moderator of the Calvinist Methodists he detected a 'hesitating note' in the life of the churches and complained of 'a wave of paganism'.[77]

The decline would have been noticeable by the 1900s had it not been for a last burst of enthusiasm in 1905. In retrospect, this came to look like the last great rally of Welsh-speaking Wales, for the revival was almost entirely a Welsh-language phenomenon and the principal preacher, Evan Roberts, was virtually a monoglot. This laid him open to ridicule from an increasingly anglicised audience. The Reverend J. V. Morgan, a critical observer, noted that Evans's lack of English was seen as a black mark. 'When requested to speak in English, he has repeatedly said that he is not prompted by the Spirit . . ."Why did he not tell the straight truth and say 'I don't know English', which I am told is the fact",'[78] Morgan reported one minister as sneering.

The revival let many ministers hope that Wales still had *hwyl* in store, and on the back of a brief surge in chapel attendance, there was a last spurt of chapel-building. But the relief was short-lived. When he analysed the revival in 1909, Morgan pronounced it a failure. It had been led by children, who had used the guidance of the 'spirit' to overthrow the authority of their parents and the ministers, he said. 'The insolence that the young were encouraged to cultivate towards their elders may be classed as one of the saddest features of the Revival.'[79] Ministers had seen 'their claims to leadership denied'. Morgan ended on a prophetic note. 'For two centuries and a half, Nonconformity has been the great bulwark that has enabled the Welsh to withstand the inroads of English habits and characteristics.' Now he as good as sang a dirge over its grave. The Bible, he said, was falling rapidly into decline and was 'less and less the book of the rank and file'.[80] He concluded: 'The fall of the spiritual thermometer is very marked.'

Nonconformity and Welsh nationalism had marched and risen together for so long that it was hard to imagine either force declining. 'As long as the gospel is preached in Welsh with growing efficiency to an increasing number of hearers, the old language cannot die,'[81] David Davies wrote in 1907. 'It is beyond all doubt pre-eminently adapted to be a vehicle of religious thought.' The drop in the 'spiritual thermometer' after 1905 had a damaging effect on a language and culture that for more than 150 years had been bound up with Nonconformity. In fact, the number of Welsh-speakers grew until 1911. In the 1890s, John Southall's book *Wales and her Language* noted that the language border between the English and Wales had held firm since the 1480s. But he also reflected that the dream of 3 million Welsh-speakers might never be realised, because the new wave of English immigrants was not being absorbed as the immigrants of the 1830s and 1840s had been. He noted that the plethora of denominations, once seen as part of the strength of Nonconformity, was now revealed as a weakness, as each one had spawned its own press that was confined to a small readership of 20,000 to 30,000 at most.

A sign of the declining power of Nonconformity was the sudden disappearance of disestablishment as a popular issue. Politicians were bemused, wondering what this might herald. In 1895 a Cymru Fydd pamphlet described 'the incubus of an alien church' as 'the greatest of all our burdens'.[82] Within a few years this could no longer be said to be the case. 'Before 1895 no meeting could be held in Wales where disestablishment did not hold the foremost place,' the MP Llewelyn Williams remarked in 1911. 'Nowadays, even at the height of a general election, one can attend meeting after meeting without hearing a word about disestablishment.'[83] When the Liberals returned in 1906, a new disestablishment bill made its leisurely way through the Commons in 1909, though the Lords blocked it until the Parliament Act of 1911 trimmed the powers of the upper house. The Liberals threw Wales a sop in the form of a Royal Commission on the Church in Wales, which compiled a vast amount of information on religious habits. This body produced evidence – unwelcome to Nonconformists – of an Anglican revival, the fruit of renewed Anglican activity and of continued English immigration. The Nonconformist churches now numbered 550,280 but the Anglicans mustered 200,000. A new disestablishment bill was introduced in April 1912 and passed in January 1913. Still nothing happened. Like the Home Rule cause in Ireland, which had triumphed at the same time, it came too late and in any case the outbreak of war in 1914 put both disestablishment and Home Rule on hold for the duration of hostilities.

Many Welsh people no longer looked on Lloyd George as the successor to Llewelyn the Great. Disappointed after the débâcle over Cymru Fydd in 1895, he had concentrated on gaining national office and toned down his rhetoric. In 1906 he joined the cabinet as president of the Board of Trade and the Welsh champion gave way to the British statesman. He hurried to make peace with his Nonconformist constituency before shaking the dust from his feet. Before an audience of 3,000 at a great Nonconformist convention in Cardiff, he swatted the doubters who cast aspersions on his commitment to the Welsh cause, referring to his controversial opposition to the Boer war. He reminded the audience that he had then risked his parliamentary career for 'a little country which I never saw, fighting for freedom, fighting for fair play'. He added: 'Am I going to sell the land I love?'[84] Nonconformist Wales was reassured – for a while.

Lloyd George was only following the path taken by Tom Ellis who left Wales to become Deputy Chief Whip and subsequently Chief Whip, a position he held until his death in 1899. Cymru Fydd's founder was the first MP to include self-government for Wales in his election manifesto and 'dreamt many dreams for Wales'.[85] But in 1892 he had decided he could best serve Wales in London, where he was instrumental in persuading Gladstone to set up the Royal Commission on Land in Wales that reported in 1896. Lloyd George also thought he could best serve Wales in London. In both cases the Welsh nationalist ended up playing second fiddle to the British Liberal.

Welsh radicals preferred the man who had savaged the Boer war and the concentration camps in South Africa to the defender of the British empire. After war broke out in 1914 the inclusion in the cabinet of Edward Carson, the Tory hammer of Irish Home Rule, left a bitter taste in Welsh mouths. Lloyd George could still hit the right note. At a dinner for Serbia at the Savoy in 1917, he declared: 'I am a believer in little nations . . . I have the honour to belong to one myself. I believe in the nation that can sing about its defeats.'[86] But there was no great elation in Wales when Lloyd George assumed the helm as British Prime Minister in December 1916. The believer in little nations had the tricky responsibility of managing the aftermath of the Sinn Fein rising in Dublin in Easter 1916. It seemed a very long time since Lloyd George had welcomed the Irish Land Leaguer and ex-convict Michael Davitt to Ffestiniog in 1886, horrifying the Liberal worthies of the town. Some could still recall the young man who had used his first election address in Caernarfon to savage the Tories' 'baton-and-bayonet rule in Ireland'.[87] Now, he was in charge of the batons. The *Welsh Outlook* was outraged. 'It is a moral impossibility for men engaged in coercing one Celtic country . . . to wax enthusiastic about the liberation of another Celtic land,'[88] it wrote in 1918, gloomily dismissing the story of Welsh politics from 1906 as 'a dismal story of lost opportunity and hopeless ineffectiveness'.[89]

The age of Liberal and Nonconformist Wales was drawing to a close. It had redefined Wales's national identity. Nonconformist religion, as its supporters maintained, was the heir to those Welsh Elizabethan church reformers like Bishop Morgan, who had seen the hand of God in the near-miraculous survival of Welsh. Nonconformity had kept the Welsh different from the English, just as Presbyterianism had kept the Scots Scottish. It had kept alive the Welsh people's self-consciousness as a Celtic people. But by 1918 Nonconformity and Liberalism were exhausted and the Welsh were discovering the new religion of socialism. The Reverend J. V. Morgan noted its advance in 1909: 'Since the [1905] revival, various Socialistic organisations have invaded the valleys and are gathering Welsh working men by the thousands to hear the "socialistic gospel",' he wrote. 'These men have already reverted to the belief that their salvation is not to come by way of the pulpit, or by the way of the churches, but by the way of the Labour Party.'[90] A decade on and the 'socialist gospel' was starting to nudge both the chapels and Liberalism out of the frame. The *Welsh Outlook* wondered in 1918 if the Labour Party might not be a much better partner for Home Rule than the Liberals, 'who are loud in their protestations of patriotism on election platforms and at eisteddfods'.[91]

CHAPTER SIX

South Wales
'A rich culture, long departed'

> *Where can I go, then, from the smell*
> *Of decay, from the putrefying of a dead*
> *Nation?*
> (R. S. Thomas, 'Reservoirs')[1]

Merthyr Tydfil, town of the martyr Tydfil, lies on the A470 about 45 minutes' drive north of Cardiff. A short but monotonous journey from the south, the approach from the north through the Brecon hills, down winding roads and around corkscrew bends, has an oddly Scandinavian feel. Pine forests line these hills and to anyone over the age of 40, raised on images of South Wales that were as black as the coal it yielded, the belt of emerald greenery has a surreal quality.

The approach road to the town brings another change of gear. The old sooty blackness has gone but the town is grey instead. Merthyr Tydfil looks desolate. Youths in baseball caps idly stroll the streets, girls not out of their teens but already with a world-weary air and often smoking, push prams. Hanging baskets add a festive air to the centre of town but in the council estates nearby, the neglected verges, peeling paint and unwanted junk strewn on pavements bear witness to a climate of indifference, as well as poverty. Government talk of the regeneration of the South Wales valleys seems to have passed Merthyr Tydfil by.

Merthyr is a town of ruined temples, dedicated to a vanished culture. No vines and creepers have engulfed the stonework as in some Latin American jungle, but there is the same air of a forgotten civilisation, and of a way of life that has not only disappeared but seems now incomprehensible. A stay in the town yielded no feeling of a community interacting with the verdant forests that have grown up around it. On the contrary, the townspeople seem to ignore, even resent, their new green belt, as if it is a badge of shame, for the greening of Merthyr is the mark of its defeat, testament to the departure of the coal kings and the iron kings who turned this upland parish into the world's first industrial town.

Little remains of the once vibrant Welsh culture of the valleys. The temples of learning have gone the way of the temples of industry and religion. Merthyr's magnificent, Edwardian-era Carnegie library remains open. But in many valley towns the love of learning that was a feature of working-class life has evaporated. Spacious Workers' Educational Association halls that once echoed to debates about socialism, trade unions, capitalism and the Spanish civil war have closed and been boarded up while once-extensive libraries eke out a hangdog existence that would have appalled their Victorian founders, some reduced to mean Portakabins that are mostly closed and stock nothing but paperback novels.

The decline in learning has gone on for decades. Welsh miners' libraries, as Jonathan Rose wrote in *The Intellectual Life of the British Working Classes*, had their real heyday between the 1880s and the First World War, when they were 'one of the greatest networks of cultural institutions created by working people anywhere in the world.'[2] Some were vast. The Tredegar Workmen's Institute library circulated 100,000 volumes a year.

Rose cited the collier's son D. R. Davies, born in 1889, who in the 1950s feared the decline in Nonconformity had helped to erode the intellectual keenness of the South Welsh working-class communities. 'The Welsh Nonconformity in which I was reared did not make for narrowness and fanaticism of mind, as so many of the frustrated, embittered critics of my generation have maintained. Today we are living upon the capital of those same "tin Bethels" and when that gives out (as it is now doing) the futility and leanness of our contemporary life will become more obvious and disastrous.'[3]

By the 1950s the miners' libraries were being dissolved. Even the flagship Tredegar Institute was broken up in 1964 and its library dispersed. The miners' culture could not outlast the closure of the actual mines and after the British Prime Minister Margaret Thatcher took on the National Union of Mineworkers in 1983 – and won – the mining industry in Wales was effectively shut down over the following decade. The last pit in South Wales closed in Mardy in 1999.

The Labour Party machine which ruled Merthyr Tydfil and the Vale of Glamorgan unchallenged throughout the twentieth century created an almost Soviet landscape. No other part of Britain has an urban landscape so close to that of Belarus or Ukraine. They all have the same air of history crushed under concrete and of culture flattened in the drive to forge a socialist society. Merthyr Tydfil's rulers went at their nineteenth-century heritage with the same furious ball-and-chain zeal that the Soviets employed in Russia. A mania for reorganising the town has torn out its guts, opening up desolate gaps and windswept spaces and leaving the odd preserved street or building looking just as marooned as the tiny Orthodox churches left sandwiched between concrete blocks in downtown Moscow or Bucharest. Street patterns have vanished in successive, waves of rebuilding. The terraced back-to-back houses of Waterloo Street, Queen Street and Taff Street have disappeared in their entirety, replaced by curling suburban 'drives' whose bland names evoke the drug-like calm of the English Home Counties.

Whereas a nineteenth-century visitor to Llanrhaeadr-ym-Mochnant would find some familiar landmarks in the modern village, a visitor from the same time to Merthyr Tydfil would think he or she had returned to the wrong town. It is as if the people of the town have turned their backs on their own past and started afresh. On a Sunday afternoon I joined an industrial archaeology tour with a local historical expert. The tour was a depressing experience, given over to discussing what had been demolished and to 'imagining' with the aid of maps the old street patterns. The walk took us over pieces of railway track, overgrown with grass, and around the darkened remains of blast furnaces – archaeological fragments of Merthyr's lost civilisation. With the best will in the world it was hard to reconstruct in my mind's eye the ironworks that had made Merthyr Tydfil the workshop of the world. The expert said there were plans to build an 'interpretative centre' around the relics of the blast furnaces but it was not certain. 'There's a worry it will be vandalised,' he sighed.

After the tour, I walked outside the town to find a beautifully preserved legacy of the Merthyr that predated the coming of the blast furnaces. Hen Dy Cwrdd chapel, though rebuilt in the 1850s, occupies a site where a Nonconformist chapel has stood since 1747, when a dispute between Arminian and Calvinist factions among the congregation at nearby Cwmglo led to the Arminian group under Richard Rees moving here. Hen Dy Cwrdd was never large. The easy-going doctrines of the Unitarians, as the Arminians became, were anathema to the Calvinistic mainstream in Welsh Nonconformity, which makes it remarkable that the chapel has survived, when larger and more recent rivals have disappeared, for the chapels that once formed a striking part of Merthyr's skyline have been largely effaced. Merthyr boasted about 30 chapels in the 1840s. On those that remain, bare roofs and buddleia growing from exposed brickwork testify to continuing neglect. The names and biblical passages carved on the outside walls are a reminder that, along with the faith, the language of faith also died. Welsh was the language of these streets at least until the First World War, but is not much heard now. The story of Hen Dy Cwrdd echoes the transition. The chapel slipped slowly from Welsh into English in the 1950s in an effort to keep the congregation. 'As the old people one by one passed to their rest . . . a fragment, as it were, of the Welsh language sank into the grave with them,' wrote the historian of the chapel, adding that the hope that English would lead to bigger congregations was not fulfilled. 'The congregation of today is composed in the main of members whose forebears were torch-bearers in the dark days of two hundred years ago, men and women . . . held together by a bond that only death can sever,' he added. 'Every year their ranks grow thinner.'[4]

No one would be more amazed, not to say horrified, by the change in Merthyr Tydfil and the Vale of Glamorgan than Edward Williams, better known as Iolo Morganwg, whose lifetime from 1747 to 1826 spanned the early decades of the Welsh renaissance of Welsh life: a revival that touched Glamorganshire in particular. Poet, historian, dreamer and master forger, this brilliant but erratic son of a stonemason dedicated his life to Welsh culture, Glamorganshire and to druidic lore, which he imaginatively embellished.

On a warm morning in August, at the National Eisteddfod in St Davids, I watched the fruits of Iolo's work being played out in front of the television cameras, as Rowan Williams, Archbishop of Wales and Archbishop-elect of Canterbury, was inducted into the Gorsedd yr Beirdd, or Company of Bards, by the Archdruid of Wales, Robyn Lewis. The hour-long ritual, which took place at dawn in a circle of improvised standing stones, seemed culled from the pages of Tolkien's *Lord of the Rings*, not least because the more intrusive signs of modern technology, such as loudspeakers, had been concealed beneath wreaths of foliage. After a fanfare of trumpets and the playing of a harp, the Archbishop, dressed in white, laid his hands on a huge sword before being escorted into the heart of the stone circle to meet the 'horn of plenty'. For all its appeal to antiquity, the rite that the company followed was one Iolo Morganwg would have recognised, since he invented it. There is no secrecy about this, and the Archdruid referred quite casually to Iolo's fertile mind the next day, while answering criticism in the English media about Dr Williams for having taken part in a 'pagan' ritual. 'Iolo did create his Gorsedd while fantasising about pre-Christian times,' the Archdruid remarked, 'but as it developed it rapidly became a mainstream

Christian organisation.' As the Archdruid said, the marriage of paganism and Christianity (at Dr Williams's induction the crowd sang 'Oh God of Our Fathers') was all Iolo's work. It stemmed from his twofold ambition to establish Glamorganshire as the historic centre of the druidic cult and to popularise druidic rituals among a firmly Christian population. Iolo did not invent all of this from scratch. He merely added to the copious existing literature on druids, much as medieval theologians span out the lives of saints from the skeletons of ancient *vitae*. What was truly novel was that he then put all of this into practice.

Iolo shared the eighteenth century's curiosity about druids and their mysteries. Where he differed most was over the common belief that the centre of the druidic cult in ancient times lay in Anglesey. He was determined to prove that this honour belonged to Glamorganshire. Apart from 'discovering' various documents and poems to support his claim, Iolo reinforced his argument by insisting he was a bard himself, the last alive in the world, having been inducted into their company by a member of the bardic order that had survived the centuries in his county alone. 'He was admitted a bard in the Ancient manner: a custom still retained in Glamorgan but I believe in no other part of Wales,' an anonymous correspondent of the *Gentleman's Magazine* (probably Iolo himself) reported reverently. 'This is by being discipled to a regular Bard and afterwards admitted into the order by a Congress of Bards . . . and being also admitted into their Mysteries.' The same article proclaimed that he and Reverend Edward Evans of Aberdare, the man who had ordained him, were 'the only legitimate descendants of the so-long-celebrated Ancient British Bards; at least they will allow no others this honourable title.'[5]

Iolo was convincing because he brooked no dissent. 'You are talking of what you don't understand,' he told quibblers, 'of what none but a Welshman, and a British bard, can *possibly* understand.'[6] Faced with such self-belief, it is not surprising that the English literary world took Iolo's claims at face value. Armed with a mass of 'mysteries' to which he alone enjoyed access, Iolo, like many essentially shy people, could be a great showman. The first 'Gorsedd' was performed before a crowd on Primrose Hill in London on 22 September 1792. 'This being the day on which the autumn equinox occurred, some Welsh Bards resident in London assembled in Congress on Primrose Hill, according to ancient usage,' the *Gentleman's Magazine* reported.

A circle of stone formed, in the middle of which was the Maan Gorsedd, or altar, on which a naked sword being placed, all the Bards assisted to sheathe it. This ceremony was attended with a proclamation, the substance of which was that the Bards of the Isles of Britain (for such is their ancient title) were the heralds and ministers of peace.[7]

That Iolo was the source for the magazine's report is suggested by its robust claim that 'the Bardic Institution of the Ancient Britains, which is the same as the Druidic, has been from the earliest times, through all ages to the present day, retained by the Welsh'. Druidism was, it added, well known to this nation and 'any Welsh regular Bard can in a few minutes give them a much better account of it than all the books in the world, and at the same time the most convincing proofs that it is now exactly the same as it was two thousand years ago'.

But Wales was a more appropriate setting for Iolo's ceremonies than any London park. Around 1814 an observer caught sight of Iolo in full flight in Pontypridd, walking behind a banner,

> at the head of a procession . . . over the great bridge and then over to the Rocking Stone on the common above. Ancient ceremonies were performed on the great stone by Iolo in the role of Y Gwyddon, or Odin, the Archdruid, not the least interesting being sheathing the State Sword of Wales to convey the valuable lesson, as in Gethsemane, that there is more credit in sheathing the sabre than in drawing it forth among the sons of men.[8]

As the reference to Gethsemane shows, Iolo fused Christian beliefs with pagan rituals for his Gorsedd. His religious beliefs were as difficult to pin down as his politics. Sometimes a republican, he also dedicated works to the Prince of Wales. Sometimes a Unitarian, others summed up his creed as 'a compound of Christianity and Druidism, Philosophy and Mysticism'.[9] But he was never anti-religious in the French style and his insistence on identifying the druidic cult with the patriarchal religion of the Old Testament helped sell the Gorsedd to the deeply religious Welsh. An overtly pagan or anti-Christian ceremony could never have attached itself to a nation gripped by an evangelical revival. As it was, Iolo glued his Christianised Gorsedd to the traditional Welsh poetic gathering known as an eisteddfod with ease.

The size of the modern eisteddfod, the big tents for the performers, the hundreds of stalls, the television cameras, the massive open-air screens, the guest 'stars' and the burger stalls with their Welsh-language menus, all create the impression of a movable feast which, updated to meet modern needs, has continued since time immemorial. This impression is heightened by the fancy-dress ritual of the Gorsedd with the swords and robes. In fact, the ceremony of the modern eisteddfod, much like the ceremony surrounding the modern monarchy, is a nineteenth-century creation, grafted on to older stocks. Since the disappearance of poets and bards from the households of the anglicised Welsh gentry in the sixteenth and seventeenth centuries, eisteddfods had continued in a mundane fashion in graveyards and in inns. Elizabeth I encouraged an eisteddfod in Flintshire in 1568, so that 'all and every Person or Persons that intend to maintain their living by name or Colour of Minstrels, Rythmers, or Bards . . . shall . . . shew their learnings thereby'.[10] But the experiment in royal patronage was not repeated and an event held in Glamorgan in the 1620s attracted an audience of only four people.[11]

The fascination of the Romantics with the poetry of the 'ancients' brought a revival, stimulated further in the 1780s when the London Welsh societies, the Cymmrodorion and the Gwyneddigion, started to offer literary prizes at these gatherings. Iolo, a member of the Gwyneddigion since the 1770s, took part in the eisteddfod it sponsored in St Asaph in 1790. Convinced that the bards (of whom he was one) descended from the druids, and that the eisteddfod was a relic of the old druidic cult, Iolo reintroduced what he considered the ritual of an ancient bardic congress to a series of rather ordinary literary proceedings conducted chiefly in hotels.

Iolo's opportunity occurred in 1818, when Thomas Burgess, the scholarly Bishop of St Davids and a friend of Iolo's, established the Cambrian Society in Camarthen, dedicated to collecting Welsh manuscripts and promoting traditional music. At the eisteddfod held in the town the next year, Iolo made his mark. Burgess was confused by the ceremonies that the bossy Iolo imposed on this event, for he

> maintained the dignity of his Order with absolute authority, standing in the midst of a circle of stones . . . from whence he commanded the several aspirants to put off their shoes before entering the circle . . . the good bishop, Dr Burgess of St Davids, was present and wished the Bard to dispense with some of the initiatory forms; but he would not permit the slightest departure from ancient usage, for within that circle he was, and would be Pontifex Maximus.[12]

The 'ancient usages' that Iolo had come up with stuck to the proceedings, as eisteddfods became less rustic and more middle class, and as a vogue for 'Ancient British' or 'Celtic' costumes spread. Cosy readings in taverns or hotels gave way to parades, which also became anglicised to suit their fashionable new audience.

By the 1840s the eisteddfods were drawing the great and the good. The eisteddfod in Abergavenny in 1843 was attended by the ambassador of the Sublime Porte, the Chevalier Bunsen of Prussia and a flock of marquesses and viscounts. Four hundred carriages drew up at the opening day and most of the women who attended the event dressed in the 'national' costume of Wales. Like the Gorsedd ceremony this was also an invention. It comprised a strikingly tall black beaver hat surmounting a frilly, white linen wimple. The ensemble ended in a long, draping red shawl. It was mainly the work of Augusta Hall, Lady Llanover, whose sketches of women in regional costume had proved very popular after they were published in the mid-1830s following her prizewinning essay at the 1834 Cardiff eisteddfod on 'The advantages of preserving the language and dress of Wales'. The Halls had energetically propagated their idea of Welsh national costume by encouraging its use on their estate at Abercarn. In 1854 the *Illustrated London News* reported that Sir Benjamin and Lady Augusta had opened a church on the estate 'for the sole use of the native cymri' and that on the arrival of the patrons, 'the native population, (to the number of about a thousand in their native costumes) . . . formed themselves in picturesque groups beneath and on each side of the church'.[13]

The 'native costume' was now a fixed item. Later in the century, Lady Llanover's costume was popularised on postcards, dolls and in advertisements. It was eulogised in paintings, most notably in *Salem,* painted in 1908 by the Devonshire artist Sydney Vosper. This iconic work depicted a group of elderly women (and a few men) in a chapel near Harlech, all dressed in their tall black beaver hats, frilly white bonnets and long red shawls. The painting purported to 'recall' a Wales that never existed in the manner suggested. In reality, Vosper dressed the main figure, Sian Lewis, in the costume, which was borrowed from a local clergyman's wife for the occasion. Lewis would never have worn it otherwise.

Lady Augusta's friend, Lady Charlotte Guest, was another formidable influence on the Welsh national movement, translating and having published the collection of eleventh-century Welsh stories known as the *Mabinogi* in three volumes in 1838, 1840 and 1849. The *Mabinogi* had escaped close attention by the great Welsh scholar at Oxford, Edward Lhuyd, who regarded them as unhistorical, but the children of the Romantic movement were more receptive to legends. The Welsh wanted their own answer to Macpherson's Ossianic poems and got them. William Owen Pughe, who had worked with Iolo on the book *The Myvyrian Archaiology*, conceived the idea of translating the stories but died in 1835 before completing the task. Lady Charlotte took up the project herself. Her dedication was addressed to her sons, Ifor and Merthyr, and heaped praise upon that romanticised Wales, 'in whose beautiful language you are being initiated and among whose free mountains you were born . . . May you become early imbued with the chivalric and exalted sense of honour and the fervent patriotism for which its sons have ever been celebrated.'[14]

Iolo had died in 1826. By then his beloved Glamorgan was in the throes of transformation, which would turn the green vale of his childhood into the soot-black vale of the twentieth century. The quiet villages he knew (he walked almost everywhere) were to be covered with houses, no longer whitewashed, but made of brick and surrounded by factories, mines, new canals and railways. Iolo had dreamed of making the Vale of Glamorgan famous for druids. In the event it became famous as the workshop of the world and as the centre of the industrial revolution.

In the story of this revolution, the upland parish of Merthyr Tydfil played the major role, for this was where coal, iron ore, water and capital fused to create an economic 'Big Bang'. Within a couple of decades between the late eighteenth and the early nineteenth centuries, the old village was covered in the detritus of the new iron factories. A nineteenth-century visitor wrote: 'Its rise from a rude struggling mountain hamlet in less than a century to the nucleus of a vast manufacturing population is one of the marvels of modern times.'[15] Painters recorded the hellish, though awe-inspiring, sight of the night sky over Merthyr glowing from the light of crimson flames. It was a place where the laws of nature and the normal course of day and night seemed to have been suspended.

Merthyr Tydfil's physical strangeness and the sheer novelty of it struck all visitors. To T. E. Clarke, who wrote an account of the town in 1848, it was more an American than a European phenomenon. The town was 'one vast assemblage of churches, chapels, houses and hamlets'. Even the outskirts were alarming, for the town was ringed by

> heaps of cinders which rise to an immense height. These heaps have been formed by the accumulation of refuse matter thrown out from the mines and furnaces. Railway embankments, compared with these tips or heaps, are mere pigmies; the great heat of the cinders causes them to smoulder for many years. In the evening they may be seen studded with beautiful

flames of various hues, caused by the burning of the sulphur which is emitted from the minerals.[16]

That was just the outskirts. The iron furnaces at the core were yet more amazing. According to Clarke: 'The scene at night is beyond conception. The immense fires give a livid hue to the faces of the workmen while sounds of blast and steam, rolling mills and massive hammers worked by machines or wielded by the brawny arms of athletic sons of Vulcan, preclude the possibility of being heard when speaking.'[17] It was 'like a vision of Hades in its milder form', E. Roberts wrote in 1852.[18]

As these observers said, nothing of the old order in South Wales had survived in Merthyr Tydfil. The parish church named after its ancient martyr survived, but its influence was insignificant compared to the dozens of newer Nonconformist chapels. Whatever cartways had run through the village had disappeared under the new terraced streets. Merthyr not only differed physically from the towns and villages of old Wales, but had given birth to a new society, based, as Clarke said, on the brawny 'sons of Vulcan'. The semi-feudal network of landed families, middle-class traders and rural peasants had been swept away by the needs of the 'iron kings'.

Merthyr's transformation began in the 1750s, when Anthony Bacon leased an eight-by-four-mile stretch of land in the village – the first major outside investor to notice the fortuitous proximity of coal, iron seams and running water to power machines. Within a few years there were several small furnaces on the banks of the River Taff, powered by bellows and water. The real advance took place in 1759, when nine investors formed a partnership to build a steam-powered furnace on the banks of the River Dowlais. William Brownrigg and Bacon then started their own similar works on the outskirts of Merthyr at Cyfartha in 1765. By then, the activity around Merthyr was attracting greater interest in England. Richard Crawshay, father of the greatest dynasty of 'iron kings' in Merthyr, had started out life as a poor Yorkshire boy selling flat irons in a London iron warehouse. When eventually he took over the business he bought a share in the Cyfartha works in 1786, buying out the other partners in 1796.

In the 1790s the construction of the Glamorganshire canal, linking Merthyr to Cardiff, boosted the town's already rapid advance. A single barge drawn by a horse was equal to a dozen wagons drawn by 48 horses and by 1803 10,000 tons of iron were being sent each year to Cardiff, rising to

39,000 tons in 1817, 50,000 tons by 1823 and 160,000 tons by 1848. By the time Richard Crawshay died in 1810, Cyfartha had half a dozen furnaces producing 50 tons of iron a week, which rose to more than a thousand tons by the mid-1840s. By then coal was overtaking iron as an export and the new railways were superseding the canals. The Taff Vale railway opened in 1841 and the Vale of Neath railway a decade later.

Cyfartha Castle, the Gothic folly built by Crawshay's grandson William Crawshay II in 1829 at a cost of £30,000, which still stands outside the centre of Merthyr, symbolised the ascendancy of the iron kings. But the Crawshays were not the only local potentates. The Dowlais works, owned by Sir John Guest, advanced at much the same rate and boasted six furnaces by 1815, while Penydarren, owned by the Homfray family, and Plymouth, owned by the Hills, were of a similar size.

The needs of the 'iron kings' inevitably created a new society. The blast furnaces needed men. Each of the 47 by the 1850s required about 400 workers, so the town started sucking in huge numbers of young male immigrants. The overall population soared. A village of a few thousand inhabitants at the turn of the nineteenth century, it contained 22,000 people by 1831, 35,000 a decade later and 46,000 by 1851. The population of Glamorganshire soared. Cardiff, also little more than a village of about 1,900 residents in 1801, had become a town of just over 10,000 people in 1841, 33,000 in 1861 and 164,000 by the turn of the twentieth century. The total population of the county more than tripled, from 70,000 in 1801 to 230,000 in 1841. It reached almost 860,000 by the turn of the century and 1,120,910 by 1911.

There was no absolute chasm between the old aristocrats of rural Wales and the meritocrats in Merthyr. The former were curious about the latter, which explains why the Grand Duke Constantine of Russia, a member of the most feudal society in Europe, toured the town in 1847. Nor did Merthyr instantly shrug off patterns of deference. When the wife of the Marquis of Bute, patron and owner of much of Cardiff, was delivered of a longed-for son, the Earl of Windsor, in 1847 Merthyr Tydfil was *en fête* with parties and illuminations. The mock-Gothic crenellation of Cyfartha Castle and the luxurious dresses the Crawshay women wore for their portraits hint at the longing felt by the 'iron kings' to ape the landed lifestyle. But if they dressed like the gentry, they did not vote like them. William Crawshay II was hostile to the Church of England and opposed tithes. 'His most memorable comment on the French Revolution of 1830,' a historian of Merthyr wrote, 'was an expression of keen regret that he had not been there with his fowling piece to pepper the backside of the fleeing king.'[19]

Another oddity about Merthyr was its tiny middle class. There were 'no men of middle station, none of the ordinary class of "residents" who are to be found more or less in number in every other town in England,'[20] a visitor reported in 1850. A community composed of a handful of ironmasters and agents and a vast mass of workers was bottom-heavy and naturally prone to riots. There were food riots in 1800, and in 1816 the dragoons had to be called in to restore order. A more serious insurrection followed in 1831, prompted, ironically, by William Crawshay II's radical sympathies, for it was the iron king who encouraged 'his miners' to sign a huge petition in support of the Great Reform Bill, as a result of which thousands of men gathered in the town on 30 May to hear speeches and unfurl a huge white banner, reading 'Reform in Parliament'. It marked the start of days of violent disturbances, which ended with huge crowds surrounding and threatening the homes of local Tories and burning local records. The 1831 rising – for this was not an ordinary riot – held the town in thrall from Thursday, 2 June to the following Monday. Very significantly for the town's future reputation as a centre of political militancy, the rebels hoisted a red flag as an emblem of revolt for the first time – a white flag that had been dipped in calf's blood. Even the arrival of the 93rd Highlanders on the Friday after the trouble started failed to disperse them. That Saturday saw a huge concentration of rioters blocking the Brecon Road northwards. The rebels were only put down when the Highlanders received reinforcements from the 110th Highlanders, the Glamorgan militia and the Yeomanry Cavalry, by which time days of fighting had killed 24 people and had given Merthyr a modern martyr in the form of 23-year-old Richard Lewis from Penderyn, the 'Dic Penderyn' of legend, who was executed in Cardiff after the rising was finally crushed.

The explosive violence that characterised social relations in the town was reflected in casual violence on the streets. 'When maddened with drink, the men fight long and furiously,' an observer noted in 1840. 'They turn out into the street, stripped to the waist and not content with blinding one another with their sledge hammer blows, they fasten their teeth in one another's ears and shoulders, and worry the flesh like dogs.'[21] Merthyr contained notorious sinks of vice, like the China district. Crime was a problem among a shifting population of young men and detection was often impossible owing to the closed clannish networks in the community, which resulted in Pembrokeshire men huddling in one area and Carmarthenshire men living together in another. The education commissioner who visited Merthyr in 1847 to assist the infamous inquiry into Welsh schooling, was struck by this atmosphere. 'This kind of clanship makes them oppose every obstacle to the detection of offenders who flock to Merthyr from all parts of Wales,' he wrote, adding that 'the district called China is a mere sink of thieves and prostitutes'.[22]

Mid-nineteenth-century Merthyr was a testosterone-fuelled world that was creating its own laws about sex as well as politics. A visitor to Penydarren works in 1850s was appalled by the open sexuality of the male and female workers, and by the community's tolerance of such behaviour. He was shocked when 'a huge giant of a fellow . . . pulled a girl to the ground . . . [and] cast himself beside her, and while she was half laughing, half screaming, and ineffectually struggling in his great grasp, he was stifling her with kisses, and although there were a dozen or twenty men and girls about, none seemed to pay the slightest attention to them'.[23]

Fresh workers continued to pour into Merthyr for the money. In spite of the perils of living on the edge of flaming mountains of ash, and the risk of succumbing to the epidemics that raged through the packed streets, there was a crazy glamour about life in the brawling town. The very lack of history, the sense of a new world being born, attracted the young and the bold. Life under the iron kings was dangerous and hard, but offered better wages than a farm. In the 1840s Clarke described a town that had money to spare. At street markets booksellers did a thriving trade, which was a sign that many workers were literate and had enough left over from their wages for non-essentials like books. Women were well dressed, not wearing rags. The town boasted a library, stationers and 'respectable' hotels to vie with the seamier attractions of the countless pubs. On Saturday and Monday nights, from about 8 to 10 p.m., the whole population took part in a *corso*, a 'sort of public promenade by the working classes', as Clarke described it.[24] The existence of such a weekly event suggests that most workers had a 'best' set of clothes to parade in and felt pride in putting them on. Truly wretched people would not have dreamed of taking part in such a public display. Historians have calculated that the average wage for an ironworker was about six times larger than the wage of the average farm worker in west Wales. Workers were not herded into Merthyr Tydfil. They chose to work there.

The constant rise in Glamorganshire's population in the nineteenth century was maintained by steady immigration from beyond its borders. By the 1860s a third of the population had been born outside the county. Glamorganshire was the prototype for a new Wales, which people migrated to, rather than from. For centuries Wales – like the rest of the Celtic fringe

– had been rural, remote and a place people left. Their docile acceptance of the Reformation had precluded the need to 'plant' loyal garrisons, as the government had done in Ulster. Instead, the Welsh had been left alone in their despised valleys and mountains.

The immigration into Wales that began in the eighteenth century was of a very different kind to the colonisation of Ulster. There, thousands of English and Scots families, settled in close proximity to one another. They marginalised the old Gaelic society and made Ulster an anglophone, British, region. The immigration to South Wales had the opposite effect, strengthening the existing language and culture, as the immigrants became absorbed into the Welsh mainstream.

The English and Welsh incomers to Glamorganshire were not a cohesive bloc, nor were they 'planted' there by the government with a view to breaking up the local society. The workers came to Wales in dribs and drabs and under their own steam, and the English among them were a minority of the immigrant population, which until the end of the century came mainly from rural west and north-west Wales. The English arrivals were at first subsumed into a Welsh milieu and became as Welsh as their neighbours, a phenomenon much noted by visitors who met families of recent English descent who now spoke only Welsh.

The world to which the immigrants came was proud and self-confident about its Welsh identity, perhaps more so than the north. An eighteenth-century observer ascribed this to geography:

> Ancient manners and customs have been more by far retained in S. Wales than in North Wales. English habits and manners prevail much more in North than in South Wales . . . the greater part of South Wales is separated from England by the Severn Sea for an extent of nearly 150 miles from Chepstow to St Davids Head, and where on the east it joins English counties, the towns the likes of the Gloucester, Hereford and Worcester are at great distances and [there is] no intercourse of trade between them and South Wales . . . but on the English side of North Wales, the Towns and Cities of Shrewsbury, Chester, Liverpool, etc, are hardly out of Wales.[25]

Even in the 1840s, after the influx of tens of thousands of newcomers and the creation of large industrial towns, visitors noted the resilience of Welsh culture in South Wales. According to Clarke, while 'the English tongue is pretty generally spoken in some of the Welsh towns . . . it is not at all probable that it will ever be so generally adopted as to supersede the native tongue.' The Vale of Glamorgan still looked to English visitors like a foreign land. E. Roberts said the arrival of an English stranger remained 'an event' in 1852 in the rural parts of the county. 'Children flock shyly to the doors, cling to their mothers' gowns and look with great wondering blue eyes upon you, not venturing in their puzzled surprise to make a comment till you are past; and then you hear them in that strangely sounding Celtic tongue, which for a moment suggests a dialect spoken only in the islands of some distant seas.'

Even in industrial Merthyr, he encountered a militant Welsh nationalism that seemed more than capable of holding Englishness at bay. In some ways it was more robust than its Irish counterpart, which at that stage paid little attention to language questions. 'They have a fear lest their language should be slighted, and diluted or annihilated,' he wrote, 'and in consequence their Druidical and literary societies and their grand Eisteddfods tend to preserve the language and all connected with it in a condition of purity.'[26] It was not just English immigrants who were drawn into the Welsh world. Even the Spanish Catholics who arrived in Merthyr in the late nineteenth century drifted from their Catholic chapel into Welsh-speaking Nonconformity.

Merthyr was always a stronghold of religious dissent. According to one tradition, it dated from the 1620s, when dissenters allegedly worshipped at nearby Blaencanaid. That may have been an invention of Iolo's, who was keen to put Glamorgan in the vanguard of every movement. But it was certainly an area of Puritan activity by the 1650s, when Walter Craddock excaimed that 'the gospel is run over the mountains between Brecknockshire and Monmouthshire as the fire in the thatch'.[27] The Anglican Church in rural Glamorganshire mirrored the weaknesses of the Church in the rest of Wales. In the see of Llandaff, parishes were too large to serve but too poor to divide. The old parish churches, situated on the tops of hills or mountains, no longer suited recent settlement patterns. Even before Merthyr exploded into a metropolis, the Anglicans had lost their way in the town. The Bishop's visitation in 1763 found only a dozen communicants in the parish church and noted with envy the existence of a 'Pompeous [sic] Meeting House erected on the northside of the village'.[28] By 1817 the number of Anglican communicants had risen to 40, but as the parish now contained 11,104 inhabitants it was not an advance.[29]

The 1851 religious census confirmed Merthyr's position as a Nonconformist stronghold. About 90 per cent of the population belonged to Nonconformist denominations compared to 7 per cent in the Church of England – a paltry advance, given the thousands of English immigrants who had moved in since the turn of the century. The bishops were partly to blame. Edward Copleston, Bishop of Llandaff in the 1830s, was typical of the prelates Gladstone later blamed for the Church's crisis in Wales. An English academic and former Provost of Oriel College in Oxford, he was at sea in the industrial environment of Merthyr Tydfil. His successor, Alfred Ollivant, bishop from 1849 to 1882, was more active but it was too late then to recreate the vanished Church of Bishop Morgan. The Welsh-speakers had long left the Church for Nonconformity and the ground could only be recovered among anglophones and English immigrants, while appeals to that constituency merely confirmed the Church's status as an alien institution among the majority.

The industrial revolution saved Welsh in the nineteenth century, much as Morgan's Bible had saved it in the sixteenth century and Methodism in the eighteenth. Nonconformity alone could not have preserved the Welsh identity if the land had remained thinly populated and mostly rural. The Welsh language would have experienced the same slow attrition as Gaelic in the Scottish Highlands. Nor would a Welsh identity have survived if the industrial revolution had begun in the anglicised border towns of Monmouth, or Chepstow. The rural Welshmen who poured in would then have adopted the dominant English culture.

The chance circumstances that brought the industrial revolution to Glamorganshire saved Welsh culture for a couple of generations, and turned Merthyr Tydfil into the first large town in Britain where English was not the main language of the streets. It was, perhaps, the first properly Celtic town of modern times. Merthyr Tydfil showed that the Welsh language could escape the fate of Irish, Scottish Gaelic, Manx and Cornish, which had retreated like mist before the advance of streets, schools, gas lamps and railway stations. For once the iron rule had been broken that insisted 'progress' spoke English.

Glamorganshire's role in the Welsh renaissance was demonstrated by the fact that by the end of the nineteenth century it accounted for one-third of the Welsh-speaking population. Moreover, Merthyr Tydfil, the industrial heart of the county and the focus of immigrants from all over Britain, contained the second-highest percentage of Welsh-speakers in the county – 68 per cent in 1891, or 75,000 of the town's 110,000 inhabitants.[30]

The iron age peaked in Merthyr in the 1850s. By the end of the decade the town felt an icy wind of competition from rivals in Counties Durham, Northumberland, Cumberland, Lancashire, Yorkshire, Lincolnshire, Northamptonshire and in Scotland. Penydarren closed in 1858. Plymouth was sold in 1863. Even the mighty Crawshays faltered. In May 1874 Richard Crawshay blew out all his blast furnaces after the enginemen and firemen refused to accept a cut of 20 per cent in wages. 'I have no orders of any kind,' he explained, 'and cannot obtain any at a price which would save my losing money unless a 20 per cent reduction took place, and it would be sheer folly to stock iron at present prices.' Cyfartha was not yet finished. The works were converted to steel production at huge cost, but the air of confidence had gone. A diamond jubilee review of Merthyr Tydfil's progress in 1897 struck a more uncertain note than earlier accounts, recalling the first drop in Merthyr's population in the late 1870s, the closure of Plymouth and Penydarren and the lockouts and strikes that followed. Immigration picked up again as steel and coal replaced iron as South Wales's main export. In the 1890s Merthyr's population surged again, echoing the rise in Glamorganshire as a whole.

But in the 1890s the factors that once worked to strengthen Welsh culture in South Wales began to undo it. Immigration had made Glamorganshire more Welsh and the number of Welsh-speaking immigrants exceeded that of English-speakers, but in the 1890s the ratio changed. As the coal mines drew in more labourers, pushing the county population over the million mark, the seam of Welsh-speakers became exhausted. Rural Wales had now surrendered its surplus youth and by 1911 the English and Irish made up the bulk of the 400,000 immigrants of Glamorganshire's 1.1 million population.[31] The balance suddenly tilted against Welsh in industrial South Wales as dense pockets of English immigrants settled whole areas and for the first time failed to learn Welsh. They planted English language and culture in the middle of Iolo's Vale.

This shift had an impact on the political culture of South Wales. For decades Wales had been Liberal territory, the Tories supported only by English-speakers, the gentry and the Anglican Church. Industrial change in the south had pulled the Liberals leftwards but Liberalism had not lost its grip. Joseph Abraham 'Mabon', MP for Rhondda from 1885 to 1918 and for Rhondda West until 1920, represented a 'Liberal–Labour' ticket that harnessed the core Liberal values of self-reliance to the new politics of trade unionism. But around the turn of the century, English immigration and increasing industrial unrest began to alter the political chemistry. Men like Mabon, equally at home in the miners' lodge, the Calvinist Methodist chapel and the eisteddfod, began to appear archaic – too parochially Welsh and neither British nor militant enough for the new times. Mabon was proud to say he owed everything 'to the Sunday School, the Band of Hope and to the Eisteddfod'.[32] The new generation of miners' leaders owed very little to any of that. They would not have been seen dead at an eisteddfod, let alone reciting the Lord's Prayer in Welsh in parliament, as Mabon did on one occasion.

The North Wales that nurtured Lloyd George, radical, Welsh-speaking and Nonconformist, started to diverge even more widely than before from the South, which became increasingly deaf to appeals to Welsh nationalism and the memory of Owain Glyndwr. Iolo Morganwg had always asserted the difference between North and South Wales, insisting on the more Welsh quality of the south. Now that was turned on its head, with the north remaining more faithful to the language, chapel culture and the Liberals, while the south shifted allegiances quite dramatically to the English language and the new Labour Party.

The socialist apostle in the south was a Scotsman, Keir Hardie, and his accidental arrival in Merthyr Tydfil resembles the legends of those Celtic saints who washed up in barrels or on leaves in Cornwall after trying to get somewhere different. Hardie won his first seat in parliament in 1892 in West Ham, in east London, following the call of the Trades Union Congress for Labour to be represented in parliament independently of the Liberals. He lost the seat in 1895 and a tour of the country in 1898 and 1899 brought him to the South Wales coalfields, where he addressed meetings at Penydarren and in Merthyr Tydfil's Temperance Hall. His Independent Labour Party quickly established itself in the bitter industrial climate there and the first branch was set up in July 1896 at the Drill Hall, under Tom Mann, while other branches opened in Dowlais and Penydarren, gaining 278 members by 1898.

The coal stoppage of 1898 was a fillip. An ugly industrial dispute, it ended in September with the miners' defeat. The conflict strained the miners' loyalty to Mabon's politics of compromise and fuelled an appetite for politics based on raw class war, not compromise. Mabon's mixture of Labour and Nonconformist values began to look irrelevant. The establishment of the South Wales Miners' Federation was a direct result of the 1898 strike, and after Hardie visited the town in 1899 a miners' meeting nominated him as their candidate for parliament, a decision reached symbolically enough in the vestry of Bethel Chapel in Abernant.

Hardie's own choice was to stand in Preston, however. It was only after losing the race there that he sped to Merthyr, campaigning for all of 11 hours before the polling booths closed. The result was a historic victory. In the two-seat constituency Hardie came second to the sitting MP, D. E. Thomas, a political freelancer, beating the other sitting MP, the Liberal Pritchard Morgan, by 5,745 to 4,104. Hardie once again entered parliament.

The result was pregnant with importance for the future of Wales. Welsh-speaking Wales had been defeated by an anglophone and a newcomer, and a confirmed chapel-goer had been vanquished by someone who saw the New Testament mainly as a call to socialism. Morgan campaigned on all the issues that once seemed dear to Wales, stressing disestablishment and Wales's right to home rule – and lost. Unwisely, he had alienated the chapels by his support for licensed victuallers, but whether or not this factor lay behind his defeat, Merthyr again showed the way. The first industrial town in Wales and the first town to hoist the red flag was the first town in Wales to elect a Labour MP.

Hardie was the right man to smooth the way from Nonconformity to socialism. No longer a Christian believer in any orthodox sense, he dressed his politics in biblical imagery, wooing many Liberals who might have been wary of continental Marxism. There was a biblical undercurrent to many of his speeches. 'I first learned my Socialism in the New Testament, where I still find my chief inspiration,'[33] the *Merthyr Express* on 29 September 1900 quoted him as saying. Socialism, he wrote in 1907, 'if not a religion in itself, is at least a handmaiden to religion, and as such entitled to the support of all who pray for the coming of Christ's kingdom on earth'.[34] He recalled his fight in West Ham with his Tory opponent Major Barnes as a battle 'between righteousness and the powers of darkness'.[35]

The moral tone was attractive to people reared on Nonconformity. One of Hardie's biographers wrote: 'His appeal to Welsh miners lay in his being able to translate socialist ethics into the imagery of popular Nonconformity. This, he claimed, was "real religion", the creed of Robert Burns, of the Ten Commandments, and the Sermon on the Mount, not of pharisaical ministers and their bourgeois congregations.'[36] Hardie made a substitute church of the ILP. Caroline Benn's biography cited his suffragette friend Sylvia Pankhurst as opining that socialism 'came to him as a revelation . . . filling him with joy and eagerness to tell the great hope to everyone he would see'.[37]

Hardie's moral fervour explained part of his appeal to a community still influenced markedly by Nonconformity. He also sounded sympathetic to Welsh nationalism. 'I like yourselves am a Celt,' he assured voters in Merthyr Tydfil just before the 1900 poll closed, 'with all the love of the homeland, its language and its literature, which every Celt feels. I love the people to whom I belong. I am one of yourselves, "yr wyf ynon o honoch chwl". I want to remove from your lives the weary burden of care, poverty and toil, which presses so heavily upon you.'[38] As MP, he affirmed those sympathies, taking the stage at the 1901 eisteddfod in Merthyr Tydfil[39] and in 1911 opposing the investiture of the Prince of Wales, the future Edward VIII, on the patriotic grounds that it reminded Wales of the conquering exploits of 'an English king and his robber barons'.[40]

Material about Jesus and the Sermon on the Mount was reserved for Welsh constituents. When Hardie addressed the other faithful, the socialist faithful, he sounded a different note, insisting he was an orthodox Marxist and quoting Engels and Kropotkin. To them, he insisted the Labour Party 'embodies the Socialist tradition of Karl Marx and the great founders of modern Socialism'.[41]

Down in Merthyr Tydfil the Nonconformist ministers did not hear that side of his thinking. Many of them rushed to support the Labour Party, under the impression they were endorsing a Christian Celtic nationalist who wanted only to deliver what the Liberals had long promised. Hardie nurtured his Nonconformist voters over the years and his election material in 1906 (when his Liberal opponent, Henry Radcliffe, was a Calvinist Methodist), and again in 1910, included endorsements from key Non-conformist leaders. The new gospel in South Wales stole the tunes of the old one, for in the 1906 election the Labour Party in Merthyr popularised socialist hymns that echoed the Christian ones, after altering the ideology:

Rise! for the dawn is breaking
Arm for the longed-for fray
Now there is no mistaking
This is the workers' day.[42]

In the 1910 election the Labour Party's propaganda in Merthyr Tydfil included the claim that most chapel ministers supported his candidacy. 'The number of pastors in the constituency who are supporting Mr Keir Hardie is greater than ever before,' leaflets announced. 'They know that socialism means the application of Christian teaching to modern life and industry.'[44] Hardie's election address that year made the same point, stress-ing that socialism had 'no relation to Atheism or Free Love'. A manifesto signed by 13 ministers denounced his opponents as 'Tories, Protectionists, Dukes and Gradgrinds'.

In 1912 the Labour Party conference opened in Merthyr Tydfil with a dedication service at the Tabernacle Baptist church at Aberdare, led by Rowland Jones. The ministers' support for the Labour Party ensured that Welsh socialists would never turn furiously on organised religion like the Spanish anarchists in Barcelona in 1905 or the Bolsheviks in Russia after 1917. Yet the Nonconformist ministers were mistaken in seeing Labour as a more efficient deliverer of promises than the Liberals. Hardie's denunciations of English kings and his verbal pledges of support for home rule and the Welsh language blinded them to the extent to which Labour was also the party of anglicisation. Labour's election material was all in English, even in 1900 when almost 60 per cent of the town's inhabitants spoke Welsh as their first language. At the most, a little phrase in Welsh was tucked in at the bottom of the leaflets and posters, purely as decoration.

The personnel of the party tended to be English. 'The new local leaders had English names,' a recent historian of South Wales has remarked, citing William Brace, A. J. Cook, Vernon Hartshorn, Frank Hodges and James Winstone among others.[44] For all his show of Celtic ardour, Hardie struck a new note by not residing in Wales, the first of many Labour Welsh grandees to represent Welsh people from far away.

The new party sold the message that to concentrate on local national issues, like the Irish parliamentary party, was bourgeois and reactionary, diverting people's attention from class politics. In theory Labour propagated an internationalist outlook. In practice its internationalism subordinated Welsh interests and concerns to those of the larger English working class. The Labour Party stealthily rehabilitated the view, much admired by the Tories, that Wales was not a country but a region.

If the ministers thought they could graft their beliefs on to the new movement they misunderstood their object. The first generation of Labour men dressed their creed with a veneer of religion, much as the early Christians co-opted pagan shrines for their own use. But the second generation dispensed with the connection. They dumped the socialist hymns along with talk about the New Testament and Celtic nationalism. Socialist lectures replaced chapel sermons. The Junior Labour League replaced the chapel youth clubs and chapel buildings and vestries were abandoned as Labour meeting places. In 1912, the Ystrad Rhondda Labour club was opened after the local ILP decided it wanted its own premises, instead of depending on the goodwill of the ministers. Their example was followed elsewhere. As the Labour Party confirmed its grip on politics in South Wales, it no longer needed to woo the chapels, and attacked ministers. A harsh open letter to the clergy of the Rhondda Valley in the *Rhondda Socialist* of 20 July 1912 even charged many of them with being reactionaries. 'In local elections, as a rule, you break your professed role of neutrality, and take sides – AGAINST THE WORKERS,' it claimed. 'If the candidate happens to be a socialist, you make the shallow and hypocritical pretence that you oppose him because of his economic creed . . . the fact of the matter is . . . you seem to regard the workers' cause with hatred.'[45]

As the population transferred their enthusiasm from the chapel to the party, religious practice fell away. In Merthyr the career of David Pughe is illustrative. This dynamic Wesleyan pastor would have been in his element in the Merthyr Tydfil of 30 years previously. But in Merthyr Tydfil on the eve of the First World War chapels were fast emptying, whether or not the ministers were any good. Pughe fought back, scrapping reserved and rented pews, and performing dramatic stunts to remind the public of the importance of the chapel. One Saturday night he even rode through the streets of Merthyr Tydfil on horseback to gain publicity.[46] He got nowhere and in 1915 he left the town in disillusion to serve as a war chaplain. Workers had once used chapels to learn to read, speak in public and manage communal finances. But now the trade unions, workers institutes, miners' welfare halls and the Workers' Educational Association halls had taken over these functions. The chapels were left with the truly religious core, which turned out to be far smaller than anyone had imagined.

The careers of Arthur Horner and Aneurin 'Nye' Bevan illustrate the character of the new political elite emerging from the mining community. Horner was president of the South Wales Miners' Federation in the 1930s and a key figure in the National Union of Mineworkers until his retirement in 1959. He inhabited a different universe to Mabon. Born in 1894 to an English immigrant father from Northumberland and a Welsh mother, Horner grew up in the anglophone, increasingly British, Merthyr Tydfil of the early twentieth century. As a youngster he felt the pull of the Nonconformist tradition, very briefly working as a preacher for the Churches of Christ, an emphatically working-class, anti-revivalist denomination, and attending their Birmingham training college in 1912 and 1913. But Horner was never a Mabon in the making. Not for him a lifetime's dedication to the chapel choir. 'Only slowly did I reach the point of accepting the materialistic conception of history and the struggle of the working-class as the only way to emancipation,'[47] he wrote. Once he did reach that point, however, the break with Christianity was final and he joined the Communist Party soon after its foundation in 1920. Entirely British in his horizons, he did not give Welsh nationality a thought.

By the 1930s there were signs that industrial South Wales, having dispensed with Liberalism and Nonconformity, might progress through the Labour Party to Communism. The mining town of Mardy gained a reputation as a 'Little Moscow'. When Horner stood as the Communist candidate in Rhondda East in 1931 he took more than 10,000 votes, nearly half the 22,000 votes won by the Labour candidate. In 1933 Horner almost won the seat, taking 11,128 votes against 14,127 for Labour.[48] If Labour was sometimes coquettish towards the old religious and national traditions of South Wales, the Communist Party was not. With every year, it seemed, the South Walians put their old allegiances further behind them.

Nye Bevan was a near contemporary of Horner's. Born in 1897 in Tredegar, he came from a more Welsh background. His father David 'loved music and hymn-singing round the organ, wrote poetry and won prizes at eisteddfodau'.[49] But though Bevan senior was ensconced in the Welsh milieu of chapels and eisteddfods, his son looked on the whole phenomenon with distaste. Nye Bevan entered parliament as Labour MP for Ebbw Vale in 1929. An outright atheist, he was a staunch proponent of centralised politics, regarding any concession to regional sensibilities as a diversion from the class struggle. Yet, to the post-Second World War generation in Britain Bevan was the archetypal Welshman, with his political militancy and tub-thumping debating style. He helped form a new image of the Welsh as differing from the English mainly in their espousal of strident, left-wing politics.

South Wales followed Merthyr Tydfil's lead in adopting the Labour creed. Wales had one Labour MP in 1900 and one in 1906. But the Liberal edifice crumbled fast after that. In 1909 the South Wales Miners' Federation formally affiliated itself to Labour, forcing Mabon, the union's president until 1912, to sever his links with the Liberals. With his love of Welsh and of the chapel he now seemed a dinosaur, a tolerated relic of a vanished world. With each industrial confrontation, the ties between the Liberals and the workers frayed, and the Tonypandy riots of 1910 dealt the alliance another blow. The 1910 by-election in mid-Glamorgan was a sign of the times. The election was occasioned by the departure of Samuel Evans, a Welsh nationalist and Liberal of the old school who was once a leader of Cymru Fydd. In 1910 he was made president of the divorce court and the seat was up for grabs. The miners wanted Vernon Hartshorn, one of the new Labour men, as the joint Lib-Lab candidate, but the Liberals balked at such a choice and fought the seat independently with a devout Quaker, F. W. Gibbins, as their candidate. The result was the public breakdown of the

Liberals' battered alliance with the trade unions and although Gibbins won by 8,920 to 6,210,[50] the margin was not impressive, given the fact that this was still a Welsh-speaking area.

The 1918 election saw Labour emerge as the official opposition in parliament for the first time, winning 59 seats, of which 10 were in Wales. The election was not a true party contest but a referendum on Lloyd George's leadership in the First World War. It was in 1922 that the true extent of the socialist takeover in Wales was revealed, when Labour took 18 seats, including every seat in Glamorganshire and Monmouthshire. In the west, Ramsay MacDonald – like Hardie, a Scotsman – won Aberavon. Only the agricultural west and north remained Liberal. The era when the Liberals were the national party of Wales was over. But Labour never became the new national party for Wales in its stead and it did not want to.

The once impregnable Welsh language crumbled along with the chapels and the Liberal Party. It disappeared most quickly in the south but by the mid-1920s, observers were shocked by the decline in the north, too. 'To anyone who knew such places as Llandudno, Rhyl and Colwyn Bay and even smaller places like Barmouth, Aberdovey and Criccieth thirty years ago, and who knows what they are like today, this situation cannot but be fraught with serious misgivings,' the *Welsh Outlook* lamented in 1926. 'A process of peaceful penetration has been taking place.'[51] A few years later the same publication lamented fresh signs of retreat. 'The Anglicising forces which wear down the national traditions and assimilate us to our neighbours were never more insistent or pervasive,' it complained in 1933. 'The press, the radio, the multiple shop, the tourist industry, the cinema, and all forms of organised sport . . . all absorb the minds of the inhabitants not only of the mining valleys but of the remotest hamlets.' It mourned the death of an 'old fashioned solid Welsh life', adding waspishly and in language that sounds controversial today: 'The erstwhile yokel affects plus-fours and affects a discriminating taste in cocktails. In town and valley the streets are thronged with well-rouged, lip-sticked emulations of Garbo or Dietrich, and these are escorted by youths who were ushered into the world to nigger music.'[52]

The retreat of Welsh-speaking Wales did not go unchallenged. By the early 1920s, when it dawned on some that Wales's culture and language were spinning headlong towards annihilation, the call arose to create a real nationalist party, which would revive the *hwyl* of the long-defunct Cymru Fydd. The Welsh Nationalist Party, Plaid Cymru, appeared in 1925 as the result of the amalgamation of a few smaller groups and made some national impact a decade later when its leader, a lecturer from the University of Wales in Swansea, Saunders Lewis, and two colleagues, Lewis Valentine and D. J. Williams, set fire to the Air Ministry's new bombing range on the Lleyn peninsula. The government's selection of the peninsula was insensitive. The area was one of the last bastions of Welsh speech and the imposition of a military base was seen as a potential cultural battering ram. To add to the insult, it was only chosen after several English localities had protested against it coming to their areas.

At his trial in Caernarfon on 13 October 1936 Lewis defended his action in otherworldly terms as a violent act undertaken 'in the light of this fundamental principle of Christendom', which was that people had a 'duty to preserve the life of a nation, and to defend it from any mortal blow'.[53] The Caernarfon jury was impressed and failed to reach a verdict. But the Old Bailey jury, to which the case was transferred, was not, and Lewis was sentenced to nine months' jail.

In spite of his arson attack, neither Lewis nor the Welsh Nationalists whom he led until 1939 had much in common with the 'physical force' tradition in Irish nationalism. He was not even an extremist, pleading merely, as he put it in his 1945 manifesto, for 'a Christian, moderate and conditional nationalism' that would dam the 'unchecked rush of English totalitarianism after the war'.[54] Under his stewardship the Welsh Nationalists were an intellectual group, European in their outlook and disdainful of doctrines of racial or cultural superiority. Lewis never suffered from the small-nation syndrome of claiming everything began and ended in Wales. On the contrary he was 'totally uninterested in demonstrating the independence of any Welsh tradition',[55] and wanted only to maintain Wales's separate and individual contribution to the stream of European thought.

Lewis was the real leader of the Nationalists long after his formal resignation as party president, but neither he nor his party spoke for Wales as the Liberals had done. There no longer was one Wales to speak for, so clearly did Welsh North Wales and socialist South Wales belong to parallel worlds. Lewis was no Lloyd George either. He never drew comparisons with Owain Glyndwr or Llewelyn the Great. He was too reclusive and bookish to be popular and his convinced Catholicism – he was a convert – went against the grain. Thanks to this, well until the 1940s the Nationalists were often thought of as 'the Pope's party'. A man of spare frame, with a gnarled, gnomish face and a scholastic tone, Lewis seemed to have been mysteriously transported from the Wales of the Middle Ages, only to become a reluctant prisoner of the twentieth century. He meant virtually nothing to most people in the industrial south, where concerns focused in the 1930s on the economic recession, pushing worries about the language even further to the periphery.

The Liberal–Nonconformist alliance in the nineteenth century had succeeded because it bound the survival of the Welsh language to a range of issues, from electoral and land reform to disestablishment, anti-slavery and temperance. The sum of the parts made up the idea of Wales, against which the Tory gentry and the Established Church could argue only feebly. Saunders Lewis, with his concentration on the language and issues such as dominion status for Wales, never articulated an idea of Welshness that appealed to the anglicised working class. When war broke out in 1939 Labour rallied Wales to the struggle against Nazism as much as any other part of Britain. As usual, Lewis and the Nationalists were out of step, calling for a negotiated peace with Germany and defending the collaborationist Vichy government of France.

The Nationalists' dependence on the Welsh-speaking population, meanwhile, trapped them electorally within a decreasing proportion of the population. In 1911, 43.5 per cent of the population spoke Welsh but by 1921 that had dropped to 37.1 per cent and by 1931 it was down again to 36.8 per cent. The first post-war census in 1951 revealed a bigger slump, to 28.9 per cent, while in 1961 it was down to 26 per cent. Between then and 1971 there was another major fall, to 20.9 per cent. It was, as one recent commentator noted with morbid humour, increasingly seen as 'a language for use between consenting adults – as with homosexuals'.[56]

The census figures showed the decline was not consistent. Like the *Titanic*, the Welsh ship let in water and then remained stable for a while, only to lurch head-down to the depths. It was only in the 1950s and 1960s that the full effects of the sea-change signified by Hardie's victory in 1900 were felt, as the Welsh-speaking generation born in the 1870s and 1880s died off. Nonconformity began to sound its death rattle at the same time. Mostly Welsh-speaking by a majority of three to one as late as 1961, the rolls of the Nonconformist denominations dropped from 400,000 in that year to 284,000 in 1975, of whom around 100,000 were Calvinist Methodists, 82,000 Independents, 65,000 Baptists, 30,000 Wesleyans and 12,700 United Reformed.[57]

Lewis's achievements at the ballot box were humble. The first contest in Caernarfonshire, fought by Valentine, brought the Nationalists 609 votes out of 38,000. It did a little better in 1935, when it took 2,534 votes and better still in 1943, when Lewis contested the University of Wales seat, losing by 1,330 to 3,098 votes. But even an institution like that, established as a symbol of Welsh nationalism, did not hand him victory. The party contested several seats in 1945 and won a derisory 1 per cent of the votes overall. The Labour landslide of 1945 was the low-water mark. A hostile portrait of Lewis in 1946 sniggered that he was under the delusion that he would turn out to be the 'Masaryk of Wales', building a Welsh state out of the ruins of Britain much as Jan Masaryk had built the Czecho-slovak state out of the ruins of Austria-Hungary. The anonymous re-viewer feigned sympathy with a party burdened by 'bitterness and hate and the (possibly unintentional) air of physical superiority with which only too many of its members have regarded the bulk of their fellow-countrymen'.[58]

Lewis's greatest achievement for his cause came long after his retirement in 1962, when he was invited to deliver the annual radio lecture for the BBC Welsh region. In a talk entitled 'Tynged yr Iaith' (The Fate of the Language), he assumed a gloomy, sepulchral tone, predicting the absolute death of the language by 2000 and describing Welsh as a language that had been 'driven into a corner, ready to be thrown, like a worthless rag, on the dung-heap'.[59] His claim that the real responsibility for this lay not so much with the English bureaucracy as with the timid and indifferent Welsh-speakers themselves touched a raw nerve. An immediate result of the furore generated by the speech was the establishment of the Cymdeithas Yr Iaith Cymraeg, the Welsh Language Society, which immediately initiated a series of publicity-seeking non-violent campaigns aimed at forcing the authorities to concede equal status for the Welsh language. They started by blocking the road bridge in Aberystwyth in February 1963 and fanned out into campaigns against English-only post offices, road signs in English, the payment of road tax licences in English, and even occupied the BBC offices in Cardiff and Bangor. The invest-iture of the Prince of Wales in 1969 in Caernarfon Castle was a convenient focus for these protests.

For the first time since the 1890s, the Nationalists tapped into the spirit of the age. Lewis had argued for the language issue at a time when it seemed frivolous to many, compared with the recession and the rise of Fascism, issues that Labour claimed to have the answers to. But nationalist grievances became respectable on the left in the 1960s, the great era of protest from Quebec to Berkeley, from Paris to Prague. Civil rights activists were on the march in Northern Ireland. The Welsh Nationalists enjoyed that fillip that comes from being suddenly crowned by the media with 'relevance'. The Labour establishment in Wales had also lost its youthful image.

Nevertheless, the popularity of nationalist protests within Wales was debatable and by the time the Welsh Language Society halted its civil disobedience campaign in 1976, it still had only 2,700 members.[60] This was well up from the few hundred of the early 1960s but only a fraction of the Welsh-speaking population and only a tiny fraction of the membership the Gaelic League enjoyed in Ireland in its heyday.

The Nationalists' track record in the elections of the 1960s and 1970s was also mixed. Plaid Cymru repeated the success of the Scottish Nationalist Party in at last capturing a couple of seats in Wales after a historic by-election victory in Carmarthen in 1966. But this was followed by a massive setback in 1979 when Wales voted overwhelmingly against the offer of devolved government put forward by the Labour Prime Minister Jim Callaghan. The powerful Labour Establishment urged a 'no' vote, while divisions within the Nationalist camp over the limited powers of self-government ensured the 'yes' campaign fared worse in Wales than in Scotland. In the years that followed that débâcle, Plaid Cymru recovered enough to hold on to about four seats and after the New Labour victory of 1997 led to the creation of the Welsh National Assembly, the party scored around 28 per cent of the votes to the new body in May 1999. It was second only to Labour on 37 per cent and well above the Tories, who gained 16 per cent.

The ups and downs experienced by the Nationalists in the elections of the 1960s and 1970s and the defeat of the 1979 devolution proposal do not tell the whole story of Plaid Cymru's impact on Welsh culture, however. Far more significant than the tally of seats won was the effect that the whole phenomenon had on central government's attitude. The SNP victories in Scotland had no marked effect on government policy on Gaelic culture because the SNP never saw itself as a Gaelic party. But Plaid Cymru did see itself as the party of Welsh-speaking Wales, so its victories elicited a rather different response. For the first time, the British government was forced to recognise the existence of a substantial non-anglophone culture, and to rethink attitudes that had been set in stone since Henry VIII's so-called Acts of Union. The new, more conciliatory attitude began under Labour in the mid-1960s but continued under the Conservatives. The Welsh Language Bill of 1967 was a milestone, for it granted Welsh equal status to English in the courts. The Council for the Welsh Language, set up in 1973, stimulated a demand for bilingual schooling and more bilingual material in the broadcast media. This in turn led in 1982 to the creation of a Welsh-language television station, Sianel Pedwar Cymru (S4C).

Welsh is more visible than ever before. The moment I drove across the Severn Bridge, signs written in a different language proclaimed I had entered a different land. It was not like Scotland, where Gaelic bilingual signs were limited to a few Highland areas. As for the Bretons in France, they can only dream of such symbols of recognition. You can live your life in Welsh now, at least in theory. The officials of the North Western Railway, who fired workers on the line from Holyhead to Chester for their inability or unwillingness to speak English in the 1890s, would have a tough time of it now. It is the English-speaking monoglot who faces a problem in trying to work in the public sector, and the language sections of universities do a booming trade in teaching basic Welsh to English professionals who have taken such posts. Saunders Lewis saved more than most people thought possible by his stirring radio address back in 1962.

I realised Welsh would not die out in my lifetime when I walked into a supermarket in Caernarfon and watched a crowd of unruly-looking teenagers march in to stock up on bottles of beer. They and the cashier who served them were not more than 20 years old but their transactions were conducted entirely in Welsh. It surprised me because in Scotland, Ireland and the Isle of Man I had never seen such mundane activities carried out in anything but English. I had seen or heard Gaelic used in churches, in music and in seminars and on signposts and in beautiful books, but I had never seen it used by what might be described as 'yobs'.

A language and a culture can only stay alive when they are worn casually and unselfconsciously. Welsh has that quality. One evening I stopped off in a pub in a north Pembrokeshire village and found myself in a crowded, smoke-filled environment where everyone was speaking Welsh. But it was an earthy, ordinary place with a jukebox in the corner churning out 1950s American hits and the crowd of men and women shouting at each other above the din spiced their Welsh almost constantly with English swear words. It all seemed alive – a natural affair, rather than some kind of cultural project.

Is Wales the last and best hope of the Celts? The end of the story is still uncertain. The battle for public visibility, important as it was, did not end the *Kulturkampf*. Wales has suffered from the same problem as the Highlands, the west of Ireland and the Isle of Man – a surge of English immigrants who do up the local houses and do down the local culture. They are not all indifferent to Welsh. At a language course in Bangor I met one couple who had moved to Wales from the English midlands in their late sixties. A decade on they were almost fluent in Welsh, having learned the

1. Welsh champion: Bishop William Morgan, translator of the Bible.

2. The Word in Welsh: title page of the first Welsh Bible, translated by William Morgan and published in 1588.

3. Vogue for druids: an eighteenth-century depiction of a sacrifice at Stonehenge.

4. (*left*) Manx patron: Thomas Wilson, longstanding bishop of Man in the eighteenth century.

5. Men of the Spirit: charismatic Welsh preachers like Daniel Rowland gave a huge fillip to Welsh in the eighteenth century.

6. Cornish celebrity: Dolly Pentreath of Mousehole famed as the last Cornish speaker.

7. (*left*) Epic victory: *James MacPherson*, engraving by C. Knight after a painting by Sir Joshua Reynolds. MacPherson's *Ossian* was an eighteenth-century best-seller.

8. Mercy killing: Daniel O'Connell, engraving published 1844, by W. Holl. The anglophone leader of early nineteenth-century Irish nationalism had little time for the Irish.

9. Ideal home: the cottage of the Gaelic revivalist Patrick Pearse in Connemara. His cult of a rural, Irish-speaking Ireland reamains unrealised.

10. The Highland cult: *Sir Walter Scott and hunting scene*, mezzotint published in 1891, after a painting probably by Sir David Wilkie.

11. A romanticised past: *Salem*, 1908, by S. Curnon Vosper. The 'national dress' was largely an invention.

12. Cornish bard: Henry Jenner, father of the modern Cornish language movement and first Grand Bard of Gorseth Kernow (the Cornish Gorsedd) at Boscawen-Un, June 1927.

13. (*left*) Tourist invasion: poster of the Isle of Man Steam Packet Company.

14. Empty islands: burial ground on Skye. The churches gave such islands their current half-deserted appearance.

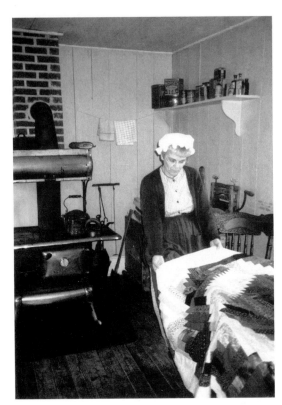

15. (*left*) The Highlands reincarnated: Gaelic museum in Nova Scotia.

16. Gaelic revival: tombs with celtic motifs at Milltown cemetery, West Belfast.

17. Memory of the saints: Bretons carrying banners of celtic saints at the *grand pardon* of St Anne in Finistère.

18. (*left*) Living tongue: Fabio Gonzales, a young Welsh speaker in Gaiman, Patagonia.

19. New Wales: a nonconformist chapel in Patagonia.

20. Colonial grave: the resting place of one of the early
Welsh settlers in Patagonia.

21. A visible change: bilingual signs in Ruthin, Clwyd, Wales.

language from scratch. They were far more motivated about Welsh culture than most of their Welsh-born neighbours, they said. It was the same with a 70-year-old father and his 40-something daughter I met on the same course. They came from the north-west of England and lived in a caravan on the Lleyn peninsula. They were working-class people with little money but were determined to 'fit in' to their new environment. A third couple I met were two women in their thirties from the south-east of England who had found work in the health service in Anglesey. After two years they were almost fluent. They worked with stroke patients and found Welsh invaluable in dealing with the elderly.

But they were not the whole picture. The problem is not energetic English immigrants who have come to live and work in Wales but the huge number of wealthy, middle-class families who have bought second homes in the 'unspoiled' north and west, ratcheting up house prices and pushing out the local people. The impact of this kind of immigration has been very marked in Snowdonia, the Lleyn peninsula and in the St Davids area, transforming quite poor Welsh-speaking areas into wealthy English-speaking ones.

Culture clashes are frequent. In the heavily colonised village of Solta near St Davids I met a shopkeeper who was in tears after a bruising encounter with a Welsh-speaking family who had berated her for her inability to speak their language. I commiserated with her account until she remarked, unthinkingly: 'Don't these people realise they'd be nothing without us?' All too many English incomers I met across Wales voiced similar attitudes. They did not mind Welsh being used in churches, or hearing it spoken in the street, especially by old women. That was charming and marginal. But they often objected fiercely to anything that signified its continuing existence as a working language.

As late as the early 1960s a commentator remarked that it was 'still possible to traverse Wales from . . . the north-western extremity of Anglesey to . . . the Carmarthen coast of south Wales without having to leave a community in which over 80 per cent of the population spoke Welsh'.[61] The next two decades, in spite of the achievements of the Nationalists in the sphere of public life, saw the break-up of that landmass into a number of vulnerable, disconnected pools. By 1981 there were no longer any concentrated Welsh areas. Even in Anglesey, where 75 per cent spoke Welsh in 1961, the number was down to 61 per cent in 1981. An almost identical drop was recorded in Carmarthen and Cardigan.[62] The trend was uniformly downward, suggesting it would not be long before Welsh-speakers were a minority everywhere. The total number of speakers had also declined, from 656,002 to 508,207.

The Welsh revival of the nineteenth century stemmed from bullish conviction about the culture's future. The primal emotion of Welsh nationalists in the twentieth century was fear. Their great bard was R. S. Thomas, a crabbed and embittered priest, whose misanthropic rhymes were an appropriate elegy to a culture that had folded its robes in preparation for death.

> Where can I go, then, from the smell
> Of decay, from the putrefying of a dead
> Nation?

he wrote in the poem, 'Reservoirs'.

> I have walked the shore
> For an hour and seen the English
> Scavenging among the remains
> Of our culture, covering the sand
> Like the tide and, with the roughness
> Of the tide, elbowing our language
> Into the grave that we have dug for it.[63]

From his father, he wrote in 'Gifts', he had inherited his weak stomach:

> From my mother the fear
> From my sad country the shame'.

The worst legacy of the century of socialist dominion over Wales was the return of shame, a restoration of embarrassment, of what Australians call the 'cultural cringe'. By the end of the twentieth century, while a wariness of Irish nationalism had banished once-common jokes about 'Micks' and 'Paddys', the Welsh remained strapped to the ducking chair, the only ethnic group in Britain that it was still safe to stereotype on television. While actors and artists with the most feeble connection to Ireland compete to assert their Irish and Celtic identity, there is no corresponding esteem about parading one's roots in Wales. There is no mileage in it. It is not 'cool'.

The depression of the 1930s, which returned in the 1980s after the Thatcher government's defeat of the miners' strike, has often been blamed for Welsh loss of self-esteem. The explanation passes the buck for Wales's ills from Labour to the mine-closing, tax-cutting Conservatives. But other countries have endured periods of severe poverty and recession without achieving the strange cultural weightlessness of modern Wales, or taking what the commentator Hywel Williams has called 'the path of rootlessness'.[64]

Little of Iolo's Wales survives in the south. 'We dare not imagine the language Iolo Morganwg would use if he came back and saw his beloved vale as it is now,' the historian Brinley Thomas wrote mournfully in the 1980s, 'almost entirely Anglicised with only a few beautiful Welsh place-names left as sorrowful reminders of a rich culture, long departed.'[65]

Wales is the only land where something survives of the pre-Anglo-Saxon culture in fairly robust form. You do not need to cross to a remote isle, or bend your head to the catch the whispers of the dying, to hear Welsh. But although the Welsh culture will survive, it is not certain if it will survive as a culture of the many or the few.

Some believe that the Welsh need to take a hard line, like the Parti Québécois, which after its historic election victory in 1976 ensured the survival of Quebec's francophone culture by passing laws aggressively promoting French at the expense of English. The Parti Québécois was accused of wrecking the economy of Montreal by driving out anglophone capital, but the brief downturn has proved to be less serious than was first thought and today Montreal is again a booming city. Wales and Quebec are different societies, however. The majority of Quebec's population has always spoken French and 'felt' French, certainly enough to vote the PQ several times into office. In Wales most people have not spoken Welsh, or perhaps even 'felt' Welsh, for a century and Plaid Cymru has little hope of winning an overall majority in the new assembly.

Iolo Morganwg's descendants are not that optimistic about their country. Robyn Lewis, the archdruid who inducted Rowan Williams at the 2002 St Davids eisteddfod, struck a pessimistic note at his own enthronement ceremony the year before. Over a century, he noted, the proportion of the population using Welsh had dropped from 54 to 18 per cent. The Government of Wales Act of 1998 had put the responsibility for the language on to the shoulders of the new, Labour-dominated Welsh National Assembly. But one of the assembly's first moves had been to appoint a non-Welsh-speaker as Welsh culture minister. It had then published a report on the future of the language, the sum of which was that English would remain compulsory while Welsh remained optional. 'I need only say this: compulsory English and optional Welsh have been the curse of Wales for centuries,' Lewis said. 'It was only by compulsion that they succeeded in decimating the Welsh language: it is only by compulsion that we shall restore it.'[66]

CHAPTER SEVEN

Cornwall
'Almost an island'

> Without the language, Cornwall is just another English county.
> (A. S. D. Smith, *The Story of the Cornish Language*)

I waited for the tide to go out before crossing the causeway to St Michael's Mount. It was a mild, wet day and the castle was half shrouded in a blanket of mist as I trudged across the shingle. A few minutes later I reached the row of cottages at the bottom of the Mount, where the staff and boatmen live, before starting my ascent through the landscaped gardens towards the mock-Gothic battlements above. The deeply indented coastline and scores of sheltered coves in Cornwall create the conditions for 'micro-climates'. Where I was staying in the village of St Buryan – close to the tip of the Cornish peninsula at St Just – cold fog shrouded the house in the morning, whilst heavy winds rolling off the Atlantic buffeted the windows and left the surrounding gardens looking blasted. Stunted oaks and hawthorns cowered away from the ocean at a 45-degree angle. It was hard to imagine soft fruit trees flourishing in such hardship. Only a few miles east it was another country, and the Mount gardens seemed semi-tropical in comparison.

At the top I found the castle's master, Lord St Levan, seated in the drawing room beside a vast pile of books. Much of Cornwall's history is interwoven with this romantic, eerie pile. Now a stately home that welcomes visitors across the shingle causeway, a Cistercian abbey dedicated to St Michael once welcomed pilgrims to a shrine. Before that Norman foundation a Celtic church stood on the site. The portraits of royal figures and statesmen that line the walls of the drawing room testify to the family's skill in retaining its possessions and its place in Cornish society from the 1640s onwards. The royal arms hanging from the chapel walls, put up in the 1660s, recall a timely shift of political allegiance from Cromwell to the house of Stuart at the Restoration. Outside, a footprint marks the place where Queen Victoria stepped ashore in 1846 – only to discover, disconcertingly, that the family was out.

Most visitors to the drawing room have eyes for one picture alone, which is certainly not of a royal personage. Painted in the style of Rembrandt's portrait of an old woman, it is an early work of the Cornish painter John Opie. The sitter is Dolly Pentreath, the eighteenth-century fishwife of Mousehole who at the end of an uneventful life achieved sudden fame as the last fluent speaker of Cornish, following her 'discovery' in the 1760s at the hands of the lawyer and antiquarian, Daines Barrington.

Lord St Levan was a genial host but more of a Cornish nationalist than I had imagined. I had expected a scion of the landed gentry, surrounded by the portraits of his illustrious ancestors, to be indulgent and dismissive of Cornish nationalism. It is a slightly humorous phenomenon to the English minority that has even heard of it. But Lord St Levan was disgruntled about Cornwall's lack of influence over events, and over government plans to incorporate the county into a devolved 'south-west' region encompassing Cornwall, Devon and lands to the east. The Labour government's recent reforms of the House of Lords and the expulsion of the hereditary peers had deprived him of the seat his family had occupied for more than three centuries. 'Now there is only the Bishop of Truro left to argue the case for Cornwall, but in the next stage of Lords' reform the bishops will lose their seats, so we won't even have him,' he said. He worried that the Cornish MPs had little clout outside the county and expressed no faith in the success of the campaign for a separate Cornish assembly. 'It doesn't have a chance,' he said quietly.

Lord St Levan told me he feared that Cornishness was dying. The strong dialect was fading. The old industries were going or had gone. For centuries beyond memory the Cornish had mined tin. But now, as in South Wales, the mines had gone. The last working mine, South Crofty, closed in 1998. The other traditional livelihood of the Cornish, which is fishing, is on its last legs, just as it is in the Outer Hebrides. It was given away by an indifferent British government in far-away London, whose politicians know that the big votes are not to be found on the Celtic fringe. Lord St Levan said he was not a member of Mebyon Kernow, 'the Sons of Cornwall', as the nationalist party is called. But he was proud to be a bard of the Cornish Gorsedd, the cultural association that was formed in 1928 to keep alive Cornwall's Celtic identity. 'Whatever I can do to strengthen Cornwall's identity as a separate nation, I will do,' he said. 'It is the only way we will ever get Westminster to listen.'

The tide had come in, so one of the Mount's boatmen rowed me back through the mist and drizzle to the village of Marazion on the mainland. As the boatman chatted away in a soft burr (no sign of BBC English intruding here), I pondered Lord St Levan's advice to track down the Archdruid of Cornwall, John Bolitho, the Grand Bard of the Gorsedd. As titular head of an organisation that exists to promote Cornish culture, I was told, he would be the man to shed more light on Cornwall's Celtic identity.

I found the Archdruid in a suburban side street in a resort town on the north coast. I thought I might find a man dressed in a toga with mistletoe round his forehead. But the Gorsedd and the bards are a workaday bunch. Nor is the annual ceremony, where new bards are created, a particularly mystical event. 'It's more like college prize-giving than anything else,' John Bolitho laughed. The Archdruid seemed a lot less interested in the meaning of Celtic stone circles than in the collapse of the Cornish fishing industry. 'If we had more control over our own affairs with our own assembly, we wouldn't be at the bottom of the pit now economically today,' he fumed. 'Our fishing industry has been slaughtered. Our government has sold the Cornish fishers out absolutely. This is the representation we have got. The port of Newlyn has been ruined.'

He added: 'It's not that we are against the rest of the United Kingdom, but the Cornish are just as at home in Brittany or Ireland ... Don't forget, we are *almost* an island.' With that his mood swung back from pensive reflection to merriment. Bolitho stood up and began singing the well-known hymn 'Eternal Father Strong to Save' in a deep baritone but not in the language I knew. He sang it in Cornish, the language of that semi-mythical person Dolly Pentreath whose portrait hung in Lord St Levan's castle.

Cornwall juts out like a long finger into the Atlantic and it is, as John Bolitho reminded me, almost an island. Sea surrounds the two longest sides of the triangle of land, while the River Tamar runs down most of the third side. The exposed position of this tapering finger means that the weather changes here with lightning speed. Mist, rain and cloud from the sea unfurl over the land within minutes, turning the blue sky first purple and then slate grey. The opposite is just as likely. A few days after walking through the mist and rain to St Michael's Mount, I was under a cobalt blue sky in the churchyard of Zennor village on the north Cornwall coast. From Zennor churchyard, the landscape of low stone farmhouses and granite boulders recalled the harsh 'karst' coastline of the Adriatic. Whatever it looked like, it did not look like England. No land has surrendered so much of its cultural identity in terms of language, among other things, and retained so much of its separateness in appearance. Part of the difference lies in the brooding presence of so many standing stones and Celtic crosses which have not, as so often elsewhere, been neatly collected and placed in a museum or in a shelter. Some have been built into churchyard walls, as at Paul, where Dolly Pentreath lies buried. But most stand where they have always stood, at the edge of fields, or beside roads, signposts to drivers on their way, as once they guided pilgrims to shrines.

Almost every writer or artist who visited Cornwall has acknowledged the peculiar, sometimes malevolent, power of the landscape, from D. H. Lawrence, who moved to Zennor in 1916, to the contemporary writer D. M. Thomas, author of the cult novel *The White Hotel*. Lawrence wrote of Cornwall: 'It has never taken the Anglo-Saxon civilisation, the Anglo-Saxon sort of Christianity. One can feel free here for that reason.' Lawrence's Cornish odyssey ended in disaster when angry locals suspected his German wife Frieda of working as a German spy and forced them out. Lawrence later decided that in fact he loathed the Cornish. They were 'like insects, gone cold, living only for money for dirt', he raged.[1] Other writers reacted equally negatively to a landscape that rarely leaves people indifferent. 'This is a hideous and wicked country,' John Heath-Stubbs wrote in a poem after his first visit to Zennor, 'sloping to hateful sunsets and the end of time.'[2] D. M. Thomas wove themes of graphic and shocking sexual violence around a Cornish landscape in his 1980 novel *Birthstone*. Not everyone was so hostile, but Cornwall has rarely inspired artists or writers with warm and sunny thoughts.

The land around Zennor looks unchanged, as if humans have only superficially affected it. It is not like the landscape of England, soft and malleable, giving off lights that constantly remind the observer of the work of human hands – evidence of centuries of loving stewardship. In Cornwall, especially on the north coast, granite pierces through the ground at every point, as if to announce the transitory quality of human endeavour. 'The most distant histories are near the surface,' the Cornish artist Peter Lanyon wrote speculatively, 'as if the final convulsion of rock upheaval and cold incision, setting in a violent sandwich of strata, had directed the hide-and-seek of Celtic pattern.'[3]

In his cosy home, over coffee and biscuits, the Archdruid insisted that the Cornish identity was bound up with a sense of place. 'Our culture is formed by our geography,' he said. 'There is such a strong attachment that every Cornishman feels. The Cornish are always homesick. We have a hankering to get back.' He had felt this as a teenager in the British merchant navy and now spent much of his time addressing that itch, visiting Cornish associations as far away as Australia, where 80,000 to 100,000 people of Cornish descent attend the get-togethers in the former gold-rush towns of Moonta and Bendigo. If the Cornish are always hankering to return home it is because ambition and cussed nonconformity drove them away in the first place. Mining is in the blood and the gold rushes in South Africa and Australia drew the Cornish in droves. They prospered and rose up the ranks of the colonial elite. The father of the Australian federation, Sir John Quick, was Cornish. Thousands of Cornish families lived on the pay that the colonials sent home.

A great many Cornish towns and villages are named after obscure Celtic saints. It is one of those marks of foreignness that instantly remind English visitors crossing the Tamar that they have entered what was once another country. The dedications remind us, as John Bolitho said, that Cornwall was 'almost an island', and that for centuries it was more easily reached by sea from Wales, Brittany and Ireland than by land from England. The saints of the Cornish churches reflect Cornwall's position at the centre of the southern portion of Celtic world, equidistant from Wales and Brittany, for few were Cornish: most were Welsh, Breton or Irish.

Petroc and Piran, the two missionaries most identified with Cornwall, both came from South Wales in the sixth century. Petroc began his mission in the north in Padstow in 518. But like the eighteenth-century Methodist leader John Wesley to whom he is often compared, he roamed all over Cornwall, inspiring numerous dedications and becoming the object of a popular cult centred on Bodmin, where his relics were housed. Piran's cult centred on Perranzabuloe, literally 'Perran in the sands', where he is believed to have first landed.

Its geographical position at the centre of the southern end of the Celtic world made Cornwall a staging post for Christian missionaries on sea journeys that began in Ireland or Wales and ended in Brittany. The brief stays of these birds of passage might be recalled in a single Cornish chapel. Samson, another Celtic missionary from South Wales, had far more impact in Brittany than Cornwall, where he is recalled only in the church at Golant. In Brittany the Cathedral of Dol-de-Bretagne was dedicated to him. Cadoc, one of the great Welsh saints and the patron of at least 25 churches there, had a great following in Brittany where he is known as Cado. But in Cornwall only a single chapel near Padstow recalls his presence.[4] Paul, or Pol, the patron of Paul near Mousehole, was another sixth-century Welshman (492–572 AD) who left a greater impression in Brittany. Like Samson he had a cathedral dedicated to him (at St Pol de Léon) and at least 10 other parishes named after him. Brioc, another Welshman from Dyfed in west Wales, is recalled at St Breock, near Wadebridge, in Cornwall. But in

Brittany he founded a great monastery and is remembered in the impressive cathedral of Saint-Brieuc.

That the Britons of South Wales had an enormous impact on Cornwall is not surprising given its proximity to Cornwall's north coast. Long before the Anglo-Saxons pushed west to Exeter, driving a wedge between the Britons of the west, they were one people. But Irish missionaries also had a great impact on Cornwall, even though Ireland lay considerably further away. Beryan, or Beriana, the saint after whom the village of St Buryan is named, was Irish.[5]

The soaring tower of St Buryan's church testifies to the prestige she enjoyed, for the tenth-century English King Athelstan honoured her cult by establishing a college of canons there.[6] Ia, after whom St Ives is named, was another female Irish missionary. The majority of the dedications in Cornwall reflect the fact that the direction of most missionary traffic was north to south, with British and Irish churchmen and women bringing Christianity to the relatively new British community in Armorica, or Brittany. But some Cornish church dedications, like Zennor's, record journeys made in the opposite direction. Zennor's dedication is not certain, but some legends connect it to Senara, or Asenora, a Breton who fled to Ireland and then later returned to Brittany via Cornwall.

It is interesting, though hazardous, to guess just how much these early missionaries crossing the 'inland sea' from Ireland to Wales and Cornwall thought of themselves as inhabiting a single cultural or spiritual space. The church and shrine dedications certainly suggest that the peoples of these lands saw themselves as part of one spiritual commonwealth with a religious treasury held in common.

The bonds between them were slow to unravel. The landmarks in that long and drawn-out process were the Saxon conquest of Cornwall which led to Cornwall becoming part of England. Much later there came the incorporation of Brittany into France, which made both peoples strangers and subjects of mutually hostile states. The Protestant Reformation in England imposed another barrier between them.

The loss of the language was the greatest blow. In 1746, Captain Samuel Barrington fancifully claimed he overheard a Cornish fisherman from Mount's Bay conversing with a Breton sailor. It was an unlikely claim, as Cornish and Breton were not mutually comprehensible.[7] But they were kin languages and easily learned from each other; even today, Welsh-speakers find it easy to learn Breton, which is extremely difficult for English- or French-speakers. The sensation of being 'at home' that many Cornish, Irish or Welsh visitors to Brittany feel even now is only an echo of the much closer ties they would have felt when they spoke similar languages.

Cornish patriots have long felt a deep sadness, or shame, over their abandonment of their Celtic language in the eighteenth century. It informs the frantic search a century later for people who possessed even a smattering of words, and the erection of plaques in the 1920s and 1930s to anyone whose knowledge of Cornish seemed to disprove the claim that Dolly Pentreath was the last Cornish-speaker. One of these plaques hangs on the outside wall of Zennor church, commemorating John Davey of Boswednack, who died in 1891 and in the cautious words of the Old Cornwall Society, 'was the last to possess any considerable, traditional knowledge of the Cornish language'.

The slow death of Cornish, and the snapping of the bonds that linked Cornwall to Brittany and Wales, drew little attention until the Celtic revival of the 1890s. As a result, earlier references to the state of the language and pace of the English advance are scant. It is usually accepted that the Saxons' westward expansion slowly cut off the Britons of the south-west from those further north and that the Battle of Deorham or Dyrham, in Wiltshire, in 577 decisively separated the two geographically. From that event dates the linguistic separation of 'Welsh' and 'Cornish' and the evolution of two separate 'alien' lands, in Saxon parlance, the 'wealas' of the north, or Wales, and the 'wealas' of Cornvovia in the south-west, which became Cornwall.

English penetration of the south-west 'wealas' began after the Anglo-Saxons pushed the Britons from Exeter and across the River Tamar in the tenth century. Under Athelstan, king from 925 to 937, the Tamar was fixed as the boundary of a Cornish earldom under the English crown and a bishopric was established in St Germans. The subjugation of the Cornish to Saxon landowners began. A. S. D. Smith, the Welsh-born Cornish linguist, believed north-east Cornwall was probably widely anglicised by the 1000s while the Domesday Book confirms that most Cornish landlords by then were Saxon or Norman.

That most medieval Cornish people spoke their native Celtic language, while the gentry were bilingual or even trilingual in Cornish, Norman French and English, is suggested by contemporary accounts of a dispute between Bishop John de Grandisson of Exeter and the parishioners of St Buryan in the 1340s. After the conflict culminated with the Bishop excommunicating the parishioners, he later travelled to St Buryan to receive their submission. The 13 leading citizens of the parish pleaded in English or

Norman French while the rest made their submission in Cornish. The reception of a bishop from far-away Exeter would have been a great event in St Buryan, so the fact that the leading citizens made their statements in English or French does not mean that was their normal speech. Cornish was still the lingua franca of the west of the county, and the fact that many medieval landed Cornish families chose Cornish mottos for their coats of arms testifies to the fact that Cornish at that time still enjoyed considerable status.[8] The attachment of many Cornish people to their native language was exhibited to the whole of England much later, when the government of Edward VI imposed the first English Prayer Book on the Church in 1549. Protestantism had made little impact on Cornwall. The Act of Supremacy in 1534 abolishing papal jurisdiction created no Cornish martyrs, nor did the suppression of the monasteries in the later 1530s.

The beginnings of a more sustained assault on the traditional beliefs at the end of the decade had a greater impact, for the cult of saints was strong in Cornwall and pilgrimages to holy wells and shrines were still an important part of Cornish religious life, as they had been since the era of the Celtic evangelists. The dismantling of Petroc's shrine in Bodmin and the suppression of countless lesser shrines must have caused real shock. It formed the background to the explosion of anger over the introduction of the first English Prayer Book.

Clearly, most people found the arrival of the new book more invasive than any of the earlier church reforms. Visits to holy wells had continued even without official sanction, as did the observance of abrogated saints' days. Holy wells occupied a key place in Cornish life even under Elizabeth I; Richard Carew's *Survey of Cornwall* of 1602 contained a detailed recent description of pilgrims at St Nunne's well at Altarnun. Long after such devotions had been outlawed and effectively forbidden in England, the sick were still coming for cures at wells in Cornwall (just as they were in Ireland, Wales and in the Scottish Highlands). Carew wrote:

> The water running from St Nunne's well fell into a square and close-walled plot, which might be filled at what depth they listed. Upon this wall was the franticke person set to stand, his backe towards the poole; and from thence, in a sudden blow to the breast, tumbled headlong into the pond, where a strong fellow . . . tooke him and tossed and tossed him, up and downe, alongst and athwart the water, until the patient, by forgoing his strength, had somewhat forgot his fury.[9]

Carew's indulgent, humorous description illustrates the degree to which basic Protestant ideas had failed to put down roots across the Tamar where traditional beliefs still held strong, several decades after they had waned elsewhere.

The Cornish ignored most of the prohibitions of the English Reformation, thanks to the tolerance of local landlords and judges. What they could not avoid was hearing Mass in English rather than Latin in their local parish church after the government of Edward VI ordered all churches to use Thomas Cranmer's new service from May 1549. The years of evasion were over. The revolt started in Bodmin and moved eastwards,[10] but the insurgents included many people from the Cornish-speaking west where, as Andrew Borde said in *The Fyrst Boke of the Introduction of Knowledge* of 1542, 'Ther be many men and women the which cannot speake one worde of Englysshe, but all Cornyshe.'[11]

Religious, cultural and social grievances cannot be disentangled in the 'Prayer Book rebellion' of 1549, as the disturbances were known. The Cornish had a history of turbulence. Within the living memory of the old in 1497 a blacksmith, *an goff* in Cornish, named Michael Joseph had led a rising in St Keverne in the south-west. These revolts had no religious dimensions. But even if many people's motives were mixed in 1549, the alien and incomprehensible language of the Book of Common Prayer was a factor. 'We, the Cornish men,' the rebels announced in their famous petition against the service that they called a 'Christmas game', 'wherof certain of us understand no English, utterly refuse this new English.'[12]

The uprising began with the murder in Helston in April 1548 of William Body, the hated Cromwellite Archdeacon of Cornwall, a month before the date established in the Act of Uniformity for the adoption of the new Prayer Book. After Easter armed crowds converged on Bodmin and the revolt swept the county. By 2 July the Cornish had crossed the River Tamar, sparking panic in London. While Archbishop Cranmer rained down his thunderbolts, the Earl of Bedford marshalled an army that finally crushed the rebels in August. The main leaders, including Humphry Arundell and John Winslade, were hanged at Tyburn.

The Prayer Book rebellion was not a wholly Cornish affair. It was almost as popular in 'Saxon' Devon as it was in 'Celtic' Cornwall and the commotion it started spread beyond the south-west into Oxfordshire. But it was only in Cornwall that the language of the Protestant liturgy emerged as a grievance.

There was no long-term resistance. After the revolt failed, the Cornish did not cling to the Mass like the Irish, who crossed themselves when they passed Protestant ministers in the road, had to be dragged into Protestant churches and put cotton wool in their ears rather than listen to Protestant sermons. Rome ignored Cornwall, presumably regarding it as a provincial backwater, and when the recusant priests began returning to England from the new continental seminaries under Elizabeth I, they concentrated on the Home Counties. Catholicism as an active force disintegrated in Cornwall during the last half of the sixteenth century. Even Cornwall's most notable Catholic martyr, Cuthbert Mayne, was a Devon man by birth, though he worked as steward to the Tregions of Golden Manor near Tregony. Discovered by the sheriff of Cornwall in 1577 he was hanged, drawn and quartered at Launceston on 30 November.[13] Like the Welsh and the Manx, the Cornish fell back into conformity to the new Church, retaining a dogged faith in certain pre-Reformation practices, such as the observance of saints' days.

Such traces of older religious practices survived even into the nineteenth century. After a journey around Cornwall in the 1790s James Forbes remarked on the survival of saints' days there long after they had vanished elsewhere. 'All the use made of their anniversary festivals is to collect the neighbouring farmers and cottagers, male and female, to eat, drink and be merry, which is seldom finished in one day,' he wrote disapprovingly. 'It occasions a good deal of excess in the country, with all its bad consequences.'[14]

The *Gentleman's Magazine* in 1790 scorned another ancient survivor known as the Furry Dance, held in Helston on 8 May. The origins were ancient, the word 'furry' deriving from the Latin (and Cornish) word *feria*, meaning feast. But the magazine dismissed it as nothing more than 'troublesome rogues [who] go round the streets with drums or other noisy instruments, disturbing their neighbours and singing parts of a song, the whole of which nobody now recollects'.[15] It was finally abandoned in the 1860s, a sign of the growing triumph of middle-class respectability.

The *Survey of the County of Cornwall* by Charles Gilbert in 1817 lamented the survival of holy days, almost 300 years after they had disappeared in England, especially the feast of St Piran on 5 March, to which the tin miners remained faithful. 'These superstitions are not so generally observed as formerly,' Gilbert noted with satisfaction, now that 'a proper knowledge of the truths of religion and a due observance of its precepts have been universally diffused among them', in consequence of which 'barbarous practices are vanquished'.[16] Gilbert wrote scathingly of the survival of another pre-Reformation relic, the miracle play, pouring scorn on the actors known as 'puffers' who 'enter in disguise into gentlemen's houses where they personate characters and carry on miserable dialogues on scripture subjects'.

The squeamish, snobbish Gilbert noted that the Cornish 'lower classes' in the early nineteenth century retained many traditional beliefs that harked back beyond the arrival of Christianity to the pagan festivals of Beltane and Lughnasa. Like the Highlanders and the Irish they lit bonfires on St John's Eve and believed in the fairy world. 'Many stories are in repute amongst them (especially the miners) respecting these puny beings, which they generally suppose to have the power of discovering the lodes in mines, and amusing them with music during their subterranean labours,' Gilbert said.[17] He also repeated the story of Anne Jefferies, a Cornishwoman who gained a strong following as a healer in the 1640s after claiming that six fairies had climbed over her garden wall dressed in green and brought her food.[18]

The Cornish historian A. L. Rowse captured the dying embers of that culture just before the First World War in his memoir, *A Cornish Childhood*. The village in which Rowse grew up was still a world apart from mainstream England. Cornish had gone but a strong local dialect, which preserved some traces of Cornish language and syntax, had survived. The lives of the villagers still revolved round a calendar of saints' days, long since shorn of any Catholic aspect, and dances whose steps had been virtually forgotten. 'We celebrated the Armistice with a Flora dance through the town,' he remembered. 'There was something instinctive, pathetic about it, like a gesture remembered from some former existence which had no meaning any more. Hardly anybody knew how to dance it by now.'[19] But harvesters still carried the last sheaf of the harvest, dressed as a figure and adorned with flowers, crying 'A-neck, A-neck', 'and some other words which my father couldn't remember: some rigmarole perhaps which went back to the Celtic past'.[20] Belief persisted in fairies, or 'piskies' as they were known, and in harbingers of doom from the spirit world. The blackbird, the bird of ill omen, the glowing candle and the corpse candle – all of which foretold the death of a family member – were common beliefs in all the Celtic lands and had lost none of their power in the nominally Christian Cornwall of Rowse's childhood. The Rowse family understood the unexpected chiming of a clock, at about the same time that an uncle was thought to have died far away in South Africa, in the traditional fashion. 'They ever afterwards took it as a "token", a signal of his death,' he wrote: 'there are many such stories in Cornish families.'[21]

Protestantism might have revitalised the Cornish identity culture as it did in Wales, through Morgan's Welsh Bible. But the Cornish were passed by.

Carswell translated John Knox's service book into Gaelic in 1567 (though Gaelic scriptures did not become widespread in Scotland for centuries). The Welsh had Morgan's Bible published by 1588. Daniel translated the New Testament and Book of Common Prayer into Irish between 1603 and 1608 (though it was not distributed). Even the Manx had a Manx Bible and Prayer Book by Bishop Hildesley's time in the eighteenth century.

The Cornish got nothing in their language, in spite of the protests they made in 1549. They had no patrons. The Cornish had no scholarly bishop at hand to take it up, for the see of St Germans had been suppressed in the eleventh century and Exeter was far away. Anglicanism in Cornwall became simply a vehicle for anglicisation. All that Protestantism achieved in cultural terms was the closure of the old springs of Cornish culture. The suppression of the monasteries and the conversion of collegiate churches into parish churches ended any role they once enjoyed as cultural centres. Where once there were several clergy, now there might be one – and, as in Wales, he was often an absentee. A particular blow was the suppression of St Thomas at Glasney near Penryn, a collegiate foundation from the thirteenth century. Miracle plays were performed at Glasney and the *Ordinalia*, a cycle of three plays that forms the most important surviving body of Cornish literature, is thought to have originated there during the thirteenth and fourteenth centuries.

Protestantism cut a swathe across the traditional north–south travel routes running from Wales and Ireland through Cornwall (often from Padstow to the Fowey estuary) to Brittany once taken by the early Christian missionaries. The Reformation wrenched Cornwall in an eastward direction towards England and cut the former close ties with Brittany. Writing in the 1680s in his *Observations on an Ancient Manuscript entitled Passio Christi* the Cornish historian William Scawen listed several factors that had contributed to the sharp decline of Cornish. They included English immigration and the failure of post-Reformation Cornwall to develop its own vernacular literature. But Scawen significantly put the disruption of contacts with the Bretons at the top of the list. He lamented as a severe blow the 'great loss of Armorica, near unto us by friendship, by cognition, by interest, by correspondence'. Now, he complained, although the Cornish and Bretons still met occasionally, we 'have not the benefit of conferences with one another in our ancient tongues'.[22]

The failure to have the Bible or Book of Common Prayer translated into Cornish condemned the language to slow death by erosion, for if the Church did not use it, who would? By the middle years of Elizabeth I's reign, Cornish was fast retreating before an incoming tide of English in the east. A snippet of a court case in the 1570s casts an interesting light on language shift among the poor. The consistory court depositions of 1572 record the testimony of William Hawyshe of Lelant who said that 'upon DEW WHALLAN GWA METTEN IN EGLOS DE LELANT, viz upon All Hallow day late about the mydds of the service, in the parish church of Lalant, Moryshe David's wife and Cicely James came into the church of Lalant together and in chiding words called Agnes Davy (–) and (–) in English and not in Cornowek' (the 'chiding words' were clearly not fit to print).[23]

It is a tantalising glimpse into the world of the 'ordinary' Cornish we know so little of, this tale of Mrs David and Mrs James marching into the church at Lelant and swearing abusively at Mrs Davy. While the cause of the quarrel is lost to us, it was clearly considered worth noting down that the women had sworn in English rather than Cornish. Even in the far west of Cornwall, the people were switching to English.

By the time Richard Carew came to write his *Survey of Cornwall* in the last years of Elizabeth I, the language had retreated to the western parishes and had lost one of its last stalwarts, for Carew wrote: 'The principal love and knowledge of this language lived in Dr Kenall [John Kenall, Rector of St Columb who died in the 1590s] . . . and with him lieth buried, for the English speech doth still encroach upon it and hath driven the same unto the uttermost skirts of the shire.'[24] In those 'uttermost skirts', however, there were plenty of Cornish monoglots, for Carew maintained that English travellers could not be guaranteed instant understanding. He said of the English speech that 'some so affect their own as to a stranger they will not speake it, for if meeting them by chance you inquire the way or any such matter, your answer shall be *mea navidna cowza sawzneck*, I can speake no Saxonage.'[25]

The miracle plays were one of the public props of the language, but they too fell into decay, an inevitable casualty of a Calvinistic Reformation that looked suspiciously on such relics of papal times. It was a testament to the Cornish affection for the plays that they survived for so long, for their counterparts in York had been suppressed in the 1570s by the simple device of Archbishop Grindal confiscating the texts. Loyalty to the plays kept them going in Cornwall for decades longer but by Carew's time the actors no longer knew the lines. He wrote: 'The players con not their parts without book, but are prompted by one called the ordinary who followeth at their back with the book in his hand, and telleth them softly what they must pronounce aloud.'[26] The plays were already in decay but the fact they were performed at all – presumably to large audiences – shows that Cornish remained the ordinary tongue of many people, for the plays had not been translated into English.

The naturalist John Ray found few speakers left in the 1660s, even in the far west, which points to the marked decline that had taken place in the six decades since Carew's account. 'Few of the children could speak Cornish so that the language is like, in a short time, to be quite lost,' he wrote.[27]

The late seventeenth century saw the final flowering of Cornish under the influence of a circle of linguists and antiquarians who, following the growing enthusiasm for 'antiquities', suddenly became aware of the implications of the death of the Cornish language. 'They saw that the language was dying before their eyes and that the forces working to that end were irreversible; what they could not save they set out to record.'[28]

This was not a language revival in the modern sense. Richard Angwin, Thomas Tonkin, William Gwavas, William Scawen and his nephew John Keigwin, and Nicholas Boson saw themselves primarily as historians and they wanted to document this history in the interests of posterity. Self-conscious members of an intellectual elite, they translated Cornish words into English, wrote letters in Cornish to each other and put up epitaphs in Cornish in churches.[29] But they were not interested in popularising their work and sadly for modern enthusiasts were infuriatingly devoid of curiosity about the living Cornish that was still being spoken yards from their doorstep by sailors and fishwives. Church services in Cornish lasted in Landewednack under Francis Robinson until 1678, much the same time that the Cornish enthusiasts were studying the language, compiling their dictionaries and translating medieval texts. But if they attended such services we know nothing of it, nor did they try to see them revived elsewhere. To charge them with intellectual snobbery would be anachronistic. They lived and worked before Macpherson's *Ossian* in Scotland sparked a vogue for collecting the language, speech patterns and beliefs of peasants. It did not occur to them to scour the alleys of St Ives in search of crones muttering in Cornish.

Moreover, they worked in a climate of pessimism. The long withdrawing roar of Cornish had been heard for so long it was impossible to imagine any ending to the story other than extinction. 'Our Cornish tongue hath been so long on the wane,' Boson lamented in *A Few Words about Cornish*, 'that we can hardly hope to see it increase again, for as the English confined it to this narrow country first, so it presseth on still, leaving it no place but about the cliff and sea . . . so it is like to decay from time to time.'[30]

The Welsh scholar Edward Lhuyd visited Cornwall in 1700 on a fact-finding mission for his *Archaeologia Britannica*, published in 1707. His visit was unfortunately brief, for it only lasted four months and coincided with a campaign against robbers and highwaymen that resulted in Lhuyd being hustled briefly into jail for suspicious behaviour. The Cornish were in 'a sort of panic and terrible apprehension of thieves and house-breakers,' he recalled.[31] Jail was an annoying waste of time, though Lhuyd still found time on his visit to copy down Cornish poems and research the neglected links between Cornish and other Celtic languages.

Lhuyd was one of the last scholars to hear Cornish spoken and was filled with melancholy at the thought of its death. 'The man with no tongue lost his land,' he mused to Tonkin in 1703, reciting one of the old Cornish poems he had learned on his trip.[32] After his departure the activities of the Cornish scholars began to sputter, for they had no successors. They had translated texts and analysed the death of Cornish and that was that. Scawen had produced the *Antiquities Cornu-Britannick* before dying in 1689. Boson died in 1703 and Keigwin in 1710. Gwavas lived until 1741.

William Borlase, Rector of Ludgvan, was the great Cornish scholar of the eighteenth century but the author of the 1754 *Antiquities of Cornwall* was not part of the circle of Cornish speakers and, in his book, he confidently pronounced that Cornish was dead. A conscientious rector, he was some-what reactionary, complaining in 1766 to his bishop that the common people of Cornwall were too well off, and had too many luxuries and clothes. Even 'common labourers' now had 'tea not once but twice a day', he grumbled. 'In short, all labourers live above their condition.'[33] His contemptuous tone may explain why he failed to note the continuing exis-tence of a few speakers of the old language.

The discovery of Dolly Pentreath, long after the publication of Borlase's *Antiquities,* was a coup. It was also the work of an outsider, Daines Barrington. Born in 1727, the fourth son of Viscount Barrington was a lawyer and antiquary of varied tastes, who headed west in search of Cornish-speakers in 1768 in the spirit of a nineteenth-century ornithologist looking for dodos. Barrington's curiosity had been awakened by his sea captain brother Samuel's claim to have heard a Cornish fisherman convers-ing with a Breton sailor. The aristocratic Barrington got down to what the Cornish scholars had scorned to do: namely scouring the backstreet inns in search of anyone with even a smattering of the language. An innkeeper in Penzance supplied the information he eagerly sought, which was the exis-tence of an elderly, foul-mouthed fishwife in Mousehole who swore like a trooper in Cornish.

Barrington made contact with his human prize and returned to London, where at a leisurely pace he published his findings in May 1773 in a paper

'On the Expiration of the Cornish Language' for the Society of Antiquaries. Barrington wanted to be the man who had found the 'last' Cornish-speaker. He had no interest in Cornish beyond that. He was more interested in Dolly's value as a curiosity, and in publicising the claim that she had not spoken English until she was 20. 'She does indeed, at this time, talk Cornish as readily as others do English being bred up from a child to know no other language,' he wrote. 'Nor could she (if we may believe her) talk a word of English before she was twenty years of age; as her father being a fisherman, she was sent with fish to Penzance when twelve years old and sold them in the Cornish language . . . she is poor and maintained mostly by the parish and partly by fortune-telling and gabbling Cornish.'[34]

Dolly Pentreath, probably the Dowryte baptised at Paul church on 16 May 1692, enjoyed a few years as a minor celebrity before her death in December 1777, by which time Opie had immortalised the features that now hang in Lord St Levan's drawing room in St Michael's Mount. The painting shows her improbably clutching a scholarly tome. The painter missed the essential Dolly, just as those who captured Peig Sayers of Blasket Island on the written page lost the vital element. In both cases the subjects were presented in refined form. Dolly Pentreath in her lifetime was better known for the scabrous abuse she dished out to people who wouldn't buy her fish than for poring over books. As the language revivalist Peter Pool wrote in *The Death of Cornish*: 'The tragedy was that neither Daines Barrington, nor anyone else, ever troubled to record her rich repertoire of fish-wifely abuse.'[35]

To the English public she was more than anything a figure of fun.

> Hail Mousehole! Birthplace of old Doll Pentreath
> The last who gabber'd Cornish.[36]

So ran the comic but cruel ode published beside her portrait in the *Universal Magazine* in 1785. Partly because of her comic status, and partly because her death robbed nineteenth-century Cornish activists of an apostolic succession of Cornish-speakers traversing the ages, it became an article of faith among some Cornish nationalists to deny that Pentreath was, in fact, the last Cornish-speaker. Barrington himself undercut the title in November 1776, when he produced a letter dated 3 July of that year. It was written in Cornish and English and came from one William Bodinar, a Mousehole sailor 19 years younger than Dolly who did not grow up speaking Cornish but, as he put it, 'learnt Cornish going to sea with old men'. He died in 1789.

It is hard to extend Cornish beyond Bodinar's death. Barrington recorded that a number of other women in Mousehole had chatted to Dolly Pentreath in Cornish. They told him they could follow her well enough but could not speak the language themselves. Possibly some of them lingered into the 1800s, taking their passive understanding of Cornish to the grave. John Davey of Boswednack, whose plaque hangs on the wall of Zennor church, and who died in 1891, could recite a few chunks of Cornish that he had learned from his schoolteacher father. Ann Wallis and Jane Barnicoat, of St Buryan, who died in the 1880s, were also credited with speaking a little.[37] The fact is that no one discovered any Cornish people who could speak more than a few phrases once the threshold of the nineteenth century had been crossed.

By then a new generation of Cornish scholars was cursing the lacka-daisical Barrington for his poor interviewing technique. But Cornish had gone. In the 1660s John Ray warned that Cornish had been pushed to the edge of the cliff. But nothing lies beyond the cliffs around St Just except the sea and no echoing sound responded to the frantic calls of the nineteenth-century hunters. No new Dolly Pentreath was waiting to be found, whisper-ing in a forgotten tongue in the corner of a neglected fishing hamlet.

There is something sad and troubling about the death of a language, for language is a way of seeing and hearing the world and with its disappear-ance, the perception it contained goes too. For Cornish activists in the nine-teenth and twentieth centuries, the language took on a totemic quality. It became like the language of elves, a whispered tongue that believers thought they could catch in the whistling of the wind through the trees and the crashing of the waves on the rocks. They could not, *would* not, believe it had finally expired and the belief endured that it must have survived in some form, providing a living link between the last known speakers in the eigh-teenth century and the language revivalists. People regularly reported hearing Cornish spoken, much as Americans in the 1950s reported sightings of UFOs. Robert Norton Nance in 1933 reported one woman who 'not many years ago' claimed she overheard some children whispering in an unknown language that was 'certainly not English' on a beach at Halsetown, and she believed the language was Cornish.[38] It was an idea straight out of *Peter Pan,* in which children fulfilled their old role in stories as intermedi-aries between the fairy and human worlds.

Henry Jenner, father of the modern Cornish language movement,[39] described his own failed search for remnants of the old tongue in the 1860s and 1870s, in the company of the enthusiastic Anglo-Catholic Vicar of

Newlyn, Wladislaw Lach-Szyrma, son of a Polish refugee who had settled in England in 1831 after the Polish uprising. Their findings, written up as 'Traditional Relics of the Cornish Language in Mount's Bay in 1875' and published by the Philological Society, amounted to a few elderly residents of the Newlyn–Mousehole area who could count in Cornish and greet each other. John Kelyack, Mrs Soady, Stephen Richards, Mrs Tregarthen and Benjamin Victor knew some words or phrases. Mrs Tregarthen knew that *veen* meant 'little', for example, while Mr Richards knew a snatch of words in Cornish from an obscure song that the fishermen sang when hauling in mackerel.[40] Mr Victor could manage a sentence about borrowing a walking stick, though Jenner judged it very corrupt.

It was not a lot to go on and when Jenner, who was born in Cornwall in 1848 to English and Scottish parents, taught himself Cornish in the early 1870s he was effectively starting from scratch and guessing the sounds. There was only a small corpus of medieval literature to work from, comprising the *Ordinalia*, the cycle of three dramas said to have originated in Glasney abbey in the thirteenth or fourteenth century, a life of St Meriasek, the oldest manuscript of which dated back to 1504, and a fifteenth-century passion poem, *The Passion of Our Lord*, comprising 259 stanzas. Jenner uncovered a new fragment in the British Museum in the 1870s. Jenner had the freedom to decide what kind of Cornish he wanted to learn – the 'late' Cornish of the era of Scawen and Boson, or the earlier language of the *Ordinalia*. He plumped for the latest known version, feeling it made most sense to link his efforts to the most recent form of the living language.

Jenner had no plan to revive Cornish as a spoken language. His interest was academic and scholarly. Like Lach-Szyrma, he initially approached the business of unearthing Cornish culture using the scientific language of an archaeologist disinterring a curious fossil. 'The language is dead,' Jenner flatly told the British Archaeological Association in 1906, adding that 'for academic and philological purposes it has been preserved, like a mummy in a museum'.[41] It was only when his work began to attract followers that Jenner decided the 'mummy' might be made to walk.

The apparent success of the Gaelic League in Ireland, of Cymru Fydd in Wales and of An Commun Gaidhealach in Scotland encouraged them to believe there was hope for a revival of Cornish spirit and identity. They were seized with the notion that Cornishness was dissolving and that action needed to be taken to recall people's attention to their roots. Nance lamented the disappearance of the Cornishman of the mid-nineteenth century, whose sense of nationality was strong even if unconscious. The Cornishman of that era, he said,

> had almost forgotten perhaps, that there had ever been a separate Cornish language, but he daily used many words of it in his own remade Cornish English speech and thought in Celtic fashion by rearranging sentences according to its rules.
>
> He had but the vaguest notion that Cornwall had ever been a separate Celtic nation, but he kept much of the ancient British spirit of independence, and scorned to imitate the ways and speech of the upcountry 'foreigner'.[42]

Anglican clergymen like Lach-Szymra played an important part in the nineteenth-century revival of interest in Cornish. Bishopless for eight centuries after the suppression of the see of St Germans in 1054, the Cornish got their bishop back (whether they liked it or not) after Edward White Benson was appointed first bishop of Truro in 1877, part of a wave of Anglican reformism aimed at recapturing the alienated Celts of Wales and Cornwall. He began soliciting subscriptions at once for the building of a cathedral on French lines, whose foundation stone was laid on 20 May 1888 by the Prince of Wales, in his position as Duke of Cornwall.

Benson was a High-Churchman with a strong feel for the Church's pre-Reformation history and the Celtic saints. As Archbishop of Canterbury he loved to 'steal away and shut himself up alone for a while in the place known as Becket's Crown where is the marble chair of St Augustine' and commune in spirit with his predecessors.[43] Not surprisingly, once in Truro he developed a sentimental regard for Cornish and sent Jenner and Lach-Szymra a message in Cornish on the occasion of the hundredth anniversary of Dolly Pentreath's death in 1877.

The role of Cornish patrons came most naturally to the Anglo-Catholic clergy. As vicars and rectors, they were automatically custodians of the oldest, most historic buildings in Cornish villages and as the Oxford movement gained strength, the dedication of these churches to a cloud of dimly remembered saints worked on their imaginations and propelled the minds of many of them back to the era of the Celtic Church.

But for all the benevolent efforts of a few individuals, the Church of England could never commandeer the Cornish revival, or make it its own. Even the stained-glass windows in Benson's new cathedral proclaimed the Church's first allegiance; they gave pride of place to Thomas Cranmer, the sworn enemy of the Cornish in the 1549 rebellion who had gloated over an English army's savage repression of the 'ignorant men of Devonshire and Cornwall'.[44]

Churchmen of Benson's stamp were curious about, and sympathetic to, notions of Cornwall's Celtic identity. But by the time that Benson reached Cornwall the Church of England there was in the same position as the Anglican Establishment in Wales – the Church of a minority. As soon as they had been offered a religious alternative, the Cornish had taken the same path as all the other Celtic peoples of Britain and Ireland, abandoning Anglicanism as an engine of Anglo-Saxon dominion. Perhaps the movement was less clear-cut in Cornwall than in Wales or Ireland, as the Cornish had no conscious sense of themselves as a separate nation. But the outcome was the same – a general stampede away from the Established Church that left the parsons in charge of buildings but not souls.

As one ecclesiastical historian of Cornwall noted, Anglicanism was not strongly rooted in Cornwall, for only six generations separated the men and women of the Prayer Book rebellion of 1549 and the crowds who flocked to hear John Wesley in the early eighteenth century. Nonconformist historians and Wesley himself played up the opposition that their mission encountered from the parsons and the gentry. Really active hostility coincided with the dying embers of the Jacobite scare and faded entirely in the late 1740s.[45]

The Methodists had a dramatic impact on Cornwall. As in Wales, the Isle of Man and the Scottish Highlands, the evangelicals brought about a revolution in popular culture. The Cornwall that Wesley encountered in 1743 was the brawling, cursing, hard-drinking world that Dolly Pentreath grew up in. It was still fairly rough at the end of his life, but as Wesley put it on his last journey to Cornwall, to Truro, in 1789:

> The last time I was here, above forty years ago, I was taken prisoner by an immense mob, gaping and roaring like lions. But how is the tide turned! High and low now lined the street from one end of the town to the other, out of stark love and kindness, as if the king were going by. In the evening I preached on the smooth top of the hill, at a distance from the sea, to the largest congregation I have ever seen in Cornwall.[46]

Methodism absorbed many of the instincts that the pre-Reformation Church had satisfied centuries before, and Wesley was widely seen as a latter-day saint. His image was even carved in stone and placed over the entrance of the chapel in Altarnun. In the 1790s, shortly after Wesley's death, James Forbes 'observed the portrait of the celebrated John Wesley in many of the poor houses in Cornwall, where his memory is held in veneration'.[47] Like St Petroc, St Samson and the other Celtic missionaries, Wesley conducted a peripatetic ministry, preaching on hillsides, beside streams and mines. The chapels became the means for disseminating a 'religion of the heart', which the Established Church had only intermittently provided since the Reformation. 'Wayside chapels again became a feature of the Cornish landscape and the people were gathered once more into intimate devotional groups, now called bands or classes.'[48]

Methodist historians have deduced many points of similarity between the Wesleyan revival and long-buried spiritual traditions of the Cornish, including 'an intensity of religious experience, a passion for holiness and awareness of the communion of saints'.[49] When Wesley famously reduced the tin miners to tears with his preaching at Gwennap Pit, they were rediscovering feelings of emotion in religion not felt since the sixteenth century. The Wesleyan feast days that the miners adopted have been justly likened to the *pardons* celebrated by Catholic Bretons, which formed part of pre-Reformation Cornish religious practice. The Methodists also appropriated and revived the tradition of grand funerals, while Sunday school processions to riverbanks marked, at least unconsciously, a return to older religious practices not seen in Cornwall since the Reformation.

The evangelical pioneers (like many of the 'Men' in the Outer Hebrides) had a simplicity that appealed to people and stirred distant memories of the Celtic saints. Billy Bray, a Cornish miner who was converted at the age of 29, 'sang and shouted and preached from one end of Cornwall to the other'. His religious awakening led him to put aside swearing, drinking and fighting, but elements of his untamed heart remained unchanged and it was said of him that 'wherever he went, he sang and danced' until his death in 1868. Bray called his dancing 'catching up his heels' and his antics inspired many affectionate anecdotes. One story ran:

> On one occasion he went to Truro to buy a frock for his 'li'l maid' and on the way back one of those upsurgings of happiness which he often felt led him to catch up his heels a bit. On his return home he handed the basket to his wife who quickly asked, 'William where's the cheel's frock?' 'I dun knaw,' said Billy, 'ed 'na in the basket?' It wasn't. 'Glory be to God,' exclaimed Billy, 'I bin and danced the frock out of the basket.'[50]

Cornish and Welsh Methodism became dowdier and more respectable in time, but as the fund of stories about Bray's life showed, it did not at first have especially censorious overtones.

The comparisons drawn between Methodists and the Celtic Church cannot be pressed too far. Although Cornish miners hung pictures of Wesley in their cottages much as the Breton farmers hung pictures of saints in their homes, the Methodists did not pray to his image, or believe in his intercession. As in all the Celtic lands, the evangelical fire destroyed as well as created. The puritan strain ran clean counter to the vestiges of half-pagan customs that had survived in eighteenth-century Cornwall, such as saints' days and the Padstow Hobby Horse and the Helston Furry Dance. Methodists had nothing to do with these pre-Reformation or even pre-Christian remnants, closing their curtains against the drinking and carousing that they were associated with.

As early as the 1750s, visitors noticed the impact of the Wesleyan reformation of manners on once-rowdy saints' days. 'The feasts used to be attended with wrestlings, hurlings and other robust exercises which often ended in murder and bloodshed,' William Wynne wrote in 1755. He rejoiced to report that these excesses had been 'happily laid aside' in his own time thanks to the efforts of the 'preachers against them'.[51] Most Cornish people in time became Methodist but the Methodists in Cornwall never had a local patriotic role like that of the Calvinist Methodists in Wales or the Catholic Church in Ireland and in Brittany. They did not see themselves as guardians of culture, traditions or language. The revivalists of the nineteenth century could not really look to any of the denominations as barriers against the decay of a Cornish identity.

The language was revived as an act of protest against this decay, and what Jenner achieved is proof of his determination, for by the 1900s the very existence of the Cornish language was almost forgotten. A Cornish glossary was published in 1882, and in 1901 a Celto-Cornwall society was established briefly under the poet and novelist Arthur Quiller-Couch. The society was short-lived, though it stimulated Jenner into producing the *Handbook of the Cornish Language* in 1904, which marks the true start of the modern Cornish language movement.

Jenner had difficulty in persuading the members of the Celtic Congress in 1904 to accept Cornwall as a bona fide member of the wider Celtic family. At their assembly in Caernarfon, he only swung it by delivering a speech in Cornish and reading out a Cornish telegram from another sympathiser. The scepticism of the outside world irritated him, as he became increasingly convinced that Cornwall was not only as Celtic as Wales, Ireland or Scotland, but more so, having – as he put it – no Scandinavian or pre-Celtic element. It was as Celtic as any of them, if you defined a Celtic nation, as he did in 1904, 'as one which, mainly composed of persons of Celtic blood and possessing Celtic characteristics and having once had a separate national existence, has preserved a separate Celtic language and literature'.[52] The characteristics were the virtues wheeled out by every Celtic revivalist since Matthew Arnold's time: 'The imaginative temperament, the poetic mind, the superstitions, if you like to call them so, the religious fervour, the generosity of heart, the kindly hospitality, the passionate nature, the absolute honesty, the thirst for knowledge, the clean spirit, the homing instinct, all these are there.'[53]

Jenner then tried to promote the fragile Celtic revival in Cornwall by introducing a version of the bardic congress, or Gorsedd, that Iolo Morganwg had invented for Wales in the 1790s. Jenner's circle were intrigued when the Breton nationalists held a bardic congress in 1899, to which Jenner was admitted in 1904 as Gwaz Mikael, 'servant of Michael'. The campaign was boosted by an exciting 'discovery' made by L. C. Duncombe-Jewell, one of Jenner's associates, of the hidden meaning of the wooden carvings of minstrels in the church at Altarnun, which Duncombe-Jewell insisted showed Cornishmen in kilts and bagpipes, providing more evidence of Cornwall's lost pan-Celtic heritage. There were numerous delays in getting a bardic congress off the ground, though, for Jenner was not even resident full time in Cornwall until he retired from his job in the British Museum in 1909. Then the First World War interposed, during which cultural activity was curtailed. It was not until the 1920s, when Jenner was in his seventies, that the move for a Cornish Gorsedd resumed and the first ceremony took place in 1928, following the nomination of seven Cornishmen and one woman as bards at the Welsh Gorsedd of 7 August at the Treorchy Eisteddfod. Jenner was no longer the real leader of the Celtic activists in Cornwall – the baton had passed by then to his disciples Nance and A. S. D. Smith, known as Caradar. But he was nominated first Grand Bard of Cornwall at the ceremony at Boscawen-Un that September for his undisputed services over several decades as father of the Cornish language revival.

The small band of Cornish linguists, never more than a few hundred strong, later split into several factions. One problem with a language recreated by one man is that his example tempts others to do the same. Why, they asked, was Jenner and Nance's version, known as Unified Cornish, necessarily the 'correct' one? The differences surfaced after Nance died in 1959 and still more after a Cornish Language Board was set up in 1968. Kenneth George, an academic, first produced and then popularised a different spelling for the language. To distinguish it from Unified Cornish it was named Common Cornish, or

Kemmyn and in July 1987 the language board formally endorsed it, splitting the ranks of Cornish-speakers in two. Old campaigners like Peter Pool were flabbergasted. 'The revival of the language [had] seemed close to immense success,' he wrote, disappointedly. 'We seemed to be approaching the promised land which Jenner and Nance had dreamed of, a land in which a good number of Cornish people would use the language of their forefathers as a living tongue.'[54] Now all was confusion. Adding to this confusion, a third secession occurred in 1988 under Richard Gendall who proposed yet another version of Cornish based on a different spelling and vocabulary, culled from the latest surviving sources of the language in the eighteenth century. This was known as Kernuack or Kernewek. Pool was deeply scornful of the criticisms of Unified Cornish and especially of the rise of Kemmyn, which he said sounded 'as if the language had been taken over by robots'.[55] He complained: 'A movement which was until recently united is now in a state of total schism and disarray, a disaster which seems beyond anyone's power to avert.'

The debate has never involved more than a few academics, all of whom, as Bernard Deacon wrote, seemed to be conducting 'a search for a holy grail of authenticity'. Each prophet insisted his version was more 'authentic' and 'real' than the other. While Gendall claimed Kernuack was 'rich, interesting and surprisingly easily learnt', George claimed that Kemmyn was a 'vibrant, living, modern everyday language'.[56]

In the streets of Truro, English remains firmly in place, facing no competition from Unified Cornish, Kemmyn or Kernuack. Most Cornish writers have never had any time for any of it, fearing that kicking over the bones of the lost dead language has led to a neglect of what until recently was a rich English dialect. Cornwall's most popular writer by far, Daphne du Maurier, was born in London but spent most of her life in Cornwall, which she used as the setting for many of her most famous novels, such as *Rebecca* and *Jamaica Inn*. She was happy to be counted a member of the nationalist group Mebyon Kernow, but was waspish about Cornish. She wrote: 'If they would turn their genuine enthusiasm to seeking ways and means of preserving Cornish individuality and independence, keeping the coast and countryside unspoiled, with people fully employed, they might in time achieve a greater miracle than restoring a dead language that never, even in olden times, produced a living culture.'[57]

A contributor to the *Cornish Review* in 1949 wrote that grumbling about the triumph of English over Cornish was absurd. English was 'the greatest of their blessings and very few Cornishmen have any interest in the revival of a Celtic language,' said Ivor Thomas. 'English is the Cornishman's mother tongue . . . it is the English dialect which these exiles (in America, and else-where) love. Few of them have any interest in the Celtic language of pre-Reformation Cornwall.'[58] Thomas suggested that the idea of a Cornish identity was in itself an invention, as most people's identities were more local than that. He was not interested in conjuring up a 'Celtic ghost world'.

The historian A. L. Rowse did not lend the former language much of a thought, either. The rebellions of 1497 and 1549 did not warm his heart. He was 'bored by popular revolts and movements', he confessed, 'such fools, led by such nit-wits'.[59] The grand march of English history, personified by Elizabeth, the Cecils, Nelson and Pitt, thrilled him far more. Rowse was fascinated by Cornwall, and was enormously interested in – and amused by – the paradox of his own identity as a working-class Celt in the upper-class, Anglo-Saxon environment of Oxford. He delighted in everything in Cornwall that genuinely distinguished it from the rest of England. But it was not the lost Celtic language but the English-Cornish dialect that engaged him and *A Cornish Childhood* is spattered with attempts to reproduce the speech patterns used by his family and their neighbours in his village. The dialect then was still interwoven with words and phrases transmitted from the older language, such as 'clickhanded' for left-handed, from the Cornish *cledh* meaning left, and 'Morgy' for dogfish, from the Cornish *mor* meaning sea, and *cil* meaning dog. Rowse recalled his grandmother as one of the last exponents of a great but fading linguistic tradition. 'In her nothing was changed,' he boasted. 'All the phrases and images and metaphors that had been used for centuries in East Cornwall, since the days when the Prayer Book and Bible had brought an end to the old Celtic language, were unspoiled and complete in her . . . her speech is alive and present with my mother . . . practically the last generation with which it is.'[60]

But the English-Cornish dialect has been neglected. It is, in fact, a cas-ualty of the upsurge of interest in Cornish. Expressions that came naturally to the lips of Rowse's uncles and aunts would sound archaic today. Who would now say they had come "ome loaded like a millerd's 'orse' unless they were on the stage or 'putting on' an accent? In Cornwall as in the rest of rural Britain, the speech of younger people contains little of the vocab-ulary or intonation of the generation that grew up before television became ubiquitous, and a wealth of expressions that sprang from the contact between people and the land has disappeared.

In the meantime, Cornish – all three variants – is gathering strength, enjoying the status it never had before. The last ten years have even seen the birth of Cornish cinema and one evening in Truro I found myself watching several Cornish-language videos at the home of an activist. One recent film, *Hwerow Hweg – Bitter Sweet*, released in spring 2002, was well received in the media columns of the national press.

George Ansell, a Cornish teacher in the village of Gwinear, told me he took a relaxed view of the divisions that have riven the Celtic language movement. He learned Cornish after moving in from England 25 years ago, stirred first of all by feelings of curiosity about the meaning of village names. For him the language was the key to a growing sense in Cornwall of a separate, Celtic identity. 'Feeling Cornish was a joke a generation ago. Now a lot of people are prepared to say they are Cornish, not English. I see it as part of a British-wide movement. Here, for example, people are asking "Why is this village called Gwinear?"'

He added: 'The language is the heart of Cornishness and Cornish culture. How can you argue a case for a Cornish identity, or even for devolution, without the language? Unlike Wales, Cornwall is not seen as a separate country, so the language has a strong political element. It is the basis on which the whole Cornish revival occurred.'

Ansell was delighted that just before the hundredth anniversary of the publication of Jenner's *Handbook on the Cornish Language* the European Union had officially recognised Cornish as a minority language. It is a decision that will guarantee greater status, access to funds and promotion of the language in schools. Ansell said he hoped he had seen the end of the days when regional television crews would fill a light-entertainment spot on the news by sending a couple of reporters on to the streets of Truro armed with a few Cornish phrases to faze bewildered shoppers.

To activists like Ansell, the spread of Cornish is the means to restore a lost Celtic identity, which will result in Cornwall receiving devolved government of its own, rather than being included in a region stretching from Land's End to Bristol. 'We need recognition of Cornwall as a Celtic nation if we are to get devolution,' he said. 'It's totally unacceptable being part of a south-west region. We don't accept that we are just a county of England.'

The most optimistic estimate I heard was that up to 3,500 people in Cornwall now have 'some knowledge' of the language, though that includes those who know only a few phrases, while about 500 can speak it with varying degrees of ability and about 100 can talk fluently. A recent academic study of Cornish reached an approximate figure of 300 speakers.[61] Cornwall has about 400,000 inhabitants, so even if the figure of 500 speakers is accepted, it is still only one-eighth of 1 per cent. Cornish activists have a long way to go before they can claim to have restored a community language.

Watching Cornish-language films in Truro, I admired the actors' perseverance, though their slow, slightly robotic tone betrayed the difficulty of wrestling with a tongue whose nuances and inflexions are unknowable, lying beyond the veil, in the grave with Dolly Pentreath.

There remains Mebyon Kernow. In November 1967 Daphne du Maurier wrote to her friend Oriel Malet in Paris about them. France was only months away from massive political upheaval. Cornwall was much quieter, but the currents were stirring, she claimed. 'I forgot to tell you,' she wrote, 'I have been made a member of the Nationalist Party of Cornwall, Mebyon Kernow (Sons of Cornwall) and given a badge to wear and a thing to stick in my car. I can hardly wait to go and blow up a bridge.'[62] Two years later Du Maurier told Oriel in another letter that she was 'having rather fun with the Cornish Nationalists, Mebyon Kernow', after writing an article for a nationalist paper. She was amused by a letter she had received from a man who was fiercely against Mebyon Kernow, warning her that the nationalists would force everyone to turn Roman Catholic. 'That is the last thing I should imagine Cornwall would do as they are nearly all chapel,'[63] she mused.

The playful, almost patronising tone was appropriate to a movement that few people in Cornwall took seriously then and which remains almost unknown outside Cornwall today. The fortunes of Mebyon Kernow have followed those of its Manx sister, Mec Vannin and the various Breton nationalist parties, rather than Plaid Cymru or the SNP, let alone Sinn Féin. Both Mebyon Kernow and Mec Vannin have sometimes capitalised enough on local grievances, especially against the influx of outsiders, to take the odd scalp in local elections. But brief successes have not been transformed into a breakthrough. The small size of both parties has left them susceptible to violent mood swings and takeovers by small fanatical groups, whose coups have merely isolated them even further from the electorate. The national party of Cornwall is, in any case, the Liberal Party, for generations the spokesman of the Celtic Nonconformist edge. The Liberals lost their grip on Wales after the First World War but they have kept their hand on Cornwall, where the unconscious Celtic reflex operates strongly against the Tories as the party of the English landlord and tithe-eating parsons. The Cornish retained what the more industrialised Welsh largely lost: an individualistic culture and a scorn of collectivist solutions. If applying socialism to Poland was, as Stalin said, like putting a saddle on a cow, Cornwall is another such cow. An instinctive non-conformity with all political projects works against socialism and in favour of liberalism as the least homogenised political creed.

The Liberals have absorbed a good deal of Cornish nationalism. They digest it naturally, as the party of local 'pavement' politics, which traditionally has opposed the Jacobin strain in socialism as well as its centralising Tory counterpart. But Liberalism cannot absorb everything. There remain the true believers that Du Maurier described meeting in the 1960s. Bookshops advertise their presence. In St Just I passed a handwritten notice in a window urging passers-by to buy a strikingly decorated book by John Angarrack entitled *Our Future is History*, whose black-and-white front cover showed a dagger being plunged through a map of Cornwall. The notice reminded people that the author was 'the hero of the nation'.

Angarrack, I discovered, after meeting him at his home, was not someone prepared to be bought off by the Liberals' unthreatening promise of regional autonomy all round the United Kingdom. He was proud to represent the militant end of Cornish nationalism, although he said he did not imagine a separate Cornish state, nor did he advocate violence (his own campaign of physical force had got no further than attempting to block the path of the Furry Dance in Helston on one occasion). But he was an aggressive advocate of what he called 'parity of esteem' with England and has campaigned fiercely against an education syllabus that has little or no Cornish input. Angarrack dated his own political awakening to an exhibition held in Bodmin to mark the 500th anniversary of the Prayer Book rebellion, whose content outraged him with its praise of a long line of English kings. After that he had set to work writing books denouncing the anglicisation of Cornwall as a fraud perpetrated on the people. The schools seemed a particular bugbear to him. 'There is complete censorship of Cornish history,' he said. 'My own two sons are taught English history in school. They are trying to remove our sense of having a shared history, and of Cornwall having a cultural tradition of its own. We are united by feeling oppressed. That's what unites Cornwall – a sense of oppression.'

Travelling round Cornwall did not confirm such an impression. It is not quite the right word for a land that has neither the anger nor the resulting energy of nationalist Northern Ireland. The Cornish identity has few institutions to rest on. There is no gaeltacht, no equivalent to the Gaelic bodies now at work in the Highlands and islands and no Church to prop it up. There is the Gorsedd, a Cornish studies institute in Redruth, a department of Exeter University and the local news service of BBC Radio Cornwall. There is no Cornish newspaper.

I did not meet many people who shared Angarrack's angry conviction, though there is a shift of mood taking place in Cornwall. The black-and-white flag known as 'St Piran's flag', which was once the exclusive property of Mebyon Kernow, flies now from church towers and town halls, as well as decorating the rear bumpers of many cars. This nationalism on the cheap, however superficial, is a new phenomenon. It reflects wider dissemination of a feeling of Cornishness. As the Cornish historian Treve Crago told me: 'Cornish nationalism was a class phenomenon before the Second World War. It didn't affect working-class families at all.'

Now it is visible, not merely in the slogans painted on bridges and the white paint daubed over municipal signs, but in the number of signatures collected for a Cornish assembly. Bert Biscoe, of Senedh Kernow, the campaign for a Cornish assembly, collected 50,000 in 2001. A veteran of the failed campaign in the 1990s to gain Cornwall a single unitary local government authority, he recalled of that business: 'We lost, but we discovered we had a massive constituency.' Biscoe dates the turn of the tide from 1998, when Cornwall won 'Objective 1' status from the EU, which entitled it to regional aid. 'The money was pretty meaningless – it was all about winning back your self-confidence,' he said. Biscoe's team handed in their petition in December 2001. However, it did not speak for the whole of Cornwall's 400,000 population. Many people care little about demands for autonomy, or suspect the motives of the campaign. Some oppose what they see as an anti-immigrant agenda, though Biscoe rejected the charge. 'It's not about Cornwall for the Cornish, it's about enhanced assistance for a peripheral region in the doldrums,' he said.

Cornwall always was poor. The annual migration of summer visitors to resorts and of second-home owners to their country cottages conceals it. Visitors to now-chic Padstow, which has a reputation as a culinary centre, or to Rock, which the media profile as a cold-water St Tropez, or to St Ives, with its Tate Gallery and artists, admire a surface patina of wealth. Private yachts bob in the bays, well-heeled crowds jostle for tables in eateries, while coaches drive bumper to bumper through 'Arthurian' Tintagel.

But as in the south of France, which was a Communist bastion before the arrival of the racist Front National, the transient presence of the wealthy accentuates the resentment of the resident mass. The Cornish, like the people of Provence, benefit from tourists and second-home owners but suffer from it, too. House prices are only a little lower than those in the English Home Counties, while a low rate of occupancy of second homes turns the resorts into ghost towns for half the year. The people of the Gaeltacht, the Outer Hebrides and west Wales have only begun to feel the effects of the invasion of second-home owners, which in Cornwall has virtually pushed local people from a host of seaside towns and villages. No fishermen live in the 'fishermen's' cottages in the prettier villages, such as St Agnes, Mousehole and Boscastle, which have been massively colonised in recent years. The piercing shrieks of the English bourgeoisie now echo down the lanes that once reverberated to Dolly Pentreath's coarse Cornish swearing. The Cornish simply cannot afford to live in their ancestral villages. In St Ives, the locals are not to be found in the old town but in the socially owned housing on the edge of town. For the most part they have been pushed into Truro and into dowdy, ex-industrial towns, such as Redruth and Camborne, which the second-home owners shun. With their dingy cafés, cheap, 'pound-stretcher' stores and signal lack of shops selling luxuries or Cornish cream teas, these towns provide a more accurate portrait of Cornish life today than the 'typically Cornish' seaside villages with their New Age bookshops full of literature on Cornwall's Arthurian legends.

Throughout history Cornwall was a land of miners, like Wales; and of fishermen, like Scotland. Now it has very few of either. The last tin mine in Cornwall, and in Europe for that matter, closed at South Crofty in 1998. Tellingly, a slogan painted on the wall of the ruined mine reads: 'When the fish and tin are gone, what are Cornish boys to do?' Much to everyone's surprise, the mine reopened in 2004, after a sharp rise in tin prices. But no one believes the future of Cornwall lies in mining.

The fishing has long been in decline. Its great days were long gone before Denys Val Baker, in *Britain's Art Colony by the Sea* in 1959, cast his mind back to the days when St Ives mustered a fleet of more than a hundred boats. 'What a sight it must have been in the old days when the fleet returned, to be greeted by hundreds of black-shawled fishermen's wives, waiting along the quay.'[64]

Agriculture is in depression, as it is everywhere in Britain. There are a few bright spots on the horizon, of course. The huge gardens of the Eden Project have proved a great success in drawing visitors; a university for Cornwall at Penryn is also anticipated. But none of these boons can compensate for the decline of all the traditional industries.

The Cornish feel that whereas Ireland and Spain have fought successfully for their fishing rights within the European Union, a British government with its attention fixed on London and the south-east has not defended the fishing communities of Cornwall, Scotland and England's north-east. There is the same resentment concerning the handling of EU aid for underdeveloped regions. The Cornish feel that Wales and Scotland have had problem areas addressed, because they are seen as 'countries', whereas Cornwall was pushed to the back as a 'county'. Lumped in with Devon when it came to applying for aid, its needs were ignored, because Devonian wealth cancelled out Cornish poverty.

It is economic resentment that is fuelling the revival of interest in Cornwall's own identity, not delayed anger at its centuries-old subjugation by King Athelstan, or regret for the death of the Cornish language. The Cornish do not want much and even nationalists are not very interested in separation or a republic. But the Cornish may not be as soft as some outsiders imagine. Daphne du Maurier warned that if the government continued to ignore Cornwall's interests, 'we may yet see a repeat of rebellion'. It sounds like hyperbole, as the Cornish have not taken up arms in defence of their rights and their culture for half a millennium. But that may be simply because they have not faced such a combination of pressures as they do now. The Archdruid of Cornwall warned against the complacent belief that the Cornish will accept a future as stewards of a tourist resort. 'Right now we are embattled,' he said. 'We have rebelled several times and were slaughtered every time. But the Cornish are a committed people. We produce martyrs . . .'

CHAPTER EIGHT

Brittany

'Plutôt comme une libération'

Nothing is left of my early civilisation but wreckage. There are still some trees but no forests.
(Pierre-Jakez Hélias, *The Horse of Pride*, 1975)

The saints went down to the sea at the *grand pardon* of St Anne in western Finistère. Some were on brilliant yellow, green and red banners, picked out with gold thread. Others were wooden statues, wobbling along in litters that rested on the shoulders of sturdy women in traditional dress, looking lost amongst the mass of white lace head-dresses. A bishop led the procession from the pilgrimage church of Sainte-Anne-la-Palud across sand dunes towards the shore. The faithful, bolstered by many tourists, cameras dangling from straps on their wrists, followed in his wake, singing hymns and canticles in Breton. 'Intron Santez Anna' (Lady St Anne), they sang, 'Mirit tud an Arvor, War zouar ha war vor!' – 'Save your Breton people, on land and sea'. They sang in a language that sounds hard to French ears. It is much more familiar to anyone with some knowledge of Welsh, for the two are sister tongues. A great deal of French has flowed into Breton over the centuries, but many Breton words are virtually the same as their Welsh counterparts. It is closer still to Cornish.

The language of the hymns was not the only reminder that Brittany is a Celtic land. The saints at the *pardon* proclaimed it. At least half the banners represented saints from the Britain of the sixth and seventh centuries. Down to the sea went St Guenole, St Mabouarn, St Pol and a host of other Welsh and Irish evangelists.

Reminders of the migration of Britons and their missionaries to Roman Armorica 1,500 years ago dot the countryside. The patron saint of Dol-de-Bretagne, in eastern Brittany, is the Welshman Samson. Pol, or Paul, another Welshman, has his cathedral in Saint-Pol-de-Léon. The port of Saint-Brieuc on the north coast honours the Welshman known in Britain as

St Breock. St-Thégonnec, famous for its magnificent church and close, recalls the Welsh, or rather British, saint known in Britain as Clonnock or St Tegoneg. The list of Breton towns dedicated to British saints is long. Many Cornish and Breton towns are named after the same saint. Samson's relative Mewan is remembered in St Mewan in Cornwall and Saint-Méen-le-Grand in Brittany, while Meriasek, or Meriadoc – Camborne's patron saint – is remembered at Saint-Meryadoc, near Pontivy, in Brittany. Petroc, another South Walian, is remembered not only in Bodmin and Padstow in Cornwall but in Loperec, in southern Brittany. Sometimes the connections are slightly disguised, for while Cornish towns often start with the prefix 'St', for saint, in Brittany this often gives way to 'plou', or 'plu', from the latin *plebs*, meaning 'people of'. So it is that the Irishman Gwinear is remembered at Gwinear in Cornwall and at Pluvigner in southern Brittany.

The wave of immigration from Britain that began in the 350s did not make Armorica a Celtic land, for it was that already. The Gauls were Celts, too, though heavily Romanised. What the immigrants did was to transplant the specific Celtic culture and language of Britain to the continent, turning it into a 'Little Britain'. From the 600s Armorica was increasingly known as Bretagne (Brittany) a cultural, ethnic and linguistic offshoot of the other Bretagne (Britain) to the north.

The forces behind the southward emigration to continental Europe remain mysterious. It was once widely believed that the Celtic Britons had fled the westward advance of the Germanic Angles and Saxons, but while this theory held obvious appeal to Celtic revivalists in the nineteenth century, they may also have been fleeing from the Irish Scoti – Celts like themselves. The result was to turn the Channel into an inland sea, linking two very similar cultures and peoples. The incomers were clearly numerous enough to overwhelm the existing society as they pushed in from their first bridgeheads on the north and south coasts, progressively conquering the interior. The line demarcating the land settled by the Britons/Bretons from that retained by the Francs remains visible. Running from just east of Dol-de-Bretagne in the north to just east of Vannes in the south, it reveals itself in the high incidence of the word *plou* (or *lan*) for settlements.

Through their churches, their patron saints and through their *pardons* at which the saints are escorted back down to the sea from which they came in real life, the Bretons recall their origins in the land to the north. But the memories have grown dim. Many centuries ago, big-power politics sliced across the old routes of communication that ran from north to south, wrenching the Welsh, Cornish and Bretons eastwards to face their mighty conquerors. The Bretons were reorientated away from Celtic kin towards France and Latin civilisation. The early medieval settlers in Brittany had at first established a kingdom of their own. But just as the Cornish and then the Welsh were unable to resist the rising power of England, the Bretons were sucked into the orbit of France. By the mid-tenth century their rulers had accepted the less than regal title of dukes, owing fealty to France. They were still effectively independent, however, until a crushing military defeat in 1488 forced the Breton Duchess Anne to marry the King of France. The Duchess did not forfeit all her rights on marriage and left the duchy to her daughter Claude, but on Claude's marriage to the next French king, Brittany passed permanently and irrevocably into France, a fact formalised by an Act of union in 1532.

Brittany was united to France at almost exactly the same time as Wales was united to England. But the outcome was not the same, for while Wales disappeared into the English county system, Brittany kept its parliament for another two and a half centuries. Not until the French Revolution of 1789 swept away the old French provinces did Brittany disappear entirely as an entity, carved up into the five departments of Finistere, Morbihan, Côtes-d'Armor, Ille-et-Vilaine and Loire-Atlantique.

To defend the existence of Brittany after that was to risk being stigmatised as reactionary, a clericalist, a royalist and a traitor to the ideals of the Revolution. Bretons did not need individual liberties, it was argued, now that they had *liberté*. Nor did they need their own language, for Breton, like Occitan, was dubbed the tongue of the disgraced priests and counter-revolutionary *notables*.

Centuries of pressure to become French and to feel French have done their work. But the memory of the connection to Wales and Cornwall has not totally disappeared. 'Ah, nous sommes cousins!' an elderly couple at the *pardon* of St Anne exclaimed on hearing they had a half-Welsh visitor amongst them. 'Nous sommes Celtes aussi!'

France has dragged the Bretons eastwards. Cornwall and Wales underwent the same process, pulled eastwards towards England and London and drawn into England's cultural, political and religious orbit. When England accepted the Reformation, Cornwall and Wales, like it or not, had to follow. The Bretons now found themselves on the other side of the religious fence from the Cornish and the Welsh. The barrier remained. When the British Celts reasserted their religious identity in the eighteenth century, it was in the context of Methodism or Presbyterian evangelicalism. The Bretons – like the Irish – became known for fervent Catholicism.

At the little *pardon* of Our Lady of Kerbader, on the south coast, I joined a few hundred people who were carrying banners and statues from a small church in a woodland clearing to a well in a nearby meadow. They trudged along a path past bog violets and rushes to the tune of a piper, halting before the well where the priest gave a blessing, before circling the well and returning to the church. It was novel, watching a well used in this way, after seeing so many in Cornwall, Wales or Ireland lying unused, overgrown with brambles or restored for visitors. No tourists visit the well at Kerbader, except on the day of *pardon* and to join the procession was to recapture some sense of the religious culture that disappeared 500 years ago in Cornwall and Wales, the lands of the Bretons' ancestors.

The Bretons underwent the same process of humiliation and rehabilitation as the Scottish Highlanders — at first feared and derided, then later exalted as noble savages. The image of the Bretons suffered for the association with royalism. It was inaccurate, for the Breton nobles had been strong opponents of royal absolutism in the eighteenth century, while in the 1790s a portion of Brittany supported the Revolution (and has voted left ever since). The Bretons rose up not against the Revolution but against the centralisation of power in Paris and the attempt to mobilise Breton men into the revolutionary army in 1793. The campaign against the Catholic Church bewildered them, for in Brittany the peasants regarded the priests as an elite sprung from their own ranks. The Jacobin 'cult of reason' was not introduced in a manner calculated to win them over. At Quimper in December 1793 the revolutionaries chose the patronal feast day of St Corentin to destroy the cathedral statues and ornaments, urinating over some of them.[1] The peasants who watched this ugly ceremony returned to their farms and, encouraged by their priests, began guerrilla warfare. They became known as *chouans*, for the owl-like calls that they used to contact each other at night. The revolt kept the revolutionary troops busy throughout the later 1790s, but even at the height of the *chouannerie*, there were parts of Brittany that spurned the royalist 'whites' and remained 'blue', the colour of the republican cause.[2]

The Bretons remained in purgatory throughout the republican era. But after the restoration of the Bourbons in 1815 counter-revolutionary barbarians mutated into noble savages. The royalist writer François-René de Chateaubriand prepared the way for the repudiation of classicism in his *Génie du Christianisme,* published in 1802, a powerful apologetic for France's medieval Christian values. Under the restored Bourbons there was a full-blooded reaction in favour of the rural and the traditional. The Catholic revival on the right led to a reassessment of the Bretons, who had suffered very publicly for their allegiance to religion. When in 1839 La Villemarque published *Barzaz-Breiz,* a pioneering anthology of traditional Breton songs, it proved very popular and a flurry of new Breton history books followed in its wake. At the same time a vogue for archaeological associations responded to – and fuelled – interest in Celticism and the Breton connection. L'Association bretonne was founded in 1843 and La Société archéologique du Finistère in 1845, while the visit of Napoleon III to Brittany in 1858 coincided with the foundation of the Société académique du Brest.

Much of the archaeologists' interest centred on the mass of standing stones near the village of Carnac on Brittany's south coast. Just as eighteenth-century England appropriated Stonehenge as a temple of Celtic druids, the French seized on Carnac as their own great Celtic temple. In reality, Carnac, like Stonehenge, long predated the arrival of the Celts, but the intellectual excitement stimulated interest in the people who lived around these monuments.

In 1828, an influential essay 'Sur l'antiquité du Département du Morbihan' claimed that Breton was linked to Persian and was widely spoken in parts of Africa.[3] If Carnac was a Celtic temple, some argued, Breton speech must be a degenerate version of the tongue of the druids in their groves and the Bretons' strange costumes must be a throwback to the druids' robes. The historian Henri Michelet exulted: 'En Bretagne, sur le sol géologique le plus ancien du globe, sur le granit et le silex, marche la race primitive, un peuple aussi de granit' ('In Brittany, on the granite and flint of the oldest geological soil in the world, stands a primitive race, a people also of granite').[4] The preface to the *Galerie armoricaine,* printed in Nantes in 1845, warmed to the theme of the *race primitive,* declaring Brittany both the ancient homeland of the Celtic peoples and the seat of the druidic religion. 'C'est là que les veritables descendants des Celtes ont conservé un costume et un physionomie . . . qui ne sont qu'un druidisme déguisé'[5] ('It is there that the descendants of the Celts have maintained a dress and a physiognomy which are but druidism in disguise'), it said.

The archaeologists' controversies attracted writers and travellers to what had been a neglected corner of France. Victor Hugo came in the late 1820s and early 1830s, but was angered to discover that the Breton peasants, far from revering the stones of Carnac, were using them to make walls. Gustave Flaubert was struck by the dirt and by the prevalence of beggars. 'Vous leur donnez, ils restent – vous leur donnez encore – le nombre s'accroît – bientôt c'est une foule qui vous assiège . . . occupés à réciter leurs prières, lesquelles sont malheureusement fort longues and heureusement inintelligibles.' ('You give them something, they remain – you give to them again – the number grows – soon there is a crowd around you, busy reciting their prayers which are, unfortunately, very long, thought happily unintelligible')[6] Flaubert's tone was exceedingly condescending but established an image of the Bretons as a people set apart by religion, superstition and folklore. He also struck a note of regret over the likely disappearance of this world, which later writers would echo.

The transformation of the Breton from reactionary to noble savage is recorded in art. The revolutionary painters hardly bothered with Breton subjects. The artistic discovery only began in the 1830s and 1840s, stimulated by the popularity of *La Galerie armoricaine*, and *Les Voyages pittoresques et romantiques dans l'ancienne France*, which came out in Paris in 1845. Fortune Abraham Dubois, in his *Voyage en Bretagne* of 1839, referred rudely to the peasants he saw in Quimper cathedral because of their 'bizarre et même barbare costume' ('strange, even barbaric apparel').[7] But as the reaction to anti-classicism took hold, the very fact that it was 'bizarre et même barbare' became an asset, marking out the Bretons as the guardians of an older, pre-revolutionary order. At a time when atheism and socialism were gaining in French cities, conservative and Romantic artists explored the theme of Bretons as defenders of Catholic values that mainstream France had foolishly rejected. The *chouans* of the 1790s became a popular theme in art, often painted like stags in Scotland 'at bay'. *Les Chouans* (1849), by Charles Fortin, showed a peasant family in their rustic home in the company of a rebel priest, fearfully awaiting the arrival of revolutionary troops. Fortin painted the Bretons as primitive but heroic people. There is no doubt where he wanted the viewer's sympathies to lie.

Until the mid-nineteenth century it took weeks for a visitor from Paris to work his way around Brittany on country roads, which explains the lack of artistic work produced before then and the glut that followed. In the 1850s and early 1860s the railway pushed west to Quimperlé, Quimper and Brest, changing an arduous expedition into a potential pleasure trip. By the early 1880s the train leaving the Gare Saint-Lazare in Paris at 9 p.m. deposited visitors rested and refreshed at Quimperlé at 9 a.m. the next morning.[8] The transport revolution had an enormous impact on art, bringing large numbers of painters to Brittany for the first time. Now they were on the spot, they no longer turned to historical themes but painted what they saw in front of them. Many seized on the *pardons* as the quintessential expression of the Breton character, which was still seen as deeply superstitious, but also in a more positive light.

Before the Second Empire, Church and state took a dim view of such celebrations. Officials saw them as a nuisance and a potential source of disorder. The ascendant Ultramontane party in the Church disliked them as semi-pagan and not quite Roman. But clerical hostility faded in the 1860s as the Church, by now battling with militant atheism among the urban workers, lost its squeamishness about *pardons*. Older clergy might object to mixing the sacred and the profane at such celebrations but by the 1870s bishops were grateful for any religious manifestation. The Church grew still fonder of Breton *pardons* after the Third Republic replaced the Empire in 1871. The more the French state distanced itself from the Church, the more the Church moved to shield the Bretons from its influence. Like the Catholic Church in Ireland, the French Church in Brittany became solicitous of the once-despised local language as a 'language of faith', a barrier to French godlessness.

The trickle of artists turned into a flood after the arrival in 1886 of Paul Gauguin. 'J'aime la Bretagne, j'y trouve le sauvage, le primitif' ('I love Brittany – I find it wild, primative'), Gauguin wrote revealingly to a friend in February or March 1888.[9] 'Ici en Bretagne,' he confided to Vincent Van Gogh in October 1889, 'les paysans ont un air du moyen âge et n'ont pas l'air de penser un instant que Paris existe et qu'on soît en 1889' ('Here in Brittany, the peasants look medieval and don't look as if they know for a moment that Paris exists and that we're in 1889').[10] Gauguin's successful exhibition in 1889 at the Café Volpini in Paris brought another surge of artists into Brittany, including the Dutch painter Jacob Meyer de Haan, Henry Moret, Armand Seguin, Maxime Maufra, the Pole Wladislaw Slewinski and the Irishman Roderic O'Conor, most of whom descended on the celebrated Pension Gloanec in Gauguin's original base of Pont-Aven before fanning out over the countryside.

The artists in the 1890s refined the Breton image yet again. Earlier artists had depicted the Bretons as rather earthy heroes – people with the hearts of lions but with mud on their fingers. It was what drew Gauguin, who had sought 'le sauvage, le primitif' among them. But in the 1890s the painters largely excised this element. As the Third Republic tilted towards left-wing anti-clericalism, they spited the left's sensibilities by painting Breton peasants as virtual angels. Jules Breton's *Pardon de Kergoat,* of 1891 was a mystical paean, showing a long procession of women dressed in elaborate and almost oriental costumes wending their way through a dark and magical forest towards a clearing and an old church. The women carry lighted tapers, while others hold aloft statues of the Virgin and other saints. There is a small concession to the theme of rural misery in the form of a discreetly positioned beggar, but he is scarcely noticeable. The overall impression was awesome: of a people as replete with mystery as the Incas or ancient Egyptians, carrying out fantastic and pharaonic rituals. Earlier paintings of the Bretons had humbly invited viewers to sympathise with their all-too-human sufferings; the *Pardon de Kergoat* commanded them to genuflect. Alfred Guillou sought a similar response in his *L'Arrivée du Pardon de Sainte Anne de Fouesnant à Concarneau*. Painted in 1887, it showed Breton women escorting an image by boat to land. Again, it gave the strong impression that the Bretons were a race of semi-divine fairies or shamans. The women escorting the image are peasants only in theory, for they have the bearing and gaze of goddesses and madonnas in dazzling white dresses, their faces pure and spotless.

The French artists in Brittany – like the British tourists to the Isle of Man or the well-meaning visitors to the Gaelic-speaking islands of western Ireland – inadvertently killed off the phenomenon they sought to record for posterity. French artists popularised Breton *pardons* to a wide audience who, thanks to the railways, then decided they wanted to see these events for themselves. The imperial family's visit to Brittany in 1858 stimulated this interest, dispelling lingering perceptions of Brittany as hostile territory. The Breton people had responded to the visit with delight. 'Avec cet élan des nations primitives . . . elle s'est portée avec enthousiasme au devant de l'Empereur' ('With all the enthusiasm of a primitive people . . . they rose to greet the Emperor'),[11] the Prefect of Morbihan reported in a patronising tone to his superiors.

By the turn of the century the ceremonies that had fascinated Gauguin's contemporaries were changing. They had already become tourist-orientated and the atmosphere was less religious. The clergy knew something was being lost. 'Nous sommes obligés d'avouer que dans nos pardons aujourd'hui on ne prie pas comme autrefois,' the abbé Gouarin noted in 1909 in the *Revue Morbihannaise*. 'On ne s'amuse plus comme autrefois.'[12] The Abbot attacked the popular press and the anti-clerical schools for having 'affaibli cette foi ardente', but while the schoolteachers may have done their bit to corrode religion, the tourists following the artists had also contributed to the change.

The Bretons in their costumes drifted from paintings to postcards and railway advertisements, becoming an indispensable part of the poster campaign of the Chemins de Fer de l'Ouest, which homed in on the women in their white lace head-dresses. They made Brittany one of the most popular French holiday resorts by the 1900s. Inevitably Bretons became self-conscious about characteristics that had once seemed natural. If for a time the interest of the tourists and painters petrified the local fashion sense, eventually the Bretons discarded items of dress that singled them out as rural and backward. The relationship between the observers and the observed was never easy. Gauguin's sojourn in Brittany ended, symbolically, in a fight with local men in the village of Concarneau. The love affair with 'le sauvage, le primitif' ended with a Breton fisherman bloodying the painter's leg with a wooden clog.[13]

The men abandoned their distinctive clothing at the start of the twentieth century. The women followed; hemlines rose after the First World War and the dresses became simpler. Only the white lace head-dress held its own, though the high towers of lace beloved by manufacturers of Breton dolls were a product of the final years of Breton dress. Far from being ancient, they were simply a fashion of the 1920s and 1930s – the last exotic fruit of a dying tree.

The writer Pierre-Jakez Hélias recorded the passing of this world in his best-selling autobiography, *Le Cheval d'orgueil,* published in 1975. Hélias, who died in 1995, grew up in the Bigouden, the semi-peninsula south of Quimper in the last decades of the 'old' Brittany. His universe was peopled by poor families who spoke Breton, obeyed priests, went to Mass on Sundays and holy days and cured illnesses by visiting holy wells and making pilgrimages. Like their rural Irish contemporaries, their culture revered death, personified as the *ankou,* or grim reaper, and they strictly observed rituals before and after a relative's or neighbour's death. Hélias said the cult of death was so strong that peasants of his parents' generation took a certain relish in their departure, lying in bed in some state in their last illness, dictating final commands to a crowd of onlookers, surrounded by candles and praying relatives. A small crowd waited outside the cottage door, crossing themselves and genuflecting every time the grave and self-important figure of the priest came and went. Departure from the world was a communal event, signalled to the whole parish and the men working in the fields by the ringing of the bells in the church. Nor were the dead left alone and forgotten after their burial, for Hélias recalled the sight of groups of women moving around the graveyards after Mass in their white coifs, murmuring 'paters' and 'aves' to the deceased.[14]

The women of Bigouden took pride in their famous head-dresses. In the *Cheval d'orgueil,* Hélias recorded his mother's attention to this indispensable item; rising at dawn in summer and well before dawn in winter, she would begin the task of fixing her coif to her head, 'which she had learned to do properly by the age of six'.[15] In the 1930s, and still more after the Second

World War, the world of the *Cheval d'orgueil* contracted and disappeared. Hélias recalled his childish amazement at the sight of a peasant woman in the 1930s removing her dress and donning the black bathing suit of a city tourist to go swimming. The woman swam into the sea with her white coif still perched on her head,[16] but this compromise arrangement – bathing suit *and* coif – could not last, and in the end the country people dispensed with their head-dresses.

The French tourist industry endeavours to persuade visitors that Breton costume, emblematic of a distinctive way of life, lingers in remote, less-visited corners, just as tourist guides to Nova Scotia coyly suggest Gaelic can still be heard in village lanes off the beaten track in Cape Breton. Breton guidebooks point visitors to Hélias's old stamping ground in the pays du Bigouden, around the village of Penmarc'h. Postcards give the same impression, depicting old women in their finery, apparently caught by chance gossiping on a harbour quay or a beach. It is all nonsense, just as the idea that Gaelic can still be heard in the lanes of Nova Scotia is nonsense. Hélias himself had no doubt that the world he grew up in was finished, totally and utterly. 'Nothing is left of my civilisation but wreckage,' he wrote. 'There are still some trees but no forests.'[17] He mourned its passing but was under no illusions about why this had happened. His own mother had gladly traded her 'traditional' life on a farm after the Second World War for a job in one of the new factories. He did not blame the young for heading to the city. They were sick of spending half their lives under their parents' roofs, he wrote, with no privacy, subject to the dictates of their fathers and of the priests.

What was dead already in Hélias's lifetime is certainly not alive now, a quarter of a century on. The Breton costume, like the world it represented, is finished. There are today no remote areas in Brittany. Highways and motorways bisect the region, pumping high-speed car traffic to the beaches and camp sites strung along the coast. A driver following the route from Quimper to Penmarc'h is quickly relieved of any lingering belief that this might still be an isolated corner of France, unawakened by mass tourism. The coastline is heavily built up, the outline of the old settlements blurred by the indiscriminate construction of thousands of holiday cottages. Mostly white and almost identical, they look from a distance like so many sugar cubes. The notion of a distinct 'peasant' culture surviving amid the criss-crossing motorways, the sugar cubes and the camp sites is absurd. A visitor is as likely to see a woman in a lace head-dress in this landscape as a man dressed in an Elizabethan ruff in London.

Costumes survive at the *pardons* but they are worn for a day only by young people and members of folk groups who borrow them from municipalities or museums. They do not wear them regularly as did Hélias's mother in the vanished Brittany of the 1930s. The handful of very old women still wearing lace hats at home are so few in number that one, Marie Paul, from Penmarc'h, born in 1912, has become quite famous, giving interviews to magazines about it. At the *pardon* of St Anne I saw one of these very old women, in her late eighties or nineties, hunched in her pew, as gnarled as her walking stick, wearing a dusty black dress and small lace cap. The ensemble was obviously her own. When she was young almost every woman attending such an event would have worn something similar. Now she looked incongruous, for even the other elderly women around her were wearing slacks and ordinary skirts.

The artists who came to Brittany concentrated on religion, and on *pardons* in their work and showed little interest in the Bretons' own work or daily life. Seen through artistic eyes, Bretons spent their lives at *pardons*, going to or from church, praying at wayside crucifixes and mourning the deaths of relatives lost at sea. These were also depicted as intensely religious occasions, featuring a friendly *curé* consoling the grief-stricken spouse.

In reality, the notion that Bretons were all devoutly Catholic, like the earlier notion that they were all royalists, was incorrect, or incomplete. The north-west of Finistère and the Vannes area in Morbihan were, and remain, Catholic and traditionally right-wing. The clergy exerted much the same political and moral influence there a century ago as their Irish counterparts. But unlike Ireland, Brittany also had a 'red belt' running through the centre, including much of Côtes-d'Armor and towns in the west of Finistère, like Brest and Douarnenez. Political divisions have remained remarkably constant since the Revolution and in this red zone, the Catholic Church is as weak as it is in the rest of France.

But the Church is now increasingly feeble outside the red zone, too. Most parishes have to share priests who are themselves mostly elderly. Asked about the state of their local parish church, the people of one remote village I encountered in a bar reacted with incredulity. 'I should not imagine more than four people go there on Sunday,' one person told me. They found the question bizarre, as the Church meant nothing to them. Faith declined in tandem with the costumes and the language in the 1950s and 1960s. The church buildings inspire more interest now than ever, judging by the number of tourists seen snapping away with their cameras in churchyards. Many parishes became wealthy in the sixteenth and seventeenth centuries, thanks to fertile agriculture and the linen trade and they celebrated their wealth by building highly elaborate parish closes that surround the church, and crucifixes known as calvaries. At Saint-Thégonnec, which boasts one of Brittany's finest calvaries, tourist officials give visitors maps to help them cover a circuit of the best in one go. But the churches are mainly museums, full of visitors on summer afternoons but fairly empty on Sunday mornings.

The decline in faith is disguised by the healthy numbers attending the *pardons*, some of which have mutated into music, food or dance festivals, with the religious element relegated to the margins. At the *pardon* of St Loup in Guingamp, the crowd attending the service in the cathedral was a fraction of the number who showed up later to watch the folk dance competition that followed. For most people it was a charming spectacle, made more pleasant by a food tent dispensing cold lager, French fries and sausages. The *pardon* of the motorcyclists at Porcarno also draws large crowds. About 20,000 bikers in black leather from all over Europe attended in the summer of 2003, few of whom were active Catholics, according to the newspapers. For most of them it was an international bikers' convention, made more enjoyable by a vague feeling that it might bring them good luck on the road. The *pardon des motorards* dates back only to the 1970s, when an inspired priest held the first event.

The *pardons* are a truly Breton experience but not a nationalist one. At the St Loup festival in Guingamp the young dancers and singers in splendid costumes drifted past the stalls selling nationalist literature without a glance. I saw no takers for the posters, stickers or piles of Irish Sinn Fein leader Gerry Adams's autobiography, *A Voice for Peace*, translated into French. The two sales people, a middle-aged man wearing a T-shirt with an Irish flag on it and a thin woman with long hair and bad teeth, sat chattering to each other with the air of people who were used to being ignored and had learned to cope with it by ignoring everyone first. They drifted off to the beer tent, leaving their stall and its wares unattended. Throughout the day I never heard one word of Breton from the audience or the dancers and singers.

The Breton language has almost vanished over the last half-century. From one of the most vigorous and widely spoken Celtic languages, it has become one of the weakest, its very survival for the next 25 years now looking questionable. At best it may linger as the language of a club of enthusiasts who communicate over the internet or meet at pre-arranged functions, like modern enthusiasts for Cornish. It has no future as a community language.

A time traveller from a century ago would be amazed at the speed with which the Breton language has contracted and seemingly committed suicide. Only a visitor from mid-nineteenth-century Ireland might nod knowingly, for the mass abandonment of Breton in the course of a few decades resembles the flight from Irish in the decades after the Famine of the 1840s. In both cases the community turned its back on the ancestral tongue: for them it had become contaminated with poverty and backwardness.

Like Scottish Gaelic and Irish, Breton was never the language of the whole community. The use of the prefixes *plou* or *lan* marks the rough borders of the territory that the Bretons originally settled. Very few lie east of the departments of Côtes-d'Armor and Morbihan; and Nantes and Rennes, which the Bretons seized in the 850s, lie well to the east. The expansion of the medieval Breton state meant that from early on it included large francophone areas. As in Scotland, the border zone spoke another tongue from that of the interior and the seat of power lay there, not in the interior. Even in the eleventh century French was the principal language of Brittany's eastern marches, while the following centuries saw the slow westward march of French. Of the five departments of post-revolutionary Brittany, only Finistère lay wholly in the Breton-speaking zone. Côtes-d'Armor and Morbihan were cut roughly in half by the linguistic frontier, while departments of Ille-et-Vilaine and Loire-Atlantique were almost totally francophone.

West of the Vannes/Dol-de-Bretagne linguistic frontier Breton remained very much a living language in the nineteenth century and French visitors routinely complained of their difficulty in being understood. The first statistical inquiry into language in 1831 in southern Finistère concluded that 80 per cent of the inhabitants were monoglot Breton-speakers while less than a fifth had any knowledge of French.[18] Monoglot French-speakers were then almost unknown. By the 1860s French was becoming more widely used in urban areas, but only by the elite. An observer in 1864 said that in Quimper and Morlaix a tenth of the adult population knew only French, a half knew French and Breton and the others knew only Breton. But the 10 per cent of the urban population who spoke only French, he added, mainly comprised government officials, foreigners and outsiders. The rural heartland, he went on, remained exclusively Breton-speaking, so much so that scarcely one person in 25 had enough French even to maintain a conversation.[19]

Brittany did not follow the pattern of the Isle of Man, the Scottish Highlands or Ireland, where the older languages rapidly receded in the face of the English advance in the early nineteenth century. It seemed more likely to follow the example of Wales, where the language was holding its own and even benefited from urban immigration. Although the French government, especially after the return of the republican regime in the 1870s, pursued a centralising Jacobin agenda, the inhabitants of western

Brittany, known as Bas-Bretagne, remained a people apart, sufficiently so to provoke the anger of the authorities. In 1902 the French Prime Minister Emile Combes, an inveterate enemy of the Church (unsurprisingly, he had once been a seminarian),[20] assailed the Breton clergy for using Breton in their sermons and catechism classes to attack the republic and ordered a new law obliging them to use only French.[21] The looming Church–State conflict stimulated research into the state of play between the languages in the diocese. A survey by the Bishop of Quimper of 19,000 children undergoing catechism in his diocese showed that 70 per cent were being instructed solely in Breton and that more than 80 per cent of churches used Breton for sermons on Sundays. The clergy estimated that just under two-thirds of the local population were incapable of understanding a sermon in French.[22] From a French point of view, Combes's nationalist rage was understandable, for the figures showed the Church was helping sustain an independent culture in southern Brittany.

The main factors behind the resilience of Breton culture were the strength of rural society and the Church. Quite unlike the Scottish Highlands, Wales, or Ireland, rural Brittany was not desperately poor or underpopulated. French visitors bemoaned the presence of beggars and many families knew poverty, but the countryside was fundamentally rich. It was flat, very fertile, highly productive and in consequence full of people. Everyone remarked on the size of Breton families and whilst many of them had to export some children to urban France to find work, Breton families never experienced the misery of their Irish counterparts in raising families who would almost all leave for foreign parts. In the 1870s the population of Brittany reached about 3 million, most of whom were rural. About 100,000 were engaged in industrial occupations, many in the port of Brest. About 700,000 were engaged in agriculture and only half the children of school age actually attended schools.[23] The statistics explain the existence of about a million Breton-speakers, for although the schools taught in French, only half the children attended them. The towns were becoming more French, but a large part of the population had little to do with urban life.

The rural population did not turn to the French-speaking schoolmaster for instruction but to the *curé*, who not only spoke Breton but often encouraged its use as a spiritual cordon sanitaire against French anti-clericalism. Jean-Marie Deguignet recorded the insulated quality of this rural life in his book, *Mémoires d'un paysan bas-breton*. Born in 1834 near Quimper, he recalled the laughter of the local mayor and his niece when as a lad he had tried to read aloud from a French newspaper, with no knowledge whatever of French pronunciation. The mayor, he remembered, advised him to learn just

enough French to survive military service. But fluent French was not necessary for a Breton. 'Pour apprendre le pur français tel qu'on l'écrit et qu'on
parle dans le monde savant, tu n'y arriveras jamais,' the mayor declared
genially. 'Moi j'ai passé quinze ans à l'école et je suis loin de le savoir' ('You
will never attain the pure French that is written and spoken in educated
society . . . I spent 15 years at school and I am far from knowing it myself').[24]

Deguignet's evolution from Breton hayseed to French republican casts
light on why the history of Brittany has been so different from that of Wales
and Ireland. It was not just that Brittany did not endure a famine, or that the
struggle over land was far less intense there. Breton nationalism confronted
a more militant, almost messianic, state ideology. French republicanism was,
quite simply, more efficient in liquidating local loyalties than Britain's
constitutional monarchy. After several years serving in the French army
Deguignet returned to Brittany a changed man. He rejected Breton culture
entirely, becoming an out-and-out atheist, republican and francophone.
'Cette race celtique est du reste condamnée à disparaître comme toutes les
vieilles races moralement et physiquement dégénerées,' he raged. 'Il ne reste
que la langue pour bavarder, argoter, blaguer, mentir en assommant de
stupidités et imbecilités' ('The Celtic race is in any case, damned to perdi-
tion like all the old races which are morally and physically decadent . . . All
that remains is a dialect used for gossiping, joking and telling lies that take
your breath away with their imbecility').[25] Deguignet's mental journey is
almost impossible to envisage in Scotland, Wales or Ireland. There, some
people may have been indifferent to the appeal of local nationalism, but they
rarely regarded their own culture as totally stupid and degenerate.

Deguignet died disappointed just after the turn of the twentieth century,
still surrounded by the imbeciles and their beloved priests. But the Brittany
he despised was, in fact, about to crack. The First World War had the same
huge impact on Breton society and culture that it had in Nova Scotia,
prising a generation of young men out of rural communities and immersing
them in a different culture. They returned home altered, fluent now in
English or French, and no longer as isolated as their parents from the urban
community. Increasingly, they moved to the towns. Rural dress disappeared. They remained overwhelmingly Catholic but the mystical fervour
that had drawn the artists of Gauguin's generation evaporated. Paintings of
pardons executed between the two world wars differ markedly from those of
30 years earlier. They show people in a mixture of urban and rural dress,
enjoying themselves in what looks like a fairground atmosphere. The
Brittany of the period was in transition. People still grew up speaking

Breton at home, which is why most people over the age of 70 in western Brittany can understand the language. But they spoke French at the schools that they now all attended. Churches held services in both languages. The barriers that had kept Bretons from being French were breaking down, and would collapse entirely after the Second World War when the self-sufficient rural economy and the culture it sustained dissolved.

The feeling of being on a sinking ship alarmed many writers, poets and clerics and prompted the growth of organised opposition. The death of so many Bretons in the First World War and the flight of so many survivors to the towns brought protests. The five Breton departments had suffered disproportionately in the trenches. About 200,000 Breton men died in the war, a large number out of a total population of 3.5 million in 1914. Part of this could be explained without recourse to conspiracy theories. As the Breton birth rate was higher than the French average, Brittany inevitably contributed a higher than average number of men to the army. It had more young men to give. But some complained that the Bretons had been used as cattle fodder. France had saved itself, they said, and dealt with the troublesome Bretons by pushing them to the front. The post-war flight of young people to the towns and to Paris exacerbated fears that the rural heartland was being bled dry. Some 300,000 men left their rural homes for the cities in the 1920s and 1930s.[26] Many villages changed out of all recognition. Busy farms were now empty, the village lanes silent and the churches suddenly full only of the old.

The decades following the First World War saw the rise of autonomist and radical separatist activists, many of them contributors to the magazine, *Breiz Atao* (Brittany For Ever), founded in 1919. They were not an altogether new force. In 1898 the Kevregidez Broadus Breiz (Breton regionalist union) had been founded in Morlaix. A conservative organisation, which enjoyed aristocratic patronage, it never went beyond politely requesting the reinstatement of Brittany's pre-revolutionary autonomy. But the fêtes and congresses it sponsored nourished more radical elements, who in 1911 founded a more aggressive group, the Stollad Broadel Breiz (Breton Nationalist Party), which campaigned under the slogan 'Breiz D'ar Vreiziz! La Bretagne Aux Bretons!'[27] They did not get far, for as one Breton historian recorded, their programme was wholly negative and gave no hint of how, practically, it might be developed.[28]

Turbulent post-war France offered nationalists more opportunities. They fed on the air of political instability, the shrill ideological confrontation between left and right, intellectual pessimism *vis-à-vis* Germany, the hope provided by Ireland's successful independence war with Britain and the suspicion that Bretons had paid too high a price for French victory in the war. *Breiz Atao* made more of an impact than previous publications, while a literary review *Gwalarn* followed, in 1925. Along with new media outlets there was a youth organisation, Unvaniez Yaouankiz Breiz (Breton Youth Union), which in 1927 stimulated the creation of a new political party, the Strollad Emrenerien Vreiz (Parti Autonomiste Breton).

The nationalists made much of the fact that the Bretons' blood sacrifice in the trenches had elicited no reward whatever in the form of autonomy or mere recognition of the Breton language. They pointed out that the increased centralisation of the French state since 1870 had been accompanied by relative demographic and economic stagnation compared to less centralised Germany. They remarked that while many of Europe's subject nationalities achieved liberty under the Treaty of Versailles, the Bretons had not even gained local autonomy. They were not calling for the break-up of France. 'Nous Ne Sommes Pas Séparatistes' was the heading of the first paragraph in the Declaration of Châteaulin, the programme the Nationalist Party adopted in August 1928.[29] They simply objected to the Jacobin policy of assimilation and demanded the granting of Swiss-style local autonomy to whichever of the old provinces wanted it.

The Breton nationalists were closer to the Welsh than the Irish in their moderation and their first electoral forays yielded results that were just as dismal as Plaid Cymru's in its early years. The autonomists' first campaign in 1930 in Guingamp brought them 376 votes out of 16,777 cast.[30] Then as subsequently, the rural masses were unmoved by those they considered townies and intellectuals.

Their tiny size did not stop them from splitting. A rupture between moderate federalists and more extreme factions hankering for an independent state led in 1931 to the formation of a new hard-line organisation, the Parti National Breton (PNB). The 400th anniversary of the Treaty of Union of 1532 uniting Brittany to France gave the hard-liners a chance to show their mettle. Just before the President of the Republic reached Rennes for the ceremony, on the night of 6–7 August, the statue of the Duchess Anne, Brittany's last autonomous ruler, shown kneeling submissively before the French King, was demolished in an explosion. The bomb brought the nationalists the attention they craved, but not much popularity. Yeats's well-known line about Ireland, in which he said 'the centre cannot hold', applied in reverse to the solid farmers of rural Brittany. There only the centre could hold and extremism and violence were generally abhorred.

The Breton nationalists made little effort to connect their demands to the rural base. Moreover, under the slogan 'Ni rouge, ni blanc, Breton seulement', they became increasingly pro-German in the late 1930s, supporting Nazi Germany's *Anschluss* with Austria and the Sudeten German demands for annexation by Germany. Ominously, they denounced in advance any attempt to call up Bretons to fight for France in a new conflict. As war with Germany loomed, the PNB's stance became increasingly controversial and in 1939 *Breiz Atao* was seized and the party dissolved in October. By then France was at war.

A rump of PNB leaders under Olier Mordrel took a fateful step, fleeing first to Brussels and then to Germany, from where they returned to France under German escort following France's surrender and the installation of a collaborationist government under Marshal Pétain in June 1940. The decision to bank everything on German victory was risky and had enormous consequences for Brittany after the war, when even the most timid expressions of support for autonomy would be stigmatised as Nazi and collaborationist. Their stance did not bring the revived PNB even short-term dividends for there was no rush to join the party, merely the tactical adherence of a few rabid anti-Semites, fanatical enemies of the pre-war, left-wing, Front Populaire and other assorted opportunists. The Germans were unimpressed and did not reward the Breton nationalists with autonomy, let alone create a satellite state on the Slovak or Croatian model. The PNB was tolerated but ignored, while the movement was torn between one side hoping to strike a deal with the Pétain government in Vichy and a rump that held out for statehood. Neither side enjoyed a following. The Bretons supplied a disproportionate number of fighters for Charles de Gaulle's Free French army in Britain, the male inhabitants of the tiny island of Sein, off Brittany's west coast, having joined up in their entirety.

The PNB fizzled out in the summer of 1944 once the Allied landing in Normandy in June made it clear that the Germans would not remain much longer in Brittany. The pro-German Breton nationalists were never more than a clique. One writer has suggested that active collaborators among the PNB numbered no more than 80.[31] But the collaboration of the handful gave the restored French state an excuse to repress virtually all Breton cultural activity. Retribution was severe. The courts handed down sentences to 3,146 individuals, including 129 death sentences.[32] Not all of these were PNB activists; many sentences were for crimes that had no connection to Breton nationalism. But a climate of revenge formed the background to the mass abandonment of Breton culture and language directly after the war.

There was more to this than shame and confusion over the links between Breton nationalism and German collaboration. France's economic miracle after the war drove a coach and horses (or rather, a TGV train) through the old rural economy of regions like Brittany. During the 'thirty golden years', as the French call the post-war decades, agriculture shrank rapidly in importance as an employer, the country was covered with Europe's most comprehensive network of motorways, and the cities were linked by high-speed trains that were the envy of neighbouring Britain. A tourism boom transformed the appearance of quiet, isolated fishing villages that suddenly became embellished with hotels, marinas and camp sites. The retail revolution weaned French shoppers from their small family stores to the vast and impersonal out-of-town hypermarkets that are now a feature of the country.

The abandonment of the Breton language was part of a cultural revolution, which also saw a collapse in church attendance. For many older people it was a bewildering time. Jean Bothorel, in his memoir *Un Terroriste breton* recalled the generation gap that opened up in the village of Plouvien in the late 1950s and early 1960s. Born in 1940, the society he grew up in was still Catholic but conscious that it was becoming less so with every passing year. The Church in Brittany, like the Nonconformist chapels in Wales, was dumping the old language of worship in a desperate attempt to appear modern. Bothorel's grandmother was confused. 'De mon temps,' she whispered, as they sat in church waiting for Mass, 'le breton et la foi étaient frère et soeur.'[33] She was in the same position as many elderly worshippers in Wales who assumed the Welsh language and the religion were brother and sister and were dismayed to see their clergy switch the language of services to English to attract the young. In Brittany as in Wales, the change did not keep the young but merely accelerated the death of the old culture. Bothorel said the sense of shame about speaking Breton was so pervasive that people gave up speaking it with relief. 'Cette volonté d'éradication de la langue bretonne leur semblait des plus légitimes, et ils ne la percevaient pas comme une agression,' he recalled, 'bien plutôt comme une libération' ('The desire to eradicate the Breton language seemed completely legitimate to them and they did not see it as an attack, rather as an act of liberation').[34]

The 'liberation' of the Bretons from their native language is more advanced now than it was when Bothorel was growing up in the 1960s. Then almost everyone living west of the Vannes/Saint-Brieuc line who was 40 or over spoke or understood Breton and there were still about 600,000 speakers. The figure was well down from the million speakers in the 1920s, let alone the estimated 2 million speakers in 1886. But it was still enough to maintain Breton as the first language of many communities.

More recent statistics contained in a bulky volume entitled *Un Avenir pour la langue bretonne* produced in 2002 by the government's Ofis Ar Brezhoneg (Breton Language Office) are alarming, to put it mildly. This puts the number of speakers at only 268,000, half the number in the 1960s. The overall drop, though rapid, hides the true extent of the crisis, for the most worrying element is the age profile. About three-quarters of native speakers are over 60, while less than 1 per cent are under the age of 30.[35] Adding in recent learners marginally brightens the picture. It still leaves 64 per cent of speakers older than 60, while 28 per cent are aged 40 to 60 and only 6 per cent under the age of 40.[36]

The statistics make it clear that almost no Breton-speakers born after the Second World War have taught the language to their children. There was what the experts call a 'cessation in language transmission', which means that only a rapid rise in the number of learners can prevent the extinction of Breton in the early twenty-first century.

The drop in numbers means Breton is no longer a community language, for the rise in learners in no way compensates for the loss of native speakers. In 1886 the 2 million speakers made up two-thirds of the total population of the five Breton departments. French-speakers were then in the minority. Brittophones dipped below the 50 per cent mark around the time of the First World War, for they made up 1.15 million out of a total population of 3 million by 1928. They then formed just over a third of the population, and still an absolute majority west of the old linguistic frontier. But by 1952 the number had dropped to 700,000, a figure which more or less held its own for three decades, as the figure had dropped only to 600,000 by 1983. The next decade witnessed the death of a substantial proportion of the last generation to be brought up in Breton, for within a space of 10 years the number of speakers had plummeted to its present level.[37]

The Breton-speakers now make up less than 10 per cent of the population of Brittany and just over 20 per cent of the population of Finistère, its stronghold. A quarter of a million speakers might still sound fairly healthy compared to the situation in Ireland, where the number of regular users of Irish (unlike the large number professing some knowledge) probably does not exceed 80,000. But Breton-speakers do not have the fallback position of a gaeltacht, a bordered area in which government, business, schools and churches co-operate to maintain the language as a means of communication. Much as Irish activists in the Gaeltacht complain of government neglect, they might like to witness the position of the language in Brittany to see what life would be like without such an area. The Bretons have no chance whatever of getting the equivalent of a gaeltacht; the whole notion runs directly counter to the Jacobin centralising ideology that has underpinned French government policy on the regions since the 1790s. In Brittany the remaining speakers are widely dispersed. There is no longer an area, or a medium-sized town, where their culture remains dominant.

Travelling west across Brittany from Dol-de-Bretagne in the east towards the port of Brest, I constantly expected to find myself in the equivalent of the Irish Gaeltacht, or of Welsh-speaking North Wales, only to find each town and village as outwardly francophone as the last.

The Jacobin legacy in France means the state gives no recognition to Brittany's existence as a historic unit. A shadowy provincial authority has come into existence since the Socialist government of François Mitterrand introduced a tiny measure of devolution, but its budget is tiny and its competences very few. Brittany has no outward visible marks whatever. Nothing advertises the historic border between Normandy and Brittany, and no sign in Breton welcomes drivers into the region in the local language, as do the signs on the Welsh border with England. It is one of the many small but significant differences between non-revolutionary Britain, with its curious respect for ancient jurisdictions, and revolutionary France, where pandering to provincial feeling is still seen as suspiciously reactionary.

I did not expect much evidence of a living Breton identity in Dol-de-Bretagne, for even if it owes its cathedral to the Welshman Samson, this land passed into the francophone pale many centuries ago. It was more disappointing to find so little evidence of the culture in the remote village of Kermaria-an-Insquit, as this lay inside the Breton-speaking area. A guidebook told me that in the village clustered around a medieval crusader church, 'You may well get your first exposure to spoken Breton'. It was not so. The only villagers in evidence were an elderly couple doing duty inside the church, mechanically informing a stream of visitors of the representation of the figures in the *danse macabre* on the wall. It was impossible to talk to them as they chanted: 'La mort! Le roi. La mort! Le patriarche. La mort! L'archevêque', and so on. Nothing was written in Breton in the church, anyway.

I pushed on north-west to the coastal port of Paimpol, but what looked on the map like an old fishing village turned out to be a major tourist conurbation, whose narrow streets were filled with the cars of irritated French tourists, many sounding car horns at each other for failing to move faster. The recent story of Paimpol is that of many villages on the north coast, where until a generation ago life revolved as it had for centuries around fishing and the annual *pardon*. Paimpol had now clearly put that way of life behind it. A *pardon* was still held there, but it competed with a performance by singers from Bulgaria and a rock concert advertised by flyers all over the walls of the town. The fishing boats in the harbour were outnumbered 10 to one by the pleasure boats of the holiday-makers whose appetites and amusement now constitute the backbone of the local economy.

Wondering if and when I would find any Breton-speakers, I gave up heading fruitlessly west and doubled back into the interior. I turned off the Brest–Rennes motorway, and was bouncing along lanes lined by cornfields, stone barns and farmhouses when a small sign reading '*chambres*' directed me to a small farm. A large piece of needlework hanging on the inside wall with a Breton motto under it confirmed that the proprietors, an elderly farmer and his wife, spoke Breton and were proud of their culture. They were not anti-French, but Breton patriots. 'Nous sommes Bretons d'abord,' the woman announced, turning up the radio and clapping animatedly to a Breton pipers' tune that was playing.

I told them I had not a heard a word of Breton spoken in the streets so far, and they said this was not surprising. They spoke Breton to their neighbours, including their young nephew who worked on a nearby farm and their daughter, but they never used it in the street or shops. It was not customary, even if they knew the shopkeeper spoke Breton. They did not know why this was, or question it. It was accepted and always had been. The woman talked vaguely of 'a certain contempt' for the language but it had not bothered them. They had done their bit by bringing up their daughter in Breton, they said, which was unusual. I spent days in their house, listening to them converse much as J. M. Synge had lain on his bunk in the Aran islands in the early 1900s, listening to the murmur of the Irish-speaking family downstairs. Like him, I was conscious that a language and a culture were fading away and that it was a privilege to be catching the sound.

In the city of Brest I tracked down a young activist, who could articulate what had happened to this once vibrant culture since the war. Ronan Hirrien, a television presenter in his late twenties, was a fluent speaker. He was fortunate in being able to use his Breton at work, which involved presenting a short Breton-language programme on French state television, France Ouest. Hirrien was a learner. Although both of his parents were brought up in Breton, typically they had brought him up in French. His parents were absolutely part of the generation that had refused to transmit their own language down the line. Hirrien learned the language himself at night school and at university. His family was far from delighted. 'My mother didn't like it and wouldn't answer me when I spoke in Breton. As for my grandfather, he was furious. "At school we were punished for talking that!" he said. He thought it was useless and simply brought a lot of pain.

'My mother was born in 1948 and my father in 1946. Those were the years when everyone made the switch to French. Partly, it was because they wanted to be modern. French was the road to modernity and a better life. The schools were crucial. They taught in French and about France. No Breton history was taught until five years ago, when the authorities allowed a book, *Bretagne, une histoire*, to be distributed.'

Hirrien worked in the nascent Breton-speaking media, but harboured no hopes of a media-based linguistic and cultural revival. His own television station bore no comparison to Ireland's TG4 or its Welsh-language equivalent. French state television's output in Breton is minute. France Ouest, which includes Brittany, provides three and a half minutes of news each day in Breton. Another hour a week is allotted to magazine programmes and half an hour to children. A viewer could watch France Ouest for months without chancing on any of the Breton programmes. Public radio produces about one and a half hours in Breton daily. TV Breizh, a private television station that started in 2000, produces more programmes in Breton than France Ouest. But the station can only be watched on cable and satellite, which puts it beyond the reach of many of the elderly and rural Breton-speakers.

It was increasingly difficult to find enough people to interview for Hirrien's programmes. 'More and more it's becoming like a club.' But Hirrien shrugged when asked if he felt any anger about the seemingly unstoppable decline of his chosen language. The Bretons have little of the militancy of the Irish and Hirrien's home city of Brest is no west Belfast. The Bretons may have given birth to the *chouans* under the Jacobin regime, but the temper of both land and people is overwhelmingly cautious, pacific and conservative. There is no public sympathy for violence. The bombing of a McDonald's restaurant in 2000 by an obscure group of extremists, killing an employee, merely underlined the isolation of the small and fragmented nationalist groups from the population. The constant, churning sense of anger and grievance that has fuelled the Celtic revival in Northern Ireland has no parallel here. Nor did Hirrien have much time for that kind of nationalism. 'The Breton language was here before the state of Brittany,' he said. 'I'm not a nationalist. I think nationalism helps to kill off languages.' He felt no anger, merely grief. 'What matters is establishing the link with my family, with this land and its people. We are going to lose a language we have had for 15 centuries. Already children in school have no idea how their grandparents lived. They have a completely new culture.'

I did not envy anyone trying to champion Breton culture in the soulless concrete mess of Brest. Like Cardiff, the city has the look and feel of an implant – a monument to the culture of foreign rulers. Dublin was rebuilt in the same way in the eighteenth century, but an Irish spirit (though not the language) conquered what remains outwardly a very British-looking, Protestant-looking, city. That cannot be said for Cardiff, which, in spite of the banners proclaiming it 'Europe's youngest capital city', stubbornly refuses to look or feel like a city, let alone the capital of anything. A dreary English provincial spirit clings to Cardiff like the most tenacious ivy, and Brest is the same, only the ivy is French. France's Jacobin inheritance means that here, as everywhere in France, the streets and avenues are all named after the same dull pantheon of male revolutionary bores. Brest was always a French island in the middle of Finistère and whatever character it ever possessed was buried in the ferocious Allied bombing during the Second World War, after which the city was rebuilt at speed in a brutal, modernist spirit.

If any city can claim to represent the heart of Brittany, it is not Brest or the old ducal seat of Nantes but Quimper, or as the Bretons say, Kemper. An old cathedral foundation established by St Corentin, its ancient skyline of steeples and pitched roofs instantly hold out the promise that more of Brittany's past traditions may be found here than in the desolate boulevards and *allées* of Brest. Quimper *is* more consciously Breton than Brest, Nantes, Rennes or Morlaix. There are stickers with Breton slogans displayed in many shop windows in the pedestrianised streets and black-and-white Breton flags flutter from the rooftops. But even here I heard not a word of Breton spoken in the streets. The manager of a Breton bookshop, which was full of Celtic music CDs and books on both the language and land, said it had changed over the last 20 years. 'Then all you heard round here was Breton, but now. . .' He shrugged, and moved off to serve a customer.

In a building beside a huge shop selling Breton pottery, I found Mark Masson, the Breton-language officer of the department of Finistère – in a sense the Breton-language officer for the Republic of France, as no other department possesses such a post. Walking into his tiny office, I compared it to the breezy complex of the Údarás na Gaeltachta in the Galway Gaeltacht, with its teams of staff. Masson took a philosophical view of his lonely position as France's only civil servant deputed to serve the cultural interests of a quarter of a million Brittophones. 'The government is more positive than it was,' he mused helpfully, 'but the ideology is still hostile to regional languages, and in France, local authorities follow the line of Paris.'

He explained that although there was interest in learning Breton, the state granted this desire very few outlets because of the strength of the revolutionary legacy, which has insisted on France's cultural uniformity. 'France does not permit the use of any other language than French in public, which is why although we have some Breton schools, they are not allowed to integrate into the state system,' he said. 'There is a great difference between France and Britain in this respect. France is ideological. The British are pragmatic.' He ended on a pessimistic note. 'In ten years time there will be less and less Breton spoken. It will be a language of societies, like an internet language – a community of interest, almost like being gay!'

'I'm sad to see this evolution. This has been the language of Brittany for fifteen centuries. Now the Bretons are becoming totally integrated into France and it's becoming just another region. It surprises me to read surveys which say 90 per cent of the people here would like Breton to survive because they don't do anything about it. They like it as heritage but in everyday life they use French.'

Masson added, though more in jest, that the Breton cause might have benefited from more physical force. 'You need violence to get anything from the state here. People who are peaceful don't get anything.' It was an uncomfortable idea, but of course force does not necessarily involve hurting anyone, let alone murder. The Welsh activists had used force when they blocked bridges and refused to pay bills or answer summonses in English. If the 260,000 Breton-speakers had been half as obstructive as their Welsh counterparts, the French state might have been less high-handed when it came to loftily forbidding the use of Breton in schools and the courts. The French state has diluted the purity of its Jacobin principles when they have become too troublesome to uphold. The Bretons are worse off proportionally in terms of schooling than the Corsicans or Basques, who live in areas where violence, or the fear of triggering violence, has dictated a more flexible cultural policy on the part of the authorities.

The schools have done most to integrate Bretons into the seamless robe of France. The republican schoolteacher was the inveterate enemy of the *curé* in the nineteenth century, and the most important agent in disseminating republican principles of *laïcité*. In most of France, the tussle pitted left against right, Church against State, and the petty bourgeois professionals against *les notables*. But in Brittany, as in Ireland, Wales and the Scottish Highlands, educational struggles had a national and linguistic dimension, for the Catholic Church spoke Breton while the republican school spoke French. As Ronan Hirrien had told me, the clergy in north-west Finistère were still more important than the teachers or mayors in their local communities as late as the 1950s.

The last half-century had seen the collapse of the Church's position and the Church as an autonomous political factor no longer exists in Brittany any more than in other parts of France. Because the catechism class is no longer a counterweight to the schoolroom, the language used in schools is more important now than ever.

A small uprising against French education began in the 1970s when a handful of charismatic activists and parents set up their own school near the village of Saint-Rivoal. Since then the number of Breton-medium schools, or mainstream schools containing a Breton stream, has grown. About 8,000 children in Brittany are now educated in Breton in Catholic schools, state schools, or wholly independent Breton-medium schools known as 'diwan' (germ) schools. Given the hostility of the French state to regional cultures, it seemed odd to hear of any state schooling in Breton. But what has happened is that in Finistère especially, where the department is most sympathetic,[38] some schools have been allowed to incorporate Breton-language streams. As these schools remain French overall, their existence can be reconciled with the law that enshrines French as the exclusive language of public life and instruction. The state also helps the 'diwan' schools in a minor way, by paying for a percentage of teachers' salaries and covering some running expenses. The system is, in fact, a muddle, as the state has tacitly accepted the existence of non-French teaching with the proviso that it is a temporary experiment, and that some matters must be left to the discretion of the department.

But if the republic has surrendered a few outlying turrets to the regional enemy, it has not handed over the keys of the castle. Far from it. One man who has run up against France in its most intransigent and centralising guise is Andrew Lincoln, an unlikely champion of Breton culture because, as the name suggests, he is in fact English. A convert to Breton through marriage, Lincoln became involved in the problems facing the 'diwan' schools when his children were due to attend nursery school, and in 1993 he joined the 'diwan' schools' governing board, tasked with regulating relations with the Ministry of Education. His modest goal was a concordat with the government that would enable all Breton-speaking schools to integrate fully into the state sector, thus gaining access to desperately needed funds, for their present voluntary-aided status grants them far fewer privileges than similar schools in Britain. Even to get access to the limited funds available to voluntary-aided schools in France, for example, a school must be up and running for five years. It is a Kafkaesque provision, for most communities cannot undertake such a financial burden for so long, which is what the authorities intend. Even if they have staggered across this bridge, and gained the prize of voluntary-aided status, comparatively little money is then available to them for investment and expansion.

For Lincoln the battle was about more than Breton rights. It was a test of French democracy and its willingness to accept diversity. The battle was lost. The Jacobin legacy in the teachers' unions proved too powerful to dislodge. After the 'diwan' schools signed an agreement in May 2001 with Jack Lang, the friendly Education Minister, the Council of State suspended the deal as unconstitutional in October. Lincoln took part in the drawing up of a new watered-down agreement, which it was hoped would not stir objections, but the agreement was suspended for a second time in July 2002. A final ruling from the Council of State in November 2003 pronounced even the revised text unconstitutional and at variance with the law dictating that the language of the Republic is French.

The result is just as the French state would like. Breton-language education limps along, underfunded, peripheral and effectively barred from expansion. But it exists, allowing France to boast that it remains the land of *liberté*. The 8,000 pupils educated every year in Breton make up about 1 per cent of the school population in Brittany and only 2 per cent of those in Finistère. It is nowhere near enough to produce a viable linguistic community. Lincoln said: 'What has happened is rather a tragedy as we had an atmosphere of hope and public support.'

For Breton teachers who want to keep their culture and identity alive it is frustrating. Many pass through the classes of Stefan Moel, a teacher-trainer for the state-school sector who lives in the western port of Douarnenez. He told me: 'The future looks bleak. When you sit down and look at it you might as well do something else, like pick strawberries.' He thought France had 'cunningly convinced people that they don't need any other identity. They have convinced people not to bother. Their identity was now French. I fear that most Bretons would now defend the use of French against Breton,' he added.

Douarnenez is an unusual place, both very Breton and very 'red' politically, which is not the normal combination. Moel said it was the only place where a type of creole speech had emerged as a mish-mash of Breton and French, and of French drawing on Breton syntax. But Douarnenez speech, like the Cornish of Rowse's childhood, the Manx of T. E. Brown's era and the English of the older generation of Irish people, is a transitional language.

It has no lasting resting place but acts as a language bridge. Moel has no faith in its durability. 'It won't last. It simply reflects the fact that this town spoke Breton until the 1940s.'

Although teachers like Moel often find it hard to believe their work is worthwhile, there are hopeful developments. In spite of the state's begrudging attitude and public indifference, the number of Breton teachers grows. Though underfunded, new Breton schools open each year and as in east-coast Ireland and South Wales, growth comes where it is least expected, in towns where the language died out long ago. Moel is a rare creature – a Breton-speaking parent of children at a Breton-medium school. 'Most of the other parents in my kids' school would not speak Breton themselves,' he said.

Stefan Moel was much more assertive about his national identity than most Bretons I met. Even when they thought they were 'Bretons d'abord', like the elderly couple I first stayed with, they seemed cowed into using French in public. Possibly it was the several years spent in Ireland, or the fact that his partner was Irish, that had grafted some Irish assertiveness on to a cautious Breton root, for Moel laughed slightly despairingly about the Bretons of his acquaintance who spent years in each other's company speaking French before finally realising they all spoke Breton at home.

In the village of Saint-Rivoal, where the 'diwan' school movement began, I met a couple who were neither teachers, civil servants nor activists working in the media, but young people who were 'out' and proud of being Breton. As almost nobody had transmitted Breton to the next generation since the Second World War, they were inevitably learners rather than native speakers. Geraint Jones was Welsh and had moved to Brittany, bringing the slightly more defiant attitude of his homeland to a new setting. His partner Gaelle was Breton, but her background was far from a traditional rural Catholic one, as her parents had been Maoists, their lives preoccupied with a great many causes, though Breton nationalism was not one of them.

In the village pub where we met, the invisible wall between the drinkers reflected the barrier between the elderly native speakers and the learners, who are often young urban intellectuals. I sat with the youngsters who, apart from Geraint and Gaelle, included the Belgian-born barman. A few feet away – but a world away – sat a trio of grizzled old farmers in cloth caps, talking quietly in Breton. For a while we fell silent, listening to their murmur. It was such a rare experience that I wanted to savour it, but they picked up on the silence, flushed and drifted unthinkingly into French. 'Nous parlons breton parce que c'est notre langue maternelle,' one of them began by way of apology. 'Mais nous aimons la langue française aussi. . .' I was as charmed by their politeness as I was depressed by their seeming need to apologise – to genuflect before the altar of French culture.

Saint-Rivoal is a community of about 180 people and as isolated a place as one could find in Brittany, but there is no unofficial gaeltacht even here, and after the old men shuffled out, their places were filled by men in their thirties and forties who were all francophones. They shrugged and laughed when asked about the language. 'Breton, maître chez toi!' one of them joked, ironically repeating the nationalist slogan I had often seen scrawled on the bridges over motorways. One man seemed distinctly offended and embarrassed by the question. 'If I spoke Breton, I would have as bad an accent as you do in French,' he said, with a sneer. He smiled, but it was a tight, angry smile, and he strode out of the bar in a huff. The sons of the village were not about to go into battle for Breton. It was up to the newer arrivals, like the Welsh immigrant and the daughter of the ex-Maoists from the city. I was reminded of the villages I had seen in the west of Ireland, where the bar playing Irish traditional music was full of German and Dutch tourists, while the local youths spent the evening singing karaoke songs to a jukebox in another pub down the road. 'People think the language is not essential to the culture,' said Gaelle disapprovingly. Geraint cut in: 'They go to a *fest noz* [music festival] and put stickers on their car. But hanging a flag in your car and dancing a dance is subject to changes in fashion. If the next fashion is not Breton music, but line dancing, that's going to be it.' 'Breton music already has gone out of fashion, to a degree,' Gaelle agreed.

I left Saint-Rivoal, full of admiration for the young people in the bar, but the situation there had summed up much of the movement to save the culture. The real enthusiasts were always learners, outsiders, from the big city, from Belgium, from Wales. They did not really connect up with the world of the old Breton farmers who actually spoke the language. There was a barrier of reserve between the two groups, and the old-timers were not much interested in preserving their culture anyway. They were content to use it among themselves, and then let it sink into the grave with them.

The Breton peasants and intellectuals have always disappointed each other. There was never much of a dialogue, which helps to explain why Breton nationalism was always weaker than its Irish or Welsh counterparts. Irish nationalism grew on the back of land hunger and under O'Connell it allied itself to the priests. Even now, with the Catholic Church so much weaker than it was before, nationalists in Ireland are reluctant to sever links entirely. Breton nationalists never allied their demands with those of the farmers in the same way. Lurching towards the extreme right before the

Second World War, then tilting hard towards the left in the 1960s, they left the farming community behind. Most Breton activists I met were anti-clerical and despised the Church, sneering at *pardons* as tourist gimmicks. They did not value the cultural identity that the *pardons* conveyed, however watered down, to many people who would otherwise know absolutely nothing about Breton culture.

I headed south to Carnac, the village famous for its fields of standing stones. Victor Hugo had visited Carnac in the 1830s, when the fashion for Celtic studies was sweeping France and when it was widely, though mistakenly, assumed that the menhirs and dolmens were druidic temples. For several years ugly metal fences have sealed them off from the public, supposedly to allow the natural environment to recover from the tourists' heavy footprints. But Carnac provided a bigger shock than the unsightly fences. Its position beside the sea obviously dictated that a holiday resort would grow up around it, but nothing had prepared me for such a sprawling conurbation. It was packed with visitors, of whom a large percentage were English. In the crowded all-day bars and restaurants English appeared to have taken over; it was the first language in which many waiters and barmen automatically addressed customers.

The visitors to Carnac's overcrowded beaches are birds of passage, alighting for a few weeks. What worries Bretons is not this phenomenon but the influx of British second-home buyers who have turned several villages into British enclaves. As house prices soar in Wales and Cornwall under the impact of the first wave of English buyers, attention has swivelled south to Brittany, now more accessible than ever owing to the rise of Brittany Ferries, which delivers visitors direct from England to Roscoff in northern Brittany, reducing driving times by several hours compared to Calais and Dieppe. Grumbles about the English invaders are audible everywhere. They are hardly surprising, as one estate agent I passed in central Brittany displayed all its information in English, giving the house prices in British sterling as well as in euro. The message was that local buyers were not wanted. As in Cornwall and Wales, the effects of the English invasion are mostly negative. House prices surge, pushing young people from the area, leading to the slow asphyxiation of the community, as second-home owners spend only a few months a year at most in their French homes. Schools, churches and small shops wither under the blight. There is little racism in this hostility, for those Britons who retire to Brittany or make it their first home are made welcome.

To some British observers, a concentration on language and culture is now beside the point when describing the state of Brittany. The British writer and journalist, John Ardagh, who has known France for decades, has a chapter on Brittany in his book *France in a New Century* entitled 'Brittany resurgent'. It is euphoric in tone. 'This formerly poor and backward province is now one of France's most modern and successful. It may have its problems but it breathes an aura of prosperity.' He added: 'Bretons are now free to express their Breton culture as they wish – and the government even helps! . . . In culture, in local affairs, in many economic sectors Bretons have won a new emancipation from Paris, and have gloriously re-asserted their identity and values.'[39]

A different pen portrait emerged in Helena Drysdale's *Mother Tongues*, a highly personal account of Europe's small language groups. Drysdale's Brittany was a rather drab, sad land that had forfeited its culture. The author found an interest in Breton only among outsiders, while the peasants were cold. Attending a *pardon* she recorded an almost brutal exchange with a man washing up glasses in the drinks tent. '"Nobody speaks Breton now," he grunted, without looking up. "We all speak French . . . it's gone. *C'est du folklore".*' He turned back to pouring rosé. I walked away, near to tears with disappointment at his indifference. All gone.'[40]

The difference in perception reflects the priority given to the economy. If what concerns you is financial, the rise of companies such as Brittany Ferries and the IT boom in cities such as Rennes, then the picture is sunny. Drysdale, on the other hand, was clearly shocked that so little of the world described in *Le Cheval d'orgueil* had survived.

I felt slightly less pessimistic than this, but none of the teachers, farmers, musicians or journalists I had met spoke of a 'resurgent' Brittany either. What would survive of the Breton identity in 20 or 30 years' time seemed so unclear. In a small town on the way back north towards Paimpol, I looked at the wares in the shop windows. They showcased books on Breton cookery, featuring pictures of *crêpes* and *moules frites* on the covers. As in Cornwall, the old Celtic saints were in fashion, and many shops displayed a book on 'the healing saints of Brittany', detailing the holy wells and the remedies for which they were famous. There were gimmicky bottles of 'Breizh Cola', 'BZH' car stickers and comic postcards of women in traditional Breton costume performing antics such as bungee-jumping or white-water rafting. The world 'Celt' has the same kind of totemic significance in Brittany as in Ireland, and is a sure aid in advertising. There were even posters for an event called 'Celti-Ping', which turned out to be a forthcoming international ping-pong competition. Bars and pizzerias sported uncomfortable hybrid names, like 'O'Keltia'.

Ronan le Coadic, who has written a book called *L'Identité bretonne*, was evasive when I asked him to predict the future identity of continental Europe's only 'Celtic land'. He said: 'It depends on what you call an identity. The general ethnic revival since the 1960s has affected Brittany. Now "Breton is beautiful" but the language is still losing ground. It won't exist as a family language in 20 years. How could it, when the level of transmission is practically zero?' The state had successfully imposed French on its border regions since the Revolution as the language of progress. 'All the others were the languages of the Church and the nobility,' he said. 'Children were taught that Breton was the language of poverty and the past. Even recently I have interviewed people who recalled their shame at school for knowing Breton.'

Music and dance had revived since the 1960s under the inspiration of singers like Alan Stivell, but this had not had any lasting political consequences. 'There are two small, opposing groups in Brittany – the French nationalists and Breton nationalists and they leave little room for most Bretons to express their opinions. Then we have no institutions, no Breton daily newspapers. There is still hostility in Paris to anything specifically Breton.'

Ronan Hirrien's account of what befell two articles he wrote for the newspaper *Progrès-Courrier* on the future of Breton summed up the obstacles that face any attempt to save the language from extinction. The articles compared the relatively healthy state of Welsh with that of Breton, which he said was likely to be spoken by only 130,000 people within 10 years owing to the age profile of the remaining speakers. 'La langue bretonne, soeur du gallois depuis quinze siècles, est à l'agonie,' he said. The first article on Welsh went into the paper untouched, but the headline on the second article about Breton was altered. The editor had refused to use a depressing headline, fearing it might alarm the readers. The paper preferred the soothing words: 'Les bretonnants attendent la relève',[41] which hardly corresponded with the author's notion of 'l'agonie'. The editor spoke for many Bretons. For generations they have prepared a quiet and dignified departure for 'la dernière langue celtique parlée sur le continent européen'[42] and many would prefer that to attempting a last-minute noisy struggle for a real revival.

PART THREE

CHAPTER NINE

Cape Breton
'Truly Highland in their ways'

Those who used to speak Gaelic well before they left have now, after being away
for a few years, ostensibly forgotten it. When I greet them with the rich sweet
language of my mother, what do they say to me but 'No Gaelic'.
(N. MacNeil, *The Highland Heart in Nova Scotia*)

At a concert in the University College of Cape Breton I watched a fiddler
in full flow. Buddy MacMaster's white hair flew around his forehead as the
hands jabbed to and fro over his instrument with increasing speed. The
audience waited, time and time again, for a sign that the performance was
about to end, but he repeatedly came back from the brink, upped the
tempo and went on until exhaustion just had to set in, the fiddle came to
a halt and the sound was shut off. The silence lasted for a second, but then
the audience rose to their feet as one, punctuating claps with cheers and
shouts of 'yee-haw!' As the fiddler took a bow, there were people in the
audience with tears streaking their faces. The emotion was too much. I
wondered if they were thinking they had witnessed one of Buddy's last
shows.

Perhaps it was, and perhaps not. At 70 he is getting on and age inevitably
starts to intervene. Fiddling is hard work. It demands a lot of energy. I could
well understand the empathy that has grown up over decades between the
people of Cape Breton and one of their best-known musicians. The tradition itself is in no danger. Cape Breton music has never been healthier. The
respect paid to MacMaster was partly a tribute to his genius and partly also
to his fidelity. He carried the flag for the fiddlers over many years when
traditional music was far less popular than now, when 'serious' audiences in
Cape Breton's towns scorned fiddling for American jazz and blues, and
when the chances of getting any remuneration for the music were almost
nil. MacMaster represents a musical tradition that has survived on this island
off the east coast of Nova Scotia for generations. Local people treasure a

legend, possibly true, that a piper was the first man to climb ashore when the first Scottish settlers reached Pictou in Nova Scotia.

That story conveys something of the importance the first settlers attached to music. MacMaster's fast and furious fiddling probably reaches back to a tradition of Scottish music that died out in the nineteenth century in the mother country, crushed by Presbyterian disapproval, the remnant tamed and changed for military bands and Victorian drawing rooms. The music historian John Gibson says Nova Scotia pipers and fiddlers were never constrained either by the demand for propriety or by the need to attune their sound and beat to the requirements of the British army. 'The typical piper immigrant to Nova Scotia from Scotland came out between 1820 and 1830 and derived from a world of music and dance which was demonstrably conservative in its exuberance,'[1] he wrote. According to Gibson, families in rural Nova Scotia passed down dance rhythms they had meticulously copied from their parents and grandparents, which suggests that the music of Nova Scotia did not depend heavily on French or New England influence for inspiration. He cites an example of this tradition in Stephen Graham of Judique, born in the 1830s, who was watched dancing by his grandson Alex, born in 1913, who in turn passed down the steps he saw to his daughter, Patsy.[2]

Of course, the music I heard at Cape Breton at ceilidhs and festivals was less conservative than this. The most 'traditional' fiddlers of Cape Breton these days have absorbed the influence of Country and Western as well as the music of the Irish immigrants and Acadian French settlers who preceded the Scots in Cape Breton. Nor has the future of Celtic music in Cape Breton always been as assured as it is now. The death of the fiddlers was foretold quite confidently in the early 1970s, when a famous Canadian television documentary of 1971, entitled *The Vanishing Cape Breton Fiddler*, said the tradition was in mortal peril. The public outcry generated by this programme ensured the reverse happened. At an open-air concert in Inverness County in July 1973 more than a hundred fiddlers went on the stage before a crowd of thousands to prove that these pundits were wrong.[3] The musical renaissance that began that summer has not faltered since.

Fiddles and ceilidhs once played a large part in the musical life of the Scottish Highlands, which is why many accounts of Presbyterian ministers and 'Men' refer to their warfare against such entertainment, or their own mastery of the fiddle before they were converted. The sound I heard pouring out of Buddy MacMaster's instrument in Sydney, Cape Breton may not have been dissimilar to the music heard throughout the Highlands before the evangelical cultural revolution silenced it.

The question is: why did the ministers who stopped the dances and burned the fiddles in the old country not repeat that success in the new Scotland of Nova Scotia? Where the Scots went, evangelical Presbyterianism followed – eventually.

One answer may be that the clergy followed the Highlanders across the ocean too late and were too weak in number to dictate the shape of the culture the settlers had established. When Bishop Joseph Plessis of Quebec came down to Nova Scotia on two rare pastoral visits in 1812 and 1815 he reported the existence 'among the Scotch' of a society used to holding what he called 'scandalous' weddings and funerals. These apparently were drunken affairs, much enlivened by dancing.[4] In Scotland the clergyman crushed the fiddle but in Nova Scotia the fiddler held his own and remained esteemed in the community. The names of master players were handed down over generations, and were every bit as famous and revered as the best-admired evangelical preachers. They were not quite a clerical caste but they were certainly seen as 'set apart' in some way. It is interesting that many of them, like priests, were unmarried.[5] No wonder the clergy looked on them as dangerous shamans and rival dispensers of power.

The first Scots in Canada were not so much unchurched as unsupervised. Most of the first settlers in Cape Breton were Catholic, as a result of which the island was predominantly Catholic for a generation until an influx of Presbyterians evened out the balance. It may be no accident that the musical heartland of Cape Breton was and remains the Catholic rural western part around the villages of Mabou, Inverness and Judique. There the fiddlers reigned supreme.

In spite of its title there was nothing very Scottish about Nova Scotia for the first century after it received its name. The title was a whim of James I and VI, a gesture to his Scottish subjects, a verbal consolation prize for the roaring success of New England. While the territory remained a debatable land contested by the British to the south and the French in Quebec, 'New Scotland' was no more than an aspiration. In reality the land, known as Acadie to the scattered community of French settlers, remained with the indigenous Miqmaq people alongside the handful of French loggers and trappers. The Treaty of Utrecht in 1713 finally awarded Nova Scotia to the British but even then Cape Breton remained French until the 1760s.

The three decades that followed the Treaty of Utrecht saw a trickle of New Englanders heading north to Nova Scotia. But it was only after the appointment of Edward Cornwallis as governor in 1749 and the foundation of the town of Halifax that systematic colonisation got under way, and it was only after the American Revolution and the flight of the defeated Tories that the colony began to flourish. Even then there was nothing noticeably Scottish about the immigrants, most of whom came from New England, Germany or England.

Immigration to Nova Scotia from Scotland started almost by accident, after the arrival in July 1772 in western Inverness-shire of John Macdonald, the laird of Glenaladale, who reached Prince Edward Island (then St John Island) with 250 Catholic clansmen from South Uist on the *Alexander*. A year later, on 15 September 1773 a boatload of disbanded soldiers and independent farmers on board the *Hector,* which sailed from Greenock, reached the tiny settlement of Pictou. As the boat dropped anchor, according to one account, 'The piper blew his pipes to their utmost power, their thrilling sounds then first startling the . . . forest'[6] and with that Scottish colonisation in Nova Scotia can be said to have begun. To this day the Nova Scotians of Highland descent look on the *Hector* as their own version of the *Mayflower*.

The arrival of the *Hector* may have inaugurated a new era of Scottish settlement in Nova Scotia, but Highlanders had been emigrating to the American colonies for far longer than that and in ever increasing numbers after the Battle of Culloden of 1746 and the dismantling of the clans. By the time Johnson reached the Highlands in 1773, the 'rage of emigration', as he put it, was already in full flow. Skye saw a substantial exodus in the 1760s, while the savage winter of 1771–72 drove off more. By the early 1770s about 23,000 Highlanders had already left for America in the space of a decade, representing the loss of about 10 per cent of the total population of the four Highland counties of Inverness-shire, Sutherlandshire, Ross-shire and Argyllshire.

The world they knew was collapsing and changing, as rents rose, farms merged and land was enclosed; and they heard of the positive opportunities of the New World. 'I see a wonder', the Kildonan poet Donald Matheson wrote of his increasingly unfamiliar world:

> I see hardships now on every side
> Families who were respected with their heads brought low
> Servants become landlords and young children heirs
> The land is full of misery, Oh God who can endure it?[7]

As the population of the Highlands increased, the strain added to rural communities. The population of Sutherlandshire grew from 20,774 in 1775 to 22,961 in 1795, that of Inverness-shire from 64,656 to 73,979 and that of the Hebrides from 49,485 to 91, 044.[8] In North Uist alone the numbers rose from 1,836 to 4,012 and in South Uist from 1,958 to 5,500.[9] Emigration released the pressure. Until the rebellion in the 13 American colonies in the 1770s North Carolina was the favoured destination for Highlanders and by the mid-1770s this colony was home to about 15,000 of them.

The first New Scotland in North Carolina fared badly after 1776. In spite of their sufferings after Culloden, the Highland emigrants remained over-whelmingly royalist, transferring the loyalty they had felt for the Stuarts to the Hanoverians. Many lost their lands, or were killed, in the American war. The poet Iain Mhurchaidh (called John MacRae in English), who arrived in North Carolina in 1774 – a real case of bad timing – had hardly got himself estab-lished before he was fighting his fellow Americans. His last-known poem, 'I have been a fugitive since autumn', was a moving cry of defiance:

> Although I am a fugitive, no charge can be laid on me,
> Except loyal service to my King to which he is entitled
> Bear my sincere greeting to the land where I ought to be
> Bear my greeting to Kintail, where there is music and song.[10]

Mhurchaidh disappeared into the maelstrom, probably killed by the American Patriots, and his poems were brought back to Scotland years later by others who had learned them. His fate symbolised the rupture between the Highlanders and America. A Gaelic-speaking community survived in North Carolina until it was well and truly disrupted by the fighting in the civil war of the 1860s, but it was no longer irrigated by a flow of emigrants from Scotland. Instead, the Highlanders began to look northwards, towards the virtually uncharted lands of British North America.

Other factors prodded the Scots towards Nova Scotia besides a strong disinclination to settle the now independent United States. Famine struck the Highlands in 1782. The first clearances took place, heralding the 'improvements' that were to turn swathes of the Highlands into sheep runs. Landlords encouraged their agents to circulate flattering descriptions of the opportunities awaiting emigrants in Nova Scotia. A rosy account from 1787, compiled by Samuel Holland, surveyor-general of British North America, painted an attractive portrait of sunny skies, salmon-rich rivers and land aplenty. It was widely circulated. At the same time first-hand reports filtered back to Scotland from disbanded soldiers who had settled there after becom-ing familiar with the terrain during the wars with the French in Quebec in the 1750s.

While Cape Breton remained French, Scottish settlers were restricted to mainland Nova Scotia. But the Treaty of Paris of 1763 transferred the island to Britain, after which Scottish settlers who were dissatisfied with the opportunities around Pictou drifted in to the island's west coast, hitherto the preserve of indigenous tribes and the Acadian French.

Highlanders began moving east from Nova Scotia into Cape Breton as they reached the New World. Many resented the lairds and tacksmen who had brought them over and who wanted them to remain tenants. By heading for Cape Breton, virtually a no man's land, they carved out an independent existence for themselves on the frontier. The tacksmen played an important role in settling Nova Scotia. The middlemen of the Highland clan system – the 'natural lieutenants'[11] of the chiefs in an earlier age – they had been progressively squeezed out of society as the clan chiefs mutated into capitalist landlords. Rendered redundant by the decay of the military side of clan life, emigration offered them an escape route.

They were natural conservatives who hoped to recreate overseas the lost world of the Highlands before Culloden. Macdonald of Glenaladale, mastermind of the Prince Edward Island expedition of 1772, was typical. By the start of the 1770s he felt hunted. On the island of South Uist his kinsman Colin Macdonald, laird of Boisdale, had turned on his family's Catholic heritage and was persecuting his Catholic clansmen. John Macdonald mortgaged his land to buy territory in St John island and set sail with 200 South Uist clansmen, with a view to protecting their common Catholic faith and perpetuating the traditional social hierarchy he had been familiar with in Scotland. But New Scotland did not live up to the dreams of the tacksmen. The tenants who sailed with Macdonald were filled with land hunger and determined never again to be prey to the threat of eviction. On landing, Macdonald's tenants rebelled against his scheme and moved east to Cape Breton, where they could be their own masters.

At first the flow into Cape Breton was just a trickle. The flood of Scottish settlers into the island did not begin for half a century after the arrival of the *Hector* in Pictou. There was no direct emigration from Scotland to Cape Breton until 1802, by which time only about 136 Scottish families had settled the western shore, clustered around Judique. In that year 415 Scottish settlers disembarked at Sydney on 2 August on the *Northern Friends*[12] and were lent 40 shillings each by the British authorities to tide them over during the harsh winter.

The flow of Scottish settlers was reduced in the years after the *Hector* landed by the government's disapproval of the Highlands being depleted of manpower, its most valuable resource. The landlords' associations, such as the Highland Society, were hostile to emigration. Harvesting and burning kelp from the seashore had become highly lucrative and the work was labour-intensive, much of it being done by women. While the price of kelp remained high it was not in the interest of landlords to see their tenants leave for Canada to become independent farmers. In response to their agitation, parliament passed the Passenger Act in 1803, setting many restrictions on the owners of emigrant ships. Highly optimistically, the Act stipulated minimum depths between passenger decks, set a requirement that passengers' bedding should be aired daily, the whole ship was to be fumigated twice weekly, and passengers were to receive minimum set daily allowances of food and water. It also became compulsory to carry a doctor on board. But the law had no teeth and was only a gesture. As one historian noted, 'the clauses relating to provisions and cleanliness were a dead letter from their inception'.[13] Nevertheless, the existence of a potential fine of £200, even if rarely applied, bespoke an intention.

The repeal of the legislation in the 1820s and the adoption of a *laissez-faire* attitude towards emigration reflected a radical shift in thinking at home. By then the overall rural population of the Highlands had reached a new high, while the interest of landlords in retaining people on the land, when sheep-grazing offered the prospect of higher incomes, had dipped. Pressure on tenants to quit their crofts after the end of the Napoleonic wars in 1815 increased as the price of kelp collapsed. As landlords lost their incentive to keep people on the land, some actually paid for the passage of tenants willing to emigrate. At the same time the government lost all interest in restraining Highlanders wanting to leave.

One other reason accounts for the change in official attitudes towards emigration. The first generation of Highland emigrants to Nova Scotia included men of 'substance' whose departure was an obvious cause of regret, as it impoverished the community. Some left with large sums of money, which helps to explain the sorrow expressed at their leaving, in newspapers such as the *Scots Magazine*. The 425 emigrants who left Maryburgh in 1773 were reported to have taken £6,000 in cash with them.[14] The *Inverness Courier* reported scenes of jubilation among these wealthy emigrants. Describing one such departure the newspaper noted that 'the crowd upon the shore burst into a long, loud cheer. Again and again that cheer was raised and responded to from the boat, while bonnets were thrown into the air, handkerchiefs were waved and last words of adieu were shouted from the receding shore.'[15] No society could afford to look on such a scene with anything but uneasiness. But the flight that started in the 1820s elicited less regret, for it involved not ambitious independent farmers and ex-soldiers but desperate crofters who had no alternative, and their removal from their homes was increasingly seen as necessary.

The numbers of Highlanders sailing directly for Cape Breton rose steadily after the arrival of the first boatload on the *Northern Friends* in Sydney in 1802. Some 238 reached Sydney in 1811.[16] The *Hope* and the *William Tell* brought another 400 or so from the island of Barra to Sydney in 1817.[17] But these official figures and are probably the tip of the iceberg. Most arrivals came unannounced and unrecorded. Ships' captains had no wish to undergo any form of inspection and they often dropped anchor in remote bays, summarily expelling the passengers. Working out the real number of arrivals in these years is, therefore, almost impossible. We know only that in 1827 there were 1,070 documented arrivals, and in 1829 another 2,413. In 1833 the reported number had dropped to 1,090 and in the mid-1830s the number dropped again to the low hundreds.[18]

The new emigrants of the 1820s did not celebrate their departure with bumper toasts and cheers. Frequently they had to wait weeks at the port of departure while the ship owners rounded up the requisite number of passengers. Many exhausted their remaining capital on renting accommodation while waiting to embark and arrived at a different destination from the port they thought they were going to. Not surprisingly, the emigrants of the 1820s arrived in worse condition and in poorer health than the earlier, wealthier emigrants. The authorities in Sydney in 1827 reported that the *Stephen Wright* had brought 170 Highlanders from the port of Tobermory on the island of Mull, of whom 40 had arrived infected with smallpox. The town surgeon wrote that the cause 'can I imagine be readily traced to the confined, crowded and filthy state of the vessels – the quantity and quality of the food . . . the scarcity of water'.[19] The authorities in Sydney learned that the master of the vessel was 'an obstinate brutish fellow [who] declares he will do nothing towards the relief or recovery of his unhappy living cargo and in pursuance of that determination perversely refuses to let air into the hold of the vessel, where it must necessarily be pestilential'.[20]

The rise in the number of Highlanders going to Cape Breton in the 1820s reflected both the deteriorating environment in Scotland and the more stable situation in Cape Breton. Until 1820 Cape Breton was a separate British colony. Relatively poor and racked by political conflict between Tory refugees from New England and more recent colonists, it was widely judged a failing experiment. The colony's charter was withdrawn and Cape Breton incorporated into Nova Scotia. Only in the more stable atmosphere that followed did it start attracting colonists in earnest.

By 1828 Cape Breton was unable to cope. The days when officials in Sydney had welcomed immigrants with 40 shillings each to tide them over their first winter were long gone. The flow of settlers had been too great to absorb and Highlanders were now wandering around Sydney in misery. The authorities noted with gloom that the newer arrivals came from a very different class than their predecessors and 'on their landing were quite destitute of food and of the means of procuring it'. The harvest that summer had mostly failed 'and those settlers who have ventured to open their doors to their relatives and ancient connections have, with their families and lodgers, a melancholy prospect before them. But great numbers of these unhappy people [the immigrants] are without friends or resources of any kind to relieve their necessities and are begging from door to door for a morsel of food'.[21]

The colonial government voted supplies to help the most desperate, but destitution continued. Much of the early poetry that came out of Cape Breton reflected disappointment. Donald Chisholm, who left Strathglass for Nova Scotia in 1803 at 68 settled near Antigonish, in mainland Nova Scotia. In the poem 'When I was young in Strathglass' ('Bha mi ogam a Strathglais') he expressed his sorrow at having to leave home in old age and his anger at the clan chiefs for betraying the old social order.

> When I was young in Strathglass
> I had no thought of leaving,
> Now that the gallant men have gone, I too, shall leave
> The coward who now rules us
> Evicted his own, few remain
> He prefers sheep in the hills to a kilted retinue.[22]

John MacLean, known as the 'Bard MacLean', meanwhile lamented the poor condition of his new land in the well known poem 'The Gloomy Forest' (A Choille Ghruamaich). This poem, written in 1819, in which MacLean complained about almost everything in Nova Scotia, was intended as a warning to potential emigrants that Nova Scotia was not the land of prosperity they imagined it to be.[23]

But as Scottish immigration continued the poets forgot their initial fury. Some began describing their joy at the sight of fish-filled rivers in the New World and the thrill of tapping sugar maple trees for syrup. They poured scorn on poets who wailed about not being able to see stags any longer, and who had forgotten that in their homeland they had never been allowed to lay a finger on those stags. 'This is the isle of blessing in which we now are,'[24] wrote Calum Ban Matheson. To Alexander McLean-Sinclair, Canada was

The new land of freedom and food
A good land in which overlords do not expel us from the glens[25]

For all the horrors experienced by some on the journey, and the disappointment felt on arrival, word continued to filter back to the Highlands
that there was land and a future for Gaels in Cape Breton. Men of advanced
years joined the exodus in the 1820s. Some may have done so with hearts as
heavy as Chisholm's, but the dominant attitude among the emigrants was
one of optimism. One such Methuselah, Allan MacLean, sailed on the *Saint
Lawrence* from Greenock to Cape Breton in 1828 aged 89.[26] Not only did
many of these ancient passengers survive the journey to Cape Breton, but
many of them lived out several more years in their new home. MacLean was
supposed to have died aged 114, after spending almost a quarter-century in
his new home in Washabuckt. Cape Breton would gain a reputation as a
land where people lived to great ages owing to the harsh but 'clean' climate.
Neil MacNeil wrote in *The Highland Heart in Nova Scotia* that, men and
women who lived into their eighties and nineties were thought of as
normal, while those who died in their seventies were considered to have
died young.[27]

From 1820 the population of Cape Breton soared, but what was almost
unique about this particular corner of the British empire was that the
emigrants came from one area – the Gaelic-speaking Highlands and islands
of Scotland. In 1802 the island mustered about 2,513 inhabitants. By 1805 the
figure had risen to 5,975, and by 1817 it stood at about 7,000. By 1819 it
reached 9,000 but by 1827 the number had jumped to 18,700 and by 1838 it
was 35,420. By 1860 it had reached about 57,000, now balanced between
about 33,000 Catholics and 23,000 mostly Presbyterian Protestants.[28] By 1871
it reached 75,483 and in 1891 the population peaked at 87,000.

From a sparsely inhabited community of Scottish, English and French
settlers and indigenous tribes, speaking several languages, Cape Breton
became an overwhelmingly Scottish Highland environment where Gaelic
was the tongue of more than three-quarters of the population. By 1871 the
50,000 Cape Breton Scots easily outnumbered around 7,000 Irish, 10,000
francophone Acadians and the small English community in Sydney. Unlike
the Irish heading to Boston or New York, Highland emigrants to Cape
Breton were not absorbed by a dominant host culture: there was no question of Gaelic-speaking Highlanders integrating with indigenous tribes or
with the Acadian French, while the anglophone society in Sydney was far
too small to overcome the culture and language of the Scottish immigrants.

It was an overwhelmingly rural society. Whereas most of the Irish settled in urban environments in America or Australia, and within a generation spoke the language of the cities, the Highland emigrants to Nova Scotia moved into a world of small villages. Cape Breton was an isolated and rural destination, with no railway until the 1890s and no bridge to the rest of Nova Scotia and Canada. Such a society was bound to be culturally more conservative than an urban environment, with its wealth of opportunities, challenges and temptations. What added to this conservative quality was that families from the same clan and island in Scotland settled areas together and were not dispersed. Catholic families from the island of Barra, many of them MacNeils, settled Iona, Washabuckt, Christmas Island and Grand Narrows. South Uist Catholics settled Grand Mira, North Uist people Mira Ferry. The Presbyterian MacVicars of North Uist settled Catalone, people from Lewis settled St Ann's and so it went on. This tradition has maintained itself. In Iona I met a member of the MacNeil family in her sixties who said her granddaughter was one of the ninth generation of MacNeils not only to live in Iona, but on one site, too. As a historian of nineteenth-century Cape Breton said: 'The successful transfer of kin groups to Cape Breton, the lack of major immigration by other ethnic groups and the relative isolation of the rural areas helped maintain the Gaelic language and culture.'[29]

There was competition of a mild variety between the denominations as the population increased. The earlier Catholic settlers in Cape Breton had the island to themselves in the early nineteenth century, which explains why the first areas they settled on the west coast remain overwhelmingly Catholic. But Presbyterian immigration added a denominational element to competition for land.

Folk legends shed light on this denominational friction, as each religious community staked out its territory. In Judique's village hall Cape Breton's best known storyteller, Jim St Clair, recounted to me one such conflict in the Mull River area which featured a famous witch called Kitty Livingston.

Livingston, née Campbell, was a Protestant, for all her witchcraft, who offered the services of her Protestant nephew Dan to her Catholic neighbours, the Beatons, to help bring in their harvest. After Mrs Beaton betrayed this gesture by converting the young man to the Catholic faith, the rest of the clan Campbell rushed up to Mrs Livingston's hilltop eyrie to demand satisfaction. According to St Clair, Mrs Livingston descended to the Beaton residence for a memorable woman-to-woman confrontation on Mrs Beaton's threshold, which ended in Mrs Beaton insolently offering to repay the services of her neighbour's family with an old cheese. The witch then put a curse on the Beatons, condemning the womb of the family matriarch to rot and dissolve like the old cheese she had carelessly hurled to the ground.[30] The curse was fulfilled and as a result the Catholic Beatons lost the battle for the area.

Throughout the mid-nineteenth century the Gaelic culture of Cape Breton developed undisturbed, facing little competition from anglophone or francophone Canada. The potato famine hit the island in the 1840s but did not devastate it for long. In fact, the only result was to dissuade Irish settlers from trying their luck there, so Highland Gaelic culture consolidated itself further on Cape Breton. The only town on the island, Sydney, remained a little anglophone colony but the nature of the rural economy meant few islanders had much contact with Sydney, or anywhere more than a few miles from their villages.

The great change began in the 1880s, as Cape Breton was discovered by the outside world. As people became conscious that the Gaelic culture was declining fast in Scotland, Nova Scotians attracted attention because they were 'still' speaking the language. A few decades earlier the use of Gaelic would have passed unnoticed, but when the editor of the *Celtic Magazine* visited Nova Scotia in 1880, the strength of the Gaelic language struck him as remarkable. At Pictou he said he found himself 'right in the centre of a county and people more truly Highland in their ways and in their speech than almost any part of the north of Scotland. Gaelic was more commonly spoken at this gathering of highlanders than you can find it now in any part of Sutherland or Ross-shires.'[31] In Cape Breton he found only two Presbyterian churches that were not using it for services.[32]

The survival of this self-contained Gaelic world inside the bosom of the British empire relied on isolation and immobility. It depended on relatively few people coming in or out and on few people travelling round within Cape Breton. P. J. Mackenzie Campbell, an elderly inhabitant of the Bras d'Or community, recalled in 1966 his upbringing at the turn of the century in a society where movement was very limited. Although only 40 miles from the bright lights of anglophone Sydney he never set eyes on Cape Breton's largest town until he was 17. 'Planning a trip of that distance in those days was as momentous as planning a trip from Cape Breton to Vancouver would be today,' he said.[33]

Campbell grew up in a village that kept to itself and decided almost everything locally and communally. Clothes were made at home on looms and then 'beaten into submission' in a process that would have been quite recognisable to Dr Johnson when he visited Skye and listened to women's 'waulking songs' in the 1770s. Marriage was not only a decision between two people, and when one marriageable middle-aged man looked like being left on the shelf, the community took the event in hand. 'Home after home which housed females of marriageable age would be visited until they would come across a girl who would agree to entrust her future to the person in particular.'[34] There was little reason to leave when almost everything of importance was made and decided locally or could be bought in the local shops. Though it was only a rural area it had three stores, a sawmill, a carding mill, a hotel and a telegraph office.[35]

Up until the end of the century, the few outside influences on Cape Breton tended to reinforce the Gaelic culture that the settlers had brought with them. The most important external factor was religion. Far more than politicians, the principal bearers of information about the world were visiting preachers from Scotland, who enjoyed the automatic deference of local society. Many of the legends recounted by storyteller Jim St Clair concern the deeds of the preachers and the tremendous impact they had on the island at revival meetings. It was highly significant for the future of Cape Breton that the religion of the island's Protestants was taken in hand by the Scottish motherland in a way that was sensitive to the island's Gaelic culture.

For several decades the first Catholic Highlanders in Nova Scotia lived virtually without the supervision of clergy, certainly without regular pastoral care. They had at first to rely on occasional visits by French clergy from Quebec, like Bishop Plessis, with whom they could barely communicate. The first priest of their own nationality, James MacDonald, reached Nova Scotia in 1791 and as late as 1815 the 7,000 Scottish Catholics on Cape Breton had only one priest to serve them.[36]

By the 1830s the lack of clergy among the newer Protestant immigrants was attracting attention in Scotland and the evangelical Edinburgh Ladies' Association under the strong hand of Isabella Mackay selected and underwrote a team of Church of Scotland missionaries for the island. By the 1850s Mackay's association was supporting five ministers, eight catechists and three teachers,[37] all doing their best to realise her ambition of creating a 'well-watered garden' of faith on Free Church lines in Cape Breton.

The distinctive features of evangelical church life in Scotland were replicated in Nova Scotia, such as the lay brotherhoods of 'Men', huge open-air communions attended by several thousand people at a time and the great public devotional exercises that customarily preceded these events. As in Scotland, these events, usually held in July or August, followed three days of devotional exercises, beginning with a day of fasting on Thursday, a day of interrogation on matters of faith on Friday, known as Question Day, the final examination of the candidates for communion and the distribution of communion tokens on Saturday and the communion service on Sunday. Like most Gaelic-speakers at home, the Scots of Cape Breton almost all followed the seceding evangelicals out of the Church of Scotland into the Free Church after the 1843 'Disruption'. Observers were struck by their indifference to harsh weather when attending religious services and their willingness to sit through hours of sermons in the blinding rain. As one eyewitness noted in admiration in 1872, after attending one of these Gaelic religious marathons: 'For five hours and twenty minutes that multitude sat upon the soaking sward as if glued to it. During the first two hours of that time the rain came down incessantly . . . every male had his head uncovered.'[38]

But for all their commitment to evangelicalism, the Protestant clergy in Nova Scotia never enjoyed the same sway over their congregations in New Scotland as their counterparts at home. The strict penalties for moral lapses were never enforced in Nova Scotia with the same severity either. 'Most of the stern traditions and harsh penalties of the kirk were moderated in Cape Breton. The kirk stools, where penitents were forced to sit, and which had become symbols of petty-mindedness and tyranny in Scotland, were not in use in Cape Breton, although public rebuke and denial of sacraments were still common actions against offenders.'[39] Significantly, women who gave birth to children outside marriage were merely 'admonished'.

The relative weakness of both Catholic priest and Protestant minister in Nova Scotia may have contributed to the survival of the traditional music that the clergy in Scotland succeeded in suppressing. In the twentieth century a number of clergy in Cape Breton, priests in particular, championed the Cape Breton fiddling tradition. But many of their nineteenth-century predecessors were just as hostile to instrumental music as their counterparts in Scotland. Nor was this animosity confined to Presbyterians. The Catholic clergy in rural west Cape Breton included notorious enemies of the fiddle, such as Father Kenneth MacDonald of Mabou, who conducted a local war with the music-makers in the 1860s and the 1870s. His campaign met with little success,[40] however, and Cape Breton never saw ceremonial burnings of fiddles and bagpipes, as happened in Skye under the instigation of the famous blind catechist Donald Munro.[41]

There were tyrannical clergy on Cape Breton who frowned on virtually everything, but they tended to be religious freelances. The most famous oddball, Norman McLeod, originally of Assynt parish in Sutherland, reached Pictou in 1817 and settled on Cape Breton in 1820 where he became 'minister, magistrate and schoolteacher' to his devoted but totally intimidated flock in St Ann.[42] McLeod fulminated against the evils of 'toddy and tobacco', interpreting the potato famine that hit Cape Breton from 1845 to 1851 as divine retribution against indulgers in both wicked habits.[43] He replicated in Cape Breton all the severity of the ultra-strict Calvinism he had admired but ultimately been disappointed by at home, typically refusing to baptise or hold communion services except very infrequently. As a result some 600 of his flock were unbaptised by the 1840s.

Men like McLeod were quarrelsome and egocentric eccentrics who in Cape Breton had to rely entirely on their charisma to maintain their sway over their congregations. A ministry like his could only flourish in a frontier society where people were making up the rules as they went along. Naturally, for all his insistence on unquestioning obedience, McLeod himself obeyed no external authority whatever. He furiously denounced the backsliding tendencies not only of the Church of Scotland but of the Free Church as well. Men like McLeod operated without the sanction of a wider society. It was significant that when he decided that God was summoning him from Nova Scotia to Australia in 1851, only a minority of his flock obeyed the call and went with him.

McLeod, Father Kennedy of Mabou and the missionaries of the Edinburgh Ladies' Association made war on aspects of traditional Highland folk culture, above all on fiddlers, witches, belief in fairies, belief in 'second sight' and addiction to 'toddy'. But they were not at war with the Gaelic language and were not an anglicising influence. Isabella Mackay had played an important role in this. In the face of considerable opposition, she insisted on selecting missionaries for Cape Breton solely on the criterion of godliness, rather than education, and she fought off all attempts to foist better-educated anglophone Lowlanders on her mission field.

Until the 1880s the Highlanders in Nova Scotia appeared to have successfully created a Gaelic society and culture that was far stronger than the one they had left behind. The Gaels of Nova Scotia did not merely talk informally and pray in church in Gaelic. For a while Gaelic was the language of print, too. The first book published and printed in Gaelic in the New World was a Nova Scotian work, the *Companach an Oganaich* (Companion to Youth), printed in Pictou in 1836. By the 1850s Nova Scotians were reading a popular Gaelic monthly, *An Cuirtear Og Gaelach* (The Gaelic Tourist), printed in Antigonish. By the 1890s, a Gaelic weekly, *Mac-talla* (Echo), was being produced in Cape Breton in the anglophone bastion of Sydney under the editorship of Jonathan Mackinnon.

The confidence felt by the Nova Scotian Gaels in their culture was aired in demands for the language to be given official status and used in schools, too. John Morrison, of Victoria County, recommended the Nova Scotia assembly in 1879 to divert funding from what he called 'contemptible worthless French' and spend it on 'the honourable Gaelic tongue'.[44] The demand elicited no response but the fact it was made at all, and at a time when the language was widely despised in Scotland, indicated the higher status it had won in Nova Scotia.

But the hopes of a Gaelic triumph in Nova Scotia were not fulfilled. A culture that seemed strong and self-confident in the 1880s declined with extraordinary speed after the turn of the new century, withering away within a few generations. The Gaelic open-air communions ceased, as did all open-air communions in the end. The Gaelic precentors who led the psalm-singing in the churches grew old and no one continued their work. The Gaelic newspapers folded or became bilingual and then monolingual again, but using English this time, not Gaelic. The language retreated from streets, pulpits and printing presses to villages, farms and kitchens, then retreated again to certain generations within those homes until – quite suddenly – all that remained were scattered pools of words, thoughts, phrases and memories that no longer linked or added up to a language.

With the language perished a culture. The 'holy geography' that the Highlanders had brought from Scotland to Nova Scotia, zoning their new environment into fairy mounds and streams, as well as the belief in 'second sight' and in witches, all of which was bound up with the language, fell away. After that, there remained only an accent. Older people retained a distinct Scottish pronunciation, a tendency to pronounce house as 'hoos' or goose as 'gus'. But even that residual memory of difference is rapidly fading. The younger generation of Nova Scotians has adopted the American intonation of English. Like young Americans, they interpolate their sentences with the repeated use of the world 'like' and emphasise the ultimate or penultimate syllable, so that many of their sentences finish with a 'like *awe*some!' or with a 'like *wow*' or with a 'like, you *know*, incredible!'

Walking around the University College of Cape Breton I found no trace among the students of the culture that had once been so dominant on this island, beyond a banner greeting that year's fresher students reading 'Ceud Mile Fáilte'. It was suspended over a door beside similar greetings in French and Miqmaq. The language of the students was pure American English, as was the dress code, featuring on men the near-compulsory peaked baseball cap turned backwards. American rock music blared from speakers in the corridors and canteens, creating an inescapable background din. Among young Cape Bretoners, like their American counterparts, the look to cultivate was that of African-American ghetto youths, carrying desirable overtones of danger, risk, non-conformity and sexual experience. Even in the college's Beaton Institute, which houses records of the Scottish community in Cape Breton, most visitors I met appeared solely interested in researching their own genealogy. I met no one who gave much thought to the dead tongue. 'Gaelic? Such a nice *family* language!' said one woman, bestowing North America's highest compliment.

At the college I attended a session that featured two very old men singing Gaelic songs of Nova Scotia. Listening to their voices, we were tapping into more than a language; into a sound, a way of thinking, a way of viewing the world, that is vanishing and will not be recaptured by students studying Gaelic culture on university courses. But the students sitting with me in the hall showed not even a flicker of recognition. There was no sign that they felt they were watching and listening to something that was part of their world. They were polite, like almost all Canadians, but they shifted in their seats – soon bored – while some whispered into cellphones and looked longingly through the glass door of the auditorium towards the cafeteria, where the distant *bam, bam, bam* of some rock tune was blaring on the sound system. By the time the old men ceased their song a large proportion of the students had already left the room.

Tourist literature on Nova Scotia (as in Brittany) makes too much of the alleged survival of the culture of the Highland Scots. Books and brochures say those wandering the village lanes of Mabou may well catch the silvery sound of the Gaelic tongue in the air. But when I put that to Jim MacDonald, a 71-year-old villager whose family has lived in Nova Scotia for six generations, he just laughed. 'My parents spoke Gaelic to each other – my father especially,' he said. 'But to us – me and my brother – never. Like most people he left the village to work – in New Brunswick. So did my mother – she went to work as a domestic in Boston. And both felt they were mocked for their poor English. And they both said they would never let this happen to their children. We never learned it and once you got to school at six you never heard it. Now I can say *Ciamar atha thu?* (how are you?) and that's about it.

'They brought a couple of women from South Uist to work in the school to try and revive the language about 20 years ago. But one went back, one stopped teaching and the other . . . well, she's a wonderful woman but . . . [he shrugged] it's gone – dead! It's a terrible thing, losing a language, but it's dead. I'd say you need about 30,000 people to keep a language alive. You would be lucky to find 500 speaking Gaelic today.'

What interested MacDonald much more was the Celtic music revival. 'Now the music, that's another thing. That was holding on by a finger 30 years ago and it was just down to Mabou. We were hayseeds, with our fiddlers. But now, my God, it's a thousand times bigger than it was.' I heard this refrain time and time again; the Gaelic language was dead but the music that the Scottish Gaels had brought with them was livelier than ever. Jim MacDonald's description of his family's transition within a single generation from almost monolingual Gaelic to monolingual English was one I also heard frequently. At a café in Mabou I met the Gaelic teacher from Scotland he had referred to. There was interest in the language, Marje Beaton said, but few school students followed it through to true fluency. At the end of the day the subject was only an option and it was not essential to matriculation. 'In 20 years the old Gaelic of this area will be dead and with it will vanish a whole vocabulary,' she said. For the young people of Cape Breton, Gaelic was only interesting as a key to the Celtic music that they liked so much.

Around me some old men nodded in agreement. 'Sure, I remember a few phrases,' said one. 'Gaelic slang really, but nothing more . . .' He wasn't interested in adding to this. He had seen Scotland as a soldier in the Second World War but when it came to exploring the Highlands, had never got much further than the bars of Glasgow. Nor were most people I encountered more engaged, even the older women who remembered the time when the language was more widely spoken. 'Oh, my grandmother spoke it,' one woman said, as if irritated by the topic. I heard the same note of boredom and slight irritation I had heard earlier in Brittany. It was as if I was trying to tap them for information about a long-dead relative who deserved to be left in peace.

The story I heard repeatedly was that families lived in villages in relative isolation until the 1940s. Few people had cars and to go a few miles was an adventure. There were few telephones to bridge the distances. One woman in Iona village recalled that in her youth the entire community had only about a dozen telephones. But now the barriers have gone and distances have shortened. When the causeway between Cape Breton and Nova Scotia was opened in the 1950s, a Highland piper stationed himself on the island side, serenading the first car drivers. But the piper had welcomed in a culture that would flatten his own. Farming, which once sustained the community, now employs a fraction of the former numbers. Only big dairy farms have survived on the island and they employ few people. Fishing has also declined. Postcards featuring the ironic greeting 'In cod we trust(ed)' refer to the collapse of the cod stocks in the North Atlantic through over-fishing, which has devastated communities in Newfoundland especially, but also Nova Scotia. In Mabou a large pulp mill is all that sustains the liveli-hoods of a large percentage of the residents.

Mabou is not really an enclave of Gaelic culture any more, for all its high profile in the Celtic music scene. A sign reading *Ceud Mile Fàilte* hangs on the outside wall of the village hall. The local museum has a Gaelic name, An Drochead, but it was shut when I passed by and a window display of bottles, pictures and papier mâché Hallowe'en figures did not suggest it was the beating heart of a local Gaelic revival. At the Mull Restaurant, in spite of the background fiddle music, the ambience was Anglo-Canadian, or American, from the sleep-inducing size of the portions of food to the 'Have a nice days' of the waitresses. This was mom-and-pop-and-two-kids land. The Americans seem to have had the last laugh in Nova Scotia, sucking the Canadians back into the homogenised goo of American popular culture. Whether the Highland patriarchs now in the old burial grounds of Cape Breton would scorn their descendants' achievements is another matter. It is a peaceful community. The Mabou area is almost bewilderingly beautiful. Liquid blue skies match the colour of still lakes, setting off the dazzling white of the painted wooden churches, the red-ochre barns and the green and luminous orange leaves of the maple forests. Scotland is bleached and grey by comparison with this Technicolor world. Apart from some early poems, there are few signs that the Scots in Cape Breton missed their home-land. They took from it what they wanted – music and their ceilidhs – and have slowly dispensed with the rest.

On 26 July 1939 Angus Macdonald, Premier of Nova Scotia, opened the Gaelic College in the village of St Ann's. Macdonald, as devoted a son of Scotland as Nova Scotia has produced, made the most of the occasion, dress-ing in a kilt. 'We honour Scotland, we are under a debt to Scotland. That is why we try to pay back that debt by erecting this memorial and by endeav-oring to preserve the language, the traditions, the music of our fathers.'[45]

The name of the new college paid tribute to the dedication of the author-ities to preserving the region's Gaelic culture. It was appropriate that Macdonald should preside over the ceremony, for his personal ascendancy was widely seen as proof that the descendants of the Scottish settlers had made Nova Scotia their own. Though not more than one-third of the population of the province, by the 1930s they seemed to have scaled the commanding heights.

The Gaelic College is still there in St Ann's and has become one of Nova Scotia's big tourist attractions. It boasts a grandiloquently titled Great Hall of the Clans, where visitors wander between glass cases of life-size mannequins dressed in the tartan of one of the various clans that migrated to Nova Scotia. The shop is a riot of tartan memorabilia and contains a clothes section where visitors can order their own bespoke kilt.

The Gaelic College and the reconstructed Highland Village in Iona, set up later, symbolise the 'tartanisation' of Nova Scotia. The founder of the Gaelic College, Angus Mackenzie, a Presbyterian minister from Scotland, made his priorities clear when he told visitors they would find there *Ciad Mille Fáilte* – but what the eye will thrill to will be the beautiful tartan woollen goods being woven on the handlooms by student apprentices – yards and yards of it . . . then, what the ear will thrill to will be the enchanting lilt of the traditional milling songs or the ever-fascinating wailing of a Phiob Mhor [bagpipe] doing duty to the steps of Cape Breton lassies who are trying to master the Highland Fling.'[46] A doubtful chronicler of Celtic revivals in Cape Breton wrote that the result was 'a tourist mecca for anti-modernist audiences who yearn to see the kilts and hear the pipes in their "natural" setting'.[47] A still more hostile observer in the 1980s dismissed it as a 'tartan circus with the attraction of tourists as the first priority'.[48]

Angus Macdonald, who dominated the province's political life from 1933 to 1954, was a fervent 'tartaniser'. He promoted Highland Games even in traditional English settlements of Nova Scotia, such as Yarmouth, where previously they had been unknown and he personally supervised the adoption of an 'official tartan' for Nova Scotia in 1953. Though he did not live to see the completion of the Highland Village, he laid the footwork after being impressed by an exhibit of a reconstructed Scottish cottage at the Empire Exhibition in Glasgow in 1938.

Begun as a venture to sustain what was then the surviving Gaelic culture and language of the Iona area, the Highland Village shed that aspect of its mission over the years. When I visited, the employees – dressed in period costumes – greeted visitors in Gaelic but many seemed startled when their greeting was actually answered. The role of the Gaelic language in the village had dwindled to events such as 'Gaelic Immersion Day'.[49] The recent direction of the modern village was set in 1988 by a team of management consultants brought in to identify priorities. They suggested focusing on the concept of 'village' as the major product. 'All other products such as entertainment, Gaelic language and Highland roots are secondary products,' they said.[50] That is what has happened. When Vince Maclean, a figure closely associated with direction of the village's entertainment side since the 1960s, was interviewed on the progress of the last 40 years, he did not address the subject of the Gaelic language, at the same time claiming that the village was 'showcasing what literally has become an explosion of Cape Breton Gaelic culture upon the world's stage'.[51]

Tartanisation gave a generic 'Scottish' character to the whole of Nova Scotia, not just to Gaels but to the descendants of English settlers and New England Tory Yankees. It obscured and disguised the slow death of the most important element of the indigenous culture: its language. While Highland Games and tartan spread over the province, the local government allowed the Gaelic language to die. James MacDonald, a Gaelic-speaker and Celtic studies professor at St Francis Xavier University in Antigonish, told me the government drove it to extinction. 'It's not just that there was no support for Gaelic – there was actual antagonism,' he said.[52]

MacDonald claimed that Gaelic had been a victim of the battle that raged in the provinces of maritime Canada between French and English. Forced by the power of adjacent Quebec into ceding bilingualism to the tiny French-speaking minority, descendants of the Acadians, the government had squeezed Gaelic out of Nova Scotia. The province had acted far more vigorously to protect the language and culture of the Acadian community than that of the far more numerous Scots. Even the once downtrodden Miqmaq people seemed to fare better over language provision, as the conscience-pricked and politically correct federal government funnelled resources into keeping the languages of what are now called 'First Nation' people alive. No one resented the protection of Miqmaq or French: what was shocking was that the culture and language of the majority of the population of Cape Breton had been allowed to wither away – absorbed into the English mainstream and diverted into music and dress. 'Interest in Scottish culture has focused instead on fiddle music and step-dancing,' MacDonald said. 'The fiddle music has, in fact, been resurrected.'

Gaelic on Cape Breton declined with the great out-migration of Highlanders that began in the 1880s. No sooner had the island filled up than it began to empty. The 'rear', as the poor uplands of the interior were known, emptied first. By the 1950s the Mabou Highlands were almost deserted and today only a diminishing number of people like storyteller Jim St Clair even know where some of the settlements once were. A drift from country to town meant that Gaelic-speaking villages leaked manpower to English-speaking Sydney, which expanded rapidly as an industrial port and steel manufacturing town. Judique had a population of 2,027 in the 1880s but only

904 remained by 1941. In the same period, Whycocomagh's population fell from 1,787 to 696;[53] Sydney ballooned from only 2,180 in 1881 to 28,305 in 1941. Cape Breton was Sydney-fied and anglicised at the same time.

If the villagers had all left their rural communities for the Sydney steel-works it might have led to the Gaelicisation of the island's biggest town, much as the influx of rural Welsh to South Wales in the industrial revolution initially strengthened Welsh language and culture in the new towns. But many of the newcomers to Sydney in the twentieth century came from outside, from the Ukraine, Poland, Italy and Yugoslavia, while the Gaels tended to stream out of the province altogether. Most went to Boston, aided by cheap steamboat fares of about $10. Boston had always been an alternative capital city for Nova Scotians, who nicknamed New England 'the Boston States' in tribute. Miners left in droves for British Columbia. Some emigrants stayed in Nova Scotia, drawn to the growing urban centres of Halifax and New Glasgow, but this was a minority. At least three-quarters of the emigrants from Cape Breton from the 1880s onwards went to the United States.[54] Those who returned from Boston tended to act much like the 'Woman who lost her Gaelic', a well-known poem composed in the 1880s making fun of a woman who pretends she cannot understand her native language on returning from Boston.[55] A writer in 1894 complained that many of the returnees despised their culture. 'Those who used to speak Gaelic well before they left have now, after being away for a few years, ostensibly forgotten it. When I greet them with the rich sweet language of my mother, what do they say to me but "No Gaelic".'[56]

As many biographers of the island's Gaelic community have said, the language only survived as long as it did because of the isolation of close-knit rural communities. But that changed for ever in the First World War. True to their loyalist, royalist roots, the Cape Breton men joined up *en masse*. The war mobilised the entire male population and the world that these service-men returned to was changed in turn by their own experience overseas. Just as the war made the Bretons more French, it made the Cape Bretons more like English Canadians and the almost self-sufficient agrarian society in which they had been brought up dissolved rapidly on their return.

The Gaelic press ground to a halt. *Mac-talla* ceased to appear in 1904. Its disappointed editor Jonathan Mackinnon complained: 'We can reach no other conclusion than that the Gaels do not want a Gaelic paper and that they are content to be classed as the only Christian race in the world who will not pay to keep up a paper in their own language.'[57] The churches declined in influence and were anglicised. Open-air communions lasted until the 1940s but the writing was on the wall for such events long before that. A busier, more comfortable and more private generation was not prepared to spend four days, possibly in the rain, sitting for hours at a stretch in wet fields. A visitor predicted their disappearance in 1903. 'That this custom should eventually become a thing of the past is indeed a pity but the remorseless march of modern ideas and the busier lives that men live today cannot but bring this about,' wrote the author of *Cape Breton at the Beginning of the Twentieth Century*.[58]

Many churches switched first to having two services – one in English and one in Gaelic – and then gradually dispensed with the Gaelic service. There had been a time when, as one historian of the Presbyterian Church in Cape Breton said, 'Many of the old people found it difficult to believe that the Supreme Being could be sufficiently addressed with becoming respect in any other language than Gaelic.'[59] Quite recently old people could still recall their shock as children on hearing God addressed for the first time in another language. Sandy Morrison in 1980 recalled his surprise on hearing English first used in church services in Wreck Cove. 'Well, my heavens I was young, you know,' he told his interviewer, 'and I was telling father when we came home – I was little by heavens – "The Lord will never understand", I said. "How is he going to understand that?"'[60] By the time he was interviewed in 1980, the tradition of precenting in Gaelic was as good as dead. 'It's just going to die and go in the ground with the dead people,' said John Alex MacDonald. 'That's the end of it, that's it. Ten years at the longest. I don't think there's a precentor in Cape Breton that is under 65 years old.'[61]

Schools had always been hostile to non-English-speakers. John Morrison's plea for Gaelic to be used in school was ignored. The schools remained anglophone and as in Scotland (and Brittany), it was the lack of schools that enabled Gaelic to survive. The colony's Common Schools Act of 1826 had inadvertently worked against the spread of schooling, by setting impossibly high benchmarks for communities in terms of the money they had to raise first. The Act entitled village schools to claim state aid but then effectively disbarred them from doing so by insisting they first build the school and then endow a local teacher with a minimum investment of £25 a year before they could apply for state aid.[62] One of the ministers sent out to Cape Breton by Isabella Mackay's Edinburgh Ladies' Association in the mid-nineteenth century thought at least half his thousand or so parishioners were totally illiterate.[63] In any case, only boys attended schools, so that at least half the population remained distant from the world of the English-speaking teachers.

The spread of schools in the early twentieth century anglicised the rising generation within a remarkably short time. The first generation to attend school immediately emerged bilingual, even if it was a pretty idiosyncratic version of English that they learned. As Neil MacNeil recalled in *The Highland Heart of Nova Scotia*, 'The average Washabuckter butchered the English language in pronunciation and syntax, and no one had any regrets about it for it was an alien language anyway.'[64]

John Rory MacNeil, of Barra Glen, who was born in 1905 and interviewed just before his death in the mid-1980s, attributed his fluency in Gaelic to the fact that his father had died prematurely, as a result of which he was withdrawn from school to work at home on the farm. School was orientated towards teaching children to love England as well as English. Children were set tasks such as learning by heart 'Ye Mariners of England', 'The sinking of the *Royal George*' and Walter Scott's *Lady of the Lake*. Gaelic stayed outside the school gate. 'It wasn't to be taught at all, and there wasn't to be a word of Gaelic spoken in the school,' John Rory MacNeil recalled. English was the language 'by which the world was operating'. By the time he was a teenager, Gaelic was more than ever the mark of the undesirable rustic. 'If you had Gaelic – especially if you went to town, well, it's from the woods you came . . . you were no more than half-animal.'[65] The teachers were not often actively hostile. They simply ignored Gaelic and so ensured it was not associated with education and advancement. 'The Gaels did not speak Gaelic because they were punished by their teachers but because the actions of those teachers (and others in authority) influenced their own beliefs about their language.'[66]

In the 1880s almost all the 50,000 or so Highlanders in Cape Breton were Gaelic-speakers and many were monoglots. By the 1930s the language was spoken by 24,000 people throughout Nova Scotia. By 1961 the figure had slumped to 7,500 in the whole of Canada, of whom about 3,700 were in Cape Breton. By that point historians and language experts were anxiously interviewing the last survivors. Kathleen Lamont in 1964 recorded her own depression on finding the culture so attenuated. 'In all my time there I did not to my knowledge meet one single fluent Gaelic speaker under the age of thirty,' she wrote. 'Even in families where the mother and father are passionately fond of the language, their children can only say a few phrases at most . . . I had thought the situation in Scotland bad enough but it seems hopeful when compared to Cape Breton.'[67]

In the early 1970s a few brave souls continued to hope this situation could be turned round. Rosemary Hutchinson warned in the pages of *Cape*

Breton's Magazine in 1972 that the language would perish unless there was a real effort to turn matters around, adding that it would mean the loss not only of a means of communication but of a whole value system. 'It's still not too late to fight,' she declared. 'That's what the current movement towards revival on Cape Breton is all about.'[68] By the time James Colin Kelly came to survey Gaelic in Cape Breton in the 1980s it was too late for even the most optimistic fighters to hope for the creation of a Cape Breton gaeltacht. But at that stage Kelly still hoped a 'massive campaign in schools' to revive the language might avert disaster.[69]

The massive campaign never occurred. In the summer of 2002 the provincial government of Nova Scotia and the Highland Council of Scotland announced a new initiative to boost Gaelic culture. A joint declaration concerning the revival of Gaelic was signed in Gaelic and English and a steering committee had been set up across the province of Nova Scotia to monitor its success. There was talk of a new Gaelic 'secretariat' and of 'innovative strategies to renew the Gaelic language and culture'.[70]

It was a little late in the day for such bureaucratic campaigns. The experience of Ireland shows that once a language has lost its grip, death is all but inevitable even when the political will is there. When I was in Cape Breton in 2002 the despairing predictions made by language and culture activists in the 1970s and 1980s had been fully realised. A 'Celtic revival', centring on fiddle music was (as ever) in full swing, attested to by the vast crowds attending the annual 'Celtic Colours' music festival and by the ever growing international fame of Cape Breton's army of fiddlers.

But many observers give this and every other Celtic revival in Cape Breton short shrift. A 1997 study of Nova Scotia Gaelic revivals by Jonathan Dembling described the 'Celtic revival' of the 1990s as an empty phenomenon. What had been the point of Nova Scotia declaring May 'Gaelic awareness month' in 1996? he asked. Dembling tore into syrupy magazine puffs, such as *Canadian Geographic*'s January 1996 celebratory article on the Celtic revival in Nova Scotia, which hailed the Gaelic signs in Mabou post office and the Scottish delicacies on the menu of the village's Mull Restaurant as evidence of a Gaelic renaissance. Dembling said newspapers and magazines had an infuriating habit of resorting to corny clichés when describing the whole Celtic phenomenon, describing ceilidhs as 'rollicking celebrations', for example, or the Gaelic language as 'bardic and musical'. As Dembling said, the basic problem with these heralds of a Celtic revival was their inability to provide hard evidence, beyond the popularity of a few famous musicians and increasing enrolments on Celtic studies courses in some universities. What was stupid about these articles was that they propagated a view of Celtic or Gaelic culture as consisting of little more than a set of 'cute' attitudes: 'songs, stories, dance, drinking, joking and partying are sometimes presented as the total Gaelic experience,' he said.[71] Dembling did not have much time for the musical revival either, suggesting that what people now thought of as Cape Breton's indigenous Celtic music owed more to modern popular music than to traditional sounds.

This was, perhaps, a harsh judgement. Cape Breton and Nova Scotia would know less – not more – about its Gaelic background without the Celtic Colours festival and its spin-offs. Big festivals and local ceilidhs suck in tourist money that keeps the fiddlers playing. Old professionals like Buddy MacMaster, it is true, worked for decades in ordinary day jobs without expecting payment for their musical gifts, but it would be unwise to bank on such attitudes surviving deep into the twenty-first century. The world of the fiddlers and 'Celtic' musicians is now virtually the only environment in which Gaelic survives in Nova Scotia. When I attended the Celtic Colours festival the performances featured many sentimental 'Irish' ballads that owed nothing and contributed little to the musical tradition of Nova Scotia. But in and among this generic Celtic musical pap were singers like Angus Wilson, who is in his teens and hammers out Gaelic milling songs with force and confidence. Purists complain about the big commercial ceilidhs, but without them the old house ceilidhs would have died off, as the arrival of television in most homes by the 1970s had sentenced that kind of entertainment to death anyway.

The language is gone, never to return as a community language. It will survive in music, in university courses, on street signs in self-consciously 'heritage' towns like Pugwash in western Nova Scotia, on numerous banners reading 'Ceud Mìle Fàilte' and at Gaelic 'Immersion Days'. But the thought-world of the eighteenth- and nineteenth-century Gaelic poets is gone and is irrecoverable. The new Gaelic language programmes are not intended, in any case, to make anyone proficient in Gaelic but to give a 'taste' of Gaelic culture. They are aimed at 'allowing people who have been assimilated into the mainstream to feel as if they were still part of an ethnic group'.[72] As one observer recently said, with deadly accuracy, it is all about providing people with 'emotionally sustaining' cultural badges.[73] What Cape Breton will keep is its music. The fiddlers go on. One of the most charming sights I saw in Cape Breton was a performance of fiddling by a veritable army of small children, some fairly dwarfed by their instruments but all fast and confident in their playing. Some of those players will be around in 70 years' time. The language the Gaels brought to Nova Scotia will have gone by then but something will have survived, if only a rhythm and a sound.

CHAPTER TEN

Argentina
'The survival of our race'

Because of this the idea of a Welsh colony came to be in the mind of those who cared for the old traditions, so they searched for an empty region to which the flow of Welsh emigration could be diverted.
(From *Book for Children of the Colony*, in Gaimán Museum)

A dead dog lay outside the main entrance to Retiro railway station in Buenos Aires in the hot sun, flies buzzing round the snout. It was ignored by the hordes of *favela* dwellers standing only a few feet away, hawking poor copies of brand-name T-shirts, rubber shoes and alarm clocks that went off continuously.

The station, the work of British engineers, was built when Argentina was a land of opportunity, when Buenos Aires was the Paris of the southern hemisphere and when the Avenida de Mayo was the equal of any boulevard in Paris or London. The station's massive columns, soaring arches and well-crafted metalwork recall the great age of steam. It is the kind of railway station that inspires the imaginative traveller with the expectation of being able to board a luxury train resembling the Orient Express and journey in comfort across deserts and through mountain ranges to far-off destinations in Brazil, Bolivia and beyond. A century ago, at the strike of a gong, three transcontinental trains left Retiro each week for the 900-mile, 38-hour journey to Chile. And if Buenos Aires was the Paris of the southern hemisphere, the railways made it so. 'Like the colossal web of a spider it sends out its strands of steel north to the border of Paraguay and Bolivia, east to the Atlantic, south into Patagonia and west across the Andes.'[1] So wrote an awestruck American visitor in 1911. The 20,000 miles of track were a worthy symbol for Argentina, a British contemporary wrote. John Foster Fraser dilated at length on the delights of an Argentine transcontinental journey – the dining cars especially, with their glamorous clientele of landowners ('estancieros'), the welcoming sight of twinkling, red-shaded lamps, the sleek black heads of the waiters bending down to murmur to the customers and the sound of bottles of champagne and Moselle being uncorked.[2]

Fraser titled his book *The Amazing Argentine* as an act of homage to a country that was the acknowledged prodigy of the era preceding the First World War. Writers struggled to find the right superlatives when describing the country. Most dispensed with comparisons to Paris, whatever the grand sweep of the boulevards and parks of Buenos Aires owed to Haussman. The sight of the skyscrapers and tramcars and the cacophony generated by continual demolition work and general bustle reminded them more of Chicago. The gloss, glamour and showiness of Buenos Aires and its citizens, the *portenos*, was seen as truly American. 'Nowhere in the world have I seen such a display of expensive motor cars, thousands of them,'[3] Fraser remarked of the wealthy suburb of Palermo. Edward VII's emissary, Sir Thomas Holdich, agreed. 'No more perfect drive exists anywhere than the long, palm-bordered drive to Palermo,' he wrote, 'where the broad roadway is occasionally so packed so full of carriages and riders as to render progress at anything but a foot's pace impossible.'[4]

Meat and wheat made this country its sudden, stupendous fortune. Nature left the vast, fertile basin around Buenos Aires perfect for raising cattle while the land further south was equally suitable for wheat. As recently as 1876 Argentina had imported wheat, but by 1880 6 million acres were under crops. This rose to 12 million acres by 1895, 43 million acres by 1908 and 54 million acres by 1911.[5] The railway made this expansion possible. Growing crops or raising livestock in such a huge country would have been pointless without the means of getting them to the coast. As it was, 95 per cent of meat exports were carried to the ports by rail. No wonder trains took pride of place at the 1910 exposition in Buenos Aires, commemorating the centenary of Argentina's independence from Spain.

But the 'colossal web' of steel is no more. It has vanished, along with the popping champagne corks and the scurrying waiters. The façade of Retiro station is all that remains. It has withstood the test of time magnificently but the real Latin America, banished only for a while, has crept up and around the building. When did the *favela* grow up behind the sidings? When did the first shacks spawn others, until first a street and then a little township came to girdle much of the building, giving it an edgy atmosphere after dark?

Retiro railway station has the air of a cathedral where the services have largely ceased. There is a lot of bustle on the outside but not much going on in the building itself. The once extensive railway network, British-built, like the station, practically vanished in the 1990s, the legacy of a botched privatisation programme and the withdrawal of government subsidies. The vast building is now embarrassingly inappropriate to the railway's only surviving function: to shuttle commuters to and from homes on the suburban lines.

Yards from the squalor of the station lie the streets in the Recoleta district, the area where Eva Peron lies buried, many of which still exude the opulence of the Buenos Aires of the 1900s. Outside elegant antique shops and pâtisseries young men walk groups of manicured poodles and German shepherds – the pets of the wealthy. But even here one cannot escape the atmosphere of crisis. A long queue snakes around the block leading from the front door of the Spanish embassy. The people in the queue are young and well dressed. The grandchildren and great-grandchildren of those who escaped the poverty of Spain and Italy for the legendary wealth of Argentina are now desperate to make it back to the 'old' country. On the other side of the road from the embassy a mestizo beggar lies sprawled on the pavement, eyeing them uninterestedly. They are going. He was most definitely staying.

While parts of Buenos Aires preserve a certain unmistakable air of glamour by day, the feeling dissipates by night. At dusk huge numbers of Argentina's *nouveaux pauvres* descend on the city centre to sift through the rubbish bins and collect paper and cardboard for recycling. The *cartoneros,* as they are called, do not look like the tough and swarthy Paraguayan traders selling T-shirts and clocks outside Retiro station. The *cartoneros* include a large segment of the ruined middle class of Buenos Aires, whose jobs and savings vanished in the economic chaos of 2000. While they sift away, outside the stately Colon Theatre where Maria Callas sang, bedraggled but distinctly bourgeois ladies stand in tattered finery waiting to accost the crowds leaving the theatre. They plead for cash in high-pitched, reedy tones that are quite unlike the megaphone rasps of the beggars in the Calle Florida, who ambush tourists. Carrying wailing babies under each arm, they bear notes in English that implausibly declare them to be refugees from Bosnia.

On a Saturday night the cinemas seemed virtually empty – the 5 peso ticket was clearly too pricey for the average *porteno* in his or her current dilemma. Evangelical churches seemed to be doing better. I watched a large congregation stream out of a hall at around 10 p.m., near an intersection of the Calle Florida and Calle Viamonte. The minister stood in the doorway. Young, good-looking, dressed in a dark suit and white shirt, his mestizo face was Inca-like in its impassivity as he talked to a frantic female parishioner. In the arc of light cast by the fluorescent strip-light inside the hall his features looked almost bluish. The woman was drawn-looking, heavily pregnant, her face a picture of anxiety. Perhaps she felt crushed by the burden of being pregnant for the umpteenth time. The pastor's lips moved, uttering, so I imagined, some tough but tender text from the Bible, which reminded her of her duty to bear her burden with joy.

Argentina is a land of lost opportunities. The day I left for Patagonia, the front page of the *Buenos Aires Herald* reported the death of a 14-year-old girl in Chaco province from starvation. 'She was suffering from breathing problems caused by malnutrition,' the newspaper reported. At her death she weighed 25 kilograms. 'She would not gain weight,' her mother Rita was reported as saying. 'We sometimes cried because we did not have enough food.' Waiting for the bus south in a bookshop I thumbed through a book of photographs. The black-and-white stills in *The Buenos Aires of Long Ago* recalled the city in its pre-First World War finery – women in ostrich-feather hats marching down the Calle Florida; a policeman in solitary splendour guarding a merchant's palace. Perhaps too much has been read into the 'golden era' that lasted from around 1880 to 1914, when wool, beef and leather briefly lifted Argentina into the ranks of the world's richest countries, sparking crazy talk of Argentina overtaking the United States. In reality, instability has been the norm, and so, on occasion, has hunger, in spite of the country's reputation as an agricultural paradise where everybody eats steak every day. Paintings in the museums of Buenos Aires tell a story of desperate poverty among many of the immigrants who crowded into hastily built cities. They show queues of people waiting for soup and scenes of savage labour unrest. Argentina has always given off different lights – one moment the most glamorous country on earth, the next, a wretched place. This was the country to which the Welsh came in the 1860s in search of their promised land. They called Argentina 'Arianin'.

There were not many people in the chapel in Gaimán that evening, perhaps no more than 30, and with the exception of the young Welsh teacher from Aberdare, it was an assembly of the elderly. Hair was white, receding or gone and voices had the quavering tone of the old. But even old Welsh voices are strong when raised together in song and the hymn-singing was lusty enough. At the end of the service they spilled out of the simple red-brick building into warm evening sunshine. The presence of a stranger excited a fair amount of interest. 'Dych yn wedi mwynheu yr gwasanaeth?' ('Did you enjoy the service?') They asked me where I was from: 'Llundain! Da iawn' ('London! Very good'). The warm smiles faded a little when it became apparent that the new visitor was not from the homeland after all, but an English-speaker with little more than childish Welsh. They turned away, bored by the prospect of a conversation in English.

In a large rambling house that looked as if it had been picked up from the Wales of long ago and dropped into the unlikely setting of Patagonia, Eluned Gonzalez, born Roberts, was making jam; jars of the stuff. While her husband quietly read the newspaper, oblivious, she and her elder sister, Tegai Roberts, director of Gaimán museum, her son, Fabio, the Welsh teacher from Aberdare and her ancient maid, a tiny village woman with a long grey pigtail and a face that looked as if it was made of old, creased leather, continued a four-way conversation. It flitted back and forth from Spanish into Welsh with occasional interjections in English for my benefit. 'Actually,' Tegai Roberts told me, 'Fabio's grammar is excellent . . . it's better than my own.' Fabio smiled. Quite capable of conversing in English, he preferred to fly in Welsh – 'the language of my ancestors', as he called it, though the phrase to an outsider sat oddly on such a Latin-looking man in his thirties with a Spanish name.

Patagonia is deceptive. There are people whose faces blush beetroot red in the southern sun and who look as if they have stepped straight off a pavement in Aberystwyth. Their names might be Mervyn or Edith and they even still dress as if they have wandered off the set of a programme about the vanished Britain of the 1950s. But the most they can manage in Welsh is a *croeso* (welcome) or a *syt dach chi?* (how are you?) before relapsing into the Spanish that is now their only real language. Then there are other more surprising encounters, with people like Fabio. At the village *locutorio* (telephone and internet shop) an olive-complexioned woman in charge came up and asked 'Dych yn siarad Cymraeg?' (Do you speak Welsh?) as I waited my turn for the net. She had caught sight of a Welsh book poking out of my pocket. At the far end of the valley, in a dusty village called 28 de Julio, I came across another woman in her twenties, thin faced and Latin looking but who started to speak halting Welsh to Eluned Gonzalez after overhearing her conversing with Fabio. How did she know the old language?, we asked. Was she going to classes? No, she had simply picked up a lot of Welsh in the farmhouse where she grew up.

We had reached 28 de Julio, the far end of the Chubut valley, on a mission to check out the state of the Welsh chapels. Eluned Gonzalez's ire had been roused by a newspaper article, which claimed they were mostly in ruins. 'Ruins?' she expostulated. 'Many are still used . . . they have teas in the grounds every 28 July to commemorate the *Mimosa*.' In searing heat and kicking up clouds of dust and swarms of mosquitoes we conducted a motorised visitation from the lower eastern end of the valley to the west-ward upper end, which marked the limit of the Welsh pale. Another Welsh settlement lay more than 400 miles to the west in the foothills of the Andes in Cwm Hyfryd, 'Pleasant Valley', but that lay well outside the day's remit. We journeyed through Gaimán to Bryn Crwn and Dolavón towards 28 de Julio with a checklist of Seions, Nazareths, Bethels, Carmels and Salems to investigate. 'So, is that a ruin?' Eluned Gonzalez would remark. 'Does that look a ruin to you? If anything it is *over*-restored, almost too English, one might say.' We took photographs as evidence for some future article that would demolish the claims of the offending newspaper report. One chapel had fallen down almost totally. A farmer had appropriated the disused build-ing and turned it into a cowshed: a stench of cowpats fermenting in the intense heat filled the air. The others stood lonely but not neglected in fields or on tops of hills, simple square brick structures, one made out of nothing more than corrugated iron, with no other decoration than a tablet proclaim-ing the name and the date of construction, or reconstruction.

The congregations that built these simple places of worship have almost disappeared. Like the rest of Argentina, the Chubut valley has not lived up to expectations. The valley was never the promised land that the Welsh emigrants were optimistically oversold in the 1860s. Where was the green-ery, or the woods they expected? There was a river, but no sooner had the Welsh mastered the art of irrigation, channelling the sluggish waters of the Chubut into the bone-dry soil, than it turned on them viciously, first in 1899 and again in 1902, flooding the valley and sweeping away years of work. There are still Welsh farming families in the rural hinterland of the Chubut valley but their numbers are fewer and the sight of what was clearly once a neat Welsh farmhouse, now gone to ruin, is common. The square red-brick dwellings are rarely deserted but many have changed hands. The Welsh have gone and their place has been filled by land-hungry peasant farmers from Paraguay or Bolivia, prepared, as the Welsh no longer are, to do battle with the blinding sun, the fierce, whipping wind and rock-hard soil. The Welsh feel little resentment towards the in-comers, just a certain sadness about the tumble-down state of their old farmhouses and a worry that the Bolivians and Paraguayans use too much pesticide and fertiliser on the land. They were not pushed off their farms; they left. They still return, as Eluned Gonzalez remarked, to the rural chapels every 28 July, the day in 1865 when the first Welsh settlers disembarked from the *Mimosa* on to Patagonian soil, and in the cold winter sunshine they remember their ancestors and drink cups of tea.

At the Patagonian Institute in Puerto Madryn I found Fernando Coronato poring over computerised records of the descendants of the first Welsh settlers, in company with a ruddy-faced local doctor named David Williams. Coronato, an Argentine historian with no Welsh ancestry, spoke fluent Welsh. Williams, who looked totally Welsh, spoke the language less well. Like many Patagonians of Welsh descent, Williams had only recently embraced a culture that his parents and grandparents discarded out of desire to fit in with the prevailing Latin culture of Argentina. Williams's forefathers were among the very first settlers who arrived on the *Mimosa,* and included one John Jones, a miner from Mountain Ash in South Wales. Aged 60 when he stepped off the *Mimosa*, he had been the oldest of all the original emigrants.

John Jones's generation of settlers brought an intense national pride to the New World. Their mission was not merely to better themselves but to build a new Welsh-speaking homeland as far as possible from England and free from the attention of Anglican parsons and English-speaking officials, judges and schoolteachers. For at least 50 years the colonists remained faithful to the founders' intentions, resisting the encroachments of Buenos Aires officialdom and sealing themselves off from the Latin and Catholic state they were living in.

With time, the emphasis on separation faded. As Wales and South Wales in particular became less Welsh and less Welsh-speaking, the homeland forgot the cause of the Welsh colony in Argentina – the *Gwladfa Gymreig* – while the colonists intermarried with the Italian immigrants and Spanish-speaking Argentines around them. In 1911 a British visitor remarked on the gap between the older and younger generations of Welsh settlers in Patagonia. He was startled by the appearance of 'red-faced, open-eyed straight-backed boys, each with a bright-coloured handkerchief around his neck and the guanaco-wool poncho hanging from his shoulders . . . the latter who are Patagonian-born seem to be part of their horses, but the elders, however excellent long practice has made them, never attain the proficiency of their sons.' The writer attributed this change to the fact that the Welsh no longer married their own. 'And so the efforts of the fore-fathers who fared overseas to found a new home shall be made null and void,' he remarked, adding that the average Argentine girl was 'rather apt to make roast meat of the hearts of the Welsh youth'.

David Williams was the product of a culture that by the 1930s and 1940s had rapidly moved away from the moorings of the Welsh chapels and the Welsh language. 'They felt a kind of shame,' he recalled of his grandparents. 'When the Italians and Spaniards began to settle in the Chubut valley, they teased people who talked differently. As a result my parents did not speak the language at all. I have had to go to school to learn Welsh!' He added: 'I have become a bit obsessed with the subject. We have become proud of our origins. Our parents did not speak Welsh, but we are speaking it.'

Attitudes had clearly changed over the past 30 years, the years of Argentina's decline. Williams felt no 'shame' about his origins and had proudly named his baby son Eric Thomas Williams. No concession to Latin culture there. Attitudes had changed because the nationalism of the older Argentinians, with its emphasis on Latin *machismo*, had folded under the impact of catastrophic economic recession and the shocking military defeat in the Malvinas or Falkland Islands in 1982. Like many people in Britain, the Argentinians had partly recoiled from a national identity that it was felt had failed to deliver. Just as many Britons with only the faintest of connections to Ireland or Scotland now parade Irish or Scottish identity, members of once-scorned minorities in Argentina have also reclaimed the identities that their parents threw aside. The Welsh Patagonians of Williams's generation are not liable to the charge their parents or grandparents often faced of possessing divided loyalties. They speak Spanish and are just as Argentinian as any of their neighbours.

Attending Welsh classes in Patagonia has become a popular pastime and in the old-fashioned bar of the Touring Hotel in Trelew I met a group of young women in their twenties and thirties who had become Welsh teachers. Theirs was not quite the language of Eluned Gonzalez and Tegai Roberts – learned from childhood and honed by years of listening to Welsh sermons. They had no connection to the old chapels and their Welsh had been learned in adulthood. They spoke with a distinct Spanish inflexion. It was no more their first language than it was mine. Fernando Coronato thought there were as many as 5,000 Welsh-speakers in Argentina today. 'It was all in decline until 1965,' he remarked, 'but then the centenary celebrations of the *Mimosa* brought a change. A great many people came here from Wales and interest revived. In the last 15 years there has been more and more. But no one thinks Welsh will ever again be a spoken language in the street. It's all about a search for identity.'

Outside the Patagonian Institute, the town of Puerto Madryn straggled untidily along an unattractive volcanic beach. Not far from the institute building a series of shallow caves lay fenced off, a sign on the top proclaiming that this was the spot where the immigrants from the *Mimosa* had landed on that cold winter's day in July 1865, when the promised land hove into view. A red stone block marked with the emblem of a red dragon crowned a hillock above the sand-filled caves, beside which dozens of Argentine holiday-makers, bronzed and glittering with sun cream, lay dozing like sea lions. 'Glaniesant yma, 1 Aros 28 Gorffenaf 1865' the sign read, followed by a long list of names – Edwyn Roberts, Amos Williams, Evan Jones, Aaron Jenkins, Thomas Harris, Daniel Evans, Richard Ellis, Evan Davies, and so on. The names of a number of identifiably single women, such as Elizabeth Wood, Ann Owen, Mary Lewis, were interspersed with the massed ranks of Roberts, Williams, Jones, Hughes and Davies families.

It was not hard to imagine how disappointing the land must have appeared to the Welsh colonists who disembarked in the depths of winter. 'It would be difficult to give an adequate idea of the dismal aspect presented by Puerto Madryn,' Hersketh Pritchard wrote at the turn of the last century, long before the sunbathers and ecological tourists arrived. 'Suffice it to say that the settlement consists of half a dozen houses and a flagstaff. The first crouch on the lip of the tide and the second shivers above the bare pampa-run . . . and there in inhospitable fashion, the little colony of human beings clings.'[6]

Even now that it has become one of the most popular Patagonian resorts, Puerto Madryn still has a dusty, slightly forlorn air. Behind the strip of concrete blocks and villas lining the greyish beach, the real nature of the Patagonian countryside immediately reveals itself – bare, brown, treeless and flat. Harsh and dry in the summer glare, it is more forbidding still in winter, when searing heat gives way to bitter winds. The Argentines have turned Puerto Madryn into a pleasure resort through sheer willpower. Determinedly ignoring the dry wind that carries clouds of dust from the beach into sunbathers' eyes, they plump their towels on the sticky grey 'sand' and soak up the rays. Few venture into the choppy, uninviting, dark green water of the South Atlantic. This is the home of the killer whale, or orca, the sea lion and the penguin. In the winter months, like those when the *Mimosa* landed, southern right whales migrate in large numbers to a bay just north of Puerto Madryn to breed and play fascinating games, waving their giant tails from the water and providing a spectacle for crowds of ecological tourists. Killer whales circle the beaches, waiting to snatch sea lion pups and sometimes even crashing their huge bodies on to the shingle to snatch a pup brazenly from the dry land. It is a landscape that still seems not quite suited to human habitation; good for tourists perhaps but not for settlers. This, the land of killer whales and penguins, was where the Welsh landed in 1865. Historians say they wore their Sunday best clothes when they stepped uncertainly ashore.

Today the town boasts a monument to the first colonists, defaced by graffiti, as well as a small museum and a few streets with Welsh names. That is about the sum of the Welsh legacy in Puerto Madryn in terms of architecture. There are, however, a few descendants of the Welsh colonists in Puerto Madryn, such as Clydwyn Jones who at nearly 90 could still recall the culturally more self-confident Welsh colony of the 1930s, before it was engulfed by the feelings of shame that Dr Williams had mentioned. 'When I went to school I knew only Welsh,' the former music teacher told me in the living room of his immaculate flat on the seafront. 'My family were farmers. Everybody spoke Welsh then. Only the farmhands spoke Spanish. In Gaimán the teachers were Welsh. David Rhys Jones, who opened the school in Gaimán in 1910 was my uncle. The chapel was in Welsh. It was full in those days.' Clydwyn was not optimistic about the long-term future of the Welsh community. 'Welsh is dying out now,' he said, sipping his tea. 'The chapels are closed. For a long time the Welsh did not go out of their circle . . . but then the children all left for Buenos Aires.' He was still an active and healthy man, prepared to drive many miles to attend irregular Welsh chapel services held at various times of the year in the valley, in the company of his Argentine wife Alicia. The musician was a symptom of what had befallen the experiment in transplanting Welshness overseas. He, too, had left the Chubut valley for Buenos Aires. And while his nonagenarian sister living in Gaimán spoke Welsh, his Argentine wife, for all her sympathy for her husband's culture, did not.

The Welsh colonists on the *Mimosa* soon left Puerto Madryn for the valley some 50 miles to the south. By the middle of September they had drawn up an Act to incorporate a settlement there. They named it Rawson, in honour of Guillermo Rawson, the Argentine Interior Minister who had done much to encourage the Welsh to settle in Patagonia in the first place and who had lent them invaluable aid in the first trying years. Rawson quickly lost its Welsh character. As the centre of government, it attracted Spanish-speaking Argentine officials and shopkeepers, often Italians, who together set the tone. There is little now to recall the town's Welsh origins except a chapel. Instead, I followed in the footsteps of the colonists to the place that the Welsh really made their own, Gaimán.

If Rawson has largely forgotten its Welsh roots, Gaimán has done the opposite. No town or village in the Chubut valley has preserved so much of its Welsh appearance, from the very un-Argentine streets of square, red-brick cottages to the well-preserved chapel beside the river and the old cemetery, where generations of Welsh colonists lie under tombstones marked in some cases with motifs of sailing ships.

The faces in the street are just as likely to be mestizo, Paraguayan or native American as Welsh but Gaimán has staked its future on its Welsh past. As the bus raced into the centre of town, I passed billboards proclaiming 'Croeso', a forest of red dragons and several advertisements urging visitors to visit a *Casa De Te Galesa* – a Welsh tea house, including the lucky establishment that Diana, Princess of Wales patronised on her brief visit to Patagonia in the 1990s.

In Gaimán Welshness is not an attractive pastime but a livelihood, and even the wholly Latin owners of the town's hotel beamed delightedly when I produced my Welsh dictionary at the dinner table, triggering approving murmurs about 'los galesas'. Gaimán does good business serving out Welshness to visiting coach parties of Argentine and foreign tourists from Puerto Madryn who stop off at one or other tea house *en route* to or from a whale- and penguin-watching expedition on the coast. The coaches mean that a steady flow of visitors circulates through the town's museum. I watched Argentine families perambulating the exhibits slowly, peering at fading copies of early Welsh newspapers such as *Y Gwerynwr* and *Y Drafod*, at the copy of the Act of the foundation of Rawson, dated September 1865, and at the plan of the valley in the 1890s, showing the subdivision of the plots among the various settlers. They stared at grainy photographs of men and women who had insisted on being photographed in the late-Victorian finery they brought with them from Britain, at the photograph of President Julio Roca visiting the colony in 1899 and at a picture of one of the first eisteddfods held in Patagonia, in Trelew, when the now bustling town contained no more than a handful of buildings. The museum displays a couple of extracts from books that were written for the colonists over the years. One, by R. J. Berwyn, for the children of the colony, neatly sums up the history of the enterprise in a couple of sentences. 'In this century emigration had become a necessity for survival to many of our race,' it read. 'Of those who left Wales, some felt like aliens in the country to which they went, others became integrated with their surroundings and lost their national identity.'

I found lodging with a Welsh-speaking widow in Gaimán. In the evenings I re-read Bruce Chatwin's 1978 book *In Patagonia*. After several decades during which the Welsh colony in Argentina had been virtually forgotten, his book did much to remind the world of its existence. But it was a couple of decades since Chatwin had moved through the valley, making arch, though not unaffectionate, observations about the inhabitants. When Chatwin stayed in Gaimán it had still been possible to encounter elderly survivors of the last influx of colonists, who arrived before the First World War. He found, or maintained he found, Welsh farmhouses with old wooden dressers covered in blue-and-white ornaments and china dogs, run by women who asked if it was true that 'the morals had gone down' in the land they called home. The book remains controversial among the diminishing number of people in the valley who recall the real Chatwin. Eluned Gonzalez and her sister Tegai did. The museum director said: 'We are all very surprised by the book . . . so superior. Looking down on us . . . a very *English* way of looking at things'. Her sister flipped the book open to a photograph of a Welsh family. They had been photographed in a somewhat squalid setting and the picture had been juxtaposed (by accident?) with one showing the splendid interior of an Anglo-Argentine *estanciero*. 'Look at that,' she added. 'This family was not photographed in their house. It was obviously taken in a *barn!*' There was no real irritation, just a feeling of bemusement, and of having being taken for a ride by a clever and self-possessed young Englishman.

Chatwin brought the Welsh settlement in Patagonia alive to millions of English-speaking readers. But it skewed the view for people visiting the valley in the twenty-first century. My host was as Welsh as they come. She talked the language continually on the telephone to her sisters and to old friends but her home was nothing like the houses Chatwin described, shrines to the Welsh taste of long ago. The bungalow was modern with not a trace of a Welsh dresser or blue-and-white china or ornamental dogs. She was a devout Christian but the biblical injunctions that covered almost every door and wall were in Spanish. She did not even attend the Welsh chapel, having long ago transferred her allegiance to one of the Spanish-speaking evangelical churches that had sprouted in Gaimán, and which attracted larger and younger crowds than the one I joined in the old chapel. I thought back to the large evangelical congregation I had seen leaving their hall in Buenos Aires that Saturday night and the stern, Inca-like features of the pastor standing in his dark suit in the doorway, dispensing advice to his crushed-looking parishioner. 'Of course I attended Welsh chapel as a child,' she said in slow, perfect English. She smiled, recalling days when Welsh congregations on summer outings to the coast entertained Argentine holiday-makers with their hymn-singing at the railway stations they passed through. The congregations had gone along with the railway (a single steam train lay parked in lonely isolation in the middle of Puerto Madryn, looking like some stuffed extinct bird). And she had also gone, quitting the dry atmosphere of the Welsh chapels with their overflowing cemeteries for the liveliness of the Spanish-speaking congregations in their bright new premises.

On the sideboard in the living room where I was staying stood two photographs. The older showed my landlady at the time of her marriage in the 1940s, her face flushed and sparkling with anticipation beside her smiling, tall, tanned husband. The much more recent photograph had clearly been taken towards the end of the husband's life. He sat there, frail and delicate. She sat next to him in the picture, still smiling – no longer with anticipation but with a look of inexpressible tenderness. Like many of her generation, she had broken the old taboo and married out, though not to a Spanish-speaker but to an Anglo-Argentine. 'We spoke English at the beginning of our marriage and Spanish at the end,' she recalled in a faintly surprised tone, as if she had not noticed this fact before. There were other photographs in the room, of her children and grandchildren. The grandchildren were good-looking, with white teeth, tanned complexions and Latin features. None spoke Welsh or lived near Gaimán. It was the story of much of the community, of dispersal and quiet assimilation into the Hispanic mainstream. What they had kept was not the Welsh language (or the English, for that matter) but evangelical Christianity.

The *Mimosa* pioneers, many of whom lie buried in Morah chapel cemetery near Trelew, would not wholly have approved of such an outcome. They did not journey to the Americas, as the English Puritans had in the seventeenth century, to find religious freedom. They had that at home, however much they disliked paying tithes to the clergy of the Anglican Establishment. They had not made the journey to the Americas to escape hunger, like the desperate Irish peasants in their hellish coffin ships in the 1840s. They had not been thrown off their land, like the Scottish Highlanders in the early nineteenth century. The Welsh journeyed to Latin America with the express intention of founding a new Welsh-speaking homeland, the *Gwladfa Gymreig*. Some may have gone in hopes of gain, but that was never their main impulse.

'I wouldn't have dared to speak Spanish inside the family home,' Elvey Macdonald told me, recalling life in Gaimán in the 1940s. 'My mother spoke Spanish perfectly well, as I did, but I never spoke it to her until the day she died.' Elvey's mother died in her nineties in 2002, resolutely preserving the Welsh character of her household to the end – a small Celtic island in a rising sea of Spanish-speaking Latins. The Macdonald family stood out when most of their generation lost faith in the original aims of the colony. Macdonald recalled feeling out of step with the prevailing culture.

'The children would shout "Pan y manteca" [Bread and butter] at us. I suppose that is what they thought we ate all day! They shouted all sorts of nasty things. It was a terrible time. By the time I went to school people were afraid even to acknowledge they spoke Welsh. Even the children you knew from the Sunday school would not speak it with you. Many Welsh parents decided not to pass the language to the next generation. My parents took a stand, but very few others did.'

The aims and fears of the mid-Victorian founders of the Welsh colony in Patagonia make sense when set against the fate of previous Welsh settlements in the United States. The numbers of Welsh emigrants was always small compared to the Irish, which was unsurprising given the job opportunities available in their own increasingly industrialised country. But they rose all the same. There were about 30,000 Welsh-born immigrants in the US by 1850 and about 45,000 by 1880. That grew to more than 100,000 in 1890, the majority concentrated in the states of New York, Pennsylvania, Ohio, Minnesota and Wisconsin.[7]

Welsh settlements in America date back to the 1790s, when 50 emigrants left the village of Llanbrynmair in Montgomeryshire for a tract of land purchased by a radical Baptist minister named Morgan John Rhys on the waters of the Blacklick and Connemaugh rivers in Pennsylvania, about 250 miles west of Philadelphia. From Cambria, as it was named, an offshoot established a new foothold in Paddy's Run, now Shandon, in the state of Ohio. At much the same time families from Caernarfonshire settled Utica in New York, while in 1803 other settlers from Radnorshire created Radnor Township in Delaware. In Ohio state, Jackson and Gallia counties in particular became a 'little Wales', where Welsh settlers were sufficiently thick on the ground by the 1830s to justify the establishment of Welsh Calvinist-Methodist synods. Minnesota became another popular destination for the Welsh in the 1850s, so much so that in 1857 the state constitution of Minnesota was translated into Welsh for the benefit of the compact Welsh farming communities in the Blue Earth and Le Sueur counties. But if the Welsh settlers of Minnesota needed a translator to understand their English constitution in the 1850s, their children did not by the 1880s. Communities changed language with astonishing speed and by then Paddy's Run and the Welsh tracts in Ohio had largely lost their Welsh character.

Welsh-language newspapers in America quickly opened, folded, adopted English, or reduced their Welsh-language coverage to a few token articles and obituaries. *Y Drych* (*The Mirror*) of Utica was published in Welsh from the 1850s until 1914 when it became bilingual. Later only the obituaries were in Welsh. The churches were anglicised at the same pace. Ohio had many Welsh-speaking Congregational and Calvinist-Methodist clergy in the mid-nineteenth century and 150 even in 1900 but the numbers dropped fast after that. By the twentieth century the Welsh Calvinist-Methodist church in the US was succumbing to pressure to throw in its lot with ideologically similar English-speaking denominations and in 1920 it duly merged with the American Presbyterian Church. After the union, Welsh-language services had no future and even the staunchest Welsh-speaking communities ceased hearing Welsh sermons in the 1930s.[8]

The pressures to anglicise had proved irresistible. It was part of the fruits of the economic and political success that made William Bebb, son of Welsh immigrant parents, governor of Ohio from 1846 to 1849. So did the urge to spread out over the country. 'Texas fever' in the 1870s, besides drawing Welsh emigrants from Wales, diluted the Welsh character of the existing American settlements, luring men from sealed communities into the cultural melting-pot of the western frontier. With the opening up of the west, many moved to Kansas or California. Where the mines opened, the Welsh, like the Cornish, were sure to follow.

The Welsh knew they were losing their cultural identity in America. They 'lose the love of their country', Henry Davies of Bala lamented to the folks at home from his new home in Kansas. 'They go to live among the Americans where they do not hear a word of their mother tongue.' Davies said loss of faith and national identity ran concurrently and they should be equally deplored. 'There are hundreds of people raised in religious houses in Wales to the sound of family prayers and religious instruction who have emigrated to this country and fallen by the wayside.'[9]

A nineteenth-century observer in Paddy's Run made the same complaint about the effects of Mammon on the faith and nationality of his fellow-countrymen in America. 'The Welsh soon forget God and become worldly in America,' he lamented. 'The mixture of languages makes the religious cause to suffer.'[10] The assimilation of the American Welsh took decades to reach completion but the trend was clear as early as the 1850s, which explains the growth in interest in founding a new settlement far from any English-speaking country. In Wales itself, where for the first time concern was growing about the eventual disappearance of the Welsh language in its homeland, nationalists decided to explore the chances of establishing an alternative focus for emigrants outside the United States.

The dream of a new Wales outside the British empire and the US attracted Michael Jones, president of the Congregational theological college in Bala. Jones, born in 1822, was bitterly hostile to the regime of Tory land-lords and their allies in Wales among the established clergy. As a young man in the 1840s he had spent time in the United States, preaching in Welsh chapels in Ohio, when William Bebb was state governor from 1846 to 1849. Bebb remained a strong supporter of Welsh emigration to the US, moving to Tennessee in the 1850s to sponsor a new Welsh settlement. But Jones changed his mind. He was increasingly convinced that compact Welsh settlements had no future in the fluid and mobile world of North America and began searching for an alternative in a more deserted corner. It was Jones who gathered a meeting of sympathisers at his Bala home in 1861 to discuss the possibility of establishing a colony in Patagonia and who started communication with the Argentine authorities. In Guillermo Rawson, the Interior Minister, he found an interested interlocutor: Rawson helped pay for two sympathisers with the project, Lewis Jones and Sir Love Jones-Parry, to undertake a mission to Patagonia and follow up Jones's written communications with Rawson. The two returned to Wales in May 1863 after paying a brief visit to the Chubut valley by sea and drawing up an agreement with Rawson in Buenos Aires.

The country that the two Welshmen visited had been independent for just over 40 years and seemed to be something of a blank canvas. It was little more than an extension of Buenos Aires and in the mid-nineteenth century its racial and even religious character was only partially determined. Although the vast majority of white inhabitants were of Spanish origin and thus Roman Catholic, the revolution of 1810 had triggered a rebellion against the past and all things Spanish. The Catholic Church had virtually disintegrated since independence, after the royalist bishops and their clergy abandoned their dioceses. A British visitor in the 1820s was amazed to find most churches in Buenos Aires completely deserted, 'and inside them only one or two decrepit old women'.[11] About half the population was made up of native people, though the government was set on reducing this percentage by a mixture of warfare, containment and massive immigration from Europe.

Just as a question mark hung over Argentina's racial and cultural identity, its frontiers were also hazy. On the other side of the Andes lay Chile. Then as now it was a not too friendly neighbour and rival for the position of regional paramount power. Chile and Argentina were both determined to claim the vast, half-empty southern cone of the continent for themselves and it was the race for control of the south that opened the door for Michael Jones and the Cambrian Immigration Society that he helped establish in Liverpool in 1861.

In the 1840s and 1850s several worrying developments preoccupied the government in Buenos Aires. In the 1830s the British had expelled the Argentine authorities from the Malvinas in the South Atlantic. As the Falkland Islands they would remain a largely forgotten British outpost for the following century and a half, until Argentina's botched invasion gave them a prominence in British eyes they had never previously enjoyed. The British seizure of the islands was not merely an irritant to national pride, however. There were genuine worries that Britain's assertiveness in the South Atlantic paved the way for the seizure of the Patagonian mainland, a development that would have boxed the new state into the basin around the River Plate. British manoeuvres were one concern, Chilean ones were another. In 1843 Chile took control of the Magellan Straits at the southern tip of Patagonia, planting the Chilean flag for the first time on the eastern shore of the continent and raising fears that the whole of Patagonia might fall into Chilean hands.

It was thus that the Welsh society's interest in establishing a colony and Argentina's interest in keeping Chile at bay began to converge. But from the start there were misunderstandings. Argentina just wanted some colonists to raise the blue and white Argentine flag over the heart of Patagonia, while Jones and his committee in Liverpool wanted a *Gwladfa Gymreig* that would be independent of any foreign power, at most accepting nominal Argentine sovereignty. There were also misunderstandings on the Welsh side over the nature of the country that they were going to settle. The Cambrian society had only a scanty knowledge of Patagonia's terrain, culled partly from Charles Darwin's account of his voyage on the *Beagle* around Tierra del Fuego in the 1830s, supplemented by more recent observations made by Lewis Jones and Jones-Parry. The assumption that the valleys of central Patagonia might afford vistas similar to those of South or mid-Wales was wide of the mark.

The two sides saw in their negotiating partner only what they wanted to see. The Welsh dealt almost exclusively with Rawson, a strong supporter of the Welsh venture but not the only voice in the government. That neither side was prepared to take note of anything that obstructed their predetermined vision was demonstrated by the fact that even after the Argentine Senate rejected the agreement to establish a Welsh colony that Rawson had negotiated, Jones and his team pressed on as if nothing had happened. In reality, the Senate's reaction was of enormous significance. The Argentines had shown then, as they would show in the future, that they had no intention of acting as midwives to the birth of a Welsh state in what they insisted was their land.

The agreement that Rawson had drawn up was hopelessly unrealistic. It stipulated that the Welsh society would supply between 300 and 500 families annually for settlement while the government would allot two square leagues of land each to 200 families for subdivision. The Welsh society had conceded the principle of Argentine sovereignty from the start by agreeing to the eventual appointment of a governor selected by Buenos Aires. On the other hand, the colony was promised the status of a province within Argentina once the population reached the 20,000 threshold. To add to the confusion the Welsh appeared to be under the illusion that provinces enjoyed far more autonomy from the central government than was the case. Nothing daunted by the rejection of their agreement in the Argentine Senate, the Welsh society solicited colonists for the expedition through lecture tours which promoted the Chubut valley as a fertile land. Prospectuses offered every colonist a substantial farm of about 106 acres, which was to come with five horses, 10 cows, 20 sheep and 'a number of fruit trees'.[12] There was no mention of the presence of indigenous people. They were told to bring beds, blankets, knives, forks, plates and boiling pots. Evidence of the society's ignorance of the climate in central Patagonia was provided in the information that 'clothing worn in Wales will do'.[13] While the Welsh society mustered interested parties for a provisional sailing in April 1865, Lewis Jones and Edwin Roberts set out beforehand in March to prepare the terrain for landing, buying livestock in Buenos Aires and driving them south to the Golfo Nuevo on the Patagonian coast. In the end the colonists did not leave Liverpool as planned on the *Halton Castle* in April but on 24 May on the *Mimosa*. They were a young group in the main and included 61 children, 32 bachelors and 12 spinsters.[14]

Disappointment that was the fruit of poor planning marred the venture from the start. After two months at sea and a journey of 7,000 miles the pilgrims on the Welsh *Mayflower* reached the uninhabited bay of the Golfo Nuevo. On 28 July 1865 they came ashore. It was midwinter and as the arrivals observed the flat, cold and treeless desert with its dreary scattered shrubs, it was clear that Patagonia was no new Wales. The welcome preparations were not inspiring. In the early 1850s a Welshman had passed through on an errand to round up wild cattle and the few flimsy wooden sheds he had built on his sojourn provided shelter for the dazed arrivals. With no trees to build homes or fences, and with no idea of what could grow in the hard soil, the mood of facile optimism surrounding the future colony soured immediately.

The first Welsh settler to be born in Patagonia came into the world on 10 August 1865, two weeks after the colonists landed. Maria Elizabeth

Humphreys, daughter of Elizabeth and Morris Humphreys, would live to a reasonable age, dying in 1928.[15] But that birth was one of few auspicious signs. Although Lewis Jones duly arrived with a quantity of livestock from the north, it was obvious they would not feed the population for more than about three months. The women had no idea how to milk the wild cattle that hired gauchos deposited at the settlement. As the fantasy of an empty lush valley transformed into the reality of a semi-desert, the hope of luring hundreds of Welsh families to Patagonia every year perished. The only question was whether the existing contingent would hang on or appeal for evacuation.

The emigrants did not remain beside the Golfo Nuevo for long but headed south-west towards the banks of the Chubut river where they established a settlement named in honour of Rawson. But their arrival in the Chubut valley did not mark an upturn in either their fortunes or morale. They were not agricultural specialists, in any case. Many had come from industrialised Aberdare, Mountain Ash and the Rhondda valley and had not been selected with reference to any special skills. Only a couple had experience of farm work. As one historian noted: 'Anyone willing to sail was accepted as a passenger.'[16]

By the end of 1865 the colonists in the Chubut valley were half starving and their clothing was in shreds. They sent a representative to Buenos Aires to appeal for aid and Rawson promised £140 a month for food and seed,[17] but the seed proved of no use and the first harvest in 1866 failed. The British authorities, who regarded the whole enterprise with bemused detachment, began to voice concern. Even if the Welsh had fled 'English oppression', the British still did not want them all to die horribly at the bottom of Argentina and HMS *Triton* was sent by the governor of the Falklands with supplies. It docked in the Golfo Nuevo in July 1866.

But these were no more than sticking plasters. There were more alarums that year. The colonists had been told nothing of the existence of native peoples and on a terrifying Sunday, scores of these people materialised outside the first chapel in Rawson, halting the minister Abraham Matthews in mid-sermon. The Welsh were fearful, though it turned out that the natives wanted nothing more than to sell them some meat, horses and ostrich skins. After the harvest failed, most of the colonists simply wanted to abandon the venture and get out, as a result of which the entire party in 1867 journeyed back to the Golfo Nuevo to await a ship to Buenos Aires. In the end they did not leave. Both Lewis Jones and Abraham Matthews persuaded them to remain, adding that if they returned to the Chubut valley the Argentine government would guarantee continued financial aid for at least a year. They went back and decided to make a go of it once more.

The year 1867 brought the invaluable discovery, allegedly made by a farmer's wife, that the valley's hard soil could be transformed by digging channels from the Chubut into the fields. But there were no human reinforcements in 1868 and 1869. Instead the colony dwindled in size.[18] At the same time the Argentine government began to complain that the Welsh colony was proving a financial burden. By then its failure was well known and being discussed in the English press as a textbook example of how not to colonise an area. 'The Welsh colony is a failure because it was from the commencement a great mistake,' the Argentine immigration secretary in London, W. Perkins, told the *Field* in 1869. 'The poor Welshmen were settled in Patagonia out of reach of civilisation and with no market for their produce . . . had North Americans been settled there the result might have been different, but with the Welsh settlers the change from their thickly populated native land to such dreary isolation unnerved them.'[19]

The commentators were premature in writing off the Welsh colony. A turning point came in the 1870s with the expansion of irrigation and the construction of a network of channels. By 1880 the colonists were producing 1,800 tons of wheat and by 1885 this had risen to 6,000 tons. The high price fetched by wheat at the time brought a real profit and for the first time a trickle of new settlers joined the hardy survivors of the *Mimosa*. The population inched up, though it never even remotely approximated the numbers predicted by the Welsh society in the heady days of the negotiations with Guillermo Rawson. A few arrivals reached the settlement in 1874 after the *Electric Spark* left New York, while the *Luzerne* brought another 27 that year. Between 1875 and 1876 the pace increased, with about 500 settlers arriving in all. The modest influx enabled the Welsh to strike out from Rawson and create a new settlement 21 miles to the west and upstream at Gaimán and this, rather than Rawson, then became the heart of the *Gwladfa Gymreig*. By 1881 Gaimán comprised only 18 dwellings but by the following year there were already 28. A third settlement named Trelew after Lewis Jones and positioned between Rawson and Gaimán followed in 1888.

The settlers then began to look beyond the small expanse of the Chubut valley. Only 100 kilometres long by about 10 wide, the usable land was all divided up by the early 1880s. If the colony were to survive it would have to expand west. In November 1883 a party of four set out on an expedition towards the Andes on a venture that ended in tragedy. A group of

Tehuelche natives ambushed John Evans, John Parry, Zachariah Jones and Richard Davies about 150 kilometres west of Gaimán at Las Plumas.

The Welshmen were victims of circumstances they had done nothing to create. The government had been waging a genocidal war against the indigenous peoples since the late 1870s, which had increased in scale after Argentina signed a border treaty with Chile in 1881. The ferocious persecution embittered the indigenous people against all white settlers. The Welsh had nothing to do with the 'war of the desert' but the Tehuelche were not in a mood to distinguish between the various white settlers at the time. Evans made a famous getaway on a horse. It was a rare and untypical example of friction between the Welsh and the indigenous people. The Welsh were never numerous enough to pose an existential threat to the Mapuche and Tehuelche, who did not live in settled communities and were not much interested in the Chubut valley. Their resources and lifestyles were different. These people were hunters and gatherers while the Welsh were tillers. Far from clashing, they usually traded happily. The Spanish-speakers exulted in the destruction of the 'Indians'. Francis Latzina, author of an emigrants' handbook in the 1880s, boasted that 'thousands of leagues of land had been snatched from the savage' as a result of the latest campaign. 'The scourge of civilisation and of the prosperity of the Argentine Republic was done away with,'[20] he wrote. The British were equally callous. Sir Thomas Holdich, sent by Edward VII to adjudicate the border between Argentina and Chile in 1902, used native guides for his expedition through Patagonia and placed photographs of them in costumes in the pages of his memoir. But his gratitude was skin deep, for he described them venomously in the text as sub-humans and savages whose imminent extermination was heartily to be welcomed.

The Welsh were horrified by such talk. The crowing, boastful tone that came so easily to the Spanish and the English was foreign to them. With no grudge against the native peoples and no desire to see them annihilated they deplored the war being waged against them and in 1883 petitioned the military to leave the 'Indians' in their homes. 'We have received much kindness by the hands of these natives since the time of founding the colony and we felt no anxiety about our safety among them,'[21] they said. The Argentines took no notice whatever.

The ambush at Las Plumas did not deter the Welsh or the new Argentine governor of Chubut, Luis Fontana, from planning new expeditions. Fontana set out in October 1885 with a party of 30, almost all Welsh, and after traversing the barren, desert-like plateau, reached the verdant foothills of the Andes in the last week of November, returning in February 1886. This was much more like the green promised land the settlers had imagined and the discoverers promptly christened the valley Cwm Hyfryd – pleasant valley. By 1891 they had established the settlement of Trevelin whose population reached about a hundred by 1894.[22]

By then the ambition of building a little Celtic state in the heart of Patagonia seemed closer to fulfilment. Another landmark was the construction of a railway connecting Madryn to the Chubut valley, running through Trelew to Gaimán and beyond. The construction work drew a large number of Welsh workers, of whom 465 arrived on the *Vista*, which left Liverpool in June 1886. Not all of them stayed after a row concerning their right to grants of 250 acres of land each once their three-year contracts expired.[23] But in the short term the influx of several hundred Welshmen had a galvanising effect on a colony of only about 1,600 settlers, while the railway boosted the development of Trelew.[24]

The Welsh started to create a network of Welsh institutions in their new homeland, such as chapels, newspapers, cultural societies and economic concerns. Capel Moriah near Trelew was inaugurated in 1880 as an Independent congregation. The Tabernacle followed in Trelew in 1889 as a Calvinist Methodist chapel. Nazareth at Drofa Dulog and Bethlehem at Treorki followed soon after. The Welsh began their own media as soon as they got to Patagonia. *Y Brut* (Chronicle) came out in 1868. It was a primitive affair, comprising a single copy containing various news items that was passed round from house to house by hand. But in January 1891 the indefatigable Lewis Jones established a proper periodical in *Y Drafod* (Mentor). The St David's Society was formed in the 1880s as a cultural and educational association. It began as Camwy Fydd – Future of Chubut – but changed its name in 1888. The same decade also saw the founding of an agricultural cooperative, the Compania Mercantil Chubut, and an irrigation company. Both bodies for the next half-century played a significant role in cementing Welsh political and economic control over the Chubut valley. The first school opened also in 1896, with 41 pupils under Robert Owen Jones.

A census taken in 1895 showed a population in the Chubut valley that now numbered 3,748 and were almost all Welsh-speakers. The colony contained four small urban settlements, Gaimán with 267 residents, Trelew with 132, Rawson with 369 and Madryn with a mere 39. The Welsh were a minority in Madryn and Rawson, the two centres of Argentine officialdom, but elsewhere there were few Latin voices in the sea of Welsh. The Welsh plant appeared to have taken root in this most unlikely setting.

Tentatively a Welsh statelet was spreading along the banks of the Chubut, far from the hostile gaze of Anglican parsons and English schoolteachers as well as from the Spanish-speaking authorities in Buenos Aires. But then nature dealt a deadly blow in the form of a flood, while Argentina imposed a series of hostile governors. After that it would never be the same again.

The problems with the government came first. The nature of Welsh autonomy in Argentina had not been satisfactorily resolved, but merely fudged. While the Argentines were afraid of the British and of Chile it suited both the colony and the government in Buenos Aires to pretend there was no dispute. But there was never a true agreement concerning what the Welsh were there for. The same suspicions about the Welsh, which had motivated the Argentine Senate to veto Rawson's deal with the Welsh society in the 1860s, returned to haunt the colony after the emergency years were over. Once it was clear that the colony was going to survive and even prosper the two sides could no longer ignore each other as before.

For the first decade of its existence the colony was entirely self-governing under its own council and president. But in 1875 the Argentine government took the first step towards consolidating its claim to Patagonia by appointing a commissioner for Chubut. It marked the beginning of a period of tension between Buenos Aires and the colonists, which exploded in 1882 with the temporary arrest of Lewis Jones for allegedly failing to collect information for a census. Jones-Parry, now a British MP, told parliament that Britain should intervene with the authorities to lessen what he called 'the oppression and disorder suffered by the Welsh colonists'.[25] It was an ironic turn of events but one pregnant with future significance. The Welsh had left Wales to escape the English. After failing to find the unrestricted liberty they expected, they were forced back into a state of semi-dependency on Britain. It was a dangerous game of brinkmanship, for while fear of British involvement cowed the Argentines for a while, it stoked suspicions that the Welsh might be a Trojan horse for British colonisation.

For a while the Welsh put their faith in obtaining provincial status for Chubut, they assumed, would dominate any elected local government. But they overestimated the degree of independence from Buenos Aires that they might expect and failed to note that governors of provinces were not elected by the population as in the United States but appointed by the government. Moreover the governors enjoyed a great deal of discretionary power.

The potential for friction was ignored temporarily in the atmosphere of relief over the granting of provincial status in 1884 and the excitement of the first elections to a council. Luis Fontana, the first governor, was a wise choice. Only 39 when he was appointed, the expedition he organised to Cwm Hyfryd with a Welsh squadron showed that the two sides could work together. But after Fontana departed in 1894 to Neuquen to head the demarcation commission with Chile the troubles of the Welsh mounted. Eugenio Tello, Fontana's successor from 1895, was determined to impress on the Welsh that they were citizens of Argentina. A fight arose over Sunday drilling. Since 1885 adult males in Argentina had been subject to compulsory, regular military exercises. Under the lax Fontana regime the law was tacitly ignored in Chubut in the interests of co-operation with the Welsh but in 1896 Tello ordered all local men between 18 and 30 to report for drill on the first Sunday in April in Rawson. There was uproar. Rawson was the least convenient place for the men of the Chubut valley to assemble and the choice of Sunday looked like provocation. As one historian of the colony put it: 'To the Welsh colonists this attitude seemed to be a desecration of the sanctity of the Sabbath, an attitude almost beyond the comprehension of the very intelligent Governor Tello.'[26] But Tello would not back down. 'I told them emphatically that the most important religion is that of the fatherland,' he informed the Interior Ministry in Buenos Aires – unaware that the Welsh did not look on Argentina as more than a tolerable evil and certainly did not accord it the status of a fatherland. 'Protestants in other Argentine provinces had not objected to Sunday drill,' the governor added. Tello was puzzled by their confused allegiances. 'If I say to them that they are English they get quite wild, saying they are not English,' he told the visiting Lloyd George in Buenos Aires. 'If they are called upon to read and write Spanish, they say they are English citizens.'[27]

Tello left in 1898 but his successor Carlos O'Donnell, governor from 1898 to 1900, was even worse in Welsh eyes and is still remembered in Chubut as 'Nero'. Under his governorship Sunday drill was enforced and accompanied by an attitude of open hostility to the Welsh that had not existed under Tello or Fontana. O'Donnell's stance anticipated the rise of a generally critical attitude among Argentines towards the Welsh as a thorn in their side. They no longer remembered that the Welsh had kept Chile out of Patagonia and only saw them as semi-British introverts who refused to be assimilated.

O'Donnell was a man of his time. He was the prototype of a new generation of militarily and culturally confident Argentines who no longer feared outside powers and were less tolerant of difference than their predecessors. The early 1900s was a time of ideological ferment in Argentina, when the seeds of authoritarian nationalism were being sown. The constant increase in immigration and growing labour unrest in the cities had spawned a nativist reaction on the right. A new generation of nationalists inveighed against 'cosmopolitanism' and Argentina as a modern Tower of Babel. They turned Catholic Spain, virtually forgotten since 1810, into an object of veneration and pilgrimage. The right's cult of *hispanidad*, and of the gaucho as an icon, bolstered by authoritarian Catholicism, was accompanied by growing racial pride in being Latin. It became increasingly clear to men of O'Donnell's generation that Argentina was a Latin state, Spanish in speech, Catholic in religion. Welsh Protestants, wedged in the centre of Patagonia, now looked like an awkward squad who were getting in the way of the business of nation-building. The Welsh were the victims of success – their own and Argentina's. Had they failed to make a go of the Chubut valley they would never have attracted any attention or drawn outsiders to the valley. Had Argentina remained the weak, underpopulated state it had been in the 1860s, Buenos Aires would never have attempted to bridle their ambitions. But O'Donnell's Argentina was a different state to Guillermo Rawson's.

Roca's 'war of the desert' against the indigenous peoples had cleared the way for immigration from Europe on a massive scale. In the 1850s the numbers had been around 5,000 a year. In the 1860s this crept up to around 10,000. In the early 1870s it reached just over 40,000,[28] but the next three decades dwarfed anything seen earlier. By the early twentieth century 300,000 immigrants were pouring into the country annually and the transformation of Buenos Aires from a provincial capital into the Paris of the southern hemisphere mirrored Argentina's changing appreciation of itself. The city of 180,000 in 1870 exploded into a metropolis of 800,000 by 1902. Even the British were awestruck by its rise. 'There is no other colonial city like it,' Sir Thomas Holdich wrote. 'Buenos Aires is now undoubtedly the capital of South America by right of its position, its wealth, its population and its magnificence.'[29] The days when Argentina had felt nervous of British or Chilean encroachment rapidly receded. The Chilean threat evaporated as Argentina's population overtook that of its neighbour. By the turn of the century the 5 million Argentinians easily outnumbered Chile's 3.5 million.

In 1899 Roca, the popular hero of the unjust 'war of the desert', visited Patagonia. The visit was a great success. Roca was genial and allowed himself to be photographed with Welsh dignitaries. He promised to deal with the dilemma posed to a Protestant people by compulsory Sunday drill. But no sooner was there some hope of closing that dispute than nature took its own revenge on the Welsh settlement. On Friday, 23 July the River Chubut, 'their ally for so many years',[30] as Holdich remarked, overflowed at

Dolavón, upstream from Gaimán. The following Monday the flood reached Gaimán. Rawson was deluged a little later while only Trelew, sited away from the river on higher ground, was spared. The scale of the flood was devastating. As the waters rose higher, farm after farm was destroyed. The governor's report to Buenos Aires on 28 July was full of foreboding. In the light of this disaster spats with the Welsh were put aside. Remarking that the provincial government had been reduced to functioning from a tent, O'Donnell wrote: 'In a few hours there has been destroyed in the Chubut valley the work of 34 years of perseverance and strenuous labour on the part of the Welsh who were its founders.'[31] The waters in the flooded valley remained for weeks. For more than a month most of the settlement was under water, and there was little to salvage when the flood receded.

The disaster of 1899 was followed by another deluge in July 1901. One natural disaster could be written off as a freak: two within such a short time could not. Though the second flood was less severe, its psychological effect on the colonists was worse. Many saw it as the last straw. They had endured the perils of the 1860s and 1870s only to enjoy a modest prosperity in the 1880s. The following decade had seen more economic progress but also a growing conflict with Buenos Aires. Then two devastating floods had pushed them back to square one. For hundreds of Welsh Patagonians the choice was not whether to leave but where to go. Initial talk of moving to South Africa came to nothing. Instead 243 colonists left Madryn on 14 May 1902 on the *Orissa* for Canada, where many found a home in Saskatchewan. The settlements they founded bore Welsh names but the Welsh language and culture did not survive there long. The whole aim of the emigration to Patagonia had been to escape the cultural and political influence of the British. Now a considerable number were moving back into the empire and the world of English-speakers. A small group left the valley for the River Negro, to the north, where their assimilation into the Spanish mainstream was also not delayed for long.

The Argentine authorities did not want the colony to die and offered money for reconstruction. For their part, the Welsh colonists offered the state of Argentina one last important service. In the 1860s their presence had secured central Patagonia for Argentina. One of the reasons why Fontana had enthusiastically backed a Welsh sortie to the west was because the Argentine frontier would travel westwards at the same time. The establishment of Cwm Hyfryd, a new Welsh community in the Andes foothills,[32] did just that. The two countries had competing claims to the area which, though it lay on the eastern side of the Andes, was closer to and better connected to Chile. The rival claims resulted in the matter being presented for British adjudication, which is why Edward VII sent Holdich in spring 1902 to survey the area and decide a border.

Holdich was welcomed into Trevelin under triumphal arches by a Welsh bard, who might just as well not have bothered, given Holdich's contemptuous reaction. 'His inspirations were as much lost on me as an Afghan ode that was once recited in my honour in the wilds of the Indian frontier,' he snorted.[33] The position of the Welsh so far to the west proved of huge benefit to the Argentine side, as Holdich called a referendum among the settlers who on 30 April 1902 unanimously decided in favour of remaining in Argentina. As a result the King-Emperor's verdict in November 1902 favoured Argentina's claims.

It was a strange outcome. The Welsh had little reason to feel gratitude to Argentina in the shape of governors Tello and O'Donnell. Relations had been marked by continuous wrangling as the Welsh defended their claim to autonomy and O'Donnell pursued an aggressive policy of assimilation. The Welsh vote in Cwm Hyfryd was not a vote of confidence in Argentina but a vote to remain in contact with their relatives in the Chubut valley. They preferred the Argentine devil they knew to the Chilean one they did not. In any case, the friction between the Chubut Welsh and the government did not concern the new settlement very much, as Holdich discovered when he visited the area. He remarked that they did not even know about the departure of several hundred Welsh colonists for Canada.[34] For all their satisfaction at the results of British adjudication, the Argentines were not eternally grateful to the Welsh, and the sniping against the Welsh resumed and intensified.

Lewis Jones died aged 69 on 24 November 1904 and was buried in the graveyard of the Moriah chapel near Trelew. Born near Caernarfon, he was the pillar of the whole experiment, far more so than Michael Jones of Bala who only visited the colony once in the early 1880s. The explorer of the Patagonian terrain with Jones-Parry in 1863, he had become the colony's first administrator, a key figure in the building of the railway in 1886 and head of the municipality of Trelew. In 1898 he had written his own account of the colony's history, entitled *A New Wales in South America*. In many senses Jones's death coincided with the dissolution of the new Wales in South America. The Welsh continued to go to Patagonia, especially from 1906 to 1913, but the title of Jones's book was increasingly anachronistic. Natural disasters, the hostility of the Argentine authorities and the contraction of the Welsh-speaking population at home combined to slow emigration to a trickle. At the same time, the process of integration into Argentina began to make itself felt. For the first half-century the Welsh had been left virtually alone in Patagonia apart from a handful of shopkeepers and officials surrounding the governor. In the last decade of the nineteenth century a flood of southern European immigrants overwhelmed them.

The change was felt at every level. The 1895 census recorded only 55 Spanish-speakers in Chubut. By 1914 that figure had jumped to 3,290. From 1905, Spanish-speaking newspapers began to appear to cater for a new market: *El Chubut, El Imparcial, El Patagonia* and in 1917, *El Pueblo*. By then the population of Chubut had soared and the Welsh found they were outnumbered by the newcomers. There were at least 23,000 inhabitants by then. The schools lost their Welsh character. From 1896 the law had insisted that schooling had to be in Spanish. The strange phenomenon arose of Welsh-speaking teachers teaching Welsh-speaking pupils in Spanish.

The self-confidence of the Welsh collapsed rapidly after that. At home in Wales the focus was moving fast away from Liberalism, disestablishment and defence of the Welsh language towards socialism and internationalism – movements that thought and expressed themselves in English. The Welsh colony, a rural world that revolved round chapel and farm, meant nothing to them and was forgotten. The colony celebrated its fiftieth anniversary that year with the opening of the St David's Hall in Trelew. But the celebrations failed to arrest the decay in Welsh confidence. Economic power in the Chubut valley was bound up with the fortunes of the co-operative society, which the Welsh set up in the 1870s, but after the First World War it was hit by a fall in the prices of wheat and alfalfa. By the end of the 1920s it was hopelessly in debt and near collapse. The blow to the farming community was enormous. Without the society they could not invest and agriculture went into decline. But the effects spread more widely. While the co-operative society survived, Welsh was the language of economic power in the Chubut valley. Without it the language was driven back into parlour and chapel.

The collapse in Welsh fortunes was accompanied by a rise in criticism in the Spanish-speaking media, which through the columns of newspapers such as *La Nación* pilloried the Welsh as an unpatriotic element. It complained of a colony in 1915 'to this day as foreign to the country as on the first day in which it was installed'.[35]

The Welsh clung on to municipal power in Gaimán and Trelew, where they continued to control the local councils, and they held the irrigation company. But they soon lost their grip on the expanding town of Trelew. From 1911, when Francisco Pecoraro took over as municipal president, few Welsh names appeared on the list of mayors, especially after John Howell

Jones's occupancy of the post from 1918 to 1922.[36] Even the stronghold of Gaimán was eventually overwhelmed. The military takeover of 1943 swept away all elected authorities in Argentina and the figures that now held the reins were invariably Spanish-speakers. Perónism was an even more authoritarian and homogenising force. The nationalisation of the irrigation company in the 1940s led to the dismissal of the old Welsh officials – the final blow to the edifice of Welsh power in what was clearly no longer a new Wales. Less than four decades after the death of the colony's founder, defender and patriarch, almost everything he had spent his life fighting for was dead. The Welsh had no love for Juan Perón or his charismatic wife, Eva Duarte. 'A horrible woman,' an old Welsh resident of Gaimán told me with a shiver. 'My mother had to wear a black armband when she died because she was a schoolteacher. In fact she despised Mrs Perón but she had no choice. The Perónists controlled everything.'

The Welsh community folded in on itself. The chapels were the last refuge. They were still full in the 1940s but attendance fell off in the 1950s as a result of intermarriage, secularisation and the rise of alternative entertainment. Elvey Macdonald recalled witnessing the change as a youngster. 'I noticed a marked decline in the fifties though there were still the odd occasions when it would be chock-a-block. Chapel was still something of a marriage agency, as you might meet families you wouldn't see again for the rest of the year. Couples still met that way.' But not for much longer, and by the 1960s services began to be held in Spanish – the start of a protracted debate over whether the chapels should cling to Welsh amid dwindling congregations, or abandon the language in the hope of attracting outsiders.

The *Gwladfa Gymreig* slumbered on through the military junta that took power after deposing Juan Perón. The wake-up call did not come from within, but from the newly invigorated Welsh in Wales, who were determined to mark the centenary of the *Mimosa* in style. 'It was so well organised and there was such enthusiasm that even the [Argentine] president came,' Macdonald recalled. The older generation in Gaimán and Trelew remember 1965 as their *annus mirabilis* when the host of Welsh-speaking visitors acted like an electric prod. The authorities were co-operative, agreeing to the erection of a number of monuments commemorating the role the Welsh colonists had played in claiming Patagonia for Argentina. The revival was not instantaneous. The military junta that followed a second experiment in Perónism in the 1970s did not encourage diversity of any sort and only after democracy returned in 1983 did the climate change for good. It was not until then that cultural diversity became fashionable rather than tolerable. 'Everyone wanted to forget everything that was oppressive,' Macdonald said. 'They went out of their way to show they were liberals. This was when the doors opened for the Welsh.'

Today the Welsh are only a small minority of the population of the Chubut valley. Trelew, a village of a thousand inhabitants a century ago, has ballooned into a small city of at least 100,000.[37] Tower blocks dwarf the single-storey architectural relics of the Welsh era. The Tabernacle chapel built in 1889 is still open, but although the minister is Welsh-speaking and Welsh-born she long ago crossed the cultural rubicon. Her services now alternate between Welsh and Spanish, as does the Sunday school. 'The new Welsh learners don't come to the services,' Mair Davies told me. 'It is disappointing because the chapel was the centre of language and culture.' But she was emphatic about her priority. Even if Welsh faded away, it was the Christian faith that mattered. 'Even if the language doesn't survive, the spiritual life must continue in the chapels. I don't want to curtail Welsh but we must encourage the Spanish youth in a way that is meaningful to them.'

In the streets of Trelew there are as many mestizo as European faces now. The town has attracted a large number of poor migrants from Bolivia and Paraguay and a dusty *favela* has sprung up on the road from Trelew to Gaimán. Here and there a recognisably Welsh face stands out in the crowd – the pale and sunburned features of the Celts contrasting with the olive-skinned majority. Though some people of Welsh descent have recently revived the culture of their ancestors, many more have slipped away. In a quiet street in Trelew I met the Edmunds family. Geraint was a Welsh Patagonian of the old type, as fluent in Welsh as Spanish, who had won prizes at the local eisteddfod for Welsh poetry. A beautifully made bardic chair sat in the front room, testimony to the esteem that his verses had won. But Welshness had reached a full stop in the Edmunds family with Geraint. His son, Eduardo, though he looked strikingly Welsh, did not know the language and shrugged when asked about it. 'I think I'd rather learn English – more useful,' he mused.

At the Patagonian Institute Professor Coronato had assured me that the Welsh had a future in Patagonia. 'It is not a dying culture, it's a fighting culture,' he said. 'There really is a revival of interest, a revival of pride in being Welsh.' But the language loses as many people as it gains as death clears away the last generation who grew up in a Welsh milieu. Though they are enthusiastic the learners come to the culture from a different standpoint. Latin and Argentinian to the core, they have no sentimental attachment to Wales. Moreover the future for the learners is uncertain. Welsh classes have flourished under teachers sent out from Wales under the joint patronage of the British Council and the new Welsh assembly. The presence of young teachers has galvanised local interest in Welsh from the late 1990s. Before then the language was identified with the elderly. But the prospects for the scheme remain hazy as the commitment of the Welsh assembly is half-hearted. There is talk of 'handing over' the classes to ill-prepared local teachers, which will almost certainly mean their decline.

The most hopeful signs are the change in attitude to things Welsh among those of Welsh descent, and the revolution in attitudes among Argentina's Spanish-speaking majority. The grandchildren of those who cried 'pan y manteca' now literally cannot get enough of just that. They flock to the Welsh tea houses whose elaborate surroundings and sumptuous array of cream cakes and home-made tarts are hardly the 'typical' Welsh produce their owners proclaim them to be. But it goes much further than a fashion for *torta Galesa*. Humbled by adversity and changed by the winds of democracy that have blown through Latin America since the 1980s the Argentines no longer despise the Welsh but show a heart-warming reverence towards their culture. In Trevelin I watched families from Buenos Aires moving respectfully round the local museum, gazing with admiration at an unexceptional collection of bric-à-brac that would hardly excite anyone in Britain. I joined one family, a bathroom-furniture saleswoman and her teenage son Luciano, touring a reconstructed Welsh mill called Nant Fach in the foothills of the Andes. The two *portenos*, mother and son, of Italian descent, were absorbed in a mission to encompass as many Welsh-related sites in the region as possible and they listened with ears cocked as the descendant of a Welsh farming family named Evans gave a guided tour of the mill and a demonstration of how Welsh settlers once ground wheat into flour. Señor Evans, a handsome, ruddy-faced man, gave the visitors a hearty *croeso* but that was as far as it went, for he, too, was a Spanish-speaker.

We returned to the waiting taxi, pausing to admire the breathtaking scenery of the snow-capped peaks in front of the mill. We drove back along unpaved roads back to Trevelin. The *portenos* wanted to try the local *Casa de Te Galesa*, a celebrated establishment whose fame had reached their Buenos Aires suburb of Belgrano. As they poured tea my new friends wanted to know if all Welsh people wore the 'national' costume they had seen on a poster in the Nant Fach mill. It showed a group of smiling women in a field holding sheaves of corn. I was stuck for an answer, not wanting to puncture their cherished illusion of a Wales in which all women wore tall black hats, worked in wooden mills beside streams, and ground their own corn. The Welsh Argentines had made their own Celtic land, half based on real memories of a way of life that existed decades ago and half pure invention. Like the Nova Scotia Highlanders they remembered what they wished to remember and had dispensed with the rest. In the corner of the tea house a tape belted out Welsh hymns. The male voice choir had a pitch and a timbre that instantly identified the singers to me as Welshmen. It was only as I listened more closely that I realised the songs were not being sung in Welsh or English, however, but in Spanish.

Conclusion

The Sea of Faith
Was once, too, at the full, and round earth's shore
Lay like the folds of a bright girdle furl'd.
But now I only hear
Its melancholy, long, withdrawing roar,
Retreating, to the breath
Of the night-wind

Matthew Arnold published 'Dover Beach' in 1867, the same year in which he delivered the last of his celebrated lectures in Oxford that did so much to shape the modern world's appreciation of Celtic culture. Arnold was not addressing the subject of the Celts in his poem but the irreversible decline of religious faith which he followed with mixed emotions. 'It expressed the sense, common in his time that the ancient supernatural world of gods and spirits which had surrounded mankind since the first dawn of consciousness was at last inexorably slipping away.'[1] Arnold was no reactionary. He did not want what had passed its time to return. He was a modern mid-Victorian whose honesty compelled him to observe that the tide of religion was going out, but whose sensitivity led him to confess to a powerful feeling of grief.

Arnold was writing about religion in 1867, but his words were just as apt when applied to his beloved Celts. Their culture once, to paraphrase Arnold, 'round Britain's shore lay like the folds of a bright girdle furl'd'. Journeying round that shore, around Brittany and two of the lands the Celts had settled in the New World, at the start of the twenty-first century, I could also only hear the sound of a long, withdrawing roar. The tide has gone out everywhere, if at different speeds. When Cornish disappeared in the late eighteenth century, Breton and Welsh were still impregnable, in spite of the challenges posed by the French Revolution and the industrial revolution. When Dolly Pentreath died, Manx remained secure in the grasp of the strange, Anglican semi-theocracy that then existed on the island. The arrival of mass tourism through the Isle of Man Steam Packet Company lay in the future. Irish was then spoken by well over half the population of Ireland. As for Gaelic, although subject to hostile attack from English-speaking schools, as Dr Johnson disapprovingly noted on his Scottish tour, it was still widely spoken north of the Highland line.

Language is not the sum total of a culture. Even after they stopped speaking their Celtic language the Cornish in the nineteenth and early twentieth centuries retained a culture that was quite separate from that of the English, even from that of their west-country English neighbours in Devon and Somerset. They kept up a distinct English, which had absorbed elements of the old language and a mass of other traditions, mannerisms, folk beliefs, memories, patterns of behaviour and religious impulses. None was maintained self-consciously. They were not Cornish nationalists. And yet, we may see the attraction of the Cornish to Methodism as part of a much wider Celtic phenomenon. The impulse to reject Anglicanism, which united the Cornish with the Catholic Irish, the Presbyterian Scots, the northern Irish and the Nonconformist Welsh, was more instinctive than intellectual. The descendants of the Scottish Gaels in Nova Scotia also kept alive a distinct culture after abandoning the Scottish Gaelic language – for the most part – in the early twentieth century. They wanted to maintain some kind of cultural continuity with their past not through language but through traditional musical instruments – pipes and fiddles. They have left behind their ancestors' verbal culture but they believe that they have kept alive the sound.

Language death is a complicated phenomenon, because, as some recent language experts put it, some languages die but 'go to heaven'. This means that their spirit and texture live on, having been transmitted into the languages that have supplanted them. Irish, Welsh and Cornish lived on in ghost form among many of the anglophones who did not know those older languages but whose English was certainly shaped by them. As T. S. Eliot put it, a people like the anglophone Irish, 'which has lost its language, may preserve enough of the structure, idiom, intonation and rhythm of its original tongue (vocabulary is of minor importance) for its speech and writing to have qualities not elsewhere found in the language of its adoption.'[2]

Many people see Ireland as a country that successfully solved the dilemma posed by abandoning the native language for English while at the same time maintaining a vigorous 'Celtic' identity. Its Celticness is assumed. Even the descendants of those parts of east and south-east Ireland that were settled over many centuries by medieval English peasant farmers have been subsumed into the Celtic whole.

But no one who looks hard at what is happening in the Irish Gaeltacht can feel confident that Ireland has, in fact, squared the circle. The media and the government propaganda machine relentlessly hail the supposed contrast between the self-confident Celtic phoenix of today and the drowsy, cowed Ireland of the 1930s and 1940s. But all they are really referring to is money. There is so much more of it around than there was, and as a result people are individually more independent than before. At the same time, early twenty-first-century Ireland is more integrated into the Anglo-American cultural mainstream than at any time in its history. In what is supposed to be a Celtic phoenix, the Celtic language continues to lose ground in its core area, the Gaeltacht, while the rich dialects in English that incorporated older inflexions are also waning – being flattened out by a metropolitan Dublin dialect that is imposing itself on the country through the broadcast media.

When I was in Ireland a thoughtful radio programme on the country's old speech patterns noted how centuries of trading had shaped regional varieties of Irish-English. The English spoken in County Wexford, for example, reflected traditional trading ties with Bristol in the west country of England. But these differences are disappearing. The influence of Bristol has become irrelevant compared to the combined influences of the Irish broadcaster RTE, the British TV stations that most Irish viewers can watch and the Hollywood American that the younger generation is relentlessly exposed to through cinema, television and popular music.

In Arnold's day the retreating tide had a majestic, orderly quality to it. Now it is faster, more hurried. The Irish bishops of the 1920s complained that an independent Ireland had turned out to be less independent than they expected. In their pastoral address from Maynooth in August 1927 they complained of a quiet invasion of dance halls, 'bad books', cinemas and 'immodest' fashions, which were combining 'to destroy the ancient characteristics of our race', and they concluded: 'One may well pray for the coming of a day when . . . true Celtic refinement will expel from our shores all these debasing fashions'.[3]

Their anger seems slightly comic now but their disappointment was understandable. When the first free Irish parliament met on 21 January 1919 and constituted itself as a 'Dáil Éireann', the renaming of institutions reflected the almost millenarian expectations of many people. The wave of religious and national euphoria that had accompanied the last phase of the independence struggle had combined to raise hopes of an entirely new start – of going back to the future. As one newspaper put it in May 1919: 'We assert that the National Person of Ireland is the Gael and that all belonging to the Irish state must be identified with and informed by the spirit of the Gael.'[4]

By the mid-1920s it was clear the new Celtic order was only a dream. The English language had not been abandoned but was increasing its grip. Free Ireland was becoming more English, not less. Some of the oldest Catholic bishops in the 1920s could remember boyhood spent in the 1860s, when the west of Ireland had been almost entirely Irish-speaking and cut off from the cultural blandishments across the water. It was a shock to them to observe the descendants of the peasant people they recalled in their youth talking English, not to mention the women cutting their hair into fashionable bobs, and everyone heading off to the cinema to watch American films.

But the pace of cultural breakdown that shocked the Irish bishops in the 1920s was nothing compared to developments that have occurred since. Economically, culturally, gastronomically, sexually, and in terms of fashion, Dublin, London and New York have practically converged. A great levelling of former distinctions has taken place. Sentimental patriotism and a disappearing accent are virtually all that now divide this homogenised society. Suddenly, the possession of a language is becoming the only barrier against total absorption into an identity that is no longer specifically English, or even American, but merely anglophone and 'white'. Eliot predicted this in the 1940s: 'For the transmission of a culture – a peculiar way of thinking, feeling and behaving – and for its maintenance, there is no safeguard more reliable than a language.'

The much-trumpeted Celtic revival lives off the accumulated cultural savings of the past. It presupposes the language's continuing existence somewhere, either in a gaeltacht, up some mountain, or in some other remote place. The existence of the language is the motor that has powered the music, poetry and art. What happens when Irish, or Welsh, or Breton or Scottish Gaelic can no longer retreat deeper, what happens when, as Nicholas Boson said of Cornish in the eighteenth century, the language has retreated to the point where it is perched 'about the cliff and sea' is hard to predict, but we will then inhabit a different landscape. For a change of language involves much more than a change of vocabulary. With its disappearance other elements vanish, too. The casualties include phrases and proverbs that provide a direct link to the past, facial gestures and body movements that accompany specific sounds and beliefs and messages that lie encoded in the structure of the words. Some may live on in the successor dialect for a while, but this is always a precarious existence, as the slow ironing out of English and Irish regional dialects has shown.

In *Spoken Here*, a study of disappearing languages all over the world, Mark Abley has described the changes that take place in a culture when the words change. Talking about Yiddish, he cites an email he received from Yonassan Gershom, a Hasidic rabbi in the American Midwest, concerning the correlation between the language and Hasidic spirit of life. In answer to his question about the importance of language to identity, the rabbi wrote:

> Yes, I think, Yiddish is important to Hasidic identity and yes, we would be less Hasidic if we lost the language. Hebrew is a harsher, more abrupt language. It does not have the same 'feel' as Yiddish. In fact it has long been my contention that if Yiddish, and not Hebrew, were the national language of Israel, the whole feel of the country would be different. The founders of Israel . . . wanted to go back to the more militant Biblical Hebrew of King David. In doing so, the softer, gentler, non-violent aspects of Jewishness were lost in Israel.[5]

This is a mind-stretching concept, for it proposes that a nation's cultural identity and political destiny, its whole character, in fact, might have been radically different if it had retained a different language from the one that its people now use. Such 'what-ifs' are impossible to test or prove. But Douglas Hyde, founder of the Gaelic League, would have recognised and agreed with the concept. Unlike Daniel O'Connell, he thought that the business of making Ireland English had involved a fundamental alteration and distortion of the Irish character, and that it was not only depriving the Irish of their identity but – ironically – making them more anglophobic than they had been. The author believes he was right on that point. Anyone travelling round Ireland will find least evidence of anglophobia among the Irish-speakers of the Gaeltacht who are secure enough in their culture not to need such props. The same comparison can be drawn in Scotland between the anglophone Lowlands and the Gaelic-speaking islands. There, too, high-octane, flag-waving nationalism is strongest among the most anglicised, urban section of society, while it appears almost irrelevant to the non-anglophone minority.

Europe needs living Celtic languages. Their disappearance has obviously impoverished the people who spoke them, as the barren cultural wasteland of South Wales – Iolo Morganwg's homeland – shows only too clearly. But their extinction also impoverishes the rest of the continent and the world, because a vital civilisation depends on contained, productive friction and diversity. Abley has described how the disappearance of Yiddish destroyed other aspects of Jewish culture. In Yiddish, he writes, certain adjectives were accompanied by a forward and downward thrust of the head, an opening of the palm of the hand, and a slight smile. 'The thrusting, opening, smiling and vibrating go along with a slow, falsetto pronunciation of the diminutive which serves to sweeten an insult or soften a criticism.'[7] So it is not just the *words* that have gone, but a mass of gestures, tones, sighs and groans – intricate patterns of human behaviour among the Jews of Europe that reflected and encoded generations of interaction between Jews and (usually hostile) European host societies.

Perhaps Cornish was not as rich and nuanced as Jewish. It may have had fewer of the attributes described above. But whatever it had will not return through a language revival. This is why the movements to bring back dead Celtic languages, like Cornish or Manx, as ordinary means of communication lack a point. So much of what was vital about these languages lies buried in the earth with the last native speakers. Not only do we not know *what* Dolly Pentreath said, because no one wrote it down, we do not know *how* she said it either. A revival, apart from diverting attention from the rich English dialects that those languages informed, can only bring back a mechanical repetition of written words divested of virtually everything that gave them life. No wonder that the recent films I saw in the Cornish language sounded rather like a conversation between a group of zombies.

There are other ways of protecting the identity of Cornwall and the Isle of Man that do not require this linguistic necromancy. It is different for the Bretons, Irish, Welsh and Scots. Their languages may yet avoid the rapid predicted extinction of about 90 per cent of the world's 6,000 or so surviving tongues. How they can survive it is still open to question. The local authorities in Connemara in Ireland appear to believe that legislation forbidding the purchase of property by anglophones is one answer. In Cornwall there are moves to impose higher taxes on owners of second homes. These are all bits of sticking plaster applied to a wound, not necessarily bad ideas but insufficient. The Celtic cultures that existed centuries ago must have been more optimistic than this. The Irish language that the Scoti brought to Scotland spread because it was a confident culture. The energy and the drive have only disappeared quite recently, and in Wales they did not fade until the early twentieth century.

Can this confidence be regained? Dissecting confidence is tricky – a bit like dissecting love – but a big element is hope. The Irish writer Nuala Ní Dhomhnaill expresses it. In her poem 'Ceist Na Teangan' (The language issue) reproduced in *An Leabhar Mòr – The Great Book of Gaelic*, she describes putting her hope 'on the water' in 'the little boat of the language' and then watching it float away,

> Not knowing where it might end up
> In the lap, perhaps,
> Of some Pharoah's daughter[8]

So, there needs to be an element of chance and uncertainty if these little boats are to be worth watching. The production of *The Great Book of Gaelic* was a sign of hope. From that gesture and from others like it, a new mood of confidence may just possibly emerge.

Notes

INTRODUCTION

1 S. Toulson, *The Celtic Alternative. A Reminder of the Christianity We Lost*, London and Melbourne, 1987, p. 57.

2 T. Davies, *The Celtic Heart*, London, 1997, p. 137.

3 P. Cherici, *Celtic Sexuality: Power, Paradigms and Passion*, London, 1995, p. 28.

4 J. Ussher, *The Religion Professed by the Ancient Irish*, London, 1631, p. 77.

5 M. Arnold, *On the Study of Celtic Literature*, London, 1867, p. 12.

6 Ibid.

7 Quoted in P. Pool, *The Death of Cornish 1600–1800*, Penzance, 1975, p. 12.

8 I. Bradley, *Celtic Christianity*, Edinburgh, 1999, p. 17, citing D. Binchy, 'A Pre-Christian Survival in Medieval Irish Hagiography', in D. Whitelock, R. McKitterick and D. Dumville (eds) *Ireland in Early Medieval Europe*, Cambridge, 1982, p. 166.

9 W. Reeves (ed.) *Life of Saint Columba, written by Adamnan*, Douglas, 1874.

10 Bradley, *Celtic Christianity*, p. 19.

11 Bede, *A History of the English Church and People*, ed. R. Latham, Harmondsworth, 1968, p. 40.

12 Nennius's *History of the Britons*, ed. J. Giles, in *Old English Chronicles*, London, 1908, pp. 408–9.

13 William of Newburgh, *The History of English Affairs*, ed. P. Walsh and M. Kennedy, Warminster, 1998, pp. 29–31.

14 L. Laing, *Celtic Britain: Britain before the Conquest*, London, 1981, p. 231.

15 R. Loomis, *Arthurian Literature in the Middle Ages*, Oxford, 1959, prologue.

16 J. Bale, *The Actes of the English Votaries*, London, 1560, p. 33.

17 Ussher, *Religion Professed by the Ancient Irish*, p. 95.

18 Caesar, *The Gallic War*, ed. C. Hammond, Oxford, 1996, p. 3.

19 Ibid.

20 Tacitus, *The Agricola* and *The Germania*, trans. by H. Mattingly, rev. by S. A. Handford, Harmondsworth, 1970 (1st edn 1948), p. 62.

21 G. Buchanan, *The History of Scotland, Translated from the Latin of George Buchanan*, Vol. I, Edinburgh, 1829, p. 99.

22 T. Habington, *The Epistle of Gildas, the Most Ancient British Author*, London, 1638, pp. 101–2.

23 H. Rowlands, *Mona Antiqua Restaurata: An Archaeological Discourse on the Antiquities Natural and Historical of the Isle of Anglesey, the Antient Seat of the British Druids*, Dublin, 1723, p. 35.

24 N. Chadwick, *The Celts*, London, 1971, p. 153.

25 Caesar, *Gallic War*, ed. Hammond, p. 96.

26 J. Spottiswoode, *History of the Church of Scotland*, I, Edinburgh, 1851, p. 4.

27 Rowlands, *Mona Antiqua Restaurata*, p. 78.

28 J. Toland, *A Critical History of the Celtic Religion and Learning, Containing an Account of the Druids . . .*, London, 1718 (?), p. 47.

29 M. Jolliffe, 'The Druidical Society of Anglesey 1772–1844', *Transactions of the Cymmrodorion, Session 1940*, London, 1941, p. 194.

30 J. G. Lockhart, *Memoirs of Sir Walter Scott*, I, London, 1900, pp. 411–12.

31 W. Lewis, *Horace Walpole's Correspondence*, IX, London, 1941, p. 407.

32 Charlotte Brooke, *Reliques of Irish Poetry*, ed. A. Seymour, Gainesville, 1970 (1st edn 1789), p. vii.

33 E. Snyder, *The Celtic Revival in English Literature, 1700–1800*, Cambridge, 1923, p. 195.

34 Arnold, *Celtic Literature*, p. vii.

35 Ibid., pp. 106–7.

36 Ibid., p. 115.

37 See L. C. Moulton, *Arthur O'Shaughnessy: His Life and Work*, London, 1894, p. 99.

38 P. Pearse, *Three Lectures on Gaelic Topics*, Dublin, 1922, p. 49.

39 M. Stoyle, *West Britons, Cornish Identities and the Early Modern British State*, Exeter, 2002, p. 24.

40 Ibid.

41 E. Morgan, *A Brief Memoir of the Life and Labours of the Revd Thomas Charles*, 2nd edn, London, 1831, p. 346.

42 [C. Anderson] *Ireland, but Still Without the Ministry of the Word in Her Own Native Language*, Edinburgh, 1835, p. 5.

43 J. Fishman (ed.) *Can Threatened Languages Be Saved?*, Clevedon and Toronto, 2001, p. 202.

44 D. Crystal, *Language Death*, Cambridge, 2000, p. 18.

45 D. Nettle and S. Romaine, *Vanishing Voices: The Extinction of the World's Languages*, Oxford, 2000, p. 5.

46 Lhuyd cited in W. Pryce, *Archaeologia Cornu-Britannica, Or An Essay to Preserve the Cornish Language*, Sherborne, 1790, preface.

CHAPTER ONE

The Scottish Highlands: 'The Auld Scottis toung'

1 Quoted in M. Todd, *The Culture of Protestantism in Early Modern Scotland*, New Haven and London, 2002, p. 185.

2 Ibid., pp. 402–3.

3 D. Mactavish (ed.) *Minutes of the Synod of Argyll 1639–1651* (Publications of the Scottish Historical Society, XXXVII), Edinburgh, 1943, p. 61.

4 W. Mackay (ed.) *Inverness and Dingwall Presbytery Records 1643–1688* (Publications of the Scottish Historical Society, XXIV), 1896, p. 268.

5 Ibid., p. 1.

6 Ibid., p. 280.

7 G. Macdermid, *The Religious and Ecclesiastical Life of the Northwest Highlands 1750–1843*, Aberdeen, 1967, p. 39.

8 S. Johnson, *A Journey to the Western Islands of Scotland*, London, 1984, p. 110.

9 Macdermid, *Ecclesiastical Life of the Northwest Highlands*, p. 186.

10 Mactavish, *Minutes of the Synod of Argyll*, p. 59.

11 W. Mackay, 'Life in the Highlands in Olden Times', in *The Old Highlands: Papers Read before the Gaelic Society of Glasgow, 1895 to 1906*, Glasgow, 1907, p. 114.

12 Ibid., p. 116.

13 Macdermid, *Ecclesiastical Life of the Northwest Highlands*, p. 206.

14 N. Douglas, *Journal of a Mission to Part of The Highlands of Scotland in Summer and Harvest 1797 by Appointment of the Relief Synod*, Edinburgh, 1799, p. 105.

15 D. Meek, 'The Reformation and Gaelic Culture: Perspectives on Patronage, Language and Literature in John Carswell's Translation of the *Book of Common Order*', in J. Kirk (ed.) *The Church in the Highlands*, Edinburgh, 1998, p. 40.

16 D. Maclean, *Life of the Revd Robert Kirk* (Transactions of the Gaelic Society of Inverness [*GSI*] 1922–1924), XXXI, Inverness, 1927, p. 347.

17 V. Durkacz, 'The Source of the Language Problem in Scottish Education 1688–1707', *Scottish Historical Review*, 57, Aberdeen, 1978, p. 32.

18 'Our Gaelic Bible', *The Celtic Magazine*, 4, Edinburgh, 1879, p. 43.

19 J. Mason, 'Scottish Charity Schools of the Eighteenth Century', *Scottish Historical Review*, 33, Edinburgh, 1954, p. 8.

20 J. Macinnes, *The Evangelical Movement in the Highlands of Scotland, 1688 to 1800*, Aberdeen, 1951, p. 244.

21 Johnson, *Journey to the Western Islands*, p. 73.

22 Macdermid, *Ecclesiastical Life of the Northwest Highlands*, p. 294.

23 *The Teaching of Gaelic in Highland Schools*, Liverpool, 1907, p. 5.

24 Macinnes, *The Evangelical Movement in the Highlands*, p. 126.

25 T. Brown, *Annals of the Disruption in 1843*, I, Edinburgh, 1877, p. 26.

26 W. Ewing (ed.) *Annals of the Free Church of Scotland 1843–1900*, I, Edinburgh, 1914, p. 5.

27 Brown, *Disruption*, I, p. 107.

28 *Speech Delivered by the Revd A. N. Somerville in the Free Church General Assembly on May 26 1887 in Connection with the Mission to the Highlands and Islands during the Year of his Moderatorship, 1886–87*, Glasgow, 1887, p. 6.

29 R. Connell, *St Kilda and the St Kildans*, London, 1887, p. 54.

30 Ibid., p. 160.

31 J. Hendry, 'The Man and His Work', in R. Ross and J. Hendry (eds) *Sorley Maclean, Critical Essays*, Edinburgh, 1986, p. 20.

32 J. L. Campbell, *The Book of Barra, Being Accounts of the Island of Barra in the Outer Hebrides Written by Various Authors*, London, 1936, p. 6, citing Bellesheim, *History of the Catholic Church in Scotland*, IV, p. 85.

33 O. Blundell, *The Catholic Highlands of Scotland, the Western Highlands and Islands*, London and Edinburgh, 1917, pp. 9–10.

34 Campbell, *Barra*, p. 14.

35 F. Thompson, *Harris Tweed: The Story of a Hebridean Industry*, Plymouth, 1969, p. 146.

36 Quoted in ibid., p. 47.

37 Raised beds of soil, built up to avoid waterlogging in the damp ground.

38 M. Powicke, *The Thirteenth Century 1216–1307*, Oxford, 1962 (1st edn 1953), p. 580.

39 Ibid., p. 576.

40 J. I. Campbell, *Gaelic in Scottish Education and Life, Past, Present and Future*, Edinburgh, 1945, p. 15.

41 E. Cowan, 'The Invention of Celtic Scotland', in E. Cowan and R. McDonald (eds) *Alba – Celtic Scotland in the Medieval Era*, East Linton, 2000, p. 6.

42 J. Spottiswoode, *History of the Church and State of Scotland*, I, Edinburgh, 1851, preface.

43 C. Withers, *Gaelic Scotland: The Transformation of a Culture Region*, London and New York, 1988, p. 5.

44 Ibid., p. 113, citing *Register of the Privy Council*, Edinburgh, 1891, X, pp. 671–2.

45 D. Defoe, *A Tour thru' the Whole Island of Great Britain, Divided into Circuits or Journeys*, London, 1752, IV, p. 241.

46 J. Maculloch, *The Highlands and Western Isles of Scotland in Letters to Sir Walter Scott*, London, 1824, IV, p. 186.

47 Ibid., p. 188.

48 Withers, *Gaelic Scotland*, p. 136.

49 Campbell, *Gaelic in Scottish Education*, p. 64.

50 D. Masson, *Church and Education in the Highlands, Transactions of the GSI, XVI, 1889–90*, Inverness, 1891, pp. 17–18.

51 Ibid., p. 21.

52 A. Farquarson, *Highlanders at Home and Abroad* (Transactions of the GSI, III and IV), Inverness, 1875, p. 16.

53 Somerville, *Speech to the Free Church General Assembly*, p. 16.

54 *Transactions of the Gaelic Society of Inverness, IX, 1879–80*, Inverness, 1881, p. 123.

55 'Statement by the Free Church', *British Parliamentary Papers, Report of the Royal Commission of Inquiry on the Condition of Crofters*, 32, Agriculture, Dublin 1969 (1st edn Edinburgh, 1884) p. 400.

56 Transactions of the GSI, XVI, 1889–90, Inverness, 1891, p. 1.

57 Ibid., pp. 6–7.

58 Transactions of the GSI, XXIV, 1899–1901, Inverness, 1904, p. 2.

59 S. Maclean, *The Poetry of the Clearances* (Transactions of the GSI, XXXVIII, 1937–41), Inverness, 1962, p. 319.

60 Campbell, *Barra*, p. 152.

61 Ibid., p. 187.

62 'Transactions of the Highland Society', *Edinburgh Review*, 4, Edinburgh, 1804, p. 75.

63 A. Mackenzie, *The History of the Highland Clearances, Containing a Reprint of Donald Macleod's 'Gloomy Memories of the Highlands'*, Inverness, 1883, p. 17.

64 R. J. Adam (ed.) *Patrick Sellar to the Lord Advocate, 24 May 1815*, Papers on Sutherland Estate Management (Scottish History Society, VIII), Edinburgh, 1972, pp. 176–84.

65 Ibid., p. 90.

66 Mackenzie, *Highland Clearances*, pp. 119–29.

67 Ibid., pp. 358–9.

68 D. Coghill, *The Elusive Gael*, Stirling, 1928, p. 32.

69 J. G. Lockhart, *Memoirs of Sir Walter Scott*, IV, London, 1900, p. 39.

70 A. Marr, *The Battle for Scotland*, London, 1992, pp. 26–7.

71 Queen Victoria, *More Leaves from the Journal of a Life in the Highlands from 1862 to 1882*, London, 1884, p. 255.

72 S. Gwynn, *The Life of Sir Walter Scott*, London, 1930, p. 73.

73 Ibid., p. 134.

74 Lockhart, *Scott*, I, p. 137.

75 Cowan, 'Invention of Celtic Scotland', p. 6.

76 J. Mackay, 'Sutherland Evictions and Burnings', *Celtic Magazine*, 9, Inverness, 1884, p. 63.

77 Ibid., p. 322.

78 E. Richards, 'Problems of the Cromartie Estate, 1851–3', *Scottish Historical Review*, 52, Aberdeen, 973, p. 160.

79 J. Hunter, 'The Gaelic Connection: The Highlands, Ireland and Nationalism, 1873–1922', *Scottish Historical Review*, 54, Aberdeen, 1975, p. 184.

80 See I. MacPhail, *The Skye Military Expedition of 1884–1885* (Transactions of the GSI, XLVIII), 1972–74, Inverness, 1976.

81 J. Hunter, 'The Politics of Highland Land Reform 1873–1895', *Scottish Historical Review*, 53, Aberdeen, 1974, p. 58.

82 J. Brand, *The National Movement in Scotland*, London, 1978, p. 184.

83 T. Devine, 'Irish Immigrants and Scottish Society in the Nineteenth and Twentieth Centuries', *Proceedings of the Scottish Historical Studies Seminar, University of Strathclyde, 1989/90*, Edinburgh, 1991, p. 24.

84 N. Ascherson, *Stone Voices: The Search for Scotland*, London, 2002, p. 286.

85 H. MacDiarmid, *Lucky Poet. A Study in Literature and Political Ideas Being the Autobiography of Hugh MacDiarmid*, Berkeley, 1972, p. 166.

86 Ibid., p. 26.

87 M. Chapman, *The Gaelic Vision in Scottish Culture*, London, 1979, p. 148.

88 A. Lang, 'Celtic Scotland in the War for Independence', *Scottish Historical Review*, 6, Glasgow, 1909, p. 326.

89 M. Fraser, 'Only 800 Infants in the Western Isles by 2016?', *Stornoway Gazette*, 2 October 2003, p. 1.

90 J. Keats, 'Touching Tongues', *Prospect Magazine*, October 2003.

91 R. Black, '20th-Century Scottish-Gaelic Poetry', in *An Leabhar Mor: The Great Book of Gaelic*, Edinburgh, 2002, p. 25.

CHAPTER TWO
Connemara: 'A vague reverence for the Gaelic'

1 C. Connolly, *Enemies of Promise*, London, 1979 (1st edn 1938), p. 173.

2 J. M. Synge, *The Aran Islands*, London, 1992 (1st edn 1907), p. 15.

3 E. Morgan, *A Brief Memoir of the Life and Labours of the Revd Thomas Charles*, London, 1831, p. 345.

4 Ibid., p. 352.

5 [C. Anderson], *Ireland, But Still without the Ministry of the Word in Her Own Native Language*, Edinburgh, 1835, p. 5.

6 D. M. Lloyd, 'The Irish Gaelic and the Welsh Printed Book', *Journal of the Welsh Bibliographical Society*, 6, July 1948, Carmarthen, p. 260.

7 J. Ussher, *The Religion Professed by the Ancient Irish*, London, 1631, p. 77.

8 D. Corkey, *The Hidden Ireland: A Study of Gaelic Munster in the Eighteenth Century*, Dublin, 1941, p. 91.

9 G. O Tuathaigh, 'Gaelic Ireland, Popular Politics and Daniel O'Connell', *Journal of the Galway Archaeological and Historical Society*, 1974–75, p. 23.

10 Ibid., p. 26.

11 Ibid., p. 23.

12 M. Legg, *Newspapers and Nationalism. The Irish Provincial Press 1850–1892*, Dublin, 1999, p. 155.

13 W. Wilde, *Irish Popular Superstitions*, Dublin, 1852, p. 15.

14 W. Wilde, *Ireland Past and Present. Lectures Delivered Before the Dublin YMCA*, Dublin, 1865, p. 222.

15 B. O'Conaire (ed.) *Douglas Hyde: Language Lore and Lyrics*, Dublin, 1986, p. 69.

16 Society for the Preservation of the Irish Language, *Annual Report 1886–7*, Dublin, 1887, p. 9.

17 Ibid., p. 10.

18 Society for the Preservation of the Irish Language, *Annual Report 1892*, Dublin, 1892, p. 1.

19 D. Daly, *The Young Douglas Hyde: The Dawn of the Irish Revolution and Renaissance 1874–1893*, Dublin, 1974, pp. 24–5.

20 D. Hyde, *The Last Three Centuries of Gaelic Literature. An Inaugural Address to the Irish Literary Society of London*, London, n.d., p. 38.

21 Daly, *Young Douglas Hyde*, p. 158.

22 O'Conaire (ed.) *Hyde*, p. 191.

23 P. Forde, *The Irish Language Movement* (read at Maynooth, 6 December 1899) (Gaelic League Pamphlet XXIX), National Library of Ireland, Dublin, p. 27.

24 J. O'Reilly, *Address to Maynooth Union, 21 June 1900* (Gaelic League Pamphlet XXIV), National Library of Ireland, Dublin, p. 4.

25 Synge, *Aran Islands*, p. 68.

26 A. Cleary, 'The Gaelic League', *Studies*, 8, 1919, p. 404.

27 R. Dudley Edwards, *Patrick Pearse: The Triumph of Failure*, London, 1977, p. 53.

28 P. Pearse, *Three Lectures on Gaelic Topics*, Dublin, 1922, pp. 45–53.

29 P. Pearse, *The Story of a Success, Being a Record of St Enda's College, September 1908 to Easter 1916*, Dublin and London, 1917, p. 69.

30 Ibid., p. 76.

31 Ibid., pp. 76–7.

32 Ibid., p. 98.

33 *Freeman's Journal*, 31 October 1918, p. 3.

34 *Freeman's Journal,* 14 December 1918, p. 3.

35 *Freeman's Journal*, 26 November 1918, p. 6.

36 *Catholic Bulletin*, November 1919, p. 231.

37 *Catholic Bulletin*, September 1920, p. 533.

38 A. de Blácam, *What Sinn Fein Stands For*, Dublin, 1921, p. 141.

39 Ibid., p. 234.

40 R. B. McDowell, *Crisis and Decline: The Fate of the Southern Unionists*, Dublin, 1997, pp. 166–7.

41 A. Cronin, *No Laughing Matter: The Life and Times of Flann O'Brien*, London, 1989, p. 134.

42 Ibid., p. 135.

43 Ibid., p. 58.

44 Ibid., p. 136.

45 Ibid., p. 135.

46 W. B. Yeats, *Memoirs. Autobiography. First Draft Journal*, ed. D. Donoghue, London, 1972.

47 Ibid., p. 120.

48 T. Brown, *W. B. Yeats*, Dublin, 1999, p. 300.

49 *Catholic Bulletin*, August 1926, p. 818.

50 H. Rope, 'The Ruin of the Gaeltacht', *Irish Monthly*, 60, 1932, p. 241.

51 *Church of Ireland Gazette*, 17 April 1931, p. 314.

52 M. Gibbons, 'The Gaeltacht Bilingual', *Irish Monthly*, 60, 1932, p. 687.

53 See M. Gibbons, 'Glimpses of the Gaeltacht', *Irish Monthly*, 59, 1931.

54 *Catholic Bulletin*, 1937.

55 P. O'Riagáin, 'The Galway Gaeltacht 1926–1981: A Sociolinguistic Study of Continuity and Change', in G. Moran and R. Gillespie (eds) *Galway History and Society*, Dublin, 1996, p. 678.

56 A. M. Thompson, *A Brief Account of the Change in Religious Opinion in Dingle and the West of Kerry*, London, 1846, pp. 104–5, cited in J. and R. Stagles, *The Blasket Islands: Next Parish America*, Dublin, 1998 (1st edn 1980), p. 99.

57 C. Moreton, *Hungry for Home: A Journey from the Edge of Ireland*, London, 2001, p. 21.

58 Ibid., p. 60.

CHAPTER THREE
Belfast: 'The liveliest Gaeltacht in Ireland'

1 J. Bardon, *A History of Ulster*, Belfast, 1992, p. 538.

2 A. de Blacam, 'Some Thoughts on Partition', *Studies*, 23, Dublin, 1934, p. 570.

3 J. Dunlop, *A Precarious Belonging: Presbyterians and the Conflict in Ireland*, Belfast, 1995, p. 3.

4 C. Hanna, *The Scotch-Irish*, I, London and New York, 1902, p. 549.

5 Ibid., I, p. 550.

6 A. Macaulay, *William Crolly, Archbishop of Armagh 1835–1849*, Dublin, 1994, p. 42.

7 Bardon, *ulster*, p. 422.

8 Ibid.

9 Ibid., p. 382.

10 See M. Rafford, 'Closely akin to Actual Warfare: The Belfast Riots of 1886 and the RIC', *History Ireland*, 7(4), 1999.

11 Bardon, *Ulster*, pp. 484–5.

12 P. Ó Snodaigh, *Hidden Ulster: The Other Hidden Ireland*, Dublin, 1973, p. 25.

13 Ibid., p. 28.

14 See G. Walker, 'Scotland and Ulster: Political Interactions since the Late Nineteenth Century', in J. Erskine and G. Lucy (eds) *Cultural Traditions in Northern Ireland*, Belfast, 1997, p. 94.

15 F. McCourt, *Angela's Ashes*, London, 1997, p. 102.

16 F. O Connor, *In Search of a State: Catholics in Northern Ireland*, Belfast, 1993, p. 240.

17 Ibid., p. 242.

18 B. Moore, *The Lonely Passion of Judith Hearne*, London 1994 (1st edn 1955), p. 99.

19 R. English, *Armed Struggle: The History of the IRA*, London, 2003, pp. 61–2.

20 Ibid., pp. 70.

21 Ibid., p. 126.

22 M. O'Doherty, 'We've Come a Long Way From the Old Austin Six', *Belfast Telegraph*, 9 June 2003, p. 12.

23 T. Hennessy, *A History of Northern Ireland 1920–1996*, London and Basingstoke, 1997, p. 240.

24 A. C. Hepburn, *A Past Apart: Studies in the History of Catholic Belfast, 1850–1950*, Belfast, 1996, p. 48.

CHAPTER FOUR
The Isle of Man: 'An iceberg floating into southern latitudes'

1 *Yn Pabyr Seyr*, 25, January 2002, p. 3.

2 S. Morrison, *Manx Fairy Tales*, London, 1911, p. 23.

3 W. Harrison (ed.) 'The Old Historians of the Isle of Man: Camden, Speed, Dugdale, Cox, Wilson, Willis, and Grose', *The Manx Society*, 18, Douglas, 1871, p. 7.

4 Harrison (ed.) 'Old Historians', p. 38.

5 Ibid., p. 99.

6 'Celtic Congress in Dublin', *Young Wales*, 7, 1901, p. 231.

7 B. Maddrell, 'The Sophia Morrison Circle', in 'Contextualising a Vocabulary of the Anglo-Manx Dialect: Developing Manx Identities', Unpublished Ph.D. thesis, University of Liverpool, 2001, p. 139.

8 M. Douglas, *This is Ellan Vannin: A Miscellany of Manx Life and Lore*, Douglas, 1965, p. 131.

9 Ibid.

10 Maddrell, 'Sophia Morrison', p. 160.

11 Ibid., p. 134.

12 A. Moore, Presidential Address, Manx Language Society – Yn Cheshaght Ghailckagh, 1899, displayed in Manx Museum, Douglas.

13 Maddrell, 'Sophia Morrison', p. 138.

14 Ibid., p. 150.

15 Harrison (ed.) 'Old Historians', p. 7.

16 Ibid., p. 106.

17 Ibid., p. 30.

18 Ibid., p. 18.

19 Ibid., p. 111.

20 J. Gelling, *A History of The Manx Church 1698–1911*, Douglas, 1998, p. 33.

21 W. Butler (ed.) *Memoirs of Mark Hildesley, Lord Bishop of Sodor and Man*, London, 1799, pp. 441–2.

22 Ibid., p 447, 3 February 1764.

23 Ibid., p. 500.

24 Gelling, *Manx Church*, p. 34.

25 Butler (ed.), *Memoirs of Mark Hildesley*, p. 599.

26 Ibid., p. 599.

27 Ibid., p. 600.

28 J. Feltham, *A Tour through the Island of Mann in 1797 and 1798*, London, 1798, p. 59.

29 M. Killip, *The Folklore of the Isle of Man*, London and Sydney, 1975, p. 181.

30 See A. S. Davis, *The Christmas Morn Carol Service of Celtic Countries: A Short Study of the Welsh Plygain, Manx Oi'e Verrey, and Cornish Carol Services*, Iver Heath, 1950.

31 F. Bazin, *Mona Douglas: A Tribute*, Douglas, 1998, p. 69.

32 G. Broderick, *Language Death in the Isle of Man: An Investigation into the Decline and Extinction of Manx Gaelic as a Community Language in the Isle of Man*, Tübingen, 1999, p. 20.

33 Ibid., p. 21.

34 Gilling, *Manx Church*, p. 53.

35 J. Shepherd, *The Life and Times of the Steam Packet*, Kilgetty, Pembrokeshire, 1994, p. 7.

36 Ibid., p. 12.

37 Ibid., p. 24.

38 Broderick, *Language Death*, p. 26.

39 Ibid., p. 38.

40 Gilling, *Manx Church*, p. 35.

41 Broderick, *Language Death*, p. 40.

42 H. Caine, *The Little Manx Nation*, London, 1891, p. 126.

43 Ibid., p. 156.

44 A. Herbert and D. Maxwell, *The Isle of Man*, London, 1909, p. 10.

45 Bazin, *Mona Douglas*, p. 2.

46 *The Collected Poems of T. E. Brown*, London, 1909, introduction.

CHAPTER FIVE
North Wales: 'The dear old language of the country'

1 W. J. Wallis-Jones, *The University College of Wales*, III, Wrexham, 1896, p. 290.
2 D. Davies, *The Ancient Celtic Church of Wales, Where Is It?*, Aberavon, 1907, p. 201.
3 *Young Wales*, I, Aberystwyth, 1895, p. 1.
4 Wallis-Jones, *University of Wales*, p. 290.
5 Ibid., University of Wales, p. 290.
6 *Young Wales*, I, Aberystwyth, 1895, p. 17.
7 L. Williams, *The Welsh Claim for Disestablishment*, London, 1911, p. 11.
8 Church Defence Association [CDA], *The Church in Wales: Five Important Speeches*, London, 1891, p. 5.
9 Ibid., p. 10.
10 K. O'Morgan, *Liberals, Nationalists and Mr Gladstone*, London, 1960, p. 39.
11 F. Owen, *Tempestuous Journey: Lloyd George, His Life and Times*, London, 1954, p. 59.
12 J. Birckbeck Morgan, *Pictures of Wales during the Tudor Period (Henry VII to Elizabeth, With Some Account of the Translation of the Bible into Welsh by Bishop Morgan)*, Liverpool, 1893, p. 26.
13 G. Curley, *Geoffrey of Monmouth*, New York, 1994, p. 50.
14 G. Williams (ed.) *Glamorgan County History*, III, *The Middle Ages*, Cardiff, 1971, p. 77, citing *Vita Edwardi Secundi*, p. 69.
15 W. Garman Jones, *Welsh Nationalism and Henry Tudor* (Transactions of the Honourable Society of Cymmrodorion, Session 1917–18), London, 1919, p. 25.
16 N. Williams, *The Life and Times of Henry VII*, London, 1973, p. 54.
17 Ibid., p. 13.
18 CDA, *Speeches*, p. 6.
19 Williams, *Glamorgan*, III, p. 160.
20 Ibid., p. 164.
21 E. William, *Upland Life in 16th Century Caernarvonshire, Ty Mawr*, National Trust, Llandysul, 1988, p. 42.
22 J. Evans, *Pictures of Wales during the Tudor Period . . . with Some Account of the Translation of the Bible into Welsh by Bishop Morgan*, Liverpool, 1893, pp. 62–3.
23 D. R. Thomas, *The Life and Work of Bishop Davies and William Salesbury*, Oswestry, 1902, p. 108.
24 J. G. Jones, 'Bishop William Morgan – Defender of Church and Faith', *Journal of Welsh Ecclesiastical History*, 5, Cardiff, 1988, p. 8.
25 C. Davies, 'The 1588 Translation of the Bible and the World of Renaissance Learning', *Ceredigion: Journal of Ceredigion Antiquarian Society*, 11, 1988–89, p. 3.
26 Ibid., p. 16.
27 I. James, 'The Welsh Language in the Sixteenth and Seventeenth Century', *Red Dragon*, 11, Cardiff, 1887, p. 432.
28 J. Southall, *Wales and Her Language*, London, 1892, p. 290.
29 G. Williams (ed.) *Glamorgan County History*, IV, *Early Modern History*, Cardiff, 1974, p. 261.
30 Ibid., p. 226.
31 T. Rees, *History of Protestant Nonconformity in Wales, from its Rise in 1633 to the Present Time*, London, 1883 (1st edn 1861), p. 9.
32 W. Williams, *Welsh Calvinistic Methodism. A Historical Sketch of the Presbyterian Church of Wales*, Bridgend, 1998 (1st edn 1872), p. 34.
33 Ibid., p. 35.

34 D. Jones, 'History of the Church in the County', in J. Lloyd (ed.) *A History of Carmarthenshire*, II, Cardigan, 1939, p. 118.

35 E. Saunders, *A View of the State of Religion in the Diocese of St David's about the Beginning of the 18th Century, With Some Account of the Causes of its Decay*, London, 1721, p. 36.

36 Ibid., p. 43.

37 J. Bulmer, *Memoirs of the Life and Religious Labours of Howell Harris, including an Authentic Account of the Calvinist Methodists in Wales*, Haverfordwest, 1824, p. 37.

38 D. Jenkins, *The Life of the Rev. Thomas Charles of Bala*, 3 vols, Denbigh, 1908, vol. 2, pp. 101–2.

39 Evans, *Pictures of Wales during the Tudor Period*, p. 67; see also E. Morgan, *A Brief Memoir of the Life and Labours of the Revd Thomas Charles of Bala*, London, 1831, p. 330.

40 T. M. Bassett, *The Welsh Baptists*, Swansea, 1977, p. 133.

41 Anon., *The History, Constitution, Rules of Discipline and Confession of Faith of the Calvinist Methodists of Wales*, London, 1827, p. 44.

42 P. Hood, *Christmas Evans: The Preacher of Wild Wales*, London, 1881, p. 17.

43 Rees, *Nonconformity in Wales*, p. 392.

44 Bassett, *Welsh Baptists*, p. 119.

45 G. Roberts (ed.) *Selected Trevecka Letters (1742–1747)*, Caernarvon, 1956, p. 66.

46 Williams, *Welsh Calvinistic Methodism*, p. 70.

47 Ibid., p. 125.

48 J. Owen (ed.) *Additional Letters of the Morrises of Anglesey (1735–1786)*, 49, Cymmrodorion, London, 1949, p. 238.

49 B. Thomas, 'A Cauldron of Rebirth: Population and the Welsh Language in the Nineteenth Century', *Welsh History Review*, 13, 1987, p. 424.

50 W. Jones, *Prize Essay on the Character of the Welsh as a Nation in the Present Age*, London, 1841, p. 67.

51 Anon., *The Welsh Looking-glass, Or Thoughts on the State of Religion in North Wales by a Person Who Travelled through that Country at the Close of the Year 1811*, London, 1812, p. 27.

52 Ibid., p. 41.

53 Ibid., p. 45.

54 J. Jones, *The History of Wales, Descriptive of the Government, Wars, Manners, Religion, Laws, Druids, Bards, Pedigrees and Language*, London, 1824, p. 143.

55 E. Roberts, *The Vitality of the Welsh Language*, Cardiff, 1886, p. 13.

56 Williams, *Welsh Calvinistic Methodism*, p. 228.

57 R. Jenkins, *The Welsh Renaissance, Vol. II: Wales*, Wrexham, 1895, p. 448.

58 Bassett, *Welsh Baptists*, p. 147.

59 Ibid., p. 308.

60 [D. Lloyd George], *Cymru Fydd, Or The National Movement in Wales, By A Celt*, Caernarvon, 1895, p. 52.

61 J. Davies, *A History of Wales*, London, 1993 (1st edn 1990), p. 454.

62 Owen, *Lloyd George*, p. 82.

63 J. C. Parkinson, *The Celtic Genius: Address Delivered at the Royal National Eisteddfod of Wales, Aberdare*, London, 1885, pp. 15–16.

64 R. W. Jenkins, *The Welsh Renaissance, Wales*, II, Wrexham, 1895, p. 553.

65 E. Fournier, 'The Pan-Celtic Idea', *Young Wales*, 5, Caernarvon, 1899, p. 1.

66 *Young Wales*, 1, Aberystwyth, 1895, p. 238.

67 Wallis-Jones, *University of Wales*, p. 290.

68 C. Betts, *Culture in Crisis: The Future of the Welsh Language*, Upton, 1976, p. 96.

69 Southall, *Wales and Her Language*, p. 58.

70 Ibid., p. 107.
71 G. Richards, 'The Early History of the Schools of Dyffryn Nantlle', *Cymdeithias Hanes Sir Caernarfon*, 24, 1963, p. 267.
72 Ibid., p. 270.
73 L. Williams, 'Free Church Debts and Free Church Progress in Wales', in *Wales*, I, London, 1911, p. 284.
74 Hood, *Christmas Evans*, p. 210.
75 Ibid., p. 98.
76 Ibid., p. 332.
77 *Welsh Outlook*, 10, Newtown, 1923, p. 146.
78 J. V. Morgan, *The Welsh Religious Revival, 1904–5, a Retrospect and a Criticism*, London, 1909, p. 144.
79 Ibid., p. 189.
80 Ibid., p. 250.
81 Davies, *Ancient Celtic Church of Wales*, p. 194.
82 [Lloyd George], *Cymru Fydd*, p. 8.
83 Williams, *Disestablishment*, p. 10.
84 Owen, *Lloyd George*, p. 153.
85 Davies, *History of Wales*, p. 454.
86 *Welsh Outlook*, 5, Cardiff, 1918, p. 227.
87 Owen, *Lloyd George*, p. 55.
88 *Welsh Outlook*, 5, Cardiff, 1918, p. 273.
89 Ibid., p. 43.
90 J. Morgan, *The Welsh Religious Revival, 1904–5. A Retrospect and a Criticism*, London, 1909, p. 255.
91 Ibid., p. 108.

CHAPTER SIX

South Wales: 'A rich culture, long departed'

1 A. Thwaite, *R. S. Thomas*, London, 1996, p. 64.
2 J. Rose, *The Intellectual Life of the British Working Classes*, New Haven and London, 2001, p. 237.
3 Ibid., pp. 239–40.
4 T. Lewis, *The History of Hen Dy Cwrdd Cefn Coed y Cymer*, Llandyssul, undated, p. 178.
5 G. Williams, *Iolo Morganwg*, Cardiff, 1956, p. 464, citing *Gentleman's Magazine*, 59(2), pp. 976–7.
6 E. Waring, *Recollections and Anecdotes of Edward Williams, the Bard of Glamorgan*, London, 1850, p. 35.
7 *Gentleman's Magazine for the Year 1792*, 62(2), London, 1792, p. 956.
8 R. Denning, 'Druidism in Pontypridd', *Glamorgan History*, I, Cowbridge, 1963, p. 139.
9 Waring, *Edward Williams*, p. 34.
10 E. Evans, *Some Specimens of the Poetry of the Antient Welsh Bards*, London, 1764, p. vii.
11 I. James, 'The Welsh Language in the Sixteenth and Seventeenth Centuries', *Red Dragon*, 11, Cardiff, 1887, p. 430.
12 I. Nicholas, *Iolo Morganwg, Bard of Liberty*, London, 1945, p. 48.
13 M. Fraser, 'Benjamin and Augusta Hall, 1831–6', *National Library of Wales Journal*, 14, 1965–6, p. 295.

14 R. Bromwich, 'The *Mabinogion* and Lady Charlotte Guest', *Transactions*, 1986, London, p. 136.

15 E. Roberts, *A Visit to the Ironworks and Environs of Merthyr Tydfil in 1852*, London, 1853, p. 44.

16 T. Clarke, *A Guide To Merthyr Tydfil, and the Traveller's Companion in Visiting the Iron Works*, Merthyr Tydfil, 1848, p. 14.

17 Ibid., p. 17.

18 Roberts, *A Visit to the Ironworks*, p. 14.

19 G. Williams, *The Merthyr Rising*, Cardiff, 1988, p. 37.

20 I. Jones, 'The Merthyr of Henry Richard', in G. Williams, I. Jones, K. Morgan and J. England (eds), *Merthyr Politics: The Making of a Working Class Tradition*, Cardiff, 1966, p. 38.

21 From the permanent exhibition in Cyfartha Castle.

22 J. Astle, *The Progress of Merthyr: A Diamond Jubilee Review*, Merthyr Tydfil, 1897, p. 119.

23 Roberts, *A Visit to the Ironworks*, p. 24.

24 Clarke, *A Guide to Merthyr Tydfil*, p. 45.

25 Williams, *Iolo Morganwg*, pp. 36–7.

26 Roberts, *A Visit to the Ironworks*, p. 45.

27 G. Williams, 'Earliest Non-Conformists in Merthyr Tydfil', *Merthyr Historian*, 1, 1976, p. 85.

28 E. Davies, *Religion in the Industrial Revolution in South Wales*, Cardiff, 1965, p. 26.

29 Ibid., p. 27.

30 See M. Llewelyn, 'A Brief History of the Welsh Language in Merthyr Tydfil', in *Merthyr Tydfil Then and Now*, Mountain Ash, 1979.

31 M. Williams, 'Observations on the Population Changes in Glamorgan, 1800–1900', *Glamorgan Historian*, 1, Cowbridge, 1963, p. 114.

32 E. Evans, *Mabon, William Abraham 1842–1922: A Study in Trade Union Leadership*, Cardiff, 1959, p. 2.

33 M. George, 'The Khaki Election of 1900. A Study of Three Towns: Portsmouth, Merthyr Tydfil and Wakefield', unpublished manuscript, Merthyr Tydfil Library, p. 63.

34 K. Hardie, *From Serfdom to Socialism*, London, 1907, p. 44.

35 C. Benn, *Keir Hardie*, London, 1992, p. 128.

36 K. O. Morgan, 'The Merthyr of Keir Hardie', in Williams et al. (eds), *Merthyr Politics*, p. 67.

37 Benn, *Hardie*, p. 108.

38 Election bulletin for circulation in the Merthyr Tydfil Constituency, Vol. I, No 3, 'A Last Word before the Poll', Kier Hardie Miscellany, Merthyr Tydfil Library.

39 See H. Edwards, 'The Merthyr National Eisteddfod of 1901', *Merthyr Historian*, 13, 2001,

40 Morgan, 'Merthyr of Keir Hardie', p. 71.

41 K. Hardie, *My Confession of Faith in the Labour Alliance*, London, 1909, p. 13.

42 Labour Representation, Merthyr Tydfil, parliamentary election, election songs (1906), Kier Hardie Miscellany, Merthyr Tydfil Library.

43 Election Bulletin for Circulation in the Merthyr Tydfil constituency, Vol. I (1910), Keir Hardie Miscellany, Merthyr Tydfil Library.

44 E. T. Davies, *Religion in the Industrial Revolution in South Wales*, Cardiff, 1965, p. 161.

45 C. Williams, *Democratic Rhondda: Politics and Society 1885–1951*, Cardiff, 1996, p. 115.

46 V. Bale, 'Wesleyan Methodists in Merthyr Tydfil 1790–1972', unpublished manuscript. Merthyr Tydfil Library, p. 120.

47 A. Horner, *Incorrigible Rebel*, London, 1960, p. 14; see also M. Casey and P. Ackers, 'The Enigma of the Young Arthur Horner: From Churches of Christ Preacher to Communist Militant (1894–1920)', *Labour History Review*, 66, 2001.

48 Williams, *Democratic Rhondda*, p. 160.

49 J. Campbell, *Nye Bevan and the Mirage of British Socialism*, London, 1987, p. 6.

50 C. Howard, 'Reactionary Radicalism: The Mid-Glamorgan By-Election March 1910', *Glamorgan Historian*, ed. S. Williams, 9, 1973, p. 38.

51 *Welsh Outlook*, 13, Newtown, 1926, p. 116.

52 *Welsh Outlook*, 20, Newtown, 1933, p. 331.

53 A. Jones and G. Thomas (eds) *Presenting Lewis Saunders*, Cardiff, 1973, p. 123.

54 S. Lewis, *Wales after the War*, Bala, 1945, pp. 17, 19.

55 Jones and Thomas (eds) *Presenting Lewis Saunders*, p. 48.

56 C. Betts, *Culture in Crisis: The Future of the Welsh Language*, Upton, 1976, p. 42.

57 Ibid., p. 57.

58 Anon., 'Saunders Lewis', *Welsh Review*, 5, Cardiff, 1946, p. 263.

59 Jones and Thomas (eds) *Presenting Saunders Lewis*, p. 139.

60 C. Williams, 'Non-Violence and the Development of the Welsh Language Society 1962–1974', *Welsh Historic Review*, 8, Cardiff, 1977, p. 450.

61 J. Aitchison and H. Carter, *A Geography of the Welsh Language 1961–1991*, Cardiff, 1994, p. 50.

62 Ibid.

63 Thwaite, *R. S. Thomas*, p. 64.

64 'Now What is Plaid For?', *Guardian*, 14 May 2003, p. 24.

65 B. Thomas, 'A Cauldron of Rebirth: Population and the Welsh Language in the Nineteenth Century', *Welsh Historic Review*, 13, 1987, p. 425.

66 Text of 28th Archdruid's address after his enthronement on 29 June 2001, *Cambria*, 5, Carmarthen, 2002, p. 18.

CHAPTER SEVEN

Cornwall: 'Almost an island'

1 M. Holloway, 'D. H. Lawrence in Cornwall', *Cornish Review*, Autumn 1949, p. 68.

2 John Heath-Stubbs, *Collected Poems, 1943–1987*, Manchester, 1988.

3 D. Baker, *Britain's Art Colony by the Sea*, Bristol, 2000 (1st edn 1959), p. 74.

4 See G. Doble, 'Saint Cadoc in Cornwall and Brittany', *Truro Diocesan Gazette*, 1937.

5 O. Padel, *A Popular Dictionary of Cornish Place Names*, Penzance, 1988, p. 61. The saint is also honoured at Berrin in Finistère.

6 C. R. John, *The Saints of Cornwall: 1,500 Years of Christian Landscape*, Padstow, 2001, p. 15.

7 See R. Morton Nance, 'When Was Cornish Last Spoken Traditionally?', *Journal of the Royal Institution of Cornwall*, 7, 1973, p. 78.

8 See P. Berresford Ellis, *The Cornish Language and its Literature*, London and Boston, 1974. For example: 'Karenze wheles karenze' – 'Love worketh love', the motto of the Polwhele family, and 'Kenz ol tra, Tonkin, ouna dev mahtern yn' – 'Above all things, Tonkin, for God and King', for the Tonkins of Trevauance.

9 D. du Maurier, *Vanishing Cornwall*, London, 1981, p. 118.

10 Mark Stoyle makes the point that whereas most previous disturbances in Cornwall centred on the far west, the 1549 rising started in Bodmin and moved east. However, as he goes on to say, the fact that the rebels rallied at Bodmin does not mean it did not

involve many from the west. See M. Stoyle, *West Britons: Cornish Identities and the Early Modern British State*, Exeter, 2002, pp. 23–4.

11 H. Jenner, 'The History and Literature of the Ancient Cornish Language', *Journal of the British Archaeological Association*, June 1887, p. 139.

12 Berresford Ellis, *Cornish Language*, p. 61.

13 M. Filbee, *Celtic Cornwall*, London, 1996, p. 102.

14 'Tour into Cornwall to the Land's End in Letters by James Forbes in 1794', *Journal of the Royal Institution of Cornwall*, 9, 1983, p. 168.

15 R. Morton Nance, 'Helston Furry Dance', *Journal of the Royal Institution of Cornwall*, 4, 1961, p. 38.

16 C. S. Gilbert, *An Historical Survey of the County of Cornwall*, I, London, 1817, p. 105.

17 Ibid., p. 106.

18 Ibid., pp. 109–10. The story enjoyed sufficient credibility to be repeated to Bishop Fowler of Gloucester in the 1690s.

19 A. L. Rowse, *A Cornish Childhood: Autobiography of a Cornishman*, Truro, 1998 (1st edn 1942), p. 7.

20 Ibid., p. 8. Mark Stoyle remarks that Rowse may be mistaken in saying the words had a Celtic origin, for they were used in England, too.

21 Ibid., p. 38.

22 Berresford Ellis, *Cornish Language*, p. 82.

23 W. T. Hoblyn, 'In English and not in Cornowek', *Old Cornwall*, Summer 1936, p. 11.

24 R. Carew, *The Survey of Cornwall*, Redruth, 2000 (1st edn London 1602), p. 64.

25 Ibid. As many observers have pointed out, it really means 'I do not wish to speak English', an error attributed to the fact that Carew was more familiar with the anglophone east of Cornwall than the west and thus knew relatively little about the language.

26 Ibid., p. 84.

27 P. A. S. Pool, *The Death of Cornish (1600–1800)*, Penzance, 1975, p. 9, citing Itinerary of John Ray, in *Memorials of John Ray*, 1846, p. 190.

28 Pool, *Death of Cornish*, p. 10.

29 Berresford Ellis suggests that Gwavas may have been responsible for the Cornish wording on the early-eighteenth-century tomb of Stephen Hutchins in Paul church, which runs: 'Bounas heb dueth eu poes karens wei/ Tha pobl bohedzak Paull han egles dei' (Life eternal is the reward of your kindness towards the poor folk of Paul and our church): see *Cornish Language*, p. 98.

30 Pool, *Death of Cornish*, p. 12.

31 R. Ellis, 'Some Incidents in the Life of Edward Lhuyd', *Transactions of the Honourable Society of Cymmrodorion*, Session 1906–7, London, 1908, p. 35.

32 Pool, *Death of Cornish*, p. 31, citing Pryce, *Archaeologia Cornu-Britannica, 1790*, p. 229.

33 P. A. S. Pool, 'William Borlase: The Scholar and the Man', *Journal of the Royal Institution of Cornwall*, 5, 1965, pp. 147–8.

34 Berresford Ellis, *Cornish Language*, p. 118.

35 Pool, *Death of Cornish*, p. 26.

36 Berresford Ellis, *Cornish Language*, p. 121.

37 Nance, 'When Was Cornish Last Spoken?', p. 78.

38 Ibid., p. 76.

39 For a summary of his contribution to Cornish nationalism, see R. Morton Nance, '"Gwas Myghal" and the Cornish Revival', *Old Cornwall*, Winter 1934.

40 H. Jenner, 'Traditional Relics of the Cornish Language in Mount's Bay in 1875', in *Philological Society Transactions*, London, 1875, p. 8.

41 W. S. Lach-Szyrma, 'Relics of the Old Cornish Language', *Journal of the British Archaeological Association*, 1906, p. 180.
42 R. Morton Nance, 'What We Stand For', *Old Cornwall*, 1925, p. 4.
43 E. Carpenter, *Cantuar: The Archbishops of Canterbury and their Office*, London, 1971, p. 360, citing A. C. Benson, *The Life of Edward White Benson*, 1900, II, p. 124.
44 D. MacCulloch, *Thomas Cranmer, A Life*, New Haven and London, 1996, p. 439. Even Cranmer's admiring biographer admits his hero's riposte to the Cornish revolt was 'unattractive in its shrill hostility'.
45 J. Pearce (ed.) *The Wesleys in Cornwall*, Truro, 1964, p. 12.
46 Ibid., p. 169.
47 'Tour into Cornwall . . . in 1794', p. 168.
48 Pearce (ed.) *The Wesleys in Cornwall*, p. 24.
49 T. Shaw, '*Saint Petroc and John Wesley: Apostles in Cornwall*, Cornish Methodist Historical Association, Truro 1962, p. 24.
50 C. Berry, 'Billy Bray: Miner, Evangelist', in A. L. Rowse (ed.) *A Cornish Anthology*, Penzance, 1990 (1st edn 1968), p. 91.
51 W. Wynne, 'A Visit to Cornwall in 1755', *Journal of the Royal Institution of Cornwall*, 8, 1981, p. 34.
52 H. Jenner, 'Cornwall: A Celtic Nation', *Celtic Review*, 1, 1904–5, London, Edinburgh and Dublin, p. 238.
53 Ibid.
54 P. A. S. Pool, *The Second Death of Cornish*, Redruth, 1995, p. 5.
55 Ibid., p. 6.
56 B. Deacon, 'Language Revival and Language Debate: Modernity and Post-modernity', *Cornish Studies*, 4, Exeter, 1996, p. 101.
57 Du Maurier, *Vanishing Cornwall*, p. 196.
58 I. Thomas, 'County or Country', *Cornish Review*, Summer 1949, p. 37.
59 Rowse, *Cornish Childhood*, p. 106.
60 Ibid., pp. 68–9.
61 Ekos Limited, Economic Consultants, *An Independent Academic Study of Cornish*, 2000, p. 45.
62 O. Malet, *Daphne Du Maurier: Letters from Menabilly. Portrait of a Friendship*, New York, 1972, p. 212.
63 Ibid., p. 225.
64 Baker, *Britain's Art Colony by the Sea*, p. 21.

CHAPTER EIGHT
Brittany: 'Plutôt comme une libération'

1 G. Oury (ed.) *Histoire religieuse de la Bretagne*, Chambray, 1980, p. 243.
2 The most substantial 'blue' zones lay around Vannes, Nantes and south of Rennes. See map of the *chouan* revolt in A. Chedeville, *Histoire de la Bretagne*, Rennes, 1997, p. 44.
3 J. Guiomar, *Le Bretonisme: les historiens bretons au XIXe siècle*, Mayenne, 1987, p. 29.
4 J. Castelain (ed.) *Pont-Aven – Gauguin, l'aventure*, Paris, 2003, p. 12.
5 *Bretagne, terre des peintres* (exhibition catalogue), Vannes, 2003, p. 11.
6 J. Euillard and R. Dantec, *Les Bretons dans la presse populaire illustrée*, Rennes, 2001, p. 15.
7 F. A. Dubois, *Voyage en Bretagne 1839*, Rennes, 2001, p. 114.
8 N. Richard and Y. Pallier, *Cent ans de tourisme en Bretagne, 1840–1940*, Rennes, 1996, p. 25.

9 Castelain (ed.) *Gauguin, l'aventure*, p. 24; see also C. Boyle-Turner, *Gauguin and the School of Pont-Aven*, London, 1986, p. 23.

10 D. Cooper, *Paul Gauguin: 45 lettres à Vincent, Théo and Jo Van Gogh*, Lausanne, 1983, p. 275.

11 Guiomar, *Le Bretonisme*, p. 166.

12 Richard and Pallier, *Tourisme en Bretagne*, p. 119.

13 For one account of the affray, see D. Sweetman, *Paul Gauguin, A Complete Life*, London, 1998, p. 390.

14 P. Helias, *The Horse of Pride: Life in a Breton Village*, New Haven, 1978, p. 104 (trans. from the French: *Le Cheval d'orgueil*, Paris, 1975).

15 Helias, *Horse of Pride*, p. 20.

16 Ibid., p. 315.

17 Ibid., p. 334.

18 F. Broudic, *Histoire de la langue bretonne*, Rennes, 1999, p. 28.

19 Ibid.

20 According to Theodore Zeldin, as a young man he was 'firm Ultramontane, a militant, it was even said, who would not hesitate to re-establish the Inquisition'. See T. Zeldin, *France 1848–1945: Politics and Anger*, Oxford, 1979, p. 320.

21 Ibid.

22 Oury, *Histoire religieuse de la Bretagne*, p. 359.

23 See D. Pierre, *Les Bretons et la Republique: la construction de l'identité bretonne sous la Troisième République*, Rennes, 2001.

24 J. M. Déguignet, *Mémoires d'un paysan bas-breton,* 1998, p. 108.

25 Ibid., pp. 428–9.

26 E. Pruvate, *Histoire de la Bretagne*, Toulouse, 1996, p. 491.

27 M. Duhamel, *La Question bretonnne dans son cadre européen*, Quimper, 1978 (1st edn 1929), p. 34.

28 Ibid., p. 34.

29 Ibid., Appendix, p. 155.

30 K. Hamon, *Les Nationalistes bretons sous l'occupation*, Kergleuz, 2001, p. 22.

31 J. Bothorel, *Un terroriste breton*, Paris, 2001, p. 48.

32 Hamon, *Les Nationalistes*, p. 228.

33 Bothorel, *Un terroriste breton*, p. 19.

34 Ibid., p. 13.

35 Ofis Ar Brezhoneg, *Un Avenir pour la langue bretonne? Rapport sur l'état de la langue bretonne*, Rennes, 2002, p. 16.

36 Ibid., p. 18.

37 Ibid., pp. 14, 17.

38 The Department of Finistère's policy on the language is set out in the Conseil Général du Finistère's handbook, *Langue bretonne*, in which it states strong support for the continued use of Breton and details the 2 million euros spent annually in the department on language projects.

39 J. Ardagh, *France in a New Century: Portrait of a Changing Society*, London, 2000 (1st edn 1999), p. 342.

40 H. Drysdale, *Mother Tongues: Travels through Tribal Europe*, London, 2001, p. 379.

41 R. Hirrien, 'Que vive la langue galloise!' and 'Les bretonnants attendent la relève, *Progrès-Courrier*, 15 March 2003, dossier.

42 Ofis Ar Brezhoneg, *Un avenir pour la langue bretonne*, p. 257.

CHAPTER NINE
Cape Breton: 'Truly highland in their ways'

1 J. Gibson, 'Traditional Piping in Nova Scotia', in C. Byrne, M. Harry and P. O'Siadhail (eds) *Proceedings of the Second North American Congress of Celtic Studies*, Halifax, 1989, p. 164.

2 Ibid., p. 163.

3 R. Gillis, *This Is Not the Mainland Either: A Bard's Tour of Cape Breton*, Halifax, 2000, p. 74.

4 K. Lamont, 'A Short Study of the History and Traditions of the Highland Scot in Nova Scotia', MA thesis, 1964, Angus MacDonald Library, St Francis Xavier University, Antigonish, p. 46, citing A. A. Johnston, *A History of the Catholic Church in Eastern Nova Scotia*, Antigonish, 1960, Vol. 1, p. 325.

5 See portraits, among others, of Dan R. MacDonald (1911–76), Johny 'MacVarish' MacDonald (*c.* 1832–1934), Johnny MacIsaac (*c.* 1867–1941), Dan MacLellan (1870–1946) and Duncan MacQuarrie (1884–1979) in A. MacGillivray, *The Cape Breton Fiddler*, Sydney, 1981.

6 D. Mackay, *Scotland Farewell. The People of the Hector*, Toronto, 1980, p. 103.

7 M. MacDonnell, *The Emigrant Experience: Songs of Highland Emigrants in North America*, Toronto, 1982, p. 23.

8 B. Kincaid, 'Scottish Immigration to Cape Breton 1758–1838', MA thesis, Dalhousie University, 1964, p. 23: copy in Angus MacDonald Library, St Francis Xavier University, Antigonish.

9 M. Adam, 'The Causes of the Highland Emigration of 1783–1803', *Scottish Historical Review*, 17, Glasgow, 1920, p. 86.

10 MacDonnell, *Songs of Highland Emigrants*.

11 M. Adam, 'The Highland Emigration of 1770', *Scottish Historical Review*, 16, Glasgow, 1919, p. 287.

12 Kincaid, 'Scottish Immigration', p. 69.

13 Ibid., p. 38.

14 Adam, 'The Highland Emigration of 1770', p. 283.

15 Mackay, *Scotland Farewell: The People of the Hector*, p. 64.

16 Kincaid, 'Scottish Immigration', p. 117.

17 R. Morgan, 'Orphan Outpost: Cape Breton Colony 1784–1820', MA thesis, University of Ottawa, 1972, p. 215: copy in Angus MacDonald Library, St Francis Xavier University, Antigonish.

18 Kincaid, 'Scottish Immigration', p. 119.

19 Ibid., p. 50, citing J. Martell, *Immigration to and from Nova Scotia*, Halifax, Public Archives of Nova Scotia, 1942, publication 6, p. 59.

20 D. Harvey, 'Scottish Immigration into Cape Breton', in *Cape Breton: Historical Essays*, Sydney, 1980, p. 36.

21 Ibid., p. 37.

22 MacDonnell, *Songs of Highland Emigrants*, pp. 64–6.

23 Ibid., p. 86.

24 Lamont, 'Highland Scot in Nova Scotia', p. 42.

25 Ibid., p. 43.

26 C. Dunn, *Highland Settler: A Portrait of the Scottish Gael in Cape Breton and Eastern Nova Scotia*, Wreck Cove, 1991, p. 21.

27 N. MacNeil, *The Highland Heart in Nova Scotia*, Toronto, 1958, p. 58.

28 L. Stanley, *The Well-Watered Garden: The Presbyterian Church in Cape Breton 1798–1860*, Sydney, 1983, p. 30.

29 S. Hornsby, *Nineteenth Century Cape Breton, A Historical Geography*, Montreal, 1992, p. 76.

30 Interview with Jim St Clair, Judique, Cape Breton, October 2002.

31 'The Editor in Canada', *Celtic Magazine*, 5, Inverness, 1880, p. 24.

32 Ibid., p. 107.

33 P. J. Mackenzie Campbell, 'The Highland Community on the Bras d'Or', typescript, Angus MacDonald Library, St Francis Xavier University, Antigonish, p. 39.

34 Ibid.

35 Ibid., p. 41.

36 Lamont, 'Highland Scot in Nova Scotia', p. 52.

37 Stanley, *Well-Watered Garden*, p. 122.

38 M. Morrison, 'Presbyterianism in Old Cape Breton', *Cape Breton's Magazine*, 42, Wreck Cove, 1986, p. 46.

39 Stanley, *Well-Watered Garden*, p. 125.

40 MacGillivray, *Cape Breton Fiddler*, p. 2.

41 Stanley, *Well-Watered Garden*, p. 15.

42 Ibid., p. 160.

43 R. Morgan, 'The Great Famine in Cape Breton, 1845–51', *Cape Breton's Magazine*, 58, Wreck Cove, 1991, p. 57.

44 Lamont, 'Highland Scot in Nova Scotia', p. 58.

45 Anon., *The Romantic Nova Scotia Highlands: Eileann Cheap Breathain*, St Ann's, 1944, p. 50.

46 J. Dembling, 'Joe Jimmy Alec Visits the Mod and Escapes Unscathed: The Nova Scotia Gaelic Revivals', MA thesis, St Mary's University, 1997, p. 52: copy in Beaton Institute, University College of Cape Breton.

47 Ibid., p. 57.

48 J. C. Kelly, 'A Sociographic Study of Gaelic in Cape Breton', MA thesis, Concordia University, Montreal, 1980, p. 73, citing *Cape Breton Post*, 5 May 1979, p. 6: copy in Angus MacDonald Library, St Francis Xavier University, Antigonish.

49 C. Sullivan, 'Forty Years of the Nova Scotia Highland Village Society', *Naidheachd a Chlachain*, Winter 2000, p. 12.

50 Ibid., p. 11.

51 'Interview with Vince MacLean', *Naidheachd a Chlachain*, Winter 2000, p. 14.

52 Interview with author, St Francis Xavier University, Antigonish, October 2002.

53 Dunn, *Scottish Gael in Cape Breton*, p. 126. J. Kelly, 'A Sociographic Study of Gaelic in Cape Breton', MA thesis, Concordia University, Montreal, 1980, p. 73: copy in Angus MacDonald Library.

54 'The Exodus, a Selection from Stephen Hornsby's New Book, *Nineteenth Century Cape Breton: A Historical Geography*', *Cape Breton's Magazine* 61, Wreck Cove, 1992, p. 80.

55 See Kelly, 'Sociographic Study of Gaelic in Cape Breton', p. 92.
   Asked how she is in Gaelic, she replies: 'You're a Scotchman I reckon/ I don't know your Gaelic/ Perhaps you're from Cape Breton/ And I guess you're a farmer.'

56 MacNeil, *Highland Heart in Nova Scotia*, p. 95.

57 Dunn, *Scottish Gael in Cape Breton*, p. 86.

58 C. W. Vernon, *Cape Breton at the Beginning of the Twentieth Century*, Toronto, 1903, p. 61.

59 Morrison, 'Presbyterianism in Old Cape Breton', p. 42.

60 'Gaelic Precenting on the North Shore', *Cape Breton's Magazine*, 27, Wreck Cove, 1980, p. 47.

61 Ibid., p. 45.

62 Stanley, *Well-Watered Garden*, p. 102.

63 Ibid., p. 103.

64 MacNeil, *Highland Heart in Nova Scotia*, p. 95.

65 H. MacNeil, 'Work and Language in a Cape Breton Gaelic Community', undated manuscript, p. 41: copy in Angus MacDonald Library, St Francis Xavier University, Antigonish.

66 Dembling, 'Joe Jimmy Alec', p. 22.

67 Lamont, 'Highland Scot in Nova Scotia', p. 154.

68 J. R. Hutchinson, 'The Future of Gaelic on Cape Breton', *Cape Breton's Magazine*, 1, Wreck Cove, 1972, p. 10.

69 Kelly, 'Sociographic Study of Gaelic in Cape Breton', p. 109.

70 'Province and Scottish Council Boosting Gaelic Culture', *Cape Breton Post*, 21 October 2002, B3.

71 Dembling, 'Joe Jimmy Alec', p. 69.

72 L. V. Cox, 'Gaelic and the Schools in Cape Breton', *Nova Scotia Historical Review*, 13, 1994, p. 34.

73 Ibid., p. 35.

CHAPTER TEN
Argentina: 'The surivival of our race'

1 N. Winter, *Argentina and her People of Today*, Boston, 1911, p. 260.

2 J. F. Fraser, *The Amazing Argentine: A New Land of Enterprise*, London and New York, 1914, p. 44.

3 Ibid., p. 27.

4 Sir T. Holdich, *The Countries of the King's Award*, London, 1904, p. 76.

5 Fraser, *Amazing Argentine*, pp. 190–1.

6 H. Pritchard, *Through the Heart of Patagonnia*, London, 1911, p. 33.

7 A. Conway (ed.) *The Welsh in America. Letters from the Immigrants*, Cardiff, 1961, p. 12.

8 P. G. Davies, 'Welsh Settlements in Minnesota: The Evidence of the Churches in the Blue Earth and Le Sueur Counties', *Welsh History Review*, 13, Cardiff, 1986, p. 149.

9 Conway, *Letters from Immigrants*, p. 135.

10 C. Taylor, 'Paddy's Run: A Welsh Community in Ohio', *Welsh History Review*, 11 Cardiff, 1983, p. 306.

11 D. Rock, *Authoritarian Argentina: The Nationalist Movement, its History and its Impact*, Berkeley, 1993, p. 28.

12 G. Pendle, 'The Welsh in Patagonia', *Wales*, 37, London, 1959, p. 14.

13 Ibid., p. 14.

14 G. Williams, *The Desert and the Dream: A Study of the Welsh Colonisation in Chubut, 1865–1915*, Cardiff, 1975, p. 36.

15 Information from the Museo Regional Pueblo de Luis, Trelew.

16 G. Williams, 'The Structure and Progress of Welsh Emigration to Patagonia', *Welsh History Review*, 8, 1976, Cardiff, p. 48.

17 Williams, *Desert and the Dream*, p. 54.

18 Ibid., p. 58.

19 W. Perkins, *Letters Concerning the Country of the Argentine Republic being Suitable for Emigrants and Capitalists to Settle in*, London, 1869, p. 18.

20 F. Latzina, *The Argentine Republic as a Field for European Emigration*, Buenos Aires, 1883, p. 9.

21 G. Williams, *The Welsh in Patagonia: The State and the Ethnic Community*, Cardiff, 1991, p. 57.

22 Ibid., p. 42.

23 K. Skinner, *Railway in the Desert*, Wolverhampton, 1984, p. 77.

24 K. Skinner, 'The Relationship between the Welsh Colonies in Chubut and the Argentine Government', Ph.D. thesis, University of Wales, 1976, p. 158.

25 Ibid., p. 72.

26 Ibid., p. 260.

27 Ibid., p. 276.

28 F. Torrome, *Emigration to the Argentine Republic – Its Advantages*, London, 1871, p. 24.

29 Holdich, *King's Award*, p. 69.

30 Ibid., p. 350.

31 Skinner, 'Welsh Colonies in Chubut' p. 314.

32 Named after the day in 1884 when Congress sanctioned the creation of national territories, see J. Fiori and G. Vera, *1902, El Protagonismo de los Colonos Galeses en la Frontera Argeninto–Chilena*, Trevelin, 2002, p. 55.

33 Holdich, *King's Award*, p. 344.

34 Ibid., p. 343.

35 Williams, *The Welsh in Patagonia*, p. 244.

36 Information from the Museo Regional Pueblo de Luis, Trelew.

37 Information from the Museo Regional Pueblo de Luis, Trelew.

CONCLUSION

1 D. Cupitt, *The Sea of Faith: Christianity in Change*, London, 1984, p. 22.

2 Eliot, *Definition of Culture*, p. 54.

3 Pastoral Address of the Archbishops and Bishops at plenary synod, Maynooth, 15 August 1927, *Irish Ecclesiastical Record*, 30 Dublin 1927, pp. 526–44.

4 *Catholic Bulletin*, 9 (May), Dublin, 1919, p. 231.

5 M. Abley, *Spoken Here: Travels among Threatened Languages*, London, 2004, p. 227.

6 Ibid., p. 212.

7 'Ceist Na Teangan', in *An Leabhar Mor – The Great Book of Gaelic*, Edinburgh, 2002, p. viii.

Bibliography

BOOKS

Abley, M., *Spoken Here: Travels Among Threatened Languages*, London, 2003

Adam, R. (ed.), *Papers on Sutherland Estate Management, 1802–1816*, Edinburgh, 1972

Adams, D., *Stage Welsh: Nation, Nationalism and Theatre; The Search for Cultural Identity*, Llandysul, 1996

Addis, J., *The Crawshay Dynasty: A Study in Industrial Organisation and Development, 1765–1867*, Cardiff, 1957

Airne, C. W., *The Story of the Isle of Man*, vol. 2, *1406 to Modern Times*, Douglas, 1964

Aitchison J., and H. Carter, *A Geography of the Welsh Language 1961–1991*, Cardiff, 1994

Alford, S., 'Knox, Cecil and the British Dimension of the Scottish Reformation', in *John Knox and the British Reformations*, ed. R. Mason, Aldershot, 1998

[Anderson, C.] *Ireland, but still Without the Ministry of the Word in her own Native Language*, Edinburgh, 1835

Arnold, M., *On the Study of Celtic Literature*, London, 1867

Ascherson, N., *Stone Voices: The Search for Scotland*, London, 2002

Astle, J., *The Progress of Merthyr: A 'Diamond Jubilee' Review, with synopsis of local information*, Merthyr Tydfil, [1897]

Baker, D. V., *Britain's Art Colony by the Sea* (1959), Bristol, 2000

Balcou, J. and Y. Le Gallo (eds), *Histoire littéraire et culturelle de la Bretagne*, Paris, 1987

Bale, J., *The Actes of English Votaryes*, London, 1560

Bardon, J., *A History of Ulster*, Belfast, 1997

Barrow, G., 'The Lost Gaidhealtachd of Medieval Scotland', *Gaelic and Scotland: Alba agus a'Ghaidhlig*, ed. W. Gillies, Edinburgh, 1989

Bassett, T., *The Welsh Baptists*, Swansea, 1977

Bazin, F., *Mona Douglas: A Tribute*, Douglas, 1998

Bede, *A History of the English Church and People*, ed. and trans. R. Latham, Harmondsworth, 1968

Behan, B., *Brendan Behan's Island: An Irish Sketch Book*, London, 1984

Bellesheim, A., *History of the Catholic Church of Scotland* . . . 4 Vols, trans. D. Blair, Edinburgh, 1887.

Benn, C., *Keir Hardie*, London, 1992

Betts, C., *Culture in Crisis: The Future of the Welsh Language*, Upton, 1976

Bliss, A., *Spoken English in Ireland, 1600–1740*, Dublin, 1979

Blundell, O., *The Catholic Highlands of Scotland: The Western Highlands and Islands*, London and Edinburgh, 1917

Bothorel, J., *Un terroriste breton*, Paris, 2001

Bradley, I., *Celtic Christianity: Making Myths and Chasing Dreams*, Edinburgh, 2001

Brand, J., *The National Movement in Scotland*, London, 1978

Broderick, G., *Language Death in the Isle of Man: An Investigation into the Decline and Extinction of Manx Gaelic as a Community Language in the Isle of Man*, Tübingen, 1999

Bromwich, R., *Matthew Arnold and Celtic Literature: A Retrospect, 1865–1965*, Oxford, 1965

Brooke, C., *Reliques of Irish Poetry* (1789), with the addition of *A Memoir of Miss Brooke* (1816), Gainesville, 1970

Brown, T., *An Account of the Isle of Man, its inhabitants, language, government, remarkable curiosities, the succession of its kings and bishops, down to the present time to which is added a Dissertation about the Mona of Caesar and. . .Tacitus; and an Account of the Antient Druids*, London, 1702

Brown, T., *Annals of the Disruption: consisting chiefly of extracts from the autograph narratives of Ministers who left the Scottish Establishment in 1843*, Edinburgh, 1877

Brown, T., *The Life of W. B. Yeats: A Critical Biography*, Dublin, 2001

Buchanan, G., *The History of Scotland: Translated from the Latin of George Buchanan*, ed. J. Aikman, 6 vols, Edinburgh, 1829

Buchanan, J., *The Lewis Land Struggle*, Stornoway, 1996

Bulmer, J., *Memoirs of the Life and Religious Labours of Howell Harris*, Haverfordwest, 1824

Buthlay, K., *Hugh Macdiarmid (C. M. Grieve)*, Edinburgh and London, 1964

Cahill, T., *How the Irish Saved Civilisation: The Untold Story of Ireland's Heroic Role from the Fall of Rome to the Rise of Medieval Europe*, New York, 1995

Caine, H., *The Little Manx Nation*, London, 1891

Campbell, J., *Gaelic in Scottish Education and Life: Past, Present and Future*, Edinburgh, 1945

Campbell, J. (ed.) *The Book of Barra: Being accounts of the island of Barra in the Outer Hebrides written by various authors . . .* London, 1936

Campbell, J. (ed.), *Highland Songs of the Forty-Five*, Edinburgh, 1984

Campbell, J., *Nye Bevan and the Mirage of British Socialism*, London, 1987

Carew, R., *The Survey of Cornwall* (1602), Redruth, 2000

Cawley, M., 'Trends in Population Settlement in County Galway, 1971–91', *Galway: History and Society; Interdisciplinary Essays on the History of an Irish County*, ed. P. Moran and R. Gillespie, Dublin, 1996

Cedeville, A., *Histoire de la Bretagne*, Rennes, 1997

Chadwick, N., *The Celts*, London, 1997

Chapman, M., *The Gaelic Vision in Scottish Culture*, London, 1979

Chapman, M., *The Celts: The Construction of a Myth*, London, 1992

Clarke, A., *The Celtic Twilight and the Nineties*, Oxford, 1969

Clarke, T., *A Guide to Merthyr-Tydfil, and the traveller's companion, in visiting the iron works. . .*, Merthyr-Tydfil, 1848

Coghill, D., *The Elusive Gael*, Stirling, 1928

Connell, R., *St. Kilda and the St. Kildians*, London and Glasgow, 1887

Connery, D., *The Irish*, London, 1968

Connolly, C., *Enemies of Promise* (1938), London, 1979

Conway, A. (ed.), *The Welsh in America: Letters from the Immigrants*, Cardiff, 1961

Cooper, D., *Paul Gauguin: 45 lettres à Vincent, Théo et Jo Van Gogh*, Lausanne, 1983

Corkery, D., *The Hidden Ireland: A Study of Gaelic Munster in the Eighteenth Century* (1925), Dublin, 1941

Coupland, R., *Welsh and Scottish Nationalism: A Study*, London, 1954

Cowan, E. and R. Mcdonald (eds), *Alba: Celtic Scotland in the Medieval Era*, East Linton, 2000

Cowan, I., *The Scottish Reformation, Church and Society in Sixteenth Century Scotland*, London, 1982

Cronin, A., *No Laughing Matter: The Life and Times of Flann O'Brien*, London, 1990

Curley, M., *Geoffrey of Monmouth*, New York and Oxford, 1994

The Cymric Language: Prize essays on the propriety of maintaining the Cymric language. . ., A subject competed for at the South Wales Chair Eisteddfod, 1879, Cardiff, [1879]

Daly, D., *The Young Douglas Hyde: The Dawn of the Irish Revolution and Renaissance, 1874–1893*, Dublin, 1974

David, D., *The Ancient Celtic Church of Wales: Where is it?*, Aberavon, 1910

Davies, A., *The Christmas Morn Carol Service of Celtic Countries: A Study of the Welsh Plygain, Manx Oie'l Verrey, and Cornish Carol Services*, Iver Heath, 1950

Davies, E. T., *Religion in the Industrial Revolution in South Wales*, Cardiff, 1965

Davies, J., *A History of Wales*, London, 1993

De Blácam, A., *What Sinn Fein stands for: The Irish Republican Movement; its History, Aims and Ideals, Examined as to their Significance to the World*, Dublin and London, 1921

Deane, S., *Celtic Revivals: Essays in Modern Irish Literature, 1880–1980*, London, 1985

Déguignet, J., *Mémoires d'un paysan bas-breton, . . .*, 1998

Delumeau, J. (ed.), *Histoire de la Bretagne*, Toulouse, 1969

Devine, T. M., *The Scottish Nation, 1700–2000*, London, 1999

Douglas, C. M., *This is Ellan Vannin: A Miscellany of Manx Life and Lore*, Douglas, [1965]

Douglas, N., *Journal of a mission to part of the Highlands of Scotland in summer and harvest 1797*, by appointment of the Relief Syno, Edinburgh, 1799

Drummond, A. and J. Bulloch, *The Church in Late Victorian Scotland, 1870–1900*, Edinburgh, 1978

Drysdale, H., *Mother Tongues: Travels Throughout Tribal Europe*, London, 2001

Du Maurier, D., *Vanishing Cornwall*, London, 1981

Du Maurier, D., *Letters from Menabilly: Portrait of a Friendship*, ed. O. Malet, New York, 1992

Dubois, F. A., *Voyage en Bretagne, 1839*, Rennes, 2001

Duhamel, M. and Y. Fouere, *La Question bretonne dans son cadre européen* (1929), Quimper, 1978

Dunn, C., *Highland Settler: A Portrait of the Scottish Gael in Cape Breton and Eastern Nova Scotia*, Wreck Cove, 1991

Durkacz, V., *The Decline of the Celtic Languages: A Study of Linguistic and Cultural Conflict in Scotland, Wales and Ireland from the Reformation to the Twentieth Century*, Edinburgh, 1983

Edwards, R. Dudley, *Patrick Pearse: The Triumph of Failure*, London, 1977

Eliot, T. S., *Notes Towards the Definition of Culture*, Glasgow, 1949

Elleray, R., *The Isle of Man: A Pictorial History*, Chichester, 1989

Ellis, P. Berresford, *The Creed of the Celtic Revolution*, London, 1969

Ellis, P. Berresford, *The Cornish Language and its Literature*, London and Boston, 1974

Ellis, P. Berresford, *The Celtic Dawn: A History of Pan Celticism*, London, 1993

English, R., *Armed Struggle: The History of the IRA*, London, 2003

Evans, E., *Some Specimens of the Poetry of the Antient Welsh Bards*, London, 1764

Evans, E. W., *Mabon: William Abraham, 1842–1922: A Study in Trade Union Leadership*, Cardiff, 1959

Evans, G., *Plaid Cymru and Wales*, Llandebie, [1950]

Evans, J. B., *Pictures of Wales during the Tudor period (Henry VIII to Elizabeth with some account of the translation of the Bible into Welsh by Bishop Morgan)*, Liverpool, 1893

Eveillard, J. and R. Dantec, *Les Bretons dans la presse populaire illustrée*, Rennes, 2001

Ewing, W. (ed.), *Annals of the Free Church of Scotland, 1843–1900*, 2 vols, Edinburgh, 1914

Falls, C., *The Birth of Ulster* (1936), London, 1996

Feltham, J., *A tour through the Island of Mann in 1797 and 1798, comprising sketches of its ancient and modern history, constitution, Laws, commerce agriculture, fishery*, Bath, 1798

Filbee, M., *Celtic Cornwall*, London, 1996

Fishman, J. (ed.), *Can Threatened Languages be Saved?: Reversing Language Shift, Revisited; A 21st Century Perspective*, Buffalo and Toronto, 2001

Fraser, J. F., *The Amazing Argentine: A New Land of Enterprise*, London and New York, 1914

Galloway, P., *The Cathedrals of Ireland*, Belfast, 1992

Gelling, J., *A History of the Manx Church, 1698–1911*, Douglas, 1998

Gilbert, C. S., *An Historical Survey of the County of Cornwall*, 2 vols., London, 1817

Gildas, *The Ruin of Britain, and Other Works*, ed. M. Winterbottom, London, 1978

Giles, J. A. (ed.), *Geoffrey of Monmouth's British History*, in *Old English Chronicles*, London, 1908

Gillis, R., *This is not the Mainland, Either: A Bard's Tour of Cape Breton*, Halifax, 2000

Guiomar, J.-Y., *Le bretonisme: Les historiens bretons au XIXe siècle*, [Rennes], 1987

Gwynn, S., *The Life of Sir Walter Scott*, London, 1930

Habington, T. (ed. and trans.), *The Epistle of Gildas: The Most Antient British Author*, London, 1638

Hanna, J., *Wales: A Land of Celts; Sketches of Land, People, and Religion*, Ohio, 1964

Hardie, K., *From Serfdom to Socialism*, London, 1907

Harford, J., *The Life of Thomas Burgess*, London, 1840

Harrison, W., *Illiam Dhone and the Manx Rebellion, 1651*, Douglas, 1877

Harrison, W., *An Account of the Diocese of the Sodor and Man and St. German's Cathedral. Also a Record of the Bishops of Sodor and Man*, Douglas, 1879

Harrison, W. (ed.), *The Old Historians of the Isle of Man: Camden, Speed, Dugdale, Cox, Wilson, Willis and Grose*, Douglas, 1871

Hearne, D., *The Rise of the Welsh Republic*, Talybont, 1975

Hélias, P., *The Horse of Pride: Life in a Breton Village*, New Haven and London, 1978 (*Le Cheval d'orgueil*, Paris, 1975)

Herbert, A. and D. Maxwell, *The Isle of Man*, London and New York, 1909

The history, constitution, rules of discipline and confession of faith of the Calvinist Methodists in Wales. Drawn up by their own Associated Ministers, London, 1827

Holdich, T., *The Countries of the King's Award*, London, 1904

Hood, P., *Christmas Evans: The Preacher of Wild Wales*, London, 1881

Hornsby, S., *Nineteenth-Century Cape Breton: A Historical Geography*, Montreal and London, 1992

Hyde, D., *A Literary History of Ireland: From Earliest Times to the Present Day*, London, 1899

Hyde, D., *Language, Lore and Lyrics: Essays and Lectures*, Dublin, 1986

Jenkins, R. and H. Ramage, *A History of the Honourable Society of Cymmrodorion and of the Gwyneddigion and Cymreigyddion 'Societies' 1751–1951*, London, 1951

Jenner, H., *A Handbook of the Cornish Language: Chiefly in its Latest Stages with some Account of its History and Literature*, London, 1904

John, C. R., *The Saints of Cornwall: 1500 Years of Christian Landscape*, Padstow, 2001

Johnson, S., *A Journey to the Western Isles of Scotland* (1st edn 1775), ed. P. Levi, London 1984.

Jones, A., *Welsh Chapels*, Stroud, 1996

Jones, A. and G. Thomas (eds), *Presenting Saunders Lewis*, Cardiff, 1973

Jones, E., *The Changing Distribution of the Celtic Languages in the British Isles*, London, 1967

[Jones, G.], *Welch Piety Continued, or a farther account of the Circulating Welch Charity Schools from Michaelmas 1747 to Michaelmas 1748*, London, 1749

Jones, J., *The History of Wales, descriptive of the government, wars, manners, religion, laws, druids, bards, pedigrees, and language*, London, [1824]

Jones, O., E. Williams and W. Pughe, *The Myvyrian Archaiology of Wales, collected out of ancient Manuscripts* (1801), Denbigh, 1870

Jones, R. B., *'A Lanterne to their Feete', Rembering Rhys Prichard, 1579–1644, Vicar of Llandovery*, Porthyrhyd, 1994

Jones, W., *Prize Essay on the Character of the Welsh as a Nation in the Present Age . . .*, London, 1841

Killip, M., *The Folklore of the Isle of Man*, London and Sydney, 1975

Kinvig, R., *The Isle of Man: A Social, Cultural and Political History* (1944), Liverpool, 1975

Laing, L. *Celtic Britain*, London, 1981

Latzina, F., *The Argentine Republic as a Field for European Emigration*, Buenos Aires, 1883

Lawson, B., *Harris in History and Legend*, Edinburgh, 2002

Lebesque, M., *Comment peut-on être breton?: Essai sur la démocratie française*, Paris, [1970]

Legg, M., *Newspapers and Nationalism: The Irish Provincial Press, 1850–1892*, Dublin, 1999

Lennon, C., *Richard Stanyhurst the Dubliner, 1547–1618: A Biography, with a Stanihurst Text, On Ireland's Past*, Dublin, 1981

Lewis, S., *Wales after the War*, Bala, [1945]

Lhuyd, E., *Archæologia Britannica, giving some account . . . of the languages, histories, and customs of the original inhabitants of Great Britain*, Oxford, 1707

Linklater, E., *The Lion and the Unicorn: What England has meant to Scotland*, London, 1935

Llewelyn, C. and H. Watkins, *Strangers in a Foreign Land: The Spanish Immigration to Dowlais*, Merthyr Tydfil, 2000

Llewelyn, M., 'A Brief History of the Welsh Language', in *Merthyr Tydfil: Then and Now*, ed. H. Williams, Mountain Ash, 1979

Llewelyn, T., *An Historical Account of the British and Welsh Versions of the Bible*, London, 1768

Llewelyn, T., *Historical and Critical Remarks on the British Tongue, and its Connection with Other Languages*, London, 1769

Lloyd, D. M., *Plaid Cymru and its Message*, Cardiff, 1949

Lockhart, J. G., *Memoirs of Sir Walter Scott*, 5 vols., London, 1900

Lomax, F. (ed. and trans.), *The Antiquities of Glastonbury, by William of Malmesbury*, London, [1908]

Loomis, R. (ed.), *Arthurian Literature in the Middle Ages*, Oxford, 1959

Lydon, J., *The Making of Ireland: From Ancient Times to the Present*, New York, 2001

MacCulloch, J., *The Highlands and Western Isles of Scotland . . . In six letters to Sir Walter Scott*, 4 vols, London, 1824

MacDonagh, O., *O'Connell: The Life of Daniel O'Connell, 1775–1847*, London, 1991

MacDonald, I., *Glasgow's Gaelic Churches: Highland Religion in an Urban Setting, 1690–1995*, Edinburgh, 1995

MacDonell, M., *The Emigrant Experience: Songs of Highland Emigrants in North America*, Toronto, 1982

MacFarlane, M., 'The Gaelic Language and the People who Speak It, in *The Old Highlands: being papers read before the Gaelic Society of Glasgow, 1895–1906*, ed. N. Munro, Glasgow, 1908

MacGillivray, A., *The Cape Breton Fiddler*, Sydney, 1981

MacInnes, J., *The Evangelical Movement in the Highlands of Scotland, 1688 to 1800*, Aberdeen, 1951

Mackay, R., *Scotland Farewell: The People of the Hector*, Toronto, 1980

MacKay, W. (ed.), *Records of the Presbyteries of Inverness and Dingwall, 1643–1688*, Edinburgh, 1896

Mackay, W. and H. C. Boyd (eds.), *Records of Inverness*, Aberdeen, 1911

Mackenzie, A., *The History of the Highland clearances, containing a reprint of Donald Macleod's 'Gloomy Memories of the Highlands. . .'* Edinburgh, 1883

Mackie, C., *Historical account of the highlands and islands of Scotland, and of the Society in Scotland for propagating Christian Knowledge incorporated by royal charter 1709. . .*, London, 1885

MacLaren, M., *The Scots*, Harmondsworth, 1951

MacLean, S., *Ris a'bhruthaich: Criticism and Prose Writings of Sorley Maclean*, ed. W. Gillies, Acair, 1985

MacNeil, N., *The Highland Heart in Nova Scotia*, Toronto, 1958

Mactavish, D. (ed.), *Minutes of the Synod of Argyll, 1639–1651*, Edinburgh, 1943

Marr, A., *The Battle for Scotland*, London, 1992

Martin, M., *A Description of the Western Isles of Scotland, circa 1695. . .* (1703), Edinburgh, 1999

McAllister, L., *Plaid Cymru: The Emergence of a Political Party*, Bridgend, 2001

McDonald, M., *We are not French!: Language, Culture and Identity in Brittany*, London and New York, 1989

Meek, D., 'The Reformation and Gaelic Culture: Perspectives on Patronage, Language and Literature in John Carswell's Translation of the Book of Common Order', in *The Church in the Highlands*, ed. J. Kirk, Edinburgh, 1998

Meek, D., *The Quest for Celtic Christianity*, Edinburgh, 2000

Moreton, C., *Hungry for Home: Leaving the Blaskets; A Journey from the Edge of Ireland*, London, 2000

Morgan, E., *A Brief Memoir of the Life and Labours of the Rev. Thomas Charles*, London, 1831

Morgan, J., *The Welsh Religious Revival of 1904–5: A Retrospect and a Criticism*, London, 1909

Morris, L., *The Celtic Dawn: A Survey of the Renaissance in Ireland, 1889–1916*, New York, 1917

Morrison, S., *Manx Fairy Tales*, London, 1911

Moulton, L., *Arthur O'Shaughnessy: His Life and his Work with Selections from his Poems*, London, 1894

Nettle, D. and S. Romaine, *Vanishing Voices: The Extinction of the World's Languages*, Oxford, 2000

Newburgh, William of, *The History of English Affairs*, ed. and trans. P. Walsh and M. Kennedy, Warminster, 1988

Nicholas, I., *Iolo Morganwg: Bard of Liberty*, London, 1945

Ó Buachalla, S. (ed.), *The Letters of P. H. Pearse*, New Jersey, 1980

Ó Tuama, S. (ed.), *The Gaelic League Idea*, Naas, 1972

Oury, G. M. (ed.), *Histoire religieuse de la Bretagne*, Chambray-les-Tours, 1980

Owen, G. D., *Crisis in Chubut: A Chapter in the History of the Welsh Colony in Patagonia*, Swansea, 1977

Owen, H. (ed.), *Additional Letters of the Morrises of Anglesey, 1735–1786*, vol. 49 of *Transactions of the Cymmrodorion*, London 1947

Padel, O., *A Popular Dictionary of Cornish Place-Names*, Penzance, 1988

Parry, C., *The Radical Tradition in Welsh Politics: A Survey of Liberal and Labour Politics in Gwynedd, 1900–1920*, [Hull], 1970

Pearce, J. (ed.) *The Wesleys in Cornwall*, Truro, 1964

Pearse, P., *The Story of a Success . . . being a record of St. Enda's College, September, 1908, to Easter, 1916*, Dublin and London, 1917

Pearse, P., *Three Lectures on Gaelic Topics*, Dublin, 1922

[Perkins, W.], *Letters concerning the Country of the Argentine Republic, South America, being suitable for emigrants and capitalists to settle in*, London, 1869

Pierre, D., *Les Bretons et la République: La construction de l'identité bretonne sous la Troisième République*, Rennes, 2001

[Pitcairn, T. (ed.)], *Acts of the General Assembly of the Church of Scotland, 1638–1842. Reprinted from the original edition under the superintendence of The Church Law Society*, Edinburgh, 1843

Ploneis, J., *La Toponymie celtique: L'origine des noms de lieux en Bretagne*, Paris, 1989

Pool, P. A. S., *The Death of Cornish, 1600–1800*, Penzance, 1975

Pool, P. A. S., *The Second Death of Cornish*, Trewolsta, 1995

Prebble, J., *The Highland Clearances*, Harmondsworth, 1976

Prebble, J., *The King's Jaunt: George IV in Scotland, August 1822*, London, 1988

Price, D. T., *A History of the Church in Wales in the Twentieth Century*, Lampeter, 1990

Prichard, H., *Through the Heart of Patagonia*, London, 1911

Pryce, W., *Archæologia Cornu-Britannica, or an essay to preserve the ancient Cornish Language. . .*, Sherborne, 1790

Radcliffe, W., *Ellan Vannin: Sketches of the History, the People, the Language, and Scenery of the Isle of Man*, London, 1895

Rae, J. (ed.), *The Ministers of Glasgow and their Churches*, Glasgow, [*c.* 1900]

Rafferty, O., *Catholicism in Ulster, 1603–1983*, London, 1994

Rees, D., *Chapels in the Valley: A Study in the Sociology of Welsh Nonconformity*, Upton, 1975

Rees, T., *History of Protestant Nonconformity in Wales, from its rise in 1633 to present times* (1861), London, 1883

Reeves, W. (ed.), *Life of Saint Columba, Written by Adamnan* (1874), Lampeter 1988

Reid, W. S., *Trumpeter of God: A Biography of John Knox*, New York, [1974]

Richard, N. and Y. Pallier, *Cent ans de tourisme en Bretagne, 1840–1940*, Rennes, 1996

Richter, M., *Ireland and her Neighbours in the Seventh Century*, Dublin, 1999

Roberts, E., *A Visit to the Iron Works and Environs of Merthyr-Tydfil, in 1852*, London, 1853

Rock, D., *Authoritarian Argentina: The Nationalist Movement, its History and its Impact*, Berkeley, 1993

Ross, R. and J. Hendry (eds), *Sorley Maclean: Critical Essays*, Edinburgh, 1986

Rowlands, H., *Mona Antiqua Restaurata, an Archæological discourse on the antiquities, natural and historical, of the Isle of Anglesey the antient seat of the British druids*, Dublin, 1723

Rowse, A. L., *A Cornish Childhood: Autobiography of a Cornishman* (1942), Truro 1998

Rowse, A. L., *A Cornish Anthology* (1968), Penzance, 1990

Saunders, E., *A View of the State of Religion in the Diocese of St. David's about the beginning of the 18th century, with some account of the causes of its decay . . .*, London, 1721

Scott, P., *Towards Independence: Essays on Scotland*, Edinburgh, 1991

[Scott, W.], *A letter to the editor of the Edinburgh weekly Journal from Malachi Malagrowther on the proposed change of currency and other late alterations as they affect or are intended to affect the kingdom of Scotland*, Edinburgh, 1826

Sheehy, J., *The Rediscovery of Ireland's Past: The Celtic Revival, 1830–1930*, London, 1980

Shepherd, J., *The Life and Times of the Steam Packet*, Kilgetty, 1994

Skinner, K., *Railway in the Desert: The Story of the Building of the Chubut Railway and the Life of its Constructor Engineer E. J. Williams*, Wolverhampton, 1984

Smith, A. S. D., *The Story of the Cornish Language: Its Extinction and Revival*, Camborne, 1947

Snyder, E., *The Celtic Revival in English Literature, 1700–1800*, Cambridge, Mass., 1923

Southall, J., *Wales and her Language*, London and Newport, [1892]

Stagles, J. and R. Stagles, *The Blasket Islands: Next Parish America*, Dublin, 1998

Stanley, L., *The Well-Watered Garden: The Presbyterian Church in Cape Breton, 1798–1860*, Sydney (Nova Scotia), 1983

Stephens, M., *Linguistic Minorities in Western Europe*, Llandysul, 1976

Stewart, R., *The Church of Scotland from the time of Queen Margaret to the Reformation . . .*, London and Paisley, 1892

Stoyle, M., *West Britons, Cornish Identities and the Early Modern British State*, Exeter, 2002

Sweetman, D., *Paul Gauguin: A Complete Life*, London, 1995

Synge, J. M., *The Aran Islands* (1907), London, 1992

The Teaching of Gaelic in Highland Schools, Liverpool and London, 1907

Thomas, D. R., *The Life and Work of Bishop Davies and William Salesbury* . . ., Oswestry, 1902

Thwaite, A. (ed.), *R. S. Thomas*, London, 1996

Todd, M., *The Culture of Protestantism in Early Modern Scotland*, New Haven and London, 2002

Torromé, F., *Emigration to the Argentine Republic: Its advantages*, London, 1871

Trevor-Roper, H., 'The Invention of Tradition: The Highland Tradition of Scotland', in *The Invention of Tradition*, ed. E. Hobsbawm and T. Ranger, Cambridge, 1983

Usher, J., *A Discourse of the Religion Anciently Professed by the Irish and British*, London, 1631

Vernon, C., *Cape Breton, Canada, at the Beginning of the Twentieth Century: A Treatise on Natural Resources and Development*, Toronto, 1903

Villiers, K., *History of Clifden, 1810–1860*, Tuthill, 1981

Waring, E., *Recollections and Anecdotes of E. Williams, the Bard of Glamorgan*, London, 1850

Watkins, C., *The History of Merthyr Tydfil*, Merthyr Tydfil, 1867

The Welsh Looking Glass, or thoughts on the state of religion in North Wales. By a person who travelled through that country at the close of the year 1811, London, 1812

Wilde, W., *Irish Popular Superstitions*, Dublin, 1852

Williams, C., *Democratic Rhondda: Politics and Society, 1885–1951*, Cardiff, 1996

Williams, G., *The Desert and the Dream: A Study of Welsh Colonisation in Chubut 1865–1915*, Cardiff, 1975

Williams, G., *The Merthyr Rising*, Cardiff, 1988

Williams, G., *The Welsh in Patagonia: The State and the Ethnic Community*, Cardiff, 1991

Williams, G., *The Welsh and their Religion*, Cardiff, 1991

Williams, G., I. Jones, K. Morgan and J. England (eds), *Merthyr Politics: The Making of a Working-Class Tradition*, Cardiff, 1966

Williams, G. J., *Iolo Morganwg*, Cardiff, 1956

Williams, N., *The Life and Times of Henry VII*, London, [1973]

Williams, W., *Welsh Calvinistic Methodism: A Historical Sketch of the Presbyterian Church of Wales* (1872), Swansea 1998

Winter, N., *Argentina and her People of Today* . . ., Boston, 1911

Withers, C., *Gaelic Scotland: The Transformation of a Culture Region*, London and New York, 1988

Yeats, W. B., *The Secret Rose,* Dublin, 1905

Yeats, W. B. *Memoirs [of] W. B. Yeats: Autobiography [and] First Draft Journal*, ed. D. Donoghue, London, 1972

ARTICLES

Aaron, R., 'The Struggle for the Welsh Language: Some Pre-Census Reflections', *Transactions of the Honourable Society of Cymmrodorion*, Session 1969 (1970)

Adam, M., 'The Highland Emigration of 1770', *Scottish Historical Review* 16 (1919)

Adam, M., 'The Causes of the Highland Emigration of 1783–1803', *Scottish Historical Review* 17 (1920)

Airey, R., 'Feltham's Tour Through the Isle of Man in 1797 and 1798 Comprising sketches of its ancient and modern History, Constitution, laws, Commerce, Agriculture, Fishery, etc', *Manx Society* 6 (1861)

Bard, M., 'Contemporary References to the Scottish Speech of the Sixteenth Century', *Scottish Historical Review* 25 (1928)

Bromwich, R., 'The Mabinogion and Lady Charlotte Guest', *Transactions of the Honourable Society of Cymmrodorion*, Session 1986 (1986)

Campbell, J., 'The Contribution of Edward Lhuyd to the Study of Scottish Gaelic', *Transactions of the Honourable Society of Cymmrodorion*, Session 1962 (1962)

Campbell, T., 'C. R. M. Talbot, 1803–1890: A Welsh Landowner in Politics and Industry', *Journal of Glamorgan History* 44 (2000)

Casey, M., 'The Enigma of the Young Arthur Horner: From Churches of Christ Preacher to Communist Militant, 1894–1920', *Labour History Review* 66 (2001)

'The Celtic Congress in Dublin', *Young Wales*, 7 (1901)

Cleary, A., 'Gaelic League', *Studies* 8 (1919)

Cox, L. V., 'Gaelic and the Schools in Cape Breton', *Nova Scotia Historical Review* 14 (1994)

Crowley, P. D., 'The "Crofters' Party"', *Scottish Historical Review* 35 (1956)

D'Albe, E. F., 'The Pan-Celtic Idea, *Young Wales* 5 (1899)

Davies, I., 'The 1588 Translation of the Bible and the World of Renaissance Learning', *Journal of the Ceredigion Antiquarian Society* 11 (1988–9)

Denning, R., 'Druidism in Pontypridd', *Glamorgan History* 1 (1963)

Devine, T. M., 'Irish Immigrants and Scottish Society in the Nineteenth and Twentieth Centuries', *Proceedings of the Scottish Historical Studies Seminar, University of Strathclyde, 1989/90* (1991)

Dewar, J., 'Bishop Carswell and his Times', *Celtic Magazine* 4 (1879)

Doble, G., 'Saint Cadoc in Cornwall and Brittany', *Truro Diocesan Gazette* (1937)

Durkacz, V., 'The Source of the Language Problem in Scottish Education, 1688–1709', *Scottish Historical Review*, 57 (1978)

Edwards, C. (ed.), 'A Visit to Cornwall in 1755 by William Wynne', *Journal of the Royal Institution of Cornwall* (1981)

Edwards, H., 'The Merthyr National Eisteddfod 1851', *Merthyr Historian* 10 (1999)

Edwards, H., 'The Merthyr National Eisteddfod of 1901', *Merthyr Historian* 13 (2001)

Ellis, R., 'Some Incidents in the Life of Edward Lhuyd', *Transactions of the Honourable Society of Cymmrodorion,* Session 1906–7 (1908)

'Emigration from the Highlands', *Edinburgh Review* 1 (1804)

Forbes, J., 'Tour into Cornwall to the Lands End, in Letters by James Forbes in 1794', *Journal of the Royal Institution of Cornwall* 9 (1983)

Fox, K., 'The Merthyr Election of 1906', *National Library of Wales Journal* 14 (1965–66)

Fraser, M., 'Benjamin and Augusta Hall, 1831–6', *The National Library of Wales Journal* 8 (1963–4)

Garmon-Jones, W., 'Welsh Nationalism and Henry Tudor', *Transactions of the Honourable Society of the Cymmrodorion*, Session 1917–1918 (1919)

Gibbon, M., 'Glimpses of the Gaeltacht', *Irish Monthly* 59 (1931)

Gibson, J., 'Traditional Piping in Nova Scotia', in *Celtic Languages and Celtic Peoples: Proceedings of the Second North American Congress of Celtic Studies*, ed. C. Byrne, M. Harry and P. O Siadhail, Halifax, 1989

Greiert, S., 'The Earl of Halifax and the Settlement of Nova Scotia, 1749–1753', *Nova Scotia Historical Review* 1 (1981)

Griffith-Jones, P., 'The Celtic Genius', *Wales* 2 (1912)

Hickey, M., 'The True National Idea', *Gaelic League Pamphlets* 1 (1898)

Hickey, M., 'The Irish Language Movement', *Gaelic League Pamphlets* 29

Hoblyn, W. T., '"In English and not in Cornowek", From the Consistory Court Depositions 1569–1572', *Old Cornwall* 11 (1936)

Holloway, M., 'D. H. Lawrence in Cornwall', *Cornish Review* 3 (1949)

Horn, D., 'George IV and Highland Dress', *Scottish Historical Review* 47 (1968)

Hornsby, S., 'The Exodus: A selection from Stephen Hornby's New Book; Nineteenth Century Cape Breton, A Historical Geography', *Cape Breton's Magazine* 61 (1992)

Hughes, J., 'The Celt, the Saxon and the Teuton', *Wales* 2 (1912)

Hunter, J., 'The Politics of Highland Land Reform, 1873–95', *Scottish Historical Review* 53 (1974)

Hunter, J., 'The Gaelic Connection: The Highlands, Ireland and Nationalism 1873–1922', *Scottish Historical Review* 54 (1975)

Hutchinson, R., 'The Future of Gaelic on Cape Breton', *Cape Breton's Magazine* 1 (1972)

James, I., 'The Welsh Renaissance in the Sixteenth and Seventeenth Centuries', *Red Dragon* 11 (1887)

Jenkin, R., 'Mebyon Kernow and the Future of Cornwall., *Cornish Review* 9 (1968)

Jenkins, R. W., 'The Welsh Renaissance', *Wales* 2 (1895)

Jenner, H., 'Traditional Relics of the Cornish Language in Mounts Bay in 1875', *Transactions of the Philological Society* (1875)

Jenner, H., 'The History and Literature of the Ancient Cornish Language., *Journal of the British Archaeological Association* (June 1877)

Jenner, H., 'Cornwall: A Celtic Nation', *Celtic Review* 1 (1905)

John, E. T., 'Wales and Self-Government., *Wales* 1 (1911)

Jolliffe, M., 'The Druidical Society of Anglesey, 1772–1844', *Transactions of the Cymmrodorion*, Session 1940 (1941)

Jones, J., 'Bishop William Morgan: Defender of Church and State', *Journal of Welsh Ecclesiastical History* 5 (1988)

Joy, J., 'Catholic Action in Ireland: The Legion of Mary', *Irish Monthly* 59 (1931)

Lach-Szyrma, W. S., 'Relics of the Old Cornish Language', *Journal of the British Archaeological Association* (1906)

Lang, A., 'Celtic Scotland and the War for independence', *Scottish Historical Review* 6 (1909)

'Llanelli Eisteddfod', *Cambrian Journal* 3 (1856)

Lloyd, D., 'The Irish Gaelic and the Welsh Printed Book', *Journal of the Welsh Bibliographical Society* 6 (1948)

Mackay, J., 'Sutherland Evictions and Burnings', *The Celtic Magazine* 9 (1884)

Maclean, S., 'The poetry of the clearances', *Transactions of the Gaelic Society of Inverness* 38, 1937–41 (1962)

Macleod, R., 'The Bishop of Skye', *Transactions of the Gaelic Society of Inverness*, vol. 53, 1985

MacPhail, I., 'The Skye Military Expedition of 1884–5', *Transactions of the Gaelic Society of Inverness* 48, 1972–4 (1976)

MacPhail, I., 'The Highland elections of 1884–1886', *Transactions of the Gaelic Society of Inverness* 50, 1976–78 (1979)

Mason, J., 'Scottish Charity Schools of the Eighteenth Century', *Scottish Historical Review* 33 (1954)

Morgan, K. O., 'Liberals, Nationalists and Mr Gladstone', *Transactions of the Cymmrodorion*, Session 1960 (1960)

Morgan, P., 'The Historical Significance of Iolo Morganwg', *Transactions of the Port Talbot Historical Society* 3 (1981)

Morgan, R., 'The Great Famine in Cape Breton, 1845–51', *Cape Breton's Magazine* 58 (1991)

Morgan, W. P., 'The Welsh in the United States', *Wales* 3 (1896)

Morrison, M., 'Presbyterianism in Old Cape Breton', *Cape Breton's Magazine* 42 (1986)

Nance, R. M., 'What We Stand For', *Old Cornwall (Journal of the Federation of Old Cornwall Societies)* 1 (1925)

Nance, R. M., '"Gwas Myghal" and the Cornish Revival', *Old Cornwall* 8 (1934)

Nance, R. M., 'The Cornish Gorsedd', *Cornish Review* 7 (1951)

Nance, R. M., 'Helston Furry Day', *Journal of the Royal Institution of Cornwall* 4 (1961)

Nance, R. M., 'When Was Cornish Last Spoken?', *Journal of the Royal Institution of Cornwall* 7 (1973)

'The Nationalist Movement in Brittany', *Welsh Outlook* 20 (1933)

O'Lúing, S., 'Douglas Hyde and the Gaelic League', *Studies* 42 (1973)

O'Reilly, J., 'What Religion has Lost by the Decay of the Irish Language', *New Ireland Review* 3 (1898)

O'Riagáin, P., 'The Galway Gaeltacht, 1926–1981: A Sociolinguistic Survey of Continuity and Change', in *Galway History and Society: Interdisciplinary Essays on the History of an Irish County*, ed. P. Moran and R. Gillespie, Dublin, 1996

Ó Tuathaigh, G., 'Gaelic Ireland: Popular Politics and Daniel O'Connell', *Journal of Galway Archaeological and Historical Society* (1974–1975)

'Our Gaelic Bible', *Celtic Magazine* 4 (1879)

Owen, J. D., 'Wales and the Celtic Movement', *Welsh Outlook* 9 (1922)

Pool, P. A. S., 'William Borlase: The Scholar and the Man', *Journal of the Royal Institution of Cornwall* 5 (1965)

Pryce, W., 'Language Areas and Changes c.1750–1981', in *Glamorgan County History*, ed. P. Morgan vol. 6, Cardiff, 1988

Rees, M., 'The Industrialisation of Glamorgan', *Glamorgan Historian* 1 (1963)

Richards, G., 'The Early History of the Schools of Dyffryn Nantlle', *Cymdeithas Hanes Sir Caernarfon (Caernarvonshire Historical Society)* 24 (1963)

Roberts, W., 'Wales During the Victorian Era', *Young Wales* 8 (1902)

Rogers, J. P., 'Cornish Saints', *Journal of the Royal Institution of Cornwall* 4 (1961)

'Saunders Lewis', *Welsh Review* 5 (1946)

Shaw, T., 'Saint Petroc and John Wesley: Apostles in Cornwall', *Cornish Methodist Historical Association Publication* 4 (1967)

Shears, B., 'The Bagpipe in Cape Breton', *Cape Breton's Magazine* 52 (1989)

Taylor, C., 'Paddy's Run: A Welsh Community in Ohio', *Welsh History Review* 2 (1983)

Thomas. B., 'A Cauldron of Rebirth: Population and the Welsh Language in the Nineteenth Century', *Welsh History Review* 13 (1987)

Thomas, I., 'County or Country', *Cornish Review* 2 (1949)

Vaughan, H., 'Welsh Jacobitism', *Transactions of the Honourable Society of Cymmrodorion*, Session 1920–1921 (1922)

Wallis-Jones, W. J., 'The University College of Wales', *Young Wales* 3 (1896)

Watson, W. J., 'The Position of Gaelic in Scotland: Inaugural Lecture 13 October 1914 in the Celtic Classroom at Edinburgh University', *Celtic Review* 10 (1914)

Wilde, W., 'Ireland Past and Present: A Lecture delivered to the Dublin YMCA, 27 April 1864', in *Lectures Delivered before the Dublin YMCA*, Dublin 1865

Williams, C., 'Non-Violence and the Development of the Welsh Language Society, 1962–c.1974', *Welsh History Review* 8 (1977)

Williams, G., 'Richard Davies: Bishop of St David's, 1561–81', *Transactions of the Cymmrodorion*, Session 1948 (1949)

Williams, G., 'The Ecclesiastical History of Glamorgan 1527–1642', *Glamorgan County History* 4 (1974)

Williams, G., 'Earliest Non-Conformists in Merthyr Tydfil', *Merthyr Historian* 1 (1976)

Williams, G., 'The Structure and Progress of Welsh Emigration to Patagonia', *Welsh History Review* 8 (1976)

Williams, G. J., 'The Eisteddfod', *Welsh Review* 6 (1947)

Williams, G. J., 'The Welsh Literary Tradition of the Vale of Glamorgan', *Glamorgan Historian* 3 (1966)

Williams, I., 'Free Church Debts and Free Church Progress in Wales', *Wales* 2 (1912)

Williams, L., 'The Welsh Claim to Disestablishment', *Wales* 1 (1911)

Yates, N., 'The Welsh Church and Celtic Nationalism', *Journal of Welsh Ecclesiastical History* 1 (1984)

UNPUBLISHED SOURCES

Bale, V. C., 'Wesleyan Methodists in Merthyr Tydfil 1790–1972', unpublished manuscript, Merthyr Tydfil Public Library

Dembling, J., 'Joe Jimmy Alec Visits the Mod and Escapes Unscathed: The Nova Scotia Gaelic Revivals', M.A. thesis, St Mary's University, Beaton Institute, University College of Cape Breton

George, M., 'The Khaki Election of 1900: A Study of Three Towns, Portsmouth, Merthyr Tydfil and Wakefield', unpublished manuscript, no date, Merthyr Tydfil Public Library

Kelly, J. C., 'A Sociographic Survey of Gaelic in Cape Breton', M.A. thesis, 1980, Concordia University Montreal, Angus Macdonald Library, St Francis Xavier University

Kincaid, B., 'Scottish Immigration to Cape Breton 1758–1838', M.A. thesis, 1964, Dalhousie University, Angus Macdonald Library, St Francis Xavier University

Lamont, K., 'A Short Study of the History and Traditions of the Highland Scot in Nova Scotia', M.A. thesis, 1964, St Francis Xavier University

MacKenzie Campbell, P. J., 'The Highland Community on the Bras D'Or', typed manuscript, 1966, Angus Macdonald Library, St Francis Xavier University

MacNeil, H., 'Work and Language in a Cape Breton Gaelic Community', typed manuscript, Angus Macdonald Library, St Francis Xavier University

Morgan, R., 'Orphan Outpost: Cape Breton Colony 1784–1820', thesis, June 1972, University of Ottawa, Angus Macdonald Library, St Francis Xavier University

Roberts, E., 'The Vitality of the Welsh Language', A paper read at Cardiff Town Hall on 2 February 1886, Cardiff

Skinner, M., 'The Relationship Between the Welsh Colonies in Chubut and the Argentine Government', Ph.D. thesis, 1976, University of Wales

Society for the Preservation of the Irish language, *Annual Report for 1886–1887*, Dublin, 1887

Index